Social Mobility and Higher Education
the life experiences of first generation
entrants in higher education

Social Mobility and Higher Education
the life experiences of first generation entrants in higher education

Mary Stuart

IOEPress

A Trentham Book
Institute of Education Press

Institute of Education Press
20 Bedford Way
London
WC1H 0AL

First published 2012

British Library Cataloguing-in-Publication Data
A catalogue record for this book is available from the British Library

ISBN 978-1-85856-508-8

Printed by CPI Group (UK) Ltd, Croydon, CR0 4YY

Contents

Acknowledgements • vi

Chapter 1
The problem with social mobility and higher education • 1

Chapter 2
Class and the life history as an account of social change • 19

Chapter 3
**A rare breed: Working-class students in higher education
before the Robbins Review** • 35

Chapter 4
The golden era? Funded growth and student grants • 51

Chapter 5
Massification without resource: The 1980s and 1990s • 69

Chapter 6
**Graduates of the twenty-first century – the new era
of higher education** • 91

Chapter 7
Gateways and gatekeepers: Mobility and class revisited • 111

Chapter 8
Social mobility and higher education in the future • 133

References • 153

Index • 165

Acknowledgements

This book would not have been possible without the generosity of all the biographers who took the time and trouble to respond to my call for life histories. Thank you all very much.

Particular thanks to Dr Lucy Solomon, my researcher, who worked on the project with me. Lucy I am grateful for all your support and friendship.

Thanks also to colleagues who provided comment on initial drafts and to Thirzah Wildman and Linda Marshall for their help in preparing the manuscript and finally to Dr Douglas Stuart and Dr Gillian Klein for their support throughout the process.

1

The problem with social mobility and higher education

Higher education and society

Until 1945 virtually any [male] student who could pass a relatively easy matriculation examination could go to university if he could find the money and if he wanted to do so. (Furneaux, 1961:xii)

The history of Higher Education (HE) in Britain extends back to the Middle Ages, but the shape, size and extent of higher education looks very different in the twenty-first century. In the Middle Ages there were only two universities in England: Oxford and Cambridge. At the time they focused largely on vocational education for clerics, doctors and so on, providing a classical education for upper-class men. Scotland gained its first institutions in the fifteenth century. Higher education remained largely unchanged until the establishment of the University of London in the eighteenth century. Towards the end of the nineteenth century civic universities in the emerging industrial cities were established to cope with the needs of commerce and industry.

Institutions remained a male-dominated domain, but during the nineteenth century and into the twentieth women campaigned to gain access to higher education, initially in separate colleges. However, institutions remained elite and dependent on families having the resources to pay to attend. As the twentieth century progressed, funding from other sources to enable study developed, but it was not until after the Second World War that a true system of higher education in the UK

1

emerged and not until the 1960s that grants were available for all who wished to study in HE (Tight, 2009).

It is the period from the 1950s through to the start of the twenty-first century that has seen the most rapid growth – in institutions, in provision and in the numbers of students and graduates. As the century turned, growth in HE became increasingly global in nature. In the last twenty years the number of students in tertiary education globally has increased from 39 million to 81 million (Schleicher, 2011).

This book charts the expansion of HE, seen through the eyes of a group of students and graduates who were the first in their families to attend higher education in the United Kingdom (UK). Once they had graduated these people either stayed on to work in higher education or returned later in life to work in the sector. Their accounts provide a special insight into the development of higher education in our lifetimes. They were what is now termed 'widening participation students', different in background from the majority of their peers as students. Their experiences provide a particular perspective on HE: what opportunity looked like for them and how they experienced becoming middle-class academics and HE administrators.

The role higher education can and should play in enabling upward social mobility is a critical debate for any society that wishes to compete in a globalised, technology and knowledge rich world, and the issue has become important in policy discussions in the UK. The Joseph Rowntree foundation (2011) argues that the problem is not that young people do not have high aspirations; it is that only some people have knowledge of the pathways that lead through education into employment. In order to make a real impact on social mobility, we must move beyond lazy stereo-types of certain communities, and focus instead on removing the barriers to people fulfilling their aspirations.

The life histories recorded for this book provide some insights into the process that enables upward social mobility. As a case study of upward social mobility they offer the beginnings of an agenda for policy interventions which can support both widening opportunity through higher education and upward social mobility in society.

Social mobility, higher education and changing society

The shape and size of social groupings in industrialised societies has changed significantly over the last hundred years, and as technological sophistication increases, the requirement for more highly skilled workers continues to grow in advanced economies. These changes in the economy have created more opportunity 'at the top' for a broader range of people which has seen the size of the working class shrink from approximately 75 per cent in the early 1900s to just over a quarter of the population in the early 2000s (Saunders, 2010). Opportunities were created for children from working-class families to move into the middle-classes as new occupations emerged. Their lives became more economically stable than those of their parents, for whom work patterns were often insecure. These social chances enabled many more to become middle-class.

Debates around social mobility focus on a concern for equity between different social groups. The argument centres on a belief in greater fairness across society where opportunity for anyone who was capable of progressing beyond their current situation is seen as an important part of a civilised society. Definitions of fairness are of course socially contingent and different societies will define fairness in different ways (Bentley *et al*, 2011). At a common sense level in Britain, the idea of meritocracy has been a key element of society for many years (Savage, 2000). Enabling upward mobility for any person who is able has led to an interest in what is termed relative social mobility, where the chances for upward mobility of different groups in society is measured to assess how fair the society is.

Social mobility is deeply entwined with the development of high level skills and education. During the nineteenth century, to support the changing workforce governments first established compulsory primary education in Britain in 1870, moved to free primary education in 1891, and extended the school leaving age to 14,15 and 16 in 1918, 1944, and 1972 respectively. Alongside these changes in school education, higher education expanded throughout the twentieth century increasing from ten universities in 1900 to 106 in 2007 (Tight, 2009). While the expansion of HE was considered important to changing society, it was not until the beginning of the twenty-first century that concern about the role higher education plays in creating social mobility became a policy issue in itself.

Researchers Blanden, Gregg and Machin argued that social mobility 'is not only declining but is also significantly lower than in some other developed countries' (2005:1). They concluded that 'the big expansion of higher education in university participation has tended to benefit children from affluent families more' (2005:2). Such findings created considerable concern in government circles following a strong consensus that access to, and participation in, higher education would lead to social mobility. Higher education received considerable investment from the late 1990s – widening participation initiatives, in particular, received targeted funding to provide less affluent young people with opportunities to progress into HE.

Concern about changes in social mobility created 'a problem' for the policy of higher education expansion and challenged the received wisdom about widening participation. It created considerable interest in both the media and political circles, and lead the government to commission a 'panel on fair access to the professions' in 2009 under the chairmanship of minister Alan Milburn. The coalition government continued this work, setting out a 'social mobility strategy' (HMG, 2011), and offered Milburn the role of 'an independent advisor on social mobility' (*The Guardian*, 15 August, 2010). In 2012 he produced an interim report on progress in access to the professions that identified some positive change but the report suggested more needed to be done (2012a).

This chapter explores the concept of social mobility and how it is understood. It also looks at the connections between widening participation and social mobility alongside the development of higher education policy in the United Kingdom over the last 70 years. The discussion provides the background and context to the life histories presented later in the book. I begin by examining the policy arguments for widening participation in higher education.

Global policy on widening access to higher education

Policy makers across the world argue that increasing overall participation in higher education and the diversity of the student population are vital to a country's economic competitiveness and social cohesion

(Delors, 1997). Higher education institutions are expected to contribute to the development of society itself, not just the development of academic knowledge. As the Association of Commonwealth Universities (ACU) points out:

> A university's mission must thus be much wider than perpetuating the life of scholarship for its own sake. The world depends increasingly on universities for knowledge, prosperity, health and policy thinking. Universities are thus required to become engines of development for people, institutions and democracy in general. (ACU, 200:i)

Significantly more people across the world are now gaining access to higher level learning, in the region of a hundred million young people (Dorling, 2010:16). However, as Osborne points out:

> ... despite a plethora of policy initiatives and the use of a variety of interventions, there is continuing under-representation of certain traditionally excluded groups in these five countries. [Finland, England, France, Australia and Canada] (2003:48)

Equally, access to higher level learning is stratified by the type of institution and qualification, as Dorling argues: 'University degrees are wonderful things, it is the arranging and valuing of them by hierarchy of institution that is problematic, when people study for a label, for a university brand, rather than actually to learn' (2010:16).

Although policy makers seek to harness the opportunities offered by HE for the benefit of their own priorities, ensuring fair access and equal opportunity are always more difficult. Access to and success in higher level study has historically been the preserve of the already wealthy and successful groups in society, but the process of widening participation to HE level study has been an endeavour of HE institutions for some time. Perhaps the first real example of widening participation in HE is the inclusion of women as students at universities in the early twentieth century. After initially studying in separate colleges, women were subject to quotas for entry in some disciplines, notably medicine where quotas restricted the number of female entrants to less than 25 per cent of the intake. Women finally gained the right to study alongside their male counterparts without quotas in the 1970s.

In the literature on widening participation and higher education there is some confusion of terminology: categories such as non-traditional, under-represented, working-class, widening participation students and first-generation entrants are often used interchangeably, despite reflecting different, but sometimes overlapping, groups of people. While several groups in the HE population are non-traditional students and are under-represented, it is the lower socio-economic groups who have caused the most concern for the UK government in recent times, as Newby points out:

> While overall participation in higher education has moved from one in seven to just one in two ..., the gap in participation rates between the top and the bottom socio-economic classes has moved only slightly ... No matter how we look at it, their life chances, in terms of their ability to access higher education and thereby graduate-level jobs remains severely restricted. (2005:5)

Earlier policies from consecutive governments, discussed later in the book, attempted to increase the number of women, ethnic minority and mature students in HE. Recent policy interventions have focused on working- class participation, but the success of widening access for women, who now dominate undergraduate entry and success rates, should not be ignored. Despite being a key feature of the debate on upward mobility, the social mobility of women is methodologically complex. In the life histories presented in this book gender issues emerge as an area of major concern across the generations from the 1950s to the present day.

Concern about the socio-economic mix of higher education students is not only confined to Britain. Since the civil rights movement in the USA, programmes to encourage people from under-represented groups studying in higher education have been common (Kahlenberg, 2004). In Australia, since the late 1980s, similar targets and programmes have featured strongly on the higher education landscape (Chapman and Ryan, 2003). In the UK, despite the previous government's commitment to changing the social mix and increasing the number of people in higher education, the gap in participation between working and middle-class students had not decreased by 2005 – although the overall number of students in HE had significantly increased (HEFCE, 2005). However, more recent research (HEFCE, 2010) suggests that the impact of policies is starting to bridge this gap. Along with current policy changes, such research is discussed in chapter 8.

Like many concerned with social justice in society, Dorling (2010) worries at the particular interest in fair access which dominates much of the debate on social mobility and higher education. Fair access, another concept which originated during the Labour administration of 1997-2010, has since been adopted by the current coalition government. Fair access focuses on students from working-class backgrounds getting into the most selective institutions in the UK. The concept mirrors concerns in the USA about needs-blind admission to Ivy League institutions.

The move from concern about widening participation in HE to concern about social mobility suggests that policy makers have become increasingly apprehensive about outcomes for graduates, not just inputs as students. While widening participation may be a precursor to upward social mobility, it does not automatically create it. For first generation students in HE who come from lower socio-economic groups what matters most is not just getting into university but succeeding there and being able to gain employment that moves them beyond their family background (Milburn, 2012b).

Over the last ten years there has been a growing interest in whether the UK has succeeded in establishing a more open society where merit, not background, creates opportunity for its members. Milburn argued that 'access to society's top jobs and professions has become less, not more, socially representative over time' (2009:18). Enabling the most creative and talented people in society to succeed is seen as vital to a successful economy and society (Goldthorpe *et al*, 1987), which explains why the issue of social mobility has become a key element in the UK's social policy during the last few years. Concerns about the role higher education plays in facilitating social mobility are more sharply focused as the costs and value of a degree are debated across society.

The task of higher education is to provide young people from working-class backgrounds with the ability to move into professional occupations by gaining a degree. Government expects higher education to play its part in creating a more open or 'fairer society' (Clegg, 2011:3). At one level, of course, everyone can and should sign up to a fairer society, but questions of social mobility are problematic and academics often contest them. The role higher education plays in creating upward social mobility is no less difficult, but the fact that education is crucial to social mobility is indisputable, as Blanden *et al* point out:

> It is well established that richer children obtain better educational outcomes, and that those with higher educational levels earn more. Education is therefore a prime candidate to explain mobility and changes to it. (2007:5)

Goldthorpe *et al* also argue: 'amongst those men who had followed direct mobility routes, the reference was almost exclusively to the expansion of educational and training opportunities of one type or another' (2003:232).

The life histories discussed later in the book reveal a complex interweaving of factors which support or hinder opportunity: personal, familial, social and wider policy decisions which enabled their upward mobility. The next section examines the academic debates on social mobility, highlighting the difficulties in understanding what is actually happening to the shape of our society.

What is social mobility?

Jut as widening participation is sometimes used to indicate slightly different things, the term social mobility can also be used imprecisely. Social mobility focuses on the size and shape of different groupings in society and how fluid or porous the boundaries between these groupings are. Social mobility is mostly examined in terms of either class or income. Later in the chapter I set out the consequences of using either methodology.

Concern about the structure and level of fluidity in society has been discussed between social scientists since the nineteenth century. Early studies of poverty such as Rowntree (1902) were interested in whether people could escape the squalid circumstances in the cities of the UK. As the twentieth century progressed, and society changed, the emphasis of policy makers shifted to an interest in an individual's ability to have a fair chance at success; in other words, concern about a meritocratic society. In 1949, Glass found that most people in the UK believed in a meritocratic society: 'hard work, good education, high ability and strong personality lead to upward social mobility' (Savage, 2000:73). The view is consistently revealed in social surveys, and this accounts for the belief that individuals can and should be able to succeed in their lives according to their ability and application. This belief is embedded in British society; the majority of people in the UK holding that social mobility, up and down, is and should be possible.

The twentieth century saw the size of the middle-class increase significantly while the size of the working class decreased. The creation of significantly more middle-class jobs provided opportunities for working-class individuals to move up into the middle-classes:

> Before 1914 ... about three quarters of all jobs in Britain were in manual work and only a quarter were 'white collar' ... with the decline of manufacturing employment, the growth of the state sector employment and the impact of technological change on routine jobs these proportions have now almost completely reversed. The shrinking of the working class and the expansion of the service class over the last hundred years has to entail recruitment of increasing numbers of working-class children into the new professional and managerial positions that were being created. (Saunders, 2010:17)

With the increase in middle-class jobs we have seen a major expansion of the higher education that provides the means for a more middle-class society. In 1940 5 per cent of people participated in HE; in 2010 that figures stood at 47 per cent. The increase in the size of the middle-class and the expansion of educational opportunities highlights the considerable success in upward social mobility that has occurred over the last 70 years. However, some academics have expressed concern that the changing shape of our society, with more middle-class jobs than before, may actually be slowing or even decreasing. As Erikson and Goldthorpe highlight: '... across the political spectrum and within the media it is widely believed that intergenerational social mobility is presently in decline or, even, has ground to a halt' (2010:212). Findings like this explain why a problem with social mobility has emerged in policy circles. The issue is hotly debated among academics, and the next section examines the different academic positions on social mobility.

Social mobility: the problematic concept

Understanding the concerns about whether social mobility has slowed or even stopped presents problems of definition and measurement. There are several aspects to this issue. Firstly, social scientists disagree considerably about what is happening to both the shape of our society and the level of fluidity within it. The debate is between sociologists themselves (Saunders, 2010; Goldthorpe, *et al*, 2003; Savage, 2000) as well as sociologists, educationalists and economists (Gorard, 2008; Blanden *et al*, 2005, 2007; Erikson and Goldthorpe, 2010).

Alongside these debates is the lack of understanding of HE's role in creating upward social mobility. Social mobility does not equate to widening access or even the successful completion of study in HE: rather, upward or downward mobility relates to an adult's economic situation. Social mobility requires a move from one part of society to another, either in relation to income – the focus for economists – or in relation to social class – the focus for sociologists. Understanding what is being measured and for what purposes is vital to gain a sense of how higher education can support an upwardly mobile society.

Beyond the question of income versus class there are other differences in measurement. Mobility can either be measured inter-generationally – that is, between parents and children – or intra-generationally where an individual's position is measured over their lifetime.

Academic debates about measurement have largely grown in response to two studies: the 1958 National Child Development Study and the 1970 British Cohort Study. Both examined children born in one week in 1958 or in 1970. Because social mobility cannot be measured imme-diately but requires time for individuals to grow up and enter the work-force, the time lag for understanding changes in society is extensive. Savage (2000) points out that most of the research has been undertaken on social mobility that is inter-generational, whereas intra-generational mobility has largely been ignored. In the 1958 and 1970 studies father and son's position and/or income were studied when they were 33 and 30 respectively.

Most research on social mobility has focused on male mobility and although Blanden *et al* (2004) attempted to include females in their analysis, other researchers such as Erikson and Goldthorpe (2010) see this as problematic since the data on women's position and incomes is incomplete. The relation between gender and social mobility is one that ought not to be ignored however. As Saunders argues: 'there is still more room at the top for women of this generation than there was for their mothers ... so women still enjoy much greater upward than downward movement' (2010:107). The life accounts in this book reflect the stories of many women who were able to use education to become upwardly mobile.

Although there is little work in the UK that has looked at questions of ethnicity and mobility, in the USA the connection between poverty and race is well documented. Questions about upward social mobility need to take account of other social divisions in society, however problematic this may be, and it is particularly at the level of the individual where social divisions are experienced that analysis becomes possible.

How to measure: income versus class

Any kind of scientific enquiry requires an appropriate measurement. How you measure and what you measure will affect your outcomes. Economists tend to focus on a single quantifiable measure – income. For example, Blanden *et al* describe how wealth affects life chances: 'better off children ... as they grow up ... achieve more at all levels of education and have greater labour market attachment in their teens and twenties' (2007:12). An income approach appears simpler than a class definition, as that involves a complex mix of factors that are often contested between academics. It is easier to provide focus and offers clear results. There are some difficulties with an income analysis however. Self-declared income may be problematic and in examining the two cohorts from 1958 and 1970, it is clear that the income data between the two surveys was gathered differently which makes it almost impossible to compare like with like.

Using class as a measurement is not without its difficulties. Although class analysis can offer a clear hierarchical occupational structure, matching occupation to class groupings which existed in both the 1958 and 1970 cohorts, class analysis has historically only examined the mobility of fathers and sons (Goldthorpe *et al*, 1987). As women's engagement with the world of work and within families has changed significantly, ignoring women within the analysis makes the process even more problematic, and it is inappropriate to view women's position solely within a household and not as individuals in their own right. Class should also include other elements beyond occupation. Indeed there is some merit in examining economic resources alongside occupational status.

There is no perfect measure, however, and the most that academics can and should do is make their approach evident. In re-examining their data, Blanden *et al* suggested that while they found income levels had fallen between the two cohorts of 1958 and 1970, this may have been the result of only comparing income at one particular age point: 'information on your parental income in the cohorts is taken on a one-shot basis and a reliable measure for permanent income is not available' (2010:2). Class analysis, including information on economic resources, could provide a more rounded view of an individual's social position, as Blanden *et al*, acknowledge: 'Economists are aiming to measure economic resource whereas class reflects workplace autonomy and broader social capital' (*ibid*).

Despite accepting that neither measure, income nor class, is perfect sociologists Boliver and Swift argue that the latter is more valuable in examining social actors. They say:

> Class boundaries which demarcate different types of occupation on the basis of employment relationships are more salient to social actors than are the relatively arbitrary cut-off points distinguishing quartiles on the distribution of income. (2011:94)

Class definitions are therefore used in this book, but with some sense of family income and economic resources available, gathered through the life stories. Issues of class definition are discussed in the next chapter.

Absolute verses relative mobility

In an attempt to understand questions of equality, Goldthorpe *et al* were keen to examine mobility in both absolute and relative terms. They state that: '... absolute or *de facto* mobility [is] the rate of mobility that we actually observe ... relative mobility [is] those that result when absolute rates are compared against [different] ... social groupings' (2003:29).

It is important to study how likely it is that a particular group will be upwardly or downwardly mobile in comparison to other groups. In absolute terms the shape of British society has altered over the last 70 years. As Goldthorpe *et al* point out:

> ... it is the case that in the more advanced stages of capitalism the intermediate strata do, taken as a whole, proportionately increase ... the middle-class thus succeeds the proletariat as an expanding class of society. (2003: 7)

Along with Goldthorpe *et al* (2003), Iannelli and Paterson acknowledge that, far from increasing in relative terms, working-class upward social mobility has remained the same over this period, that: 'the relative advantage of belonging to a middle-class family compared to a working-class family in acquiring higher occupational positions has remained constant' (2005:4). Savage explains what this middle-class advantage means in practice: 'only 7 per cent of the 'high ability' sons of large business owners and managers worked in manual occupations when they were aged 33, compared to 38 per cent of the 'high ability' sons of unskilled manual workers (2000:91). Although Saunders argues that the middle-classes' relative advantage is based on their ability to ensure that their children do not 'fall down' (2010:40), there is no level playing field and the issue of equality of opportunity for people from working-class backgrounds remains.

Further debate about whether Britain is relatively less socially mobile than other countries continues. Blanden *et al* (2010) argue that Britain is less mobile than others while Breen and Luijkx (2004) say that of twelve countries analysed, in only five – France, Sweden, the Netherlands, Hungary and Poland – has there been an increase in social fluidity. The authors did point out however that these findings have to be read in a context of substantial commonality across time and countries in men and women's fluidity. In other words their view is that the differences are slight. Gorard (2008) also argues that Britain is no worse than most advanced societies.

Policy makers' dilemmas

For policy makers hoping to create interventions that work, these disagreements present difficulties. It is very hard to establish exact and real co-relationships between changes in one area and changes in another. Is it, as Saunders argues, that 'overall the big shift in the occupational system from manual to mental labour appears to be behind us' (2010: 107), that the number of middle-class jobs available has flattened out? Is it that there is real inequality, as Dorling (2010) suggests, or is it both? Savage points out that in relation to what causes upward or downward social mobility of individuals; '... such is the inter-correlation of these variables with each other that we can never be sure that they are in fact reliable measures acting independently of each other' (2000:77).

As these debates between academics continue, the UK's coalition government has established a 'social mobility strategy' which includes sections on early years, school, transition (including a discussion on higher education) and adulthood (HMG, 2011). They have set out 'leading indicators for success' (p67) with milestones to measure improvements. In the case of higher education, the indicators refer to getting more young people from state schools into the 33 per cent most selective higher education institutions and ensuring that a greater percentage of students on free school meals (which are assessed by parental income) at age 15 go on to higher education by age 19 (p70).

Researchers in Scotland and Wales have also been looking at the issue of social mobility. Iannelli and Paterson (2005) found that while education played an important role in mobility it was not the only factor. Recruitment policies for middle-class jobs were also important, which suggests that education alone may not alone alleviate disadvantage and that more work needs to be done with employers. Paterson and Iannelli (2007) found that the current rate of absolute social mobility has slowed but the decline was slightly steeper in Wales than in England and Scotland. As with earlier studies, they found no change in relative social mobility: the fluidity of our society remains the same. For policy makers, the solutions to relative social mobility may need to be tailored to different parts of the country and for different sectors of society.

The social mobility strategy might seek to address a range of issues including child poverty, education and employment, but while a growing body of evidence suggests that early interventions are crucial to raising attainment amongst working-class children, evidence of other interventions across the life cycle remains insufficient.

Widening participation, fair access, social mobility and higher education

Social mobility can only be studied with a long view. While it is evident that higher education qualifications can enable white collar employment, it is not a precondition, nor does it guarantee it. As Patterson and Iannelli point out:

> The dynamics of the differences among these three countries in mobility to current class, and of the changes in it over time, must derive, not mainly from

14

initial experiences in the labour market, but from its subsequent effects on people's careers and from the ways in which it rewards characteristics not captured by formal credentials, some of them indeed built up during careers themselves. (2007:5)

The role of higher education therefore is not to create a socially mobile society; it is to support widening participation and work with students to gain graduate employment. Evidence suggests that employment out-comes for different social groupings are variable.

Graduates with highly qualified parents are more likely to obtain a first-class honours degree, while those with less qualified parents are more likely to hold an upper second-class degree, leading to similar proportions of students with a good degree across socio-economic backgrounds (Blasko, 2002).

Graduates with parents in partly skilled occupations were found to be 30 per cent more likely than others to have a non-graduate job 18 months after graduation; and for graduates who had no employed parents this risk increases to 80 per cent. Graduates from higher socio-economic groups were also shown to move into occupations with salaries one to three per cent higher than those from lower socio-economic groups (Smith *et al*, 2000; Smith and Naylor, 2001).

While social mobility debates have focused particularly on class, other social divisions are also worth considering. Women are more likely than their male peers to obtain a good degree (HESA, 2007; Richardson and Woodley, 2003; Rudd, 1984; Smith and Naylor, 2001; Richardson, 2008b). Female graduates were more likely than male graduates to have entered employment or further study six months after leaving UK HE (Connor *et al*, 2004). For first-generation graduates, males reported less job satis-faction while females were more likely to report that their qualification was unnecessary for their graduate job (Blasko, 2002). However, UK male graduates were found to be earning 12 per cent more than their female counterparts (Chevalier, 2004).

Recently, there has been considerable concern about outcomes for ethnic minority students in higher education in the UK. Despite their increasing participation levels in UK HE, ethnic minority students are less likely to obtain a good degree than their white counterparts (Broecke and Nicholls, 2007; Connor *et al*, 2004; Elias and Jones, 2006;

Leslie, 2005; Naylor and Smith, 2004; Owen *et al*, 2000; Purcell *et al*, 2005; Richardson, 2008a).

Connor *et al* (2004) found that six months after leaving UK HE in 2000, 94 per cent of white students had obtained 'successful' graduate outcomes – success being defined as either entering employment or further study. These were closely followed by the Indian, Black Caribbean and Black Other groups. The Black African group, however, had the lowest success rate. Ethnic minority graduates faced greater difficulties in obtaining an initial job and were more likely than white graduates to obtain graduate level positions after a longer time period (Blasko, 2002; Brennan *et al*, 2003). Asian graduates were the most likely to be in professional or managerial positions, although such positive employment outcomes were not reflected in higher salaries or greater job satisfaction (Blasko, 2002).

The outcomes for different groups of people suggest that the benefit of a higher level qualification is experienced differently and it is therefore important that widening participation, or fair access, to HE is not confused or conflated with upward social mobility. Higher education does have a role to play in ensuring fair outcomes for graduates, but it needs to operate in partnership with employers who must also examine their practice.

A growing system: Higher education from the 1940s to the present day

Higher education has grown from an elite system in the 1940s to a mass system in the twenty-first century, with the number of young people engaged in higher education at age 18 increasing from 5 to 47 per cent (*Times Higher Education*, 28 March, 2012). This growth in HE was also reflected in the growth of the public sector at the time. Since this was also a period of significant upward social mobility, it is valuable to explore working-class engagement with HE across this timeframe.

There were two particularly rapid phases of growth: between 1966 and 1970 and between 1988 and 1993. The first phase saw significant increases in the raw numbers of working-class entrants into HE, although the proportion of the classes remained the same. This can be partially explained by changes in the size of the middle and working classes, but not completely as in social mobility terms the middle-classes are 'stickier' (Saunders, 2010:52) – they have been better at ensuring that their children benefit from the expansion of HE than those from working-class backgrounds (Ross, 2003). Understanding this fact has led to considerable concern amongst policy makers about the make-up of the student body in higher education during the first decade of the twenty first century. But the focus has largely been on inputs: that is, getting working-class students into HE. The fair access agenda, however, which focuses on getting working-class students into the most selective institutions, has become increasingly important in policy circles, as despite progress to widening participation across the sector, less progress has been made in the most selective institutions (Harris, 2010). There is little comment about the outputs, ie moving working-class people into middle-class jobs, although this has now been high-lighted in the latest Milburn reports (2012a and b).

In 1978 the department for Education and Science (DfES) suggested that higher education should widen the pool of potential applicants to include 'children from manual workers' (p8) and mature entrants. During the 1980s, the latter were given places in many HE institutions recognised their prior experience even if they did not have A-levels. Access courses for mature returners were also developed. This route increased the number of women in higher education substantially and by 1992 there were equal numbers of male and female students in HE for the first time. Women who had not been able to develop their potential earlier in the century now found routes into HE and went on to progress into middle-class careers. As Savage points out:

> Women's occupational destinations are considerably less affected than men's by the class of their fathers once their ability is taken into account ... Women rely more exclusively on having high ability and converting this into good educational qualifications while the sons of service class fathers have other resources at their disposal to allow them the chance of moving themselves into the privileged classes. (2000:92)

Students from working-class backgrounds have increased from 5 per cent in 1970 to 15 per cent in 2005. By 2010 they accounted for nearly 20 per cent of the overall student population. Over time, HE institutions have genuinely widened participation.

It is difficult to predict how widening participation will be affected by the significant changes to funding in HE across all parts of the UK in the last three years. The new funding environment is discussed in greater detail in the final chapter of the book and some evaluation of the future of widening participation in HE and its effects on social mobility is attempted.

This chapter has set out some of the issues relating to social mobility. While there is clear interest in the issue of social mobility in our society, there is less clarity about trends in mobility. The majority of academics, who focus on a class analysis for measuring mobility, argue that absolute mobility has increased significantly over the last 70 years but that the rate of change may be slowing, while relative mobility has remained unchanged throughout the period. Colleagues who use income as a measure argue, however, that mobility may have decreased.

All these studies tend to focus on comparative inter-generational data rather than looking at individual changes over a lifetime. The debates about social mobility form the backdrop to this book, which details the personal histories of individuals who grew up in working-class families and who transformed their lives and now work in higher education as lecturers, managers and administrative staff. Each story is unique, but patterns emerge which suggest that there are some key elements that can make a difference to widening participation and social mobility. These themes are examined through the life histories and are discussed in chapters 3 through 7. The next chapter examines the approach taken in collecting the material for the book and the value of a life history methodology.

2

Class and the life history as an account of social change

I grew up in the North East of England. I spent my childhood in an old County Durham mining town, Tow Law, and as a teenager in west Newcastle. I was very fortunate. Like so many others of my generation I was the first in my family to go to university. It changed my life. A child of a council estate I was lucky enough to end up in the Cabinet. I was born at the right time. The '50s and the '60s saw Britain finally emerging from the aftershocks of the war years. Social Mobility was in full swing. (Milburn, 2011:1)

In speaking about his own life history, Alan Milburn draws out how social change can be embodied within one individual's experience. He highlights how the changes to social structure discussed in the previous chapter affected his own life, enabling him to move from a working-class background, through university, to become a leader in society.

This chapter is about the life history method, its value and how life histories can reveal qualitative detail to explain aspects of social change. The people represented in the research for this book are all currently working in higher education and all were the first in their families to study in higher education. They produced their own autobiographies for this research so I refer to them throughout the book as 'authors', 'respondents' or 'participants' to highlight their contribution.

As discussed in chapter 1, there are two basic ways of measuring mobility: income or class. Based on Boliver and Swift (2011) and Erikson and

Goldthorpe (2010), I argue that class can provide a more rounded picture of the measurement of social mobility. Class is a contested term within the social sciences however, but as it is central to the themes of the book, it requires some attention. In chapter 7 I look at it from the point of view of the participants but here I discuss it from a theoretical perspective and explore some of the debates surrounding class and how perceptions of it have changed over time. I argue that beyond the objective measure of class based on occupation, class is also a lived experience, encoded within the individual. Taking this position suggests that when analysing social mobility a life history approach can provide a richer and more nuanced sense of class experience than a record of someone's occupation (Archer, 2003).

It was noted in the previous chapter that most of the work on social mobility has focused on inter-generational movements. However it is widely believed 'that there is more diversity of work-life mobility trajectories than might be assumed from the standard mobility tables which compare class at one moment in time with offspring's class at another' (Savage, 2000:92). Personal history accounts can explore individual trajectories throughout the course of a life and while they do not provide macro level evidence for mobility within a lifetime they can offer detailed micro evidence of movement or stasis between classes.

As well as class, age, gender and ethnicity are important divisions in society which affect an individual's chances of being upwardly mobile. Such social divisions are discussed throughout the life histories presented in this book. This chapter sets out how the data for the book was collected and the scope and nature of the material in the life histories. It highlights the value of using a qualitative approach to enhance our understanding of the impact of policy and changes to social mobility in society. I begin by setting out the current debates on social class.

Class definitions and boundaries

Debates about the nature of a classed society have shifted in focus from class struggle and class reproduction to class identities (Archer *et al*, 2003). Increasingly, class analysis sees class as being embedded within individuals. Discussing it in relation to social mobility, Savage argues that 'class does not stand like a puppet-master above the stage pulling the strings of the dolls from on high: rather it works through the medium of the individualised processes' (2000:95).

This conceptualisation influenced how class itself is measured and has specifically affected the way class is discussed within social science literature on higher education as a field for analysis.

The most influential set of definitions of class was known as the registrar general's six level occupational class system, described as social classes I-V (class III being divided into IIIM and IIIN, depending on the level of skill attached to the occupation). This system was established at the beginning of the twentieth century and is still used in some of the literature on participation rates in higher education. Goldthorpe *et al* (1987), who produced the most comprehensive evaluation of social mobility in Britain in the latter half of the twentieth century, used a five class schema similar to the registrar general's classification. In the literature on higher education, concern about levels of participation of social class IIIM to V, ie the manual or working class, is regularly expressed.

More recently, after extensive research into the changing social structure of society, Rose and Pevalin (2005) created an updated classification system NS-SEC with a broad framework of 30 categories grouped into seven core occupational classes. This set of classifications attempts to bring into the schema categories that were not accounted for before, such as 'never been in work'. The Rose and Pevalin revised definitions highlight that the measurement of class is complex and open to change. As society alters, and employment changes, so too must definitions of occupational class. When measuring social mobility in society, such mutability is clearly significant.

Marxist definitions of class can accommodate occupational categories, but they tend to focus more on the nature of relations between the classes as the dynamic for society than on the more Weberian notions of status groups and continuities between classes. Marxists' views of class work at a high level of analysis, between the owners of the means of production or the bourgeoisie and those that sell their labour, the working class. However, the appreciation of class as a lived experience is shared by many writers irrespective of their theoretical perspective. E P Thompson, writing from a Marxist perspective, put it this way:

> By class I understand an historical phenomenon, unifying a number of dis-
> parate and seemingly unconnected events, both in the raw material of ex-
> perience and in consciousness. I emphasise that it is an *historical* pheno-
> menon. I do not see class as a 'structure', nor even as a 'category', but as
> something which in fact happens (and can be shown to have happened) in
> human relationships. . . . Class is defined by men as they live their own history,
> and, in the end, this is its only definition. (1964:9)

Writing about class inscribed within individuals and between generations, Bourdieu (1977) draws out the importance of other forms of capital to support the maintenance of economic resources in the middle-
classes. He argues that the middle-classes are able to maintain their
status through cultural and social practices which attune to the organi-
sational structures of capitalist society. For Bourdieu the middle-classes
particularly use the education system and its habitus (Bourdieu, 1985) to
enhance and maintain their position through the generations. Bourdieu
and Wacquant refer to this alignment between middle-class values and
culture and the education system as enabling middle-class children to
feel 'like a fish in water' (1992:127). By contrast, working-class culture is
less at home in this habitus.

In any grouping, culture develops and is passed between the generations, inscribing within the individual a sense of who they are and where
they are located. An individual's cultural practices become taken-for-
granted and cement aspects of their identity. Bourdieu (1984) argues
that middle-class culture aligns with institutional structures within
capitalist society which creates a smoother transition into middle-class
adulthood for middle-class children. This reproduces social divisions
within society as it is much harder for working-class youngsters to 'fit in'
with middle-class institutional practice since it is not embedded in their
culture. Scheff (1990) illustrates how the education system supports this
process by validating levels of ability, creating a sense of either esteem or
shame in the individual.

Bennett *et al* (2010) indicate that people's preferences for certain activities and attitudes cluster together, so taste and choice of lifestyle are
seen to relate to particular groups of people linked to different classes
in society. Bourdieu (1984) argues that as well as the social capital they
have acquired through their membership and professional relations,
the middle-classes are able to exploit these inscribed codes or cultural

capital to extend their influence across the generations, without being particularly aware of the power of their activities. In social mobility terms this is what Saunders means when he refers to the middle-class as 'stickier' (2010:52): they are more able to keep their position within the middle-classes for their children. Riddell (2010) describes this as a sense of entitlement, a right to a particular lifestyle.

Focusing on class identity as the level of analysis creates further complexity since the lived experience of individuals is never one dimensional, as Archer points out:

> As with identities, structural inequalities (for example of class, race, and gender) are never complete or absolute. They are both material and discursive, shifting and socially/historically constructed, and differently constructed and enabled across time and context for different individuals and groups. (2003:14)

In the previous chapter I argued that class analysis was more inclusive in any evaluation of social mobility than a one shot income measure as class definitions will draw out a range of aspects connected to people's social position alongside income and occupation. The relationship between economic resources and class provides fruitful insights when thinking about access to mobility. Savage (2000) argues that an individual's economic resources link to their class position. While the economic resources available to an individual would include wages from employment, they would also include the individual's level of economic stability and security. The accounts of mobility in this book focus firstly on transitions from working-class occupations to professional occupations in higher education. They also reveal complex relationships to economic resources between and within the generations. While more middle-class jobs often meant more stability and security, this was not always the case. For example, although it is clear that working in the higher education sector as an academic or administrator is middle-class employment, there is a difference in job security between permanent and temporary or full and part-time employment. The employment positions of the authors are discussed in chapter 7.

While no measure provides a complete picture of an individual's position, I remain convinced that a class-based form of analysis explains some aspects of the workings of our society. Divisions do exist between different groups in society and, as Archer highlights:

> Class identities and inequalities are shifting and changing, yet inequalities persist and endure ... the boundaries of classed identities and inequalities are thus indiscrete 'fuzzy' and stratified by race and gender. (2003:20)

According to Archer, class is articulated within a wider discourse of other social stratifications such as race, ethnicity, gender, age, disability and sexuality. A life history approach enables a greater understanding of the inter-dependencies between these stratifications within individual lives. The research methodology adopted to collect the data for this book required individual authors to self-report their class position over time. This was triangulated with other self-reported data on changing family and personal occupations, as well as data on social deprivation such as housing and family economic resources.

I do not intend to adopt any one particular position on class: rather, in this chapter I set out the broad debate and seek to live with the complexity, highlighting the role of class and other social divisions in shaping individuals' ambitions, abilities and pathways in life.

Sayer (2002) argues that it is often difficult for respondents to talk about their class and responses routinely reflect what they feel their class position should be. Savage emphasises this point:

> Evidence from surveys and qualitative material is consistent. People are ambivalent about class ... they wish to pursue 'ordinary' lives in which they are treated fairly and equally, as individuals on their own terms ... [individualisation theory] alerts us to the way that people seem keen to invoke a distinction between their personal lives in which class is rarely seen as a salient issue – and the world out there, the world of politics, the economy, the media and so forth. (2000:71)

In order to create a common framework to enable comparisons, class position has been defined by parental occupation and related social deprivation indices in this book. Although class definitions were first and foremost evaluated using occupation, other factors discussed in the narratives were also taken into account. For example, one of the respondents, Pauline, who went to a new university in the 1970s, says she came from a working-class background but her father was an office manager, making him middle-class. However, Pauline describes the family home environment as poor, as her mother did not work and she remembers having hand-me-downs into her teenage years. Her perception was that they had very little. She says:

> Growing up in the 1960s we always seemed to have to scrape by ... mum didn't work and there were four of us kids. We didn't go on holiday expect to see family members.

Pauline's account indicates that she had a deprived background, despite her class position. Payne *et al* highlight that deprivation cannot automatically be equated with class position, although class position in the labour market is often a key determinant of family wealth. Pauline's story is an example of Payne *et al*'s argument that class analysis often ignores 'the conditions and causes of poverty and social exclusion' (1996:17).

Over the last forty years access to resources has increased and society's level of affluence is now much greater than it was in earlier generations (Gazeley, 2003). This experience is reflected in many of the respondents' life histories. In any analysis, issues of poverty and wealth should be explored alongside definitions of occupation. These issues are discussed in the following chapters.

The life histories also draw out changes to intra-generational mobility in some families. As Savage (2000) points out, changes in social circumstances through a lifetime are often significant and need to be explored alongside inter-generational changes. Life history accounts allow for this level of analysis. Where intra-generational changes have been observed these are described and discussed. If the participant became a student in HE after the age of 21, their own occupational status and living conditions were used to define their class.

Chapter 7 examines the authors' own sense of class, ambiguities and class transformation in more detail. Many of the accounts are highly reflective and reveal important aspects of the effects of upward social mobility on different individuals' identities.

In the research on widening participation there are further complications. In Forsyth and Furlong's study of working-class students moving into HE, it was found that:

> The majority of the sample in the research, those who got as far as Scottish Highers were female. Also nearly half were more advantaged i.e. parents not manual workers. (2003:4)

Forsyth and Furlong argue that even in 'working-class areas', like Glasgow where the study was conducted, it is the more advantaged within the working class who are more likely to succeed. While many of the authors' family backgrounds in this study were from manual backgrounds, there were a significant number who did record some upward social mobility during their childhood.

An example of changing family circumstances through childhood can be seen in the story of John, who came from a manual working-class background. John's father was a miner. Growing up in the late 1950s, life was hard. They had few 'extras' and meals largely consisted of staples like 'stovies', a potato dish with very little meat. However, when they moved to Northern Ireland, his father's position improved and John could see they were better off than many around them. His family had strong trade union and deep religious affiliations, so education was important to the family and seen as way of bettering yourself (Hall, 1999). The importance of these social ties and connections, or 'social capital' (Field, 2008), are discussed in chapters 6 and 7.

The mix of complex stratifications which form part of our identities, such as gender, ethnicity and class, are thus written into the changing nature of our society. As Savage highlights, the importance of individual experience cannot be under-estimated:

> Class processes are best seen not as 'macro-social constraints' but as working biographically through the individual. Individual factors mediate the relationship between class position and social mobility. (2000:73)

It is through individuals themselves that class experience and class movement or stasis is lived out and understood.

Although it is possible to identify class characteristics and class position, even if in complex ways, many people do not identify with their class. Class might be inscribed in our lives but we tend increasingly to live our lives with a sense of being individualised. As Beck observes in relation to our current society: 'the individual himself or herself becomes the reproduction unit for the social in the lifeworld' (1992:130).

This individualisation brings with it a different level of risk for particular groups in society. As the state has receded, with the impact of globalisation individuals have had to take sole responsibility for their actions. '...

Individuals are more likely to blame themselves for life inequalities' (Archer, 2003:16). However as Beck says, it is also the case that these risks are borne unevenly:

> The history of risk distribution shows that, like wealth, risks adhere to the class pattern, only inversely: wealth accumulates at the top, risks at the bottom ... Poverty attracts an unfortunate abundance of risks. By contrast, the wealthy (in income, power and education) can purchase safety and freedom from risk. (1992:35)

Such considerations suggest that class is still a vital part of the explanation for social divisions, social mobility, or lack of it, and the unequal distribution of life chances. Class is embedded in our biographies and is experienced through our day to day lives. Class has consequences or, as Bennett *et al* put it in their research on cultural practices, 'class [still] matters' (2010:52). In an analysis of the life accounts of people whose experience was to move class, it is therefore important that we explore how that movement is understood by them. The next section examines how using life histories can throw light on the process of social mobility.

The life history approach

> ... it is not surprising that a new focus on individuals is having influence on the methods in the social sciences. In such a climate the time seems right for a methodological turn towards the study of individuals, a turn to biography. (Rustin, 2000:34)

Sociology in America produced an early flowering of life history work through what was often termed 'the case study' at the beginning of the twentieth century (Shaw, 1966; Platt, 1981). However, its more recent history grew out of a re-evaluation of history and sociology during the 1960s. It began with a set of new methodologies around oral history, based on a determination to record and capture ordinary people's accounts of their lives. Some of the most influential books on oral history that emerged in this period came from Howard Becker (1970), a sociologist in the USA, Ken Plummer (1975), a sociologist in the UK, and Paul Thompson (2000), a historian in the UK. All set out strong arguments for the value of personal accounts, which interviewed ordinary people about their experiences. Becker stated that 'the life history more than any other technique ... can give meaning to the ... notion of process (1970:vii). Plummer argued that as a method we ignore life history 'at our peril' (1983:149).

Since then a raft of related methodologies – the analysis of biographies, autobiographies and so on – has developed. These have created a suite of methodologies to record and analyse life experience in our time. Life history methodology is based on a belief that subjects seek to make sense of their own lives and can provide, through linking life experience with particular events, deep insight into life choices and chances as well as providing explanations for social change. As Armstrong says:

> The life history method assigns significance and value to the person's own story, or to interpretations that people place on their own experience as an explanation for their behaviour. (1987:8)

Although personal stories, life histories also provide rich detail of the interface between the personal and the social, as individuals describe their encounter with society and engagement with heritage and culture. Rustin points out that biographical studies offer particular insights in this area:

> Ethnography and biography explore process, rather than merely structure. It is because it is through single cases that self-reflection, decision and action in human lives can best be explored and represented that the case study is essential to human understanding. (2000:49)

In his large scale analysis studying social mobility in Britain, Goldthorpe quoting Becker (1970), was particularly keen to ensure there was a qualitative element to his investigations. He argued:

> This [life history approach] was one which could be regarded as especially apt to our purpose of eliciting our respondents' own understanding of the mobility ... the distinctive feature of the life history approach Becker argues, is in 'assigning major importance to the interpretations people place on their experience' and its distinctive value is in 'giving us insight into the subjective side of much studied institutional processes'. (Becker, 1970:66 quoted in Goldthorpe *et al*, 2003:218)

The life history approach provides a both richness and a level of understanding that cannot be gained from survey data because it is the heart of the individual's experience. Goldthorpe *et al*'s (2003) analysis of the survey work found levels of absolute upward social mobility in British society, but it was only through the life history interviews he conducted that he discovered what this upward mobility meant for those who had moved class position. For example, he found that the upwardly mobile individuals in his sample were able to be 'overwhelming recognised – in contrast to those stable in class 1 – major social differences between themselves and their fathers' (2003:227). In other words upwardly socially mobile individuals were more aware of differences between themselves and their fathers. The qualitative data adds new dimensions to the meaning of changes in the shape of British society, to under-standings of class identity and to the experience of social mobility. It adds a particular nuance to the context of the embeddedness of class in individuals' identities.

This book is based on the life stories of more than 130 individuals who grew up between the 1940s and 1990s in the UK, all of whom currently work in higher education. They were the first in their families to study in higher education and their family background was mostly working-class. The life histories provide insight into the changes in British society and British higher education since the 1950s in particular. The book enables the authors to speak for themselves, using their words to illustrate the discussions of social change recorded in their accounts. The next section describes how the life histories were collected.

Gathering the stories

The research began in 2003 and was completed in 2010. The idea for the project developed after I read the autobiography of William Woodruff. Born in 1916 into a cotton mill workers family, he left school at 13 but went to Oxford University in 1936, later becoming a professor of History in the USA (Woodruff, 2002, 2003). His life story demonstrated that with the right conditions working class people could use education to move up the class structure, despite considerable obstacles. I wanted to understand how this process of upward social mobility worked for suc-cessful first generation entrants to HE.

I began to seek out life histories of people working in HE who had grown up in working-class households. I established two different tech-niques to gather data. In the first instance, I made contact with large numbers of people through education email forums. The forums target people working across the further and higher education sector, which naturally confines the study to a particular group – those who work in post compulsory education. However, since education as a whole, and further and higher education in particular, are sectors which have grown considerably in size and scope since the 1950s, the study's focus seemed appropriate for the following reason: if social mobility was achieved by increasing the middle class by creating more middle-class jobs, this sector should have brought in more people from working-class backgrounds.

I posted a message to the groups asking for volunteers. I asked for people who would be prepared to participate in a research project that looked at the life experiences of people who had come from a working-class background who were the first in their families to attend higher education and people quickly made contact. I was surprised by the degree of interest in the research and pleased by the age range and diversity of those who responded.

Drawing on the extensive and well known work of the Mass Observation Archive (Sheriden, 1993), which provides a detailed and rich data source on social life in Britain, a 'directive' – a series of prompt questions – was sent to the respondents asking them about their family, community, school and HE experiences. A statement of confidentiality was attached to the directive, so all the names in this book are pseudonyms, although I have not altered detail on institutions or geography. All the authors now work in the HE sector in various positions: administrators, student union staff, researchers, part-time and full-time lecturers as well as senior managers. Such variety meant that the sample contained people across the professional/administrative divide but none who were employed in manual jobs.

To gain access to students who were more recent entrants into HE, the same directive was used, but students were contacted through teaching faculty in two different institutions, one new and one old university. A total of 28 students sent in their life histories. These individuals have since progressed through HE and are discussed in chapter 6.

The respondents in this research are clearly interested in 'telling their story'. Many described the act of writing their life story as 'cathartic'. A lot of the stories contain rich detail of life from the 1940s to the turn of the century and therefore chart considerable social change. Many of the earlier stories document a greater level of poverty than the later stories, because living conditions for all classes improved into the 1960s. As Dorling points out:

squalor in the 1940s was life in crowded damp accommodation with inadequate hygiene, no hot running water and often no inside toilet ... [deprivation] in 2007 [is where] a quarter of households had no access to a car, whereas thirty percent had two or more cars (2010:212).

Like social mobility, poverty can be seen in absolute terms – not enough food to eat, no fixed housing etc – or relative terms – in relation to others. In moving across time and spanning changes to British society, these life stories provide detail of the experience of those changes.

Counting and categorising individual lives

The total number of life histories received was 139. Some wrote their autobiography in a free-flowing style while others used the prompts more directly. Of the 139, 96 were female and 43 were male while 15 respondents who were from ethnic minority backgrounds. While some respondents spoke about being dyslexic, none identified themselves as having a disability.

Forty-eight people had gone into HE as mature students, some having tried to gain a degree more than once. One hundred and thirty-two had been, or were, full-time students and seven were part-time.

Respondents entered higher education during the following periods:

Period of Entry	Number
Pre 1963 (Before the Robbins universities)	13
1964 – 1979 (Considered the 'golden period of HE', much of the time with full grants for students)	46
1980 – 1996 (The period of massification and reduction in the unit of resource for institutions)	52
1997 – 2007 The introduction of fees paid first upfront and then largely by loans which were paid back once the student was in employment earning over £15,000.	28

The life histories were analysed using qualitative software to draw out key themes in the material. They extract the commonalities between the respondents as well as what makes each one unique. Examples of social mobility within generations as well as between them are also recorded. For example, one respondent said her family background was upper-class, although she had grown up in rural poverty when her mother decided to leave her father and both families disowned her. This suggests a downward movement in her family background. Others talked about seeing their families' life chances improving as they grew from small children into teenagers. Most of the sample reported growing up with some experience of real poverty, particularly if they grew up immediately after the Second World War. The examples they cited include having secondhand clothes and toys, not being able to afford holidays or any nights out, having free school meals, not having a television, or being unable to pay the rent and being forced to move home in the night to avoid the rent man.

Many of the stories used metaphors of movement to describe the changes in their lives. Conceptions of education as 'a passport to a different life', or 'escape', and descriptions of 'moving away from dead end jobs' were common. This sense of symbolic movement was further heightened by many stories of actual physical movement, travel and moving away from working-class communities. Movement therefore became a theme that emerged from the data and has been used as a central concept in exploring meanings.

Life histories provide unique insights into people's perceptions of their experience and reflect how British society has changed over the last 70 years. While each account is unique, taken together they reveal detail of the changes in society: how the role and perceptions of women have altered, how lifestyles and attitudes have changed and how employment and the world of work has shifted along with the growth and development of higher education across the UK. These accounts therefore provide a particular record of life over the last 70 years through the lens of social mobility and higher education.

This chapter has reviewed current debates on class differences and class perceptions in our society. It has highlighted the value and role of life history accounts as a mechanism to provide detail and richness to wider quantitative work on the social structures in society. It has set out the scope of the research undertaken for the book and detailed the range of life histories examined. The next chapter begins to examine the life histories in detail, starting with accounts of growing up during and immediately after the Second World War. All the authors in this age group entered higher education immediately after completing their secondary education and were part of a 'rare breed' of university graduates.

3

A rare breed: Working-class students in higher education before the Robbins Review

> I was born ... in 1941 so grew up in the forties. This means I remember the bombing of the Clydeside, gas masks, sweets rationing and sugar rationing, standing in queues, 'baby' orange juice, delicious milk puddings made with National dried milk, ration books, unwinding old jumpers and re-using the wool, lipstick with a funny taste, [and my single most important memory from my childhood was] the German bombing and rushing down so many times of the night to the unpleasant smelling concrete air-raid shelters. (Helen)

Now over 70 years ago, the Second World War still has huge resonance in our society. Helen is one of thirteen people who entered higher education between 1955 and 1963 who wrote her biography for this book. Her account has much in common with the others who grew up in this period. The war was a difficult time, not just the rationing, air raids and bombing, but the disruption for families. Many describe war-time experience as a childhood of women, of being brought up by mothers, grandmothers, aunts, and several talk about only meeting their fathers on their return from the armed forces when they themselves were older.

Surprisingly, rationing brought some positive consequences for the working classes. The period during and immediately after the war saw the end of the desperate poverty which had existed in the 1930s. The very fact of rationing created a sort of rough equality, as Gazeley points out:

The impact of wartime controls on food consumption was generally positive and class differentials in the nutritional adequacy of diets were significantly less pronounced than they had been prior to the Second World War. (2003: 157)

That is not to say that there was no poverty after the war, but in comparison to the earlier part of the twentieth century, the post war era provided greater economic security for people from lower socio-economic groups. The changes to social policy and the creation of a welfare state with the establishment of the National Health Service in 1948 heralded a different social settlement between the state and its people. Alongside these social changes, the economy and the world of work altered significantly.

In employment terms, wage differentials between higher and lower paid workers decreased and Britain had near full employment through the late 1940s and into the '50s. By 1961 women again became more active in the labour market, with the figure rising to 37 per cent in work. This period also saw the development of more highly skilled and professional work opportunities and this, as discussed in chapter 1, brought more working-class people into the middle-classes (Goldthorpe *et al*, 2003). Increased earnings meant that people had more income at their disposal. Gazeley records that 'by 1953 in the case of households with two adults and five children the real value of surplus income ... was ten times its 1935 value' (2003:167). The education system also developed considerably during this period.

The Education Act of 1944 was implemented in 1947 and raised the school leaving age to 15. The Act established what became known as the 11 plus examination which graded children at age 11 and earmarked them for either an academic or a non-academic route. This process created grammar schools for the academically able and technical and secondary modern schools for other children. Some working-class children did go on to grammar schools, although this was by no means automatic even if they did pass their 11 plus. A bright working-class student may not have gone on to the grammar if their parents did not want them to or could not afford the costs of attendance. In the life histories in this book there are several accounts of parental refusal to let students attend grammar school and only many years later, as mature students, were they able to go on to study in higher education. There were accounts of parents not being able to afford the required uniform which prevented the child from attending the grammar school. Such accounts of mature returners to HE are discussed in Chapter 5.

While attending a grammar school in the 1950s did not guarantee a student going on to university, not attending one severely restricted the possibility of going on to higher education directly from school. Many who attended the secondary modern schools did not study the relevant syllabus required to pass the university entrance examination and although the 1944 Education Act envisaged different pathways for technical and vocational education the technical route was never fully developed. In the twenty-first century the desire to develop different routes through education into higher level skills remains a concern in the UK, despite successive governments' attempts to deal with the problem. In other European countries such as Germany, by contrast, technical education is well served and students are easily able to access to higher level skills through this route.

Immediately after the war university education in the UK was limited. In 1948 there were only eighteen universities but by 1965 this had grown to 35 (Tight, 2009). Teacher education took place in predominantly single sexed colleges of education which were affiliated with universities through the 1944 Education Act. The same act also saw the development of advanced technical colleges, or CATS as they were then known, in addition to affiliations between some redbrick universities and technical colleges. Overall, approximately 97,000 students were at university in 1954 but, with the increase in the number of institutions, by 1964 these numbers grew to 160,000 (Tight, 2009). The vast majority of students were full-time, with approximately 13 per cent of the student population engaged in part-time study.

Women were still significantly under-represented in HE during this period; in 1945 the ratio of female to male students was less than 1:2. Some institutions would not accept women at all and there were quotas for women in subjects such as medicine. This trend continued until 1965, so despite increases in the overall numbers, women students still accounted proportionately for only about half the number of their male counterparts. In other words, while growth in HE participation was evident for both males and females, the expansion benefited men more than women.

Funding for students was fairly haphazard. Dyhouse sets out the situation until the '60s:

> Student grants came in the form of state, municipal and county scholarships, all hotly competed for. State scholarships were highly prized, few and far between and tended to go to students setting their sights on Oxford or Cambridge. ... [local authority provision] was patchy and inconsistent ... the most important source of funding for students from poorer homes ... came from grants from the Board of Education, made in return for a 'pledge' ... to teaching as a career. (2008:3)

Even if students showed considerable promise at school and got into and through the grammar system, it was extremely difficult for people from working-class backgrounds to enter higher education at this time if their families were not fully committed. To have done so would have required families to make significant sacrifices support their children into and through higher education.

At 2 per cent and 8 per cent of the population in 1945 and 1966 respectively (Mayers, 2011) overall participation in HE was low. These statistics explain why higher education was truly elite during this period. Cotgrove (1958) indicated that working-class students in his survey were often part of the small number of part-time students already in work in technical colleges. Even by 1971, when grants had been introduced, Abbott – whose survey looked at three universities: Edinburgh, Durham and Newcastle – tried to explain why there were few working-class students:

> The failure of the working class to take advantage of educational opportunity and the reason for the corresponding expansion of the lower middle-class students may be attributed to cultural factors at work at grammar school level. (1971:552)

In the 1950s and early 1960s working-class students at university were a particularly rare breed. Female students were also under-represented so their participation was even rarer. Although there may well have been 'cultural factors at grammar school level' as Abbott suggests, until the full introduction of grants in the mid-1960s, funding remained difficult. Dyhouse describes how parents did other people's 'washing, took in lodgers, kept chickens and went charring to scrimp resources' (2008: 4). Alongside this was a clear class divide in terms of which institution students would attend. Stories highlight that 'public school boys would rather go straight into business ... or to a foreign university ... than go to a Redbrick university' (Sampson, 1962:206). Although now part of the elite Russell Group of universities, where public school children dominate, during the 1940s and 50s Redbrick universities were thought to attract a lower class of student.

While the life histories of people who entered university during this period talk of hardship they also describe changing times and improvements in their family circumstances through their childhood. All but one of the thirteen respondents went straight to university, with one attending teacher training college before she later fulfilled her dream of going to the London School of Economics (LSE). All the respondents who attended university during this period are now in senior positions in universities. Their roles include pro vice chancellor, a professor of politics, another in physics, a senior lecturer in engineering, a dean, associate dean and a head of widening participation. The next section sets out the main themes which emerged from the experiences of the participants in this era.

Childhood, growing up and school

All the participants described themselves as having a working-class background, but for two of the group their families became upwardly socially mobile during their childhood. The family of one opened a successful business, while another bought his own house and moved to the suburbs when he was still a teenager. Poverty was something every participant was aware of and all mentioned 'going without' from time to time. One participant, Pat, put it this way:

> Father was a school keeper, mother a milk lady. My parents were deserving rather than feckless poor, ie they were very frugal and avoided debt. This was clearly a product of long periods of unemployment (in the pre-welfare era) which their fathers had both suffered in my parents' formative years.

All participants were very aware of their class position as children. Their parents' occupations included a fireman, waitress, gardener and carpenter. Most of the time, despite having low wages from their fathers' income, only one of the mothers worked full time; others did intermittent part-time work to lessen the burden of difficult financial situations. John who went to Hull University in 1960, stated that class permeated his entire life as a child:

> All my school age memories are inflected with a strong sense of class difference between me and the others at the school. I didn't have the things I should have for games, kit and things. The teachers complained and the other kids were particularly awful about it.

The participants grew up in different parts of the UK from Scotland down to South London. All were part of a two-parent family but during the war they were brought up in environments that were often female-only. One participant, Sue, commented that: 'I was brought up by my mother and the female lodgers to begin with, calling them Auntie x, etc, so much so that I called my dad 'Auntie Daddy' when he came home on leave [from the war].'

This lifestyle did not seem to create any difficulties for the children however. While acknowledging the experience of air raids and rationing, all felt their childhoods were positive and their family were supportive and loving.

The environments the authors describe while growing up belong very much to a child's world: very seldom did they ever go out with their parents, with one participant Peter describing always being outside with friends because there was no room inside the house: 'We lived on the street, in backyards and alleyways ... always out ... the house was simply too small'. Activities which required money were uncommon but occasional visits to the cinema were mentioned. One participant explained that in the 1950s they would sometimes get to go the cinema with their parents to avoid the cost of babysitters. Others had extended families, grandparents who would care for them while the parents went out or were at work. Only one participant, David, describes his mother going back to full-time work after he was born.

Comments relating to activities within the community varied. Some enjoyed being part of their community but all described the impact passing the 11 plus examinations had on their local friendships: 'I moved away, and without realising it in a year I had no friends in my area ... all my friends were from the other side of town now' (John).

All the authors describe being involved in community activities as children and teenagers: church groups, cubs, scouts or girl guides and political groups such as the young communists and young socialists. Such activities often gave the children a sense of different possibilities. Helen talked about her church group: 'going to the seaside ... it was wonderful ... seeing the sea for the first time ... imagining boats and travel, set me dreaming'. These imaginings offered a different view – alternatives to the daily lives they led – and in many cases ignited in their imaginations a possible alternative to the lives of their parents: 'At the young socialists we talked about a different world. We believed we could and would create it' (Peter).

Most describe music, boyfriends and girlfriends as their main interests when they became teenagers. This was the 1950s and youth music was just beginning to take off. Most loved jazz or the new rock and roll. Again the authors record a growing sense of belonging to something different to their parents' world: 'It felt like a new generation was emerging ... we had different ideas and wanted more' (David). Through their community group involvement many went to camps and were involved in amateur dramatics or Sunday school teaching. Urry (2007) draws out the importance of mobility, real or virtual, in creating new social meanings. In these stories and accounts through the generations of the twentieth century, the language of movement and place resonate. This theme of 'mobilities' is discussed in chapter 7.

The overall impression from this group of respondents is one of engagement in many different activities, in their communities while young and at school, and a loving family environment – a springboard from which to grow and change. Although most of their parents were unable to help in terms of their learning – 'it was not that they were unwilling but they were unable' (Paula) – there was financial support and encouragement and a general commitment to education as a means of a better life and upward social mobility from all but one set of parents. In this period parents had both aspiration and a belief that education could make a difference to their children's lives. Helen's parents were able to help and she described her family's attitude as 'positive to any type of learning, we played number and word puzzles and did jigsaws etc. [They were] also positive to formal education'.

She said that her father taught her to speak French, which he had learned during the war, and she joined the book club with her mother, who encouraged her to read as much as possible. All were strong readers who saw reading as 'an escape' (Helen). Books and reading feature throughout the life stories and their significance is discussed in chapter 7.

The life of the school and the life of the families were described as 'miles apart ... a different world' (Peter). The school did not communicate with the family other than via school reports. None of the authors describe their parents attending any parents evenings despite their aspirations for their children. There is a sense in these accounts that while parents were supportive of education, they did not see any need to engage with their children's school, nor did they wish to: 'Although my mum took me to the library regularly, she never came to the school. That was not her territory ... we just had to get on with school. I think they were sort of in awe of it all' (Paula). Studying at home was particularly hard for the participants as houses were crowded with no private space. Peter wrote: 'there simply was nowhere quiet to do so even if I wanted to study as I shared a minute bedroom with my brother'.

Segregation between students from different backgrounds was common at grammar school, although most enjoyed their time there. There were two exceptions, however, most notably Peter, who said: 'If I had had my way I would have left school at 15.' Peter claimed to have very few positive memories of school:

> I hated the discipline and I hated the middle-classness of the place from which I felt both excluded and alienated, but even though my dad hadn't had an education, he made me stay on, said I needed to get an education and I was clever enough. He was right of course.

Paula, who was also aware of class at school, commented that 'class distinctions were rife', but that this created in her a determination to succeed: 'Much of my later life was governed by 'I'll bloody show them'. Others, while noting class distinctions in the school, enjoyed their education and describe special teachers and good friends. David talked of an 'inspirational head' for whom there was only one standard, 'the best whoever you were. That had a real impact on me and made me work hard.' Helen stated that she was unaware of the importance of studying at school, but that she was inspired to do so by 'a couple of helpful teachers and a six girl close friendship group'. Jenny discussed her and her friends' attitude to school, saying that they were 'mostly obedient, some cheeky, all anxious to do well.' She stated that she was taught by 'a couple of spell-binding teachers who could weave their lessons into one's imagination and make it so easy to learn and understand.' Most of the authors were clear that the grammar school helped them to move on into higher education as although their parents wanted them to do well, actually deciding to go to university for this group was more to do with the culture of the grammar school. This is discussed in the next section.

Going into higher education

The decision to continue studies at university level was almost exclusively influenced by schools and teachers. All participants said their schools gave them little option other than to continue their studies. Everyone who went into the sixth form was expected to move on into higher education. As Riddell points out, taking on an aspiration to change their lives is important to enable young people from working-class backgrounds to take on higher level study. He says:

> They need to grow into a view of themselves which includes assumptions of the normality of such aspirations [to go to university] for people like them and the associated understanding and confidence to achieve them. This is to be their aspirational identity. (2010:47)

Developing in these working-class young people was a sense that continuing on to university was a new entitlement not based on their family background but rather on ability (Riddell, 2010). University was not the only destination for this continuation of study however; for young women in particular teacher training college was also seen as a respectable destination, which highlights social attitudes about women at the time. Paula took this route because her parents did not want her to move away from home. Her teachers also thought it the appropriate route as she could go to the college locally, but after several years teaching and the birth of her own child, she fulfilled her aspiration and went to the LSE. 'Although it was only actually eight miles away, that was seen as a long way from home so I acquiesced and went to teacher training college locally.'

The university experience

There were not many universities in the 1950s and they were mostly civic or ancient universities. The participants went to university between 1958 and 1963 attending Bristol (founded 1909), Hull (1954), Glasgow (1451), Birmingham (1900), Leeds (1904) and the London School of Economics (1895). One student, John, attended an Oxford College (1300s).

All the participants remember very little contact with their universities in advance of starting their degrees, but what comes through all the stories of those who went 'away' to university is the sense of freedom which going to university gave them. Peter described it this way: 'University and Hull were much better than home and Ilford.' Nearly all students gained a local authority grant to attend university and some talked about seeing paper money of their own for the first time. Grants were not a right at the time and were hard won based on a range of criteria including ability and status. With the exception of Paula, who attended LSE as a mature student with a child, and David who found that his life changed when he married his girlfriend who had got pregnant at the end of year one. All the other participants made friends and joined in the life at university but worked during vacations to make ends meet in a variety of jobs from postmen to factory workers.

In some cases the stories are very much of their time. John, who went to Oxford, pointed out that his college was male only, while Helen who attended Glasgow, spoke of their being a Director for Women Students since females were so much in the minority and regarded as needing special attention. Of the 500 students studying sciences in Helen's year, only twenty were women and all were 'made to sit at the front of lectures.' In other respects the authors recounted many similar activities while at university: joining clubs and societies, spending time with friends, visits to the pub and so on. All describe finding the first year difficult but several refer to this as 'not being unusual.' Although many thought of leaving early none did; some because they said they 'could not afford to ... I had won a grant, very difficult in those days and I just couldn't afford to pay it back' (Peter), while others simply settled in. The accounts of these authors' lives at university highlight the very different experiences of studying in higher education in the 1950s and early '60s and the significant contrast in experience of male and female students.

To provide some sense of the issues the next section looks at three of the life accounts in some detail.

Life at university: different experiences

Helen went to Glasgow University and studied pure science. She described herself as a good student who attended almost everything and who worked consistently hard throughout her degree. Because she was taking a science degree her timetable was full. She says she had 'three lectures every weekday morning and two chemistry and one physics labs in the afternoons.' Students were arranged alphabetically by name and women were made to sit at the front in lectures and in labs. Helen remarked that her lecturers were: 'a real mixed bag: some old and mumbling, some callow and stuttering, some brisk and efficient with wit, some sexist remarks/jokes, some women of the harsh, restrained clipped kind.'

Support came from other students both male and female, but Helen reported sadly that many female students dropped out when they became pregnant – 'contraceptives were extremely difficult to buy then'. Women were significantly in the minority at university and still faced considerable challenges, not least wanting the freedom that university allowed but which often came without the support to enable them to complete their studies.

Helen was extremely involved in extra-curricular activities which she found highly enjoyable. She was actively involved with the students' union:

> I loved Glasgow students' union (the women's union was called Queen Margaret Union after the queen of that name who introduced women's education to Scotland), debates, even impersonating Millicent Martin during a Question Time stunt, all wonderful stuff.

The friendships and support from the union enabled her to keep going, particularly in the early stages when she was not doing as well as she had hoped. When Helen was studying at Glasgow women made up a quarter of all students in Universities (Dyhouse, 2006). Men were only admitted to Queen Margaret Union in 1979.

Unlike the majority of the other students , Helen did not get a grant. Her parents supported her financially, having to go without at home in order to help her through university. Despite not understanding what degree level study required, they believed a degree was a pathway to a better life and wanted to help her: 'My parents were a bit bewildered but rather proud of me and made sure they saved to pay for what was needed and they wanted me to have the best life possible.' Helen supplemented their financial situation by working during the summer break and went on to study for an MSc in biochemistry.

John went to Oxford. He describes how 'family and friends mainly thought it a bit odd and over indulgent of my parents' to let him go to university. Because he was aiming for Oxford, which required applicants to pass an entrance examination, he had to do a third year in his sixth form to prepare and to 'learn Latin', which was also required at the time. However, he said he did not recall deciding to go to university as such:

> At a time when only a minority of school pupils went to university (or indeed, stayed in school after 15 – something that stopped some of my contemporaries taking up a place at the grammar school), it gradually became clear that I could expect to and it was accepted that I would. Family and friends mainly thought it a bit odd.

Following school John decided to take a gap year where he worked in a research laboratory. He was 20 when he went to Oxford, starting in 1958 and graduating in 1961.

John's experience at university was entirely positive. He talks of 'meeting people on my first day who subsequently have become lifelong friends'. He found the college very welcoming and did not experience feeling like an outsider. He wrote: 'In interaction with my fellow undergraduates, the first year was a great success ... the tutorial system guided us through the essential lectures and books, so we did not have to attend lectures to know what the syllabus was.' He also noted that:

> one of the merits of a college system is that you can reasonably expect to get to know all your contemporaries. Of mine, 90 per cent had been to private schools. A few like me had come from ordinary backgrounds. I don't recall that ever causing a problem or ill feeling; once there, the differences were less obvious.

John clearly enjoyed his time at university. The issue of gender is also highlighted in his story as his college was male only. He found lecturers' performance variable, but since attendance was not compulsory, he chose to attend only good lectures. Socially, John enjoyed life. He ran the college cricket club and was active in a range of other clubs and societies. He described himself as a 'gentle', not a 'hard', student. After graduating John went into industry and later took up a post in a university as a professor of physics.

David grew up in Surrey but had a father who worked as a gardener. As he earned so little, his mother went back to work when David was 18 months old. Like the others in this group he passed his 11 plus and went to grammar school: 'I remember when I went to the grammar that I tended to drift away from those who went to the secondary modern ... it was a real sifting of children – the 11 plus.' Like the others he almost 'automatically' went on to university: 'The expectation was that all pupils in the top set would go and the appropriate forms were supplied by the school.' He chose to study subjects he had been good at – languages – but hated the subject when he arrived at university and changed within a week to economics and politics. David went from Surrey in south London to Bristol University. He commented: 'There was very little in the way of induction. It felt strange at first, but I made a few friends reasonably quickly.' He described the teaching as hugely variable with some inspiring lecturers but others 'positively shambolic.' He regarded reading as vital to his success at university and felt that the university teaching 'could have been enhanced by more appropriate teaching strategies'.

David's first year at university was exciting. He had a good social life and enough money from his full grant to get by. By the end of the first year, however, his girlfriend, also at university, became pregnant and they got married during the summer. Unlike the women Helen described at Glasgow, his wife stayed on at university, but living on his grant with a baby made money very tight, especially as his wife's parents were unsupportive of her remaining at university. Like others David worked during vacations, at the post office and as a dustman. Having a small child meant they didn't go out much. By managing their finances the family avoided debt throughout their studies. David and his wife now work as economists at different universities.

All the participants are now in senior roles in universities across the country. They see the considerable influence they have in their roles and recognise that they have moved from one class position to another, all highly aware of their upward social mobility. They saw their own experience as radically different to their parents' situation as the 1950s and early '60s was a time when people's lifestyles improved (Gazeley, 2003). From these stories the key element which seemed to enable their social mobility was passing the 11 plus. Grammar schools were a vital although not absolute gatekeeper to higher education, paving the way for these individuals to become part of the growing middle-class in the UK. Their stories chart some of that development.

From access to HE to social mobility

When this cohort of students graduated, universities were expanding and considerable opportunities for employment as academics existed, especially for the male graduates. Peter, whose father was a fitter on the railways, went on to do an MA and later a PhD. He says: 'In 1966 when I had done my MA, I had three offers of jobs.' Peter commented: 'The alternatives looked to be all-round interesting but I kind of regret not going into TV in the '70s when I had nods and winks that were close to solid offers.' David, whose father was a gardener, said that it was 'fairly easy. I only applied for one job in Bristol where we were living and was successful.' John, whose father was a farm labourer, describes how he became 'hooked on research' as a student and carried on to do a PhD. He also commented that at the time it was easy to get a job in HE with a PhD: 'I had four offers from good universities.' Mike, who completed his undergraduate degree in 1964, said working at a university was:

> just what I wanted to do ... [people at the university] were very supportive, they gave me part-time teaching. I then got a two-year contract at another university and finally a permanent position after completing my PhD.

Gender and social mobility

Categorising the upward social mobility of women has been problematic for many social scientists because households were categorised by the class or income of the main breadwinner, a position not traditionally occupied by women. Unlike their male counterparts, who generally found employment in HE easy, the accounts of young female graduates told a different story. The challenges started young as there were quotas for girls to get to grammar school, a practice that continued into the 1980s in some parts of the UK. Even if girls were able to go to an academic school, progress to university was even more complex. As with the 11 plus, there were quotas in some subjects at university for women and they found they were often singled out and thought to require special attention, something Helen described.

Perceptions about pregnancy outside marriage forced women to drop out and even when such values were resisted and these women chose, as David's wife did, to stay on, the experience of completing a degree with a young baby while being very poor presented a further challenge. Most female graduates did not go into academic jobs in HE immediately but went instead into teaching in schools. This was common for women at the time, who were often encouraged into teaching as a 'suitable profession for a woman' (Paula). Helen, on the other hand, did get a job in HE, taking up a technician's post at an HEI in 1967. She was promoted to a lecturing post but missed out on a senior lectureship and had to leave her post in 1971 when she became pregnant, as the idea of maternity leave was, of course, non-existent. Helen was told that the post went to a 'male colleague who was less likely to leave and so supposedly lose the post to the department'. Helen is now a professor, having later returned as a mature student and studied religious education.

Another example of unequal treatment between men and women comes from Martha's biography. Martha married during her first year of university 'to get away from the pressure from my family of me living in sin'. Her husband was a year ahead of her and on completion of his degree, for which he gained a 2.2, he went on to do an MA. Martha commented: 'I remember when I went to see my university tutor about what I was going to do after university, he said that since I was married I would not be likely to need a career for very long.'

After completing her degree she joined her husband: 'I worked as a cook in a pub during the day and typed his thesis in the evening.' Taking on casual hours wherever she could, Martha's support for her husband meant he finally completed his PhD and went on to acquire a lectureship at a university. Like many other female graduates, Martha went into teaching. Several years later during the 1990s, she took an MA in education, finally getting a job as a widening access officer while studying for her own PhD.

The themes that emerge from this set of stories from 1945-1963 illustrate the levels of inequality for women in education and employment. As Meeham points out: 'Women have had to fight for entry as students and academics, and for recognition that their academic qualifications and potential are as credible as those of their male colleagues' (1999: 35). The accounts of female graduates in the 1950s and early '60s draw out the taken-for-granted Victorian attitudes towards women that still prevailed. Gender discrimination affected every one of the female authors and was further exacerbated by issues of class and finance.

Examining the gender issues from a position of economic resources, it is clear that these working-class entrants into HE were more vulnerable than their middle-class peers but that the female graduates were even more vulnerable. Gaining employment in HE was much more difficult for the women, often a consequence of the prejudicial attitudes towards married women – as in Martha's case – or social attitudes about what was acceptable women's work – as when Paula was made to go to teacher training college – or having to leave her job because she was pregnant, as happened to Helen.

Women's economic resources at the time were less secure than men's and this restricted their ability to succeed. The questions raised around social mobility and gender are threaded throughout the accounts in this book but the accounts of women who grew up in this period are particularly poignant and reveal much of the social context of their experience. Many young women in this period were unable to get through the system. The life histories reveal many accounts of women who grew up in the 1950s returning to higher education as mature students in later decades. Their histories are discussed in chapter five.

Women are often invisible in the literature on social mobility because of the methodological challenges of categorisation. This research highlights the transformation and the challenges women have faced in taking their place in middle-class society over the last 70 years. Their biographies are a testament to their persistence in difficult circumstances. The next chapter discusses the life stories of the authors who went through HE during the next wave of HE change, from Robbins until the massification of HE in the early 1980s.

4

The golden era? Funded growth and student grants

In 1963 the Robbins Report on higher education was published in the UK. Still regarded as a major watershed in the development of HE policy, it set out the parameters for growth in universities and the establishment of several new universities. Robbins argued that 'courses of higher education should be available for all those who are qualified by ability and attainment to pursue them and who wish to do so' (Committee on Higher Education, 1963:8). This statement became known as the 'Robbins principle' and it held true more or less into the twenty-first century when growth in demand outstripped available places. The Robbins principle dominated HE policy for over 40 years. His review altered the perception of higher education which had until then been regarded as only relevant to a limited pool of talent within the wider society.

In other parts of the Western world, higher education also saw growth during this period. In particular, in the USA, the GI bill in 1944 had invested in higher education immediately after the Second World War, giving servicemen the right to a higher education. During the 1960s and 1970s the civil rights movement ran significant campaigns to address the inequalities for Black students. Growth in HE was also seen in Australia where the number of universities grew from nine to fourteen in the 10 years between 1956 and 1966, enabling university numbers to treble (Beddie, 2010). Hence this period is seen as 'the golden age' for HE in other western countries as well as the UK.

The Robbins Report captured the spirit of the age. During the 1950s higher education had already started to establish a number of new institutions such as the University of Hull in 1954 and the University of Sussex in 1961. The Anderson Review of 1960 had recommended that there be a single system of means-tested grants for students, rather than the haphazard system of national and local grants that had operated before. The 1962 Act enshrined the Anderson recommendation and 'for nearly 30 years after the Education Act of 1962, student finance ceased to be much of an issue' (Tight, 2009:228). During the 1960s and 1970s students had their fees paid by their local authority and were able to access a means-tested grant for living. This created provision for students whose parents could not afford to pay for their children to go to university.

There were of course some who argued against the idea that HE should be available to all who qualified and wished to go. As Tight observes:

> This continuing expansion was viewed as a mixed blessing by those who believed in the existence of a fixed 'pool of talent' ... a view famously summed up by the author Kingsley Amis in the phrase 'more means worse. (2009:64)

The arguments about widening participation in the early twenty-first century had their roots in this period. The debate about the Robbins Review therefore marked the start of a wider debate about access and class. Similar arguments to Amis's had been made about women entering higher education in the 1900s and, as we saw in the previous chapter, female students remained in the minority in higher education from the 1960s until 1992. The Colleges of Advanced Technology (CATs), established in the 1950s were brought into the university system during the '60s, and later in the decade the government established polytechnics:

> The other key development of the 1960s which Robbins neither recommended, or really foresaw, was the creation of the polytechnics. ... They formed the other half of what was termed the binary policy, counterbalancing the university sector, and focusing more on applied and vocational forms of study. (Tight, 2009:70)

All this culminated in an expansion of the number of students in higher education, as Layard *et al*, report:

> From 1962 to 1967 the number of students in full time higher education grew in Britain from 217,000 to 376,000 and the increase over these five years was greater than over the proceeding twenty-five. (1969:13)

In 1969 the government announced the establishment of the Open University, a national university for open and distance learning. The number of students in higher education continued to increase into the 1970s, peaking at 14 per cent of the age participation rate in 1973. The 'golden age' of British higher education was a funded expansion of HE, providing resources for new institutions, 31 polytechnics and 24 universities, along with student funding from the public purse. Polytechnics were not as well funded as universities, but funded growth was still the over-riding feature of this period. The expansion was based on an increase in raw numbers at different institutions, with the Universities Grants Commission (UGC) believing that universities should not grow beyond an upper limit of 10,000 students per institution. This led to the development of a building programme of new universities.

During the 1970s the age participation rate stopped increasing at the expected rate. Peaking in 1973 at 14.2 per cent of the population, by 1981 it had dropped to 12.9 per cent. The raw numbers continued to rise however, following an overall increase in the size of the age group. But while absolute demand continued to grow, funding began to reduce and for the first time in the 1970s institutions faced 'efficiency gains' or cuts.

Public perception of the 1960s is often one of the radical periods of change in British society:

> The 1960s seem easily recalled as the decade of hippies and youth culture, where free love music and pop art glamorously take priority in general recollection over the less palatable actualities of the time. (Foster and Harper, 2010:2)

Students in particular were seen as pivotal to these changes and this is to some extent reflected in the life histories Margaret, for example, wrote: 'When it came to applying to university, I think I was very lucky to have been born at the time I was. I was 17 in 1968. It was all very exciting and change was in the air.' Despite the developments of the 1960s, however, it was not until the 1970s that these changes in social life were cemented and not until the 1980s that the impact of the legislative changes took effect. For example, in the 1970s equal rights for women were established in legislation but it was not until 1975 that the Equal Pay Act was enacted and the Sex Discrimination Act was passed. Similarly, while the student protests of 1968 are particularly well documented, many students were active in the feminist and gay rights movements of the 1970s, which continue to influence in our society today.

The political landscape of the two decades differed greatly. While the 1960s were largely dominated by a Labour-led government (1964-1970), the 1970s featured a Conservative government until 1974, and a Labour government until 1979. With a miners' strike that led to a three day week in 1974, and a raft of strikes during the 'winter of discontent' in 1978 the '70s were a period of much labour unrest. However, the accounts written for this book show that both decades were good times to be a student and a distinct flavour of change and freedom can be found in nearly all of them.

The first wave of higher education expansion

The period's expansion of higher education was not targeted at any particular group but grew out of a belief in a meritocracy. If you had the ability to study at university level and wished to do so, you ought to be able to go to university. This had been the central principle of the Robbins review: expand the system and the able would find their way into the expanded sector. But, even by 1977 'the age participation rate for social class I, II, and IIIN was just over 30 per cent and the age participation rate for social classes IIIM, IV and V was around 6 per cent' (Gorard, 2008:22). Working-class participation in higher education during the 1960s and 1970s was still very low compared to those from more affluent backgrounds, although levels were far higher than in the 1950s. The 1960s and 1970s were decades of rapid upward social mobility in British society as more middle-class jobs were created and the public sector expanded. Public policy and the changing nature of the economy created a greater need for graduates, and as higher education grew and new institutions were established, suitably qualified academics and administrative staff were required. The accounts of participants discussed in the previous chapter reflected such changes, with the male graduates all gaining the first job they applied for in HE. But while overall employment levels were high and demand for graduates even higher, working-class people were still much less likely to progress to HE or into a middle-class job.

By the late 1970s questions were starting to be asked about the composition of the student body in higher education and new ideas for enabling entry for different groups – particularly the development of access routes – began to emerge. However, despite the gap between higher and lower socio-economic groups in higher education evident in the 1950s, some working-class young people did progress into HE. Overall numbers of these entrants continued to rise – they simply failed to do so as rapidly as those of middle-class entrants. The next section draws out how this overall expansion in higher education was experienced by the authors in this book who were the first in their families to go into higher education during the 1960s and 1970s.

Students of the 1960s and 1970s

Unlike the previous generation who went to civic universities, this cohort tended to go to newly established institutions. Universities such as Warwick, York, and Sussex are mentioned, and polytechnics like Preston and Portsmouth, which offered sandwich courses with links to industry, emerged. For the first time some of the participants were mature entrants into higher education, following the access movement of the 1970s. Their stories are described in this chapter.

Despite the establishment of comprehensive schooling in 1965, grammar schools and the 11 plus still feature strongly in the accounts. However, unlike the previous era, where a grammar school education was vital to getting into university, the comprehensive school offered significantly more opportunities for students to progress into HE than the secondary modern did (Boliver and Swift, 2011).

Following on from the previous set of authors, these accounts reveal a great deal about the social changes at the time, one of the most significant being the emergence of the 1960s culture:

> [I grew up in the 1950s and 1960s] The '50s are mostly faded memories with little sense of time or order. The 1961 New Year Beano comic though carried a nice Biffo the Bear front page about how you could turn 1961 upside down and it was still 1961. That, perhaps, (along with my transition into secondary school the same year) marked my move into the 1960s. Of

course the 60s didn't really start until the middle of the decade, when I went to university, but I remember walking past a butcher's shop near where I lived in the evening to see a little poster of the Beatles laid out on the marble slab; about a month later the Beatles had their first number one.

From 1964 to 1969 nineteen participants – eight female and eleven male – went to university at age 18 or 19 while 27 – twelve female and fifteen male – started at 18 or 19 between 1970 and 1979. Their current roles in HE include principal lecturers, a head of a careers service, several widening participation officers, several deans of faculty, senior lecturers and heads of teacher training. Their fathers' occupations include tram driver, factory workers, printer, painter and decorator, labourer, maintenance fitter, train driver and joiner. In the 1950s cohort only one mother worked full time but among the 1960s and 1970s entrants this pattern changes. Some of the participants' mothers were in unskilled or semi-skilled work, as were their fathers, but a significant number were in clerical typing posts. This indicates the development of women's work during this period and is a real example of small levels of upward social mobility for these families.

The changing family and interest in learning

Most of these authors grew up in the 1950s or early 1960s. Many of them would have still been living with rationing and their childhoods, as they describe, would have been simple and relatively poor. The majority of the participants lived in council houses or private rental accommodation. Some mentioned their older siblings going out to work and contributing to the family income at home. Over time, as the nation became more affluent, consumer goods began to feature in the stories of the participants, who saw them as quite precious and hard-won. One of the participants, June, illustrates this well when she says: 'our house was furnished very simply and we are simple too. The arrival of the washing machine, the three-piece suite, the TV are all strong memories', meaning that they were not taken for granted but were regarded as special objects.

Like the previous generation, this group of authors had been involved in scouts, guides and youth clubs as young people. Martha, for instance, came from a strong trade union family while the mother of another, Donald, was both a parish councillor and an active member of the Labour party. He wrote:

We all went to the Mere Lane Working Men's Club and went on club trips to the seaside – dozens of double decker buses laden with families. My paternal grandfather was secretary to the working men's club and my dad was a shop steward.'

These connections into communities and groups offered these participants opportunities which others simply did not have. By contrast, Margaret, another participant who went to York University in the late 1960s, stated that: 'we had no extended family to act as a safety net and my father, as chief breadwinner, was sometimes ill and was also made redundant twice during my childhood, [so] I often felt that we were financially on the edge.'

One of the striking differences between this group and the earlier entrants is the number who commented that their father or mother had passed their 11 plus but had either left at 15 as the family could not afford to keep them there or had not gone to grammar school at all. The expenses necessary were cited as the reason for this. These parents were particularly aspirational for their children and were very supportive of their academic development. Martha's father was one such parent:

My father did well at school in spite of being absent for a long period of time because of rheumatic fever. He passed his 11 plus (or its equivalent then) but he could not go on to the grammar school because his parents did not have the money to send him.

As with the previous generation, books and reading were important. Most had few books at home, but there are many accounts of regular visits to the public library where they chose books on a weekly basis. Comments included 'not many books at home but I was an avid devotee of the public library' (Mark) and 'I was an avid reader, mainly from the public library. There were some books at home and I read what was available, as well as the Daily Mirror every day from cover to cover' (Martin). Frank also spoke about the importance of the public library:

We had no resources for study at home and very few books. But by the time I was about 10 or 11 I became an avid reader and I made massive use of the public library. I'd sometimes borrow three books and finish them within the day and be back at the library the next day. ... These were not heavy books, more adventure stories.

Schooling, homework and the role of teachers

One of the biggest challenges for the 1960s and 1970s entrants was study at home. Pat described a difficult home life with little encouragement for her studies. She said that locking herself away to do her homework was a means of escaping her father's escalating alcoholism. Joan, on the other hand, said that her father helped her with her homework, but for most there was little practical help beyond providing space and equipment. As Joan explained:'there was great respect for it [education] and for my teachers. Support for homework – bought me a desk when I was 14 so I could do homework in my bedroom.' The entrants mostly describe general encouragement towards education but reveal that their parents were ill-equipped to help in any constructive way. Martha pointed out that while education was considered vital, there was little understanding of the work she had to do:

> I would say that my parents were very much pro-education, but my school life was very much my own and my parents did not help me with homework. Not because they did not want to, I think, but because they didn't know much about it

Judy also commented that her parents encouraged her to do her best at every level but they themselves had not been academically successful:

> We were always encouraged to attend and do as we were told by teachers … both my parents had left school with no qualifications. Dad truanted a lot and mum had a lot of time off with health problems. They were keen that we should attend fully and not 'miss out' as they had done. They always viewed education as a means to improving our lives.

As discussed in chapter 1, research in the UK suggested that people believed in a meritocratic society and saw education and hard work as important drivers to achieve success and upward social mobility. These participants' parents held this view.

Homework was largely the young people's own business as their parents were not able to offer support because of their own lack of education. Frank put it this way: '.. There was no-one telling me not to do the homework (this happened with some of my friends). It was me spending hours, sometimes, puzzling over what I had to do what was needed.' What these parents mostly seemed to know was that their children needed time and space to study, although some could not provide specific study space: 'I always did my homework on the kitchen table around people. There was never any space for study' (Pam).

In the 1960s cohort all participants attended a grammar school. Most describe their time there as positive and several recall a social hierarchy within the school between middle-class and working-class children. However, one participant describes how he hated grammar school:

> [I have] almost exclusively negative memories. I was not happy at school and the attitude was summed up after I had finished O levels at age 16. I was expected to leave school at that point, although I had no clear idea what I wanted to do and do not recall any careers advice ... However I did better than expected at O levels. The school, while not explicitly saying so, did not believe I was capable of this ... there was a clear hierarchy and this was based on class although I could not have expressed this at the time ... some children travelled a long way to go to this school and tended to be from wealthier backgrounds, to travel together on the train and sit together in school. Others came by bike from 'better off' parts of the town and formed another clear group. There were a small number of people like me who walked in from the locality. There was continuing tension and occasional outbreaks of violence between these groups. The playground was at times a social minefield, and you knew which bits you didn't go near. (Mark, who went to university in 1969)

Almost all the other participants described positive memories of school. Judy was typical of the majority: 'I enjoyed school and always felt very comfortable there, ... I got on well with my teachers ... I had a strong group of friends ... who were all high achievers and all went on to university.' Such circumstances made most of the cohort committed students. They worked hard at school and never truanted, although one participant, Karen, highlighted that truancy was quite complex:

> I never truanted with others or went off on my own. I was too scared to do something like that. However, and especially during the years [when I was] 14-16 years old I was often off school with the consent of my mother. Maybe because we had no money for bus fares and maybe because the other reasons due to family issues but I was definitely off some days. Classic example of parental complicity in school absence.

By the 1970s, with changes in school education, the authors begin to describe attendance at the new comprehensive schools: 'Mine was the first year not to do the 11 plus in Bristol' (Kate). Kate later describes her comprehensive school:

> At secondary school I enjoyed the lessons, especially English, History, Geography and Home Economics, as I love cooking. In the '70s I can remember being a bit ashamed of the latter as it seemed very uncool and non-academic ... Although I attended a comprehensive school there was a distinct social hierarchy which I became aware of when I ventured off the estate. ... As I went up through the school and was placed in the higher 'sets' I became aware that my classmates were not the same social mix as on entry. More of my friends were from middle-class households in the 4th and 5th years.

Changing social class

Class distinction was evident to many of the authors and as they moved into more academic groups, working-class students found themselves with more people from middle-class backgrounds. Paul told it this way:

> After 14 [leisure time consisted of] hobbies, sports, underage drinking, girls, general hanging out, but by that time I had no peer group on the estate: all my social life was with boys from school, girls from the local grammar and circles around them.

Martin developed an identity that 'fitted in.' He wrote:

> I went down an ultra-academic and arts route – I was going to use my abilities like that ... it hasn't made me unhappy that's for sure and I don't dig the roads or come home soaking wet after a day in the open like my father and grandfather did and that is a real plus.

Others were also aware of differences between the classes at school and how they were placed in relation to their peers. George reflected that:

> ... in primary school, totally inappropriately we sat in mixed pairs, brightest top left, weakest bottom right. My 'pair' was the bank manager's daughter; we got on well, but competed like hell! My two best friends, respectively sons of a diplomat and a research scientist, sat nearby. We all took and passed the 11+ but I was the only one who stayed in the state sector ... I was the only kid from the estate at the grammar.

The authors' growing identification with a more middle-class world is striking across all the accounts from the different eras. It seems as if this sense of leaving behind previous class associations was a prerequisite for their success in education, seen by many of the families as 'a way out' of working-class insecurity and poverty. Their parents' disappointment at not being able to go to a more academic school because of their own family background made these families highly aspirational for their children and they approved of them moving from one class to another.

For those who chose this route themselves, such as Martin, it was a conscious decision to 'fit in', using their academic abilities to create a kind of entitlement to a new world.

For most of those in the 1960s and 1970s cohorts, the decision to go on to university was the result of expectations of their peers or teachers. Several commented that teachers were the most influential people who helped them decide to go to university, although parents also featured highly. Some said there was little or no encouragement to go into HE. John reflected that: 'there was no encouragement or support to apply to HE. I had to find it all out for myself and I now think that I was incredibly lucky. It could easily have passed me by.' Most of the male participants said the decision to apply to university had been made late in their school careers when some already had jobs lined up.

Their female counterparts, by contrast, had always intended to go to university, some saying the decision was taken 'as early as I can remember – it was my passport out from the poverty and Scarborough' (Jane). David said that he continued with his academic career after finishing school because he knew that 'some good jobs really needed a degree.' His comments echo a group of respondents who were aware that HE was a route to upward social mobility. Some described it as 'a passport' (Judy), others as 'getting away from home and poverty' (Kevin); George also felt this way and commented that university offered an: 'escape. [I had] a lifelong aversion to the boredom too many jobs appear to offer.'

Many of the accounts across the generations use a striking number of metaphors of travel and movement to describe the transformation in the authors' lives. Words like 'escape' suggest a dramatic breaking with the past where they had felt trapped by poverty. Another image used is that of higher education offering 'a passport.' Although a travel metaphor it also evokes images of authorisation or entitlement: education providing a new citizenship in a new life, a more middle-class life. The language of travel and mobility is discussed in chapter 7.

Into another country: at university

The accounts of life at university during this period focus on a different way of life to that of their home environment; they describe positive experiences of being away from home and a sense of freedom which is often associated with having a grant:

> I went to Reading University and got involved in all the things that were going on at the time – sex and drugs and rock and roll ... by this time, like many others, I had become somewhat estranged from my parents. I hardly communicated with them, and hardly ever went home, even though they were only about 25 miles away. It was a world apart. (Marie)

Frank, who went to Hull University, put it this way:

> The first year was ... about politics and parties and concerts (Bowie, The Who, for a couple of weeks I went out with someone whose brother used to beat up Peter Townsend when they were at school – the nearest I've ever got to fame – Pink Floyd and so on) and drinking and table football and snow-ball fights and fell walking and breaking up with my girlfriend (who had gone to teacher training college in Darlington) new friends and hitch hiking all over England and working in a brewery in Hull over the summer and, of course, the course itself (and a very nice Geography field trip to Holland at the Easter).

Comments like these from George, Mark and Jane draw out the importance of the grant that had been implemented in the early 1960s. 'My family were passive supporters, but the decision was mine. Would it have happened without a full grant (£375 pa if I remember correctly)? I doubt it' (George). Mark said that financially he was 'ok, had a maximum grant' and Jane said 'I had a generous grant.' Students who came from poorer backgrounds received a means-tested grant at this time which in most cases gave them more money than they had had before.

These students enjoyed the freedom from having to work while studying as most had had jobs before they went to university. Most describe only working during the summer holidays while at university: 'I worked in the holidays in a shop' (Peter); 'I worked in the summer; it meant I didn't need to go home' (John).

Upward mobility

The authors' time at university seemed also to cement the cultural mobility from working class to middle class that began for many when they went to grammar school. Moving away from their parents while at university severed the last link with their working class community.

Writing powerfully about this change, Martin said:

> I really can't think how to answer this one, there is no one thing and I don't want to be pretentious in my answer but I am tempted to say that I decided to become middle-class. But this had started before going to HE with the music I liked and books and things and was added to with films and other things and I did learn to change speech patterns and certain words and phrases I used so as to 'fit in.'

Martin followed a less conventional route than other participants in this era. He left his grammar school after O levels and went to the technical college to do a business OND. After completing the programme he applied for a job with which came an HE place at Portsmouth Polytechnic where he studied on a four year sandwich degree. Martin's experience points to changing opportunities for working-class students. Polytechnics were more focused on links with business and directly fulfilled the requirements of the changing economy as new middle-class employment began to emerge.

Employment in universities had been easy for the male participants who completed their studies at the end of the 1950s. Accounts from students in the 1960s and '70s record the employment of young lecturers. As the university sector developed there was a great need for new academics. Chris read geography at Sussex in the 1970s: ... [Lecturers were] 'young, there really wasn't much between us – with hindsight – most are still there now.' Lecturers varied: 'some were very good and I was inspired to do a PhD because one young lecturer made the subject come to life.' This was a very different response to those who went to university in the 1950s when there was a strong divide between lecturers and students.

Gender issues were still prevalent in the accounts of the 1960s and 1970s cohorts despite the explosion of the feminist movement and legislation for equal pay and anti-sex discrimination. Attitudes during this period remained sexist. Marie recalled being: 'told by my headmaster that 'girls like you don't go to university.'

The battles women fought for their rights to be regarded as equals in education and work did not immediately affect their lives, but by the 1980s policy changes were taking hold. This section has focused on the stories of young entrants into universities during the 1960s and 1970s, but the period also saw the development of routes into HE for mature students. The following section looks at the experiences of these students and provides a different perspective on widening participation and social mobility.

Gender, age and class: Different pathways into higher education

There are ten participants who went to university in the 1960s and 1970s as mature students, six men and four women. Two went to university in the 1960s and the rest in the '70s. All were from white working-class backgrounds and some had quite complex family relations. Ron, who was born in 1945, reported that: 'I was brought up by my grandparents and an aunt. For most of my childhood, my granddad and my aunt did not speak. Granddad was a miner and only he worked in the house.' Alan was also brought up by his grandparents: 'I lived in my grandparents' small tenement house with outside loo.' The other eight authors all lived with their parents. Family occupations varied from agricultural labourers to miners, cleaners, toolmaker and a nanny.

One participant, Cathy, explained, however, that her family were upwardly mobile during her childhood: 'My father first followed my grandfather being a tool maker but then set up his own business in the '60s making spectacle frames ... My mother was a cleaner then moved to office work.' These participants are currently in HE in a mix of administrative positions such as director of corporate and external relations, or academic posts such as senior lecturers and heads of department. All have been upwardly mobile through a career in higher education.

For the female authors, childhood included the development of a love of reading. Cathy talked about reading at home:

> My father joined the communist party when I was very young and he started to 'educate' himself by reading Marx, Lenin etc. I read avidly throughout childhood, and had books bought for birthdays and Christmas and used the public library weekly.

By contrast, not one of the male mature students read books, visited the library or had books in the home, neither did they enjoy school. These students talk of 'teachers who didn't rate me' (Ron) and 'regarded school as a pain barrier one had to endure' (Paul). George was critical of his grammar school: 'Obviously there were sets for each subject and although I was in the top set I was not the very best student. Although it was a grammar school they were really training people to be clerks. A poor school all round.' Dave, who went to a secondary modern school, said that:

> ... secondary was a nightmare with appalling behaviour problems, low aspiration and achievement and truancy. It was quite a violent place and I can remember teachers trying to get out of the gates before the students!

Ron talks about being bullied by teachers: 'They used to pick on me, especially the PE teacher because I was large for my age and couldn't do some of the gymnastics things. I hated it. There was also a bit of a 'hard lad' culture.'

While the accounts of the male mature students do provide clues as to why they did not persist and continue on to HE from school, it seems odd that the women ended up attending university as mature students, since they all studied and passed A levels and had enjoyed school. The answer lies in the fact that all went to teacher training college:

> I did two A levels and got Bs. This meant I went to teacher training college – I couldn't think of anything else to do. I don't recall anyone mentioning university (unless you were a posh blue stocking type) and this seemed something well out of my scope. (Sue)

> On reflection there was probably a lot of gender stereotyping at my grammar school – my girl friends who continued post 18 went into teacher training and one to the Lycee to train as a bi-lingual secretary and the boys who continued went to university. (Cathy)

The teacher training college route was still seen as a suitable trajectory for young women. Once they realised that university was an option for them, these mature entrants looked to find a way in, a point well illustrated by Jane. Having completed her teacher training Jane decided she did not fit in with other teachers and became enthused about the social sciences and university by her boyfriend:

When I was in my early twenties and saw what my boyfriend had learnt compared to me [I decided I would go]. He was a working-class boy who had got into Cambridge as part of a sort of early widening participation project in the late 1960s. I wanted to learn more about society. Boyfriend got a research post at Durham – so I went there to university – I paid for myself during my degree by teaching home tuition.

Jane is an example of someone who did not get a grant but found a way, by living 'in the cheap north' (Jane), to finance her way through university. Self funding is more possible for mature students who have other skills and experience as they are more likely to gain employment that could help finance a degree.

The men in the cohort all decided to go to university because they felt it would improve their career prospects. Some were told to do a degree by work colleagues, such as Paul, who said: 'I was about 21 and was told at work that I wouldn't get promotion unless I went to college.' He decided to apply after feeling that he wanted to 'get on in life.' Paul did not do A levels but was accepted onto a degree course because the admissions tutor could see he had potential. He wrote:

I had quite a lot of 'ooh get him' from some friends who thought I was 'going posh' on them. I have no contact with friends from that time and feel a bit 'culturally homeless.'

Paul went on to work in local government before he became head of estates at a university. Ron also did not do A levels and, like Paul, went to university when he was 21. He studied chemistry on day release but did not pass the qualification. Determined to succeed however, he took a pharmacy degree and went on to complete a PhD later in life. Another participant who left school at 16 to 'get away from home' later did A levels by correspondence, going to UEA at the age of 30, after a career in the services. Rob said:

I actually read the entire Robbins Report and realised that I still had a chance to get on to a degree course. I liked studying A levels, and I did quite well. An RAF education officer strongly encouraged me to try. I do believe that if my parents had been more encouraging and my teachers and school more supportive I would have stayed on at grammar and gone straight to university but I got there in the end. I was so glad that there were ways back into education for me.

The interplay between gender and class continued to dominate the experience of these participants as they moved into employment. This is discussed in the final section of the book.

Employment in higher education: routes and pathways

Higher education employment remained strong during the 1970s, and for many of graduates in this cohort, gaining employment in HE was simple. Frank, who left university in 1973, said:

> After being an undergraduate I almost became a planner but I decided to do a PhD at Cambridge in part because I wanted to move back to the South. Then after Cambridge I ... was offered HE teaching and research jobs in various places but liked the idea of being on the south coast. Staying in HE was the path of least resistance like water finding its way to the sea.

Jonathan also found moving into HE easy: 'I held PGCE places at Exeter and Chelsea college ... In the end I saw a salaried research assistantship at a polytechnic advertised, applied and was appointed.' Jonathan is now the principal at a HE college.

An increasing number of graduates took up administrative roles as the higher education sector professionalised. Amanda was typical of this group: 'It was sort of accidental as I just took a temporary admin post then it grew from there.' Amanda is now the head of the careers service at a university. Carla was another who took the administration route:

> I gained my first and Master's degrees in the mid-70s as the expansion of HE began to wane so I started in administration and sort of took to it. I quickly realised that I really enjoyed working with people and making a difference to people's lives, gave up writing my PhD and have never looked back!

Carla is now the head of academic development at a university college. We have seen that the route from teaching into higher education is prevalent amongst this group of respondents. Rosie was typical:

> I worked as a teacher for many years but decided HE would be less exhausting than school. I came into HE as a PGCE teacher and began my research career at age 42 and am proud to say I am now a reader in education.

For the graduates in this era, working in further education emerges as a route into HE. The sector had also been subject to significant changes in policy during the 1960s and its expansion provided employment for many graduates as they came out of university or the polytechnic. Martin explained his pathway in this way:

> I did well in my degree ... I found a subject I liked in sociology of industrial relations, which became my honours specialism ... I worked quite hard for the finals and I ended up getting a first class, quite unexpectedly. I had always assumed that after the degree I would carry on working for the electricity board for the foreseeable future and sure enough I got a job with them, but I knew there was some unfinished business with the academy. I got a PhD scholarship at LSE. I had no desire to stay in HE after three years at LSE, that was enough for me, so a friend suggested a lectureship in FE. I fairly quickly got a lecturing job in FE. Later on I decided I had been wrong about HE and eventually got a senior lectureship in HE.

Another route into employment in the sector was to move from industry into HE. Typical of this group is Tom. He studied at Oxford, became very involved in the broadcasting society and went to work for the BBC after completing his degree, where he worked for 15 years until he was made redundant in the early 1990s. Tom then went to work in further education before becoming an HE lecturer in media production.

All these accounts highlight that there is no magic bullet to enable success for working-class students. Each story is particular, but each individual is living within the social constraints of their time. In these stories of the 1960s and 1970s, different routes into and through HE emerge and we see people taking advantage of this. We also see the important role of the public library for many of these students. They were avid readers and this, they all said, helped them with study techniques and with aspiration by seeing into different worlds.

It is still the case that during this period issues of gender, whether for mature or younger students, affected decisions about progressing to university and on into employment in the sector. While the authors' accounts described in this chapter detail changes in society, they also draw out the fact that gender inequality in education and employment remained. Despite the challenges, these students found their way into the middle-classes. The next chapter examines the experiences of students who went to university between 1980 and 1997. Again the social climate and policy environment can be seen to be lived out in their life stories.

5

Massification without resource:
The 1980s and 1990s

Towards the end of the 1970s, Britain entered a severe recession leading to a 'bailout' from the International Monetary Fund, a winter of major strikes in 1978 and the return of a Conservative government under Margaret Thatcher in 1979. For HE the 1980s saw the beginning of the reshaping of higher education from being relatively well resourced to having its funding significantly cut.

Cuts in university funding were announced by the government in 1981: '...in the period December 1980 to March 1981, was a decision to reduce annual expenditure on home students by amounts totalling 8.5 per cent by 1983-84' (Sizer, 1988:79). Cuts were implemented on a selective basis and some institutions suffered more severely than others, notably Aston, Salford and Bradford (Shattock, 2003). However, growth in student numbers was considered important and the government later produced a new white paper on education in 1987 which sought to increase the number of people in higher education:

> The 1987 White Paper reiterated the primary economic purpose of higher education along with the need to further improve quality and efficiency. Yet it also ... committed the government to a policy of increasing participation in higher education by both young and older people. (Tight, 2009:79)

The largest proportion of the life accounts received in this project went to university between 1980 and 1996. Fifty-two of the participants went through higher education during this period. Thirty-three of them were women and nineteen were men. Of these, 35 were mature students and seventeen went straight into higher education from school. Five of the respondents were from ethnic minority backgrounds.

The second major expansion in HE in the UK took place between 1988 and 1994. It doubled the number of people in higher education, moving the participation rate from almost 15 per cent to 30 per cent.

Unlike the expansion in the 1960s, this growth was not funded and most of the additional students went into the polytechnic sector with no increase in the unit of resource. Hence the massification of HE in the UK took place without additional resource and when student finance moved from a straightforward grant system to a top-up loan system. Government continued to implement changes in HE, with another bill in 1992.

This new Further and Higher Education Act encouraged competition between institutions by removing the binary divide between polytechnics and universities that had been established in the 1960s. This meant that polytechnics could now become universities, which most of them did almost immediately.

Until this period, policy in higher education had not been concerned about the composition of the student body in the sector. In 1961, when the issue of the make-up of the student body was raised, Furneaux argued that while he acknowledged that social class must play a role in who studied in universities, he placed the blame on children's earlier experiences: 'all the important efforts have already occurred by the time a student enters the upper-sixth form' (1961:101). Certainly, Robbins believed increases in overall student numbers were sufficient to secure the right mix in HE. Women's position in HE was finally equalised when the last restrictions on female students in medicine were removed in the 1970s, increasing women's participation significantly in the overall student body to 39 per cent by 1981. The following decade (1982-1992) saw a major increase in the number of women studying as mature students and the overall number of female students finally equalised with that of their of male counterparts in 1992. In 1975-6 the ratio of female to male students 'was 0.46:1 whereas by 1999-2000 this had reversed to 1.20:1' (Reay *et al*, 2005:45).

This period of massification was thus driven and led by women, some of whom had been denied access to HE earlier in their lives. Access courses which became popular in the 1980s offered alternative routes into higher education and new universities embraced the Access movement more than the old universities did. The increase in female students in HE, and indeed the development of Access provision, are reflected in the life accounts of working-class women from this research.

Savage points out that 'women rely much more exclusively on having high ability and converting this into good educational qualifications' (2000:92) than men have done – statistically they use education as a route to mobility more than their male counterparts.

The life stories of the female participants who entered higher education in the 1980s and 1990s are examined in the following sections.

Women students in HE: 1980 to 1996

Clear themes emerge from the life stories of the women entrants. Some, as in other decades, went straight into higher education following school. For these students the same themes emerge as in previous decades: encouragement from parents, even if they did not understand their school work, support from peers and teachers, a love of reading and the availability of books at the local library, as well as what Riddell calls an 'aspirant identity' (2010:65) – a significant self-determination to succeed.

A good many of the respondents who went into HE during this period were mature entrants. Several of the women talked about their childhoods in the 1950s and 1960s, mentioning parents who were openly hostile to study; others highlighted low aspiration for their future or poor schooling which they hated; while some talked about traumas in their lives which affected their schooling and teenage years and prevented them from continuing their study. There were examples of the opposite of an aspirant identity, where for one reason or another individuals had not developed the necessary self-belief as youngsters. These life stories of mature students are discussed later in the chapter. This first section deals with the accounts from those who progressed through to HE from school.

Seeking to be upwardly mobile: developing an academic entitlement

Students who went into HE straight from school during this period had grown up in the 1960s and 1970s – a time when poverty was reducing and lifestyles were better for most people. These improvements became evident in some of the life stories. June grew up in a family that had high aspirations. Her father started his working life as a factory worker, and as a young family they lived with her grandparents on a council estate. Her father saved and managed to buy a small house in a new suburb outside Birmingham:

> [My childhood provided me with] a general feeling of security, of opportunity, of freedom, of moving on because we were out of Birmingham. My family were aspirational as they saw the move ... as a step forward to better things. ... My father ... would recite Shakespeare, poetry and tell stories based on Greek mythology.

By the time she was a teenager June had already made the decision to move beyond her family's position, particularly as her father was developing a drink problem:

> From around 14 schoolwork became an escape from an increasingly alcoholic father and the dullness of small town life. I liked nothing better than to stay in my small bedroom for hours at a time devouring George Elliot, the Brontes, Jane Austin and Dickens ... A group of 6 of us seemed to live like this – through novels and after school clubs, slightly cut off from our families. ... we came across many more children from surrounding suburbs who were much more middle-class ... the children of doctors, factory managers and teachers, however we seemed to mix fairly well and I suppose because academically I felt able, I was fairly confident ..to interact across the range of peers.

Like participants in the previous era, June describes slowly distancing herself from her background, seeing education as a way out from boredom and an increasingly unhappy family situation. She studied with a full grant at Kingston Polytechnic during the 1980s. By the time she was studying in HE, culturally she had moved completely away from her family background:

> [while a student] I lived fairly frugally. I ate pasta (for the first time!) made curries (having never had spicy food before). ... It was fashionable to get clothes from second hand shops at the time and I felt very bohemian and

urban returning to Bromsgrove along with an art school boyfriend. ... As for my family, I don't think my parents really understood at all. They were un-impressed when I decided to go on and do a Masters.

June is now a senior lecturer in education at a university but her story throws up many issues. Although she came from a more working-class background, her father had some understanding of the classics: 'He was self-taught – always hoped for more but turned against education per se as I became more independent and as he became more alcoholic, but he did give me my first love of literature.'

There are narratives of working-class parents which suggest wholly negative attitudes to education and learning and while some are dis-cussed later in this chapter, others present different and often more complex pictures. June's story resonates with other accounts – it is almost as if her family could imagine so far but no further. Her account details an entire change of life, encompassing not just changes in her education or occupation but also in her culture and diet. As her whole lifestyle altered, she was placed far away from her background.

Morag and Susan also went on to university straight from school, Morag in 1985 and Susan in 1990. Morag grew up on a farm in Scotland where her parents lived. He father was a farm labourer. She now works as a widening participation officer at a university. Reading and the library were very important to the development of her education:

> We were taken to the library and encouraged to read. There were a limited amount of books at home but ... my parents both read and it was some-thing I enjoyed doing.

Morag describes a group of friends she had at school who 'all saw HE as a natural progression. We all took it very seriously and enjoyed school ... we got on well with the teachers and were all seen as quite a unique bunch.' She went on to Aberdeen University in 1985 at the age of 18.

Susan grew up in Hull. Her father was also a farm labourer and her mother worked from home as dressmaker. She says: 'we were not well off but never hungry or in debt'. Susan is now a programme leader for social sciences. Again, books played an important part in her childhood and she enjoyed school and had good friends. By the time she was in the sixth form, 'my friends ... were from middle-class backgrounds with parents working at Hull University – I think they were influential in raising my aspirations.'

Both Morag's and Susan's families gave them a good start with reading and later the role of friends became important. Having friends from middle-class families helped them see university as a natural next step. These women had developed a sense of entitlement based on their abilities which supported their move into HE.

Another student, Janet, thought she would become a hairdresser until her English teacher told her she was university material. She went on to study at Keele. Janet's teacher saw a different future for her and gave her a new self-belief in her abilities.

Believing you are capable can make a significant difference to an individual. This belief in who you are and your abilities is shaped socially and culturally, as can be seen in Kathy's life. Kathy was also a strong reader, enjoyed school and went into the sixth form. Born in Wolverhampton her father was a fitter and her mother worked as a cook in the local college. However, her parents were less supportive of her:

> I had the ability which, though not nurtured at home, was encouraged at school. I went to university ... but was unable to cope psychologically with succeeding. I dropped out and did unskilled work for several years before I was encouraged to return to education by a very nurturing partner.

Kathy finally completed her degree at Wolverhampton in 1999. She said:

> In essence I've become aware of a whole load of psychological factors, a lot of unconscious stuff which made the whole HE thing difficult for me and made it impossible for me to go straight from school and straight through. These are all of course inextricably bound up with class and gender. Simply put, the early messages I got were all telling me I was hardly an individual, let alone someone who was entitled to a career and all the rest.

Kathy had no sense of self-worth. Her parents consistently undermined her abilities:

> They would say there was no point in me studying as for a girl learning was no use. They told me: 'people like us never get on.' A terrible thing really – what did it say about my parents as well?'

Class and gender structures inscribed within an individual's sense of themselves create barriers that are self-defined. Class structures work as much within people as they do outside them. Kathy's childhood and first attempt at university demonstrates this operation but she overcame it to become a marketing manager at a university.

This absence of entitlement and self-belief is strongly evident amongst many of the female students who went to university as mature students. The next section looks at their stories.

Women returners in the 1980s and 1990s

Many of the accounts of mature students in higher education (West, 1996; Johnson and Merrill, 2005; Merrill *et al*, 2002) draw out key factors that affected students' ability to continue in study and indicate why they returned to education, often with insecurities about learning, later in life. The accounts in this book highlight three key themes that affected these women's lives: problems with their school environment; problems with their home environment; and personal traumas which affected their teenage years. From this research it is clear that psychological and social identity issues heavily influences whether a student progresses on to higher education in the first instance. Individuals from working-class families can develop identities that enable them to progress into HE, but such narratives are based on personal achievement, not on the 'natural' entitlement that middle-class children have (Bourdieu and Wacquant, 1992). This notion of personal achievement is easily destabilised. As Riddell points out:

> The young people do not routinely encounter the narratives of such aspirations being normal for them in any of the social contexts of their lives. (2010: 64)

Just as equality legislation took hold in the UK in the 1980s, many women who had felt unable or had not had the chance to go to university straight from school began to return to education, seeking a new entitlement to study. Reflecting back on earlier attitudes to young women and learning when she was a teenager, Heather commented:

> We had some very good teachers but none really encouraged us to go to university or college. When I looked on 'friends reunited' website it is interesting to see old friends who have done so well. One even said it's surprising that so many have degrees now and are teaching, even though we were all given up on at school and not given any confidence that we could do well.

Arnot, David and Weiner argue that until the 1980s girls' education was based on lingering Victorian values. These accounts of women who returned to education in the 1980s and 1990s present evidence that girls were often seen as 'different from (and inferior to) men not only biologically, but socially, intellectually and psychologically' (1999:35). The next section examines the barriers that prevented the authors going into HE as young people.

Barriers to development part one – the school

If the basis of entitlement is rooted in academic ability for working-class children then the role of the school as a gateway to mobility is significant. For many of the mature returners to HE, school was a prominent barrier. The problems relating to school fall into two categories: either the school and teachers did not recognise or believe in the young women's ability to go on to university – these were, in other words, 'an environment of low aspiration for those sorts of girls' (Stephanie) – or the young women themselves found the school environment oppressive and stifling.

Where the school had low aspirations, parents were seldom able to challenge these beliefs since they themselves did not understand what was required to succeed in education. Kim said: 'My parents believed in education in principle but had no idea about study or what was needed.' She attended seven schools during her education and left without any A levels, despite attending sixth form.

Monica, who studied for an Open University (OU) degree when she was 30, went to a school that had only one pupil studying A level despite having a sixth form, 'and he was held up like some sort of genius.' She enquired about doing physiotherapy at school but was told 'no chance, you will need A levels for that. I left school at 17 and went to work.' She did hold on to a comment by one teacher in her secondary school however, who told her she was 'bright enough to go to university', saying:

> I laughed it off at the time, it also scared me a little but I never forgot this.
> Deep down, I always felt I could achieve but did not know how. The OU
> offered me the opportunity to try.

Monica now works as a researcher at a university. Low or high aspiration is not inherent in any group of people but becomes inscribed in individuals through social interaction. Riddell argues that 'at least part of what we think about ourselves involves taking on the expressed views of others about us' (2010:51). In Morag's case having even one teacher who believed in her gave her the chance, later in life, to return to education and gain a good degree.

A similar account of low aspiration and lack of belief comes from Jill: 'It was expected I would work in the local factory, get married and have children. Of course that was exactly what I did without gaining any qualifications at all.' Jill's experience highlights education's retention of Victorian values where 'motherhood was seen as the supreme vocation for women' (Arnot *et al*, 1999:35).

Liz 'loved school' but followed the 'route that all the girls did – left school at 16 and went to work in low paid manual jobs'. Later at 27 she took her A levels and decided to go to university in 1987.

Some respondents like Michelle did take A levels but never thought they could go to university. Her father was a boot and shoe repairer in the 1950s. Her mother worked part-time in catering jobs while her grandmother brought the children up. Her parents always believed you should work hard at school but were unable to help with schoolwork and both her sisters left school at 16, one to be a hairdresser and one who went straight into work. Michelle passed her 11 plus and went to the grammar. She worked hard, did well and went into the sixth form where she completed two A levels, but said: 'I had done better than my sisters and no-one ever suggested I carry on to university. I just drifted into work. That is what I thought I should do.'

In 1982 when she was 33 and had decided she 'couldn't bear the thought of doing dead end/uninteresting jobs for the rest of my working days', Michelle took an Access course and a further A level 'to make sure I was ready for university.' She now works as a principal lecturer at a university.

Anna followed a different route. Growing up in Leeds with her sewing machine mechanic father and her mother who was a cleaner, she left school at 16 despite passing her O levels. She said: 'The school did not expect people like me to carry on. 'Careers' consisted of where will you work next year?' She went into work but was put on an HNC at the local college by her employers. 'I only realised it was an HE qualification when I moved to work at the Poly. They then allowed me to top it up and gain a degree.' These students' schools did not believe the children they taught were capable of higher level study, even though many had exceeded the expectations of their parents, who had mostly left school at 14.

Most of the stories discussed so far have reflected a positive attitude towards school from the pupils, despite the lack of encouragement for them to continue in education. But some stories, where truanting features regularly, are of girls who hated school. Typical of these authors' accounts is Janet's:

> Not many of them [friends] liked school or went every day. Lots of my friends at secondary were encouraged to take time off school to look after younger siblings or help with the house ... it appeared to be normal practice in the older part of town ... I often took days off with them without my mother's knowledge or consent if I could get away with it.

She described why she hated school:

> I disliked systems and conformity that went with school life. At home, I was always allowed to contribute to discussion and my opinions were always valued by my mother who allowed me to be mature when I wanted to be. At school I could never sit still and listen, preferring to do things to learn. I was always fairly confident and talkative and this was not acceptable in school in the 70s.

Janet went to university when she was 37 and agrees that it was better for her to do so as a mature student: 'If I had gone from school ... I do not think I would have had as much to offer university life. I had negative learning experiences and was very hostile towards academic learning at the time.' Despite her views on her experience Janet is now a widening participation officer at a university. 'Just because it wouldn't have been right for me to go straight from school doesn't mean there aren't kids out there who should.'

While many of the life histories recount loving parents who were positive about the opportunities education could provide, the next section examines those stories where parental negativity played a significant part in putting up barriers to completing school and going to university.

Don't get above yourself: Barriers to development part two – the family

> Older sister didn't like school, failed her 11 plus, I passed mine – this didn't go down too well for me. I was put down a lot for being successful. ... I had to work in my father's bakery which I hated. My parents made me work extremely long hours ... my parents exploited me.

This quote from Barbara is fairly typical of this group of mature women graduates. She went on to study later in life and is now a senior lecturer in psychology.

Anne talked about the ambivalence in her parents' attitude to education. She said:

> My mother seemed to have a complex attitude towards education. She encouraged us to make the most of education but in arguments would throw out phrases like 'college education' in a clearly derisory tone which was meant to imply we were trying to get above our station ... I think she felt threatened by the bond that reading and learning gave my father and us and felt excluded by anything to do with education.

Shelly also talks about her parents 'encouraging me to challenge the teachers – 'they don't know a lot *you* know', they would say'. Her parents did not let her take the 11 plus as they did not believe in grammar schools so she went to a secondary modern and left school at 15.

Born in 1953, Frances had a complex family background. Her mother maintained that she came from a middle-class background and her father rose to be a wing commander in the Royal Air Force during the war. However, early on in her life her father had been in prison and the family were reduced to poverty. When he came out of prison he became a building labourer, while her mother was an alcoholic. She says of their attitude to education:

> When studying for my GCSEs I'd shut myself in a room upstairs to work and my mother would choose to assume (and inform anyone who asked) that I was obviously masturbating! This sums up the parental attitude to study ... I was often kept away from school to look after my younger sisters.

Frances returned to study English at age 33 and is now a lecturer in English literature at university.

Lisa, who grew up on a farm, talked about her parents actively discouraging her from doing her homework: 'I had to hide it – they didn't believe that you should be trapped inside but rather go out and mix with other people – not that easy on a farm.' Jenny was told that if she stayed on to do O and A levels she would also have to work and pay board at home. Margaret, despite passing her 11 plus, was sent to a secondary modern school and was made to go to work at 16 under her father's instruction. She later went on to university at Kent, saying:

> I saw it [university] as a route to freedom and independence. I watched my grandmother devote her life to her ungrateful and demanding adult children (my father being one) ... I saw the hard life that came with no education. I had ambition to go to London ... I wanted to prove to them that they were wrong about me not being able.

Eloise spent her life in foster and care homes where aspiration was very low: 'Keeping quiet was enough in most cases. I went to so many different schools as I was moved around the whole time.'

These stories highlight the importance of family encouragement, even if it was passive. Families have a great deal of power over their children. Although most loved education and recognised its value, all of the authors in this group were failed by their families. Recent research indicates that regardless of the economic background you grow up in, strong committed parenting that supports and values learning can make a significant difference:

> When parents in lower social classes are able to provide a high quality home environment this can to a large extent overcome the disadvantages of living in a low income family. (IPPR, 2008:14)

Many accounts in this book show this kind of family environment to have been prevalent and that it made a difference to the children's development and progress. When families are not supportive it becomes harder to succeed. Events in children's lives can equally have a significant impact on their progress, particularly when the difficulties are not recognised early on. The following accounts illustrate this.

Dealing with trauma

Many experiences affect young people as they grow up and if these are traumatic they can affect their life chances considerably. Two of the mature women returners talk about being raped as teenagers, an event that significantly affected their school career and confidence. Wanda was a highly academic student and considered a 'swot' by her class-mates. Her parents were extremely positive about education: '... my mother, father and grandmother all regarded education as a key to a better life. It was seen as a necessity not a luxury.' She read a great deal and visited the library regularly. However, as a young teenager she was raped by a neighbour. After the attack Wanda began to truant:

> I was raped ... around this time and started to have panic attacks but didn't tell anyone so this may have triggered the behaviour ... I think it is safe to say I was a confused teenager. I lost confidence and interest in most things and left school with no qualifications.

Wanda went back to study at 17 but failed to gain her O and A levels. In 1995, at age 28, she decided to go back into study and took an Access course. Taking an A level in psychology, she went to Aston University to do applied psychology. Wanda now works on a research project at a university and has completed a PhD.

Susan was raped at the age of 13. She says:

> Unfortunately I think that the most important [memory] would have to be the one that changed my life dramatically and was very damaging to my life and that was being raped at age 13. The reason it is important is because it affected so much of my life, my school work suffered and never got back on track, my feelings for the male members of my family changed (it was not a member of my family but a stranger) my entire self-perception changed and I developed all sorts of behavioural problems and started drinking a dangerous combination of alcohol and the anti-depressants that the doctor dished out. For many years even into adulthood I constantly felt frightened.

Susan had been a very inquisitive child. She spent hours looking at the books in her grandmother's house on her regular visits there. 'I could tackle quite difficult texts – I had been singing psalms since I was five.'

Primary school was successful and she was head girl by the end. Her secondary education started well but after the rape she began to truant:

> By the fourth year I was attending about 2 days a week and in the fifth year I had all but left and they pretty much left me to it. There was no recognition of my position. It was shaming, I had become difficult and the school just ignored me.

When she was 25, Susan decided to go to university, a decision she made with her partner:

> I had met the man who is now my husband. We were both single parents and had been unemployed since we were teenagers. I became pregnant and we already had two children between us and we sat down to think of a strategy as to how we would survive and provide for our children. We decided that one of us needed to get qualifications to increase our earning potential and as I wanted to study we decided that I should go for it.

Susan now works as a widening participation officer in HE. These accounts of women who found their way back to education later in life highlight the need for opportunities for study to remain open to people of any age. As well as recognising the necessity of a second chance education, these accounts further confirm the importance of being able to develop a sense of self that offers a level of personal confidence, self-belief and entitlement. In these accounts the sense of entitlement grew slowly, as many of the building blocks were not in place when the women were young. As Riddell points out: 'aspirations for students from working-class backgrounds develop through ... iterative social processes' (2010:58).

Male students in the 1980s and 1990s

Nineteen respondents who went to university during the 1980s and 1990s were male: seven mature students and twelve who went straight from school. The histories of the mature male students bear some similarities to the women's stories. Here too, the main reasons for not continuing with study were either personal hatred of the school's culture or parental opposition to education. Donald is typical of the participants who had no support from their parents. He grew up in a household in the West Midlands during the late 1960s and early 1970s. His family lived on benefits as his mother was ill and his father stayed at home to look after her. His home situation meant that he was: 'largely left to my own devices and was not encouraged to stay on to do more qualifications. University wasn't even thought about, it was a different world.' He talked about the shame of having to take school meals:

> Every Monday morning finding an excuse to leave the classroom whilst others handed in their dinner money and I didn't because I had free school meals, acutely embarrassing.

Donald did what was expected of him: 'My parents thought I should get out of school and earn a wage so I left at 16 with one O level.'

He describes the years he spent in vulnerable work during the late 1970s and 1980s – a time of high unemployment. He said:

> In my teens, twenties and early thirties I went through a cyclical process of being in work, being made redundant, then seeking work whilst claiming dole, then being in work again; all due to the economic climate at the time. At 32 I decided after being made redundant again that I would retrain/re-educate.

Donald says it was his wife who convinced him to think about further study. She joined him in study after an Access course and they went to university together. He now works in administration in a university.

Like Donald, Mike grew up in the late 1960s and early 1970s. His father was a dustman and his mother an office cleaner. While the family expected their children to go to school – not least to ensure they were 'minded while parents were at work' – they had no understanding of the potential of education and Mike felt that 'school was simply a fact of life. We had no awareness of it.' He does not have many positive memories of school:

> I did well at primary school – I was head boy and everything – but never valued that kind of thing. Secondary school had no value to me at all and I lost interest. My memories of secondary school are all negative – I don't think it challenged me at all, it had no rewards, and very rapidly became pointless.

Mike was an avid reader, however, and remembers 'sitting in cemeteries reading early Samuel Beckett novels – seriously, I did!' while he was truanting from school. The truant officer visited his home and he recalls his father's reaction this way:

> I came home one day at the end of a three month period of truanting and found that the truant officer had visited my parents that day. In an ordinary tone of voice my father said 'Oh you've got to go to school, y'know.' That was all that was ever said about it. It's probably a measure of how much he valued schooling.

Mike went on to study philosophy at Middlesex Polytechnic in 1991. He talked about how this happened despite having no qualifications at all:

I was in a pub with a friend. I was bemoaning my lot. She said: 'What would you do if you could do anything?.' I said, 'I'd study philosophy full time.' She asked; 'well why don't you then?' I had no answer. I applied to Middlesex soon after and she wrote me reference.

He got in to Middlesex via a mature student route and went on to do postgraduate study. He now works as a lecturer in a university. Mike's story again reiterates that although formal education provides routes into HE, informal learning is a vital part of enhancing ability and encouraging aspirations for the future. His description of reading Beckett while truanting highlights that with no encouragement from school or family, abilities are left unrecognised and can often go to waste.

Eleven men went into university directly from school. Their reasons for continuing to study correspond to those described by traditional entrants discussed in this and previous chapters. The key foundations seem to be a belief in the power of education to transform lives, an ability to gain access to books to foster an independent love of learning and a curiosity about life, and a peer and school environment which was conducive to going on to university.

Kev is typical of this group. His father worked in a factory until he became a milkman in the 1970s following redundancy. His mother worked part-time at the local swimming pool. Despite not understanding what was required for success in school his parents were very positive about school, having being forced to leave school themselves when they were 14: 'My father ... wanted me to stay on at school for as long as possible.' Kev developed a love of science and his parents provided space for him to study at home. He recounts that while most of the pupils at school: 'were killing time before they could leave', he had good relationships with the teachers, particularly in the sciences: 'they became role models for me'. Kev decided to do A level science subjects and went to Leicester University to study Biology when he was 19. He was a 'consistent hard worker' at university, 'different to school where it had been effortless, but I loved the subject so that was fine.' He is now a senior lecturer in biological sciences.

Peter's story is similar. He talks of wanting to go to university 'as soon as I knew such places existed.' His parents also saw education 'as a ticket to a more affluent and happy life'. Scott was also encouraged to go to university from an early age as his parents knew a distant family member who had gone to do maths and got a job at a university. He said: 'My parents were supportive of the school and also well-liked by the teachers.'

The daily lives of these youngsters re-inforced the value of education and their own abilities, and provided horizons beyond their current situation. This combination created the ladder of opportunity required to succeed academically. Issues of class and gender intersected in these accounts at times and created additional barriers to success. As women took up their rightful place in higher education concern about young men and their engagement in education grew, an issue that remains in the twenty-first century.

Class and gender are not the only influence that can affect people's ability to continue in education, however. During the 1980s and 1990s ethnic background was of considerable interest in education, particularly in schools. The next section examines the life accounts of ethnic minority students from working-class backgrounds who went into higher education during the 1980s and 1990s.

Ethnicity, class and prejudice

Concern among the Caribbean immigrant community about the treatment of their children in British schools simmered during the 1960s. Some local authorities began bussing Black and Asian children to dilute what was deemed to be too high a concentration in certain inner city classrooms. Protests by Black parents eventually put a stop to bussing and the community rallied behind a book published by Grenadan teacher Bernard Coard, who was teaching in a school in Hackney. He titled his book: *How the West Indian Child is made Educationally Subnormal in the British School System* (1971).

In 1979 the government commissioned an inquiry into the education of West Indian children, and an Interim report, the Rampton Report, appeared in 1981. It identified racism, 'intentional and unintentional' among teachers and found discrimination in the education system. By the final report of 1985, the terms had changed. This, the Swann Report, looked at children from all the major immigrant communities. It found that all groups were significantly 'underachieving' in education.

The attitudes to all children from visible minorities remained predicated on their 'underachievement', despite the criticism of the school system presented in a burgeoning literature led by Maureen Stone (1981), Barry Troyna – notably *Racism, Education and the State: the racialisation of educational policy* (1986) – and, from in 1990, David Gillborn. Inservice training for teachers on 'multicultural education' began in the 1980s but was uneven in quality and in some cases resented. Increasingly expert provision was made for children whose first language was not English but nothing changed for Black children and, as Arnot *et al* put it, 'Black students [were] often portrayed as the problem' (1999:145).

Several teaching unions sought to tell their members what Black pupils were facing in schools and what needed to be done. The National Union of Teachers, for example, published a pamphlet in 1979 challenging prevailing attitudes to race, and later *Combating Racism in Schools* (1989). The Eggleston Report, which followed hard on the heels of the Swann Report, presented evidence of discrimination and racism, including a chart showed the 'marked decline' in the academic attainment of Black pupils during their first five years at one secondary school (1986:166).

None of the knowledge in the literature appeared to make much difference to the prejudice and discriminatory provision experienced by Black pupils. Racism was overtly expressed by pupils – and sometimes teachers – making school an uninviting learning environment for ethnic minority pupils. Teachers and schools, with a few exceptions, subscribed to the stereotype of Black pupils, especially boys, as not very able and potentially troublesome. Such views were reflected in the school experiences of the ethnic minority authors in this book.

As the century came to an end, the government began to pay more attention to this longstanding racial injustice. In 1996, Ofsted published Gillborn and Gipps's *Recent Research into the Achievement of Ethnic Minority Pupils* to update information on this decades-long issue and found some improvement, but not a great deal. The DfES commissioned and published research by Maud Blair and Jenny Bourne in 1998. They showed that intervention schemes, such as the DCSF's Aiming Higher programmes, significantly improved the achievement of the Black pupils lucky enough to be targeted. But for most, provision continued as usual so they still lagged behind in the league tables. When the inquiry into the murder of black teenager Stephen Lawrence reported (Macpherson, 1999), the committee found 'institutional racism' characterised all public services, including educational institutions.

The accounts from the ethnic minority participants in the cohort reflect the institutional racism of schools in general. They encountered the familiar pattern of teachers' low expectations and stereotyping. The findings in the body of literature about the issues of race and education in the latter half of the twentieth century also explain why there are disproportionately few ethnic minority authors in this book. In the accounts that were recorded there are two authors whose stories reveal much about the impact of prejudice and racism on their educational opportunities.

Eugene was born in Glasgow to Nigerian parents. His father was a machine operator and his mother a dinner lady. When he was 2 he moved to Liverpool with his family. He had four brothers and sisters and when his parents divorced when he was 12, his mother took care of all the children, living on her wages as a dinner lady. While Eugene was growing up in the 1970s racial unrest spread throughout the country and this was felt in the school environment as well:

> We were one of only two black families at school, which meant that we needed to be able to care for ourselves and stand up for ourselves. I remember the National Front leafleting our school and I also remember the school's indifference to the racism we suffered from pupils and staff. I learned very quickly not to expect support from the school in that respect.

Despite his mother's belief in education for her children, the school decided that Eugene should not be entered for O levels and wanted to enter him for CSEs only. The experience described by Eugene exactly mirrors research in the literature. Playwright Kwame Kwei-Armah, for example, describes how his mother removed him from a school where his teacher saw him as, 'too clever for a Black kid' (Richardson, 2005: 165). In the Eggleston Report researcher Cecile Wright presents charts showing how in one school, teachers decided who should sit O levels and who would only sit CSEs which they based not strictly on the students' examination results but on their colour. The same subjective criteria were used in banding children in year 9, so affecting their academic career (1986: 150-161).

Eugene's mother was one of the parents who objected to the attitudes of her son's teachers and recognised the threat to his future opportunities. She was determined to ensure her son had a chance to do the higher qualification. If Eugene only gained CSEs his chance to go on to the sixth form, where he could study for university entry via A levels, would have been blocked. His mother understood this and asked for him to be entered:

> The school refused [to enter me] so my mother offered to pay the entry fee for O level subjects so I ended up double entering for both CSEs and O Levels. I managed to achieve 7 O level passes and I remember revising quite hard for my exams.

Eugene did go on into the sixth form and took A levels in history, economics and sociology. He noted that most of the students were 'middle-class kids who were mainly girls and I learned that we got on quite well. There were very few boys in sixth form, about 10 out of 80 odd.'

Eugene's experience of the teachers' low expectations is reflected in many of the stories of the mature students, as well as in the literature, eg. Richardson (2005). Although his mother was so 'desperate for all of her five children to go [to university] that she took it upon herself to pay for her son to do O levels', she should not have had to do so. As Eugene points out, black students suffered a great deal of racism. His teachers' lack of belief in his abilities is part of that racism.

With his mother's encouragement Eugene decided to go on to university. He talked about having been determined to do so when he went into the sixth form.

> I don't really remember why or what I was going to do there [university] but I was aware that I was black, aged 16, it was 1981 and youth unemployment in Liverpool was sky high. There were few options open to me so sixth form seemed a good one.

Eugene went to Liverpool Polytechnic to study social sciences in 1984. He later took an MA at Liverpool University and now works as the manager in the widening participation team. All his brothers and sisters followed him into HE level study.

Not all black students were able to challenge the school's authority however. Bella grew up in Manchester in the 1970s. Her father was a painter and decorator and her mother worked as a catering assistant. Her parents believed education was important but did not understand how to help their children, and while Bella attended school she was often asked to stay home to look after her younger brother when her parents were at work. Her parents had no contact with the school and when Bella was in the secondary comprehensive matters deteriorated. She says she has 'mostly negative memories. I was always in trouble. The teachers blamed me for things that I did not do because I was black I suppose. Anyway I began to rebel.'

Bella describes how the culture of the school quickly separated students into groups of those who would achieve and those who 'were written off.' She became less and less interested in school and began truanting: 'I used to visit my older sister or hang around with my cousin. It seemed at the time a nicer way to spend my days.'

Defiant behaviour and truanting were common forms of resistance by Black pupils, as many have later acknowledged (see eg. Richardson, 2005). In Bella's case she finally went to the University of Central England in 1994. She is now a health researcher at a university.

Bella's and Eugene's stories highlight the complexities and intersections of class and race. It was only through his mother's determination that Eugene was able to continue straight through into HE. Bella, by contrast, had no support and gave up. Her parent's lack of social capital to argue with the system meant that she was unable to progress until she was a mature student. Both students experienced racism at school in the form of teachers' attitudes that implied they were incapable of achieving, not just because of their class background but also because of their ethnicity. As Arnot *et al* argue:

> ... the performance culture at school ... tended to either pathologise black working-class youth as having problems or to 'deracialise' the situation – to refuse to see race problems ... (1999:145).

Despite the challenges, the participation in HE of people from lower socio-economic groups, ethnic minority groups and women all increased during this period of unfunded expansion, as Tight records:

> While 8.4 per cent of the 18+ cohort in socio-economic groups I, II, and IIn ... entered higher education in 1940, the proportion of groups IIIm, IV and V

was only 1.5 per cent. By 1950, the respective proportion were 18.5 per cent and 2.7 per cent and by 1995, 45 per cent and 15.1 per cent. (2009:266)

Students from working-class backgrounds were still much less likely to get into HE than their middle-class peers, but many more of them were now gaining places in HE. Many more of these students used the mature entrant route to come back into study. A significant number of the students who entered HE during this period came through the polytechnic and later new university sector. It is these institutions which grew considerably during this time and it is these which particularly embraced the Access route for mature students. The higher education student population was changing, just as HE institutions were changing.

Government and HEIs became increasingly concerned about the future funding of higher education as the sector massified. Alongside these funding concerns, people were increasingly concerned about the relative differences between the class backgrounds of entrants into higher education, for although students from working-class backgrounds were increasingly getting into HE, the gap in participation rates was still large. This concern led to drastic changes in policy and interventions between 1997 and 2009. These two themes – funding and participation – have dominated and continue to dominate HE policy. The authors in the next chapter all went into HE during this period.

6

Graduates of the twenty-first century – The new era of higher education

By the beginning of the 1990s, higher education systems across the globe were being reshaped. Developing nations began to invest significantly in developing a more skilled workforce. The international student market began to expand as students moved around the world to gain the best education they could afford. Western nations such as the USA, Britain and Australia benefited significantly from this growth as international student numbers and their fees increased. At the same time, the expansion of home student markets continued. By the early 1990s countries like the USA had nearly 50 per cent of their population entering higher education.

By 1994 there was an understanding between all political parties in the UK that the expansion of higher education, which had led to over 30 per cent of the age participation rate entering HE, was becoming a challenge for the public purse. In addition it was understood that HE itself was in need of additional resource to remain competitive in a growing global higher education marketplace:

> Higher education funding (and particularly student funding) was, necessarily, a key issue for all major parties who were supportive of the policy of further widening participation. (Tight, 2009:84)

The government consequently set up a review of higher education under the chairmanship of Sir Ron Dearing. Heralded as the first major review of HE since Robbins in the 1960s, the scope of the review was extensive: it was to examine the purpose, structure and shape of higher education. The Report of the National Committee of Inquiry into Higher Education (NCIHE), or the Dearing Review, as it became known, sought to find a solution to the continued expansion of HE within an environment of funding restraints. Reporting in 1997, NCIHE was concerned about the drop in the unit of resource caused by the swift expansion of HE student numbers between 1988 and 1994 when funding for higher education had been cut and the number of students had increased. The report emphasised that the funding of HE was already shared between the public purse and individuals and employers:

> The taxpayer meets a large part of the costs through grants to universities and colleges and through support to individual students. Individual students may pay part or all of their own tuition costs if they are studying part-time or at postgraduate level and employers may pay their employees' fees or allow them paid leave to pursue higher education. Students ... may over time repay loans for their living costs. (1997:85)

In other words, the review argued that as 'others' beyond government tax revenues already contributed to HE funding, the contribution of others' contributions could increase and full-time undergraduate students, in particular, should contribute to the cost of their study. The committee determined that:

> ... those with higher education qualifications are the main beneficiaries, through improved employment prospects and pay. As a consequence, we suggest that graduates in work should make a greater contribution to the costs of higher education in future. (1997:29)

It may have been a significant shift in thinking about HE at the time, but it was not unprecedented. The period of means-tested grants for full-time undergraduate students was in fact short-lived in the history of higher education. Chapter 3 discussed the period before universal grants in the 1950s, and even before the Dearing report was published, top-up loans had been introduced in 1988. Dearing proposed that all students should contribute to the cost of their study as they had done in the past. The report was completed as the government in the UK changed, from Conservative to Labour. As in the case of Robbins, a different government would decide how to implement the proposals from the commission. Under New Labour an upfront fee of around

£1,000 a year was introduced for students on full-time undergraduate courses, although some means testing for students from poorer backgrounds remained and some did not have to pay fees at all.

By 2000 most universities had seen a considerable drop in their number of mature students and in some institutions they had all but disappeared. The Labour government's policies were focused more on getting young first generation entrants into HE. Starting with the Excellence Challenge, which set a target that by 2010, 50 per cent of 18 to 30 year olds should have some experience of higher education, they developed a set of policy initiatives to increase numbers of young people in HE. These included the introduction of a new higher education qualification, the foundation degree, a two year, vocationally focused qualification which was generally offered by further education colleges across England, and the development of programmes to increase school attainment and aspiration for children from poorer backgrounds. These were often part of partnerships between schools and HE institutions.

Devolution of some legislative powers to the four nations in the UK was introduced during this period, giving Scotland, Wales and Northern Ireland authority over education policy, including higher education. Between 2000 and 2010 education policy began to diverge across the UK, although the different funding bodies continued to learn from each other.

In 2003 the Labour government introduced another HE bill, for England, which changed the fee regime from upfront fees to loans paid back once students had graduated and were earning a wage of £15,000 or more. Fees were increased from just over £1,000 to just over £3,000 per annum. Means-tested grants for students from poorer backgrounds had been in place under the Labour policy of upfront fees but the costs had deterred such students from going into higher education. In the new funding regime means-tested grants remained part of a package of financial support for people from low income backgrounds. Scotland did not follow the fee increase and had already achieved the 50 per cent participation target, largely because of its strong HE provision within the further education sector.

As the English Act passed through parliament there was much concern that the increase in fees would deter people from lower socio-economic groups from entering HE, just as upfront fees had done. When the Higher Education Funding Council for England published the statistics on entry into HE in 2010 however, they showed that not only had the overall number of students increased, albeit proportionately, but that the number of young people from working-class backgrounds applying was also increasing (HEFCE, 2010). Despite the initial concern, it appeared that the new system has not deterred people from working-class backgrounds as the upfront fee system had.

As female participation in higher education increased and women now constituted the majority of HE students, concern was raised over the educational outcomes for young men. The key policy focus for the government was on working-class participation in HE however, which despite having increased, was still disproportionately low in comparison with middle-class participation. Like the authors' accounts in previous chapters, these policy changes are reflected in the life histories of the people who entered HE during the decade from 1997 to 2007.

The accounts discussed here thus span two different fee regimes in England: upfront fees and deferred fees. In both systems working-class students received financial support, although it is clear from the authors' accounts that there was misinformation about what support was available. These life histories, like the other accounts from previous generations, highlight a range of factors besides money that influence decisions about higher education. These are now discussed.

The new graduates

In the previous chapter I highlighted the importance of self-belief to enable people from working-class backgrounds to feel they are entitled to a middle-class life. Along with self-belief, a sense of personal determination and persistence is strongly evident in the life histories discussed in this chapter, but the significance of friends and friendship with regard to success is seen to be almost equally important. Despite the common elements with earlier accounts – reading and books, family attitudes to education and the role of teachers and supporters – this chapter focuses on the two, slightly contradictory, themes of personal determination and friendship, since these stand out as crucial determinants for this particular cohort of graduates. The themes provide a different perspective on how these authors developed their new identities as middle-class graduates, drawing out the interplay between self and other in identity-building. As the widening participation programmes developed through this period there are some indications that a few of the authors participated in these activities and these are discussed later in the chapter.

Of the 28 respondents who entered higher education after 1997, 23 were female and five were male; five were from ethnic minority communities and 23 were white. Four were mature students. While almost all respondents were from working-class backgrounds, four accounts were from people who grew up in middle-class homes, although they were the first in their families to attend university. In chapter 2 I discussed the difficulties of using the parental occupation category. Margaret, for example, who went to university directly from school in 1998, described herself as middle-class even though her father is a lorry driver who works for a firm of road hauliers. Following her parents' divorce when she was 8, Margaret lived with her mother who subsequently married a man who owned his own scaffolding business, making him middle-class. Margaret did not have access to the cultural capital at home that most middle-class children have, however. Her stepfather and mother could not assist her with homework:

> ... it was miles away from their experience and they had no friends or contacts that had been to university making the concept quite alien to them: 'I told them I wanted to go to university and they were surprised, asked me why. It was a little awkward but in the end they agreed.

Another illustration of the complexity of defining class comes from Sara. Her father is a double-glazing salesman, an occupation which places him and her as middle-class. When Sara's father forced her to leave home when she was 16 though she had nowhere to go, however, she lived on the streets for several years before returning to study in her mid-twenties. Her experience led her to find herself in one of the most vulnerable groups in society, where her father's background was irrelevant. While Sara grew up in a relatively secure financial environment, her father disowning her as a teenager meant she had to rely on her own abilities to survive. She found a refuge where the manager took an interest in her life and helped her get back into education.

The other two middle-class authors are Henrietta and Tom, both of whom had some of the advantages of middle-class cultural capital because although their parents had not been to university, their professional status brought them into contact with people who took university study for granted.

In chapter 1 I identified a much larger middle class in the UK in 1990 than existed in 1945. In the following chapters I commented on the increase in the number of universities and university places which supported this growing middle-class. Since its growth was swift, however, people from working-class backgrounds could move into middle-class jobs without obtaining a degree.

Henrietta's mother worked part-time in a school. Her father was a lecturer in hotel and catering management at an FE college, having worked in the hotel industry for many years 'starting in the kitchens' (Henrietta). His own father had been a miner.

Tom's father also lacked a degree, even though he had a job as an accountant in a law firm. He, too, had worked his way up the firm, taking his qualifications as he progressed. His father had been a dock worker. Although these students were the first in their family to go to university, their parents' upward mobility had made their families middle-class. Nowadays, of course, these professions would require degree qualifications.

The knowledge and experience provided by the social networks these two families used to support their children into and through HE is discussed later in the chapter. All the other authors were from working-class backgrounds: care workers, shop assistants, carpenters and cleaners. Respondents all record the role of peers and friendship in their lives as they grew up and the next section examines these stories.

Friends and friendship

Brooks comments that despite the significance of such relationships, 'the influence of young people's friends and peers has remained undertheorised' (2003:238). In his study of working-class youngsters in the north of England, Miles (2000) points out that for the sake of their friends young people would forgo parental approval, get into debt and engage in criminal activities .

While some respondents mentioned teachers as important role models, as others from previous generations had done – 'There were one or two important teachers' (Kelly, who went into HE in 1998) – the comments about friends are more common in this generation: 'Friends were the most positive part of school' (Kayleigh, who went to university in 2005); 'I have a few negative memories of primary school but once I'd moved schools it was mostly positive due to the friends I made' (Jane who started in HE in 2000). Friends were important not simply for solidarity and support but also because friendship groups are constructed into social hierarchies. The authors were very aware of this differentiation between their peers. 'At primary school everyone seemed to be the same but as we got older a social hierarchy definitely emerged as people segregated into their own groups' (Abi, who went to university in 1998).

Peer relationships can play a significant part in shaping young people's identities (Riddell, 2010). Social interaction influences how we see ourselves and locates us within the social hierarchy. Respondents were very aware of how they 'fitted' and were conscious of their position in relation to others.

Tom remarked that: 'hierarchies are at every school and to some extent this is harsh to live with but I guess it is a way of life for teenagers.' Peer groups could be both positive and negative; in Sara's experience was that fights between rival groups often broke out: 'There was a regular hit list, who to target, who to avoid. There were fights with other schools usually at lunch time.'

Sara and Tom's comments about peer relations echo certain of the recollections from the authors writing decades earlier and highlight that debates and even about fights about social position begin at an early age in the playground.

Their friends and enemies shaped the identities of this group of young people. The significance of friendships is illustrated through the histories of George and Alex presented below. Although they grew up with poverty, their experiences were quite different though both their futures were shaped by the friends they had during their teenage years. Alex went to university straight from school, while George went back to study much later.

Born in 1954 to Jamaican parents who had come to Britain to work, George was taken into care at an early age: 'I still feel angry that they took me away.' He began his studies in HE in his fifties as the 'first time to have the opportunities as an ethnic minority in this country [with] few chances.'

George spent most of his working life supporting people in care, acquiring the qualifications he needed to get into university over the course of many years. Because of his life experience George decided to study social work. He spoke about the lack of support his carers provided when he was a child: 'I had no direction from my carers really. They just insisted I was good at school but did not press me to do well. I did my homework myself, no-one helped or cared.'

Being in care put George in unusual circumstances. However, the distinction between being 'good' and 'doing well' is a common feature of many accounts across the generations. Families and carers found imagining academic success difficult but were clear that they wanted their children to behave correctly.

George felt his friends were important: 'I was very sporty and so were my friends. I played a lot of football and did athletics. The only way to get out of the home was to play football.'

He escaped in another way too: 'I read many, many books to fanaticise ... There were a lot of books in the home and that is one thing I did a lot of, fictional reading.' George's love of reading pointed to his potential, but the care home did little to develop his abilities, and although he behaved well at school and did not get into trouble, he was unable to gain any qualifications.

George was popular: being good at football gave him some standing with his peers, as his friendship group was only interested in sport: 'We played all the time. We didn't think about schoolwork.' It may have been rational to focus on the abilities he had in sport, but George's decision to neglect his schoolwork was partly because he 'could not see the point in it'. We can see how his peers influenced his choices as to where to direct his efforts. With no-one explaining to him that he could or should work hard, George gained respect from his friends because of his success at football.

He went on to work as a care assistant, and there he began taking qualifications, which finally led to university at the age of 50: 'It had been in my head for over 20 years, the 'what if' question. I longed for higher education and when the opportunity came along to take time out I decided to do it.'

Alex, by contrast, went into university straight after A levels, starting in 2004, the same year as George. Her parents separated when she was young and she grew up living with her mother in the south of England: 'I come from a single parent household, my father is a carpenter and I live in an ex-council house – can't get more working-class than that!.' She said her mother is very clever but never had any opportunities to study. As we have seen in other accounts, Alex's mother could not help her with difficult homework: '... towards A levels mum didn't really know what it was all about though this is fair enough, she hasn't done it before.' She kept in touch with her father and was close to both her parents, although she describes her relationship with her father as 'difficult at times.' Neither of her parents engaged with her school: 'I was always good in school so they never got involved in school matters, eg. open days, parents evenings, simply because I was alright and wasn't in any trouble.' Although the circumstances are different, the attitude of Alex's parents resembles that which George described at the care home: being good was all that mattered. At school Alex realised that she needed friends who were committed to learning:

> I hated lower school ... because at that point my friendship groups were changing and becoming more important. Once I began spending more time with people who worked harder ... than the people I had spent time with before who were rebelling and hating school and becoming frustrated with having to be there when they could be out earning, ... things got better then. Those students weren't as well off as the hard [working] ones and I could see patterns arising, so deciding to be friends with hardworking individuals really benefited me.

Alex decided to place herself in a middle-class friendship group who were 'well off' and 'hardworking.' She developed her academic entitlement through the membership of her friendship group and used this social capital to find out about going to university.

Although she cared about her family, they were unable to provide the support Alex needed to develop her academic abilities: 'I was the one who put pressure on myself to do well, as I guess I wanted to prove something.' Despite feeling close to her father, his attitude to her academic abilities was negative and he did not believe that she would be able to get into university: 'He kept saying his kids wouldn't be bright enough.' Her father also argued with Alex over fees, thinking he would have to pay for her: '... he told me 'I can't pay for you' ... he just kept on saying it. I was downhearted ... thank goodness for my friends telling me I wouldn't have to pay.'

Alex gained a grant and a full loan, but her father did not know this was possible. Misinformation of this kind could have prevented Alex from going to university despite achieving top grades in her A levels. Her father 'asked me if I was lying when I said I got three As. He was shocked – just couldn't believe I could do it.'

Because she wanted a different life Alex deliberately chose a friendship group that contrasted with her background. George, however, stayed with the peer group who idolised football above everything else. Alex had no friends in her local community because they had all given up on school. The decision to change friendship groups to acquire the academic and emotional support she needed to succeed is also mirrored in accounts from previous generations where the respondents talk about deliberately deciding to 'become middle-class' (eg. David). Such a conscious decision at an early age to become middle-class is discussed further the next chapter.

Alex commented on how students divided in secondary schools were divided along class lines. She felt sorry that people from the area where she lived did not do as well as she did:

> I feel the school could have done more for the students from backgrounds like me, who don't have the determination/will power like I had to do well. I think the school let them become apathetic towards study, as did the wider community, and more could be done to combat this and keep them in school and help them achieve.

It was her friends who virtually enabled her to move on to higher education, guiding her through the application process and telling her she would not have to pay fees: 'I really didn't know anything about it [getting into university] but my friends said it was easy and that I shouldn't have to pay, their parents had told them.'

Early friendship groups provided two important elements of personal development for these authors: friends offered solidarity and support and located the young person in the social hierarchy. Such location was a crucial influence in enabling progression to HE – Alex's group of friends were 'automatically going to university, that helped me.' George's friends on the other hand 'saw no point' in school work and he therefore did not work hard at school. But later, influenced by people who had been to university, he was prompted to ask the question 'why not me?'

Some of the authors in this period took part in activities developed as part of the initiatives to support working-class student progression into HE. Kayleigh, who started university in 2005, went on a residential summer school while studying for her A levels: 'I had already decided to go to university but I guess it helped me decide to move away from home and stay in residence. I was very independent and I enjoyed it so much I thought this is the only way to go...' Claire went to university in 2007 after retaking her A levels on the advice of a mentor she had been matched up with through an AimHigher programme between the local university and her college: 'She told me it was worth repeating, that there was no shame and it helped me convince my parents to support me for one more year. That was hard but she [the mentor] helped me at a difficult time.'

Once at university friendship was also important in contributing to the participants' success. 'I rely on my friends to help relax me after working hard' (Jenny, who studied from 1999-2002). 'The students are great. I have made some really good friends' (Jack, who went to university in 2004).

While friendships provide solidarity and support when you 'fit in', in cases where they are more precarious, accounts detail a greater feeling of insecurity about being at university at all:

> I thought Uni would be great and I would meet a whole new group of friends. I knew the work would be hard, but I thought, it would be worth it for the social life. It's not as great as I thought- haven't met many people I click with. (Kelly)

In their study of universities in Scotland Christie *et al* found social isolation to be a significant factor in non-completion:

> The non-continuers reported more difficulties in meeting new people, getting involved in student activities and were more likely to perceive the environment as alienating. (2004:625)

Kelly is from a working-class, single parent family. She talked about her home life: 'I was really close to my mum. She believed in me but she wasn't quite sure what that meant, didn't get school as she had left as soon as she could and had me pretty soon after that.'

Thomas (2002) argues that experiences such as Kelly's may well relate to the middle-class habitus (Bourdieu, 1985) evident on many university campuses, where middle-class values are taken for granted and held by the majority of the student body. Many of the authors already developed a middle-class identity as part of the process of deciding to go to university, but those who did not were perhaps at a greater disadvantage if they got through to HE. Her class background made it more difficult for Kelly to find like-minded people. By her second year, however, she had become friendly with two young women:

> In my second year I did an option on child development and met my two best friends, Kate and Hayley. We still go everywhere together. Kate's very intelligent and helped me think things through. I don't believe I would have survived the third year without her.

Kelly's account draws out how valuable friends can be in encouraging persistence. Kate might have helped her with her studies, but Kelly's account indicates her friends helped her to acclimatise to university psychologically, enabling her to develop an identity as a university graduate. On completing her psychology degree Kelly took a a master's degree in 2001 and is now studying for a PhD, while teaching part-time in HE.

Although he was a mature student, friendship was important at university for George as well. He regards his social life as a vital way of maintaining his self-identity: 'It was a huge part of who I am today and allows me to be me.' He was actively involved in the students' union in the Afro Caribbean and Africa Society and the United Nations Society. Unlike many other mature students who find university isolating (West, 1996),

George has developed his own community of friends. As he says: 'despite the age differences there are no differences.'

George received a full loan and had saved some money towards his studies so he only worked five hours part-time in a local care home. After completing his studies in 2005, George gained a place on an MSW and now teaches part-time on the BA degree in social work.

Alex also recalls the importance of social interaction at university:

> I didn't realise how important the social life would be to me. I said I would come to university with the aim of studying and socialising didn't matter but actually I have a great time and I go out all the time, probably more than some students who seem to do less work than me!

She is actively involved in the ski and snowboarding clubs and goes on trips abroad with these groups:

> I am a hard working student but I also go mad and drink a lot, I burn the candle to an extreme extent, at both ends. I love studying though and the reason I can go out as much is because I am so organised and forward thinking.

University has more than lived up to Alex's expectations and her friendships and social life have been 'a real added bonus.' She used her friendship group to support her academic development and to gain access to vital information, as well as to realise her aspirations. She sees herself as hard-working and determined but recognises that she has gained much from her friends. The social capital in her friendship group has enabled her to bridge the gap between her family's experience and the world she has entered. Alex completed her degree and is now a postgraduate admissions officer at a university.

The role of peer support in creating educational success has been used extensively by Coleman (1994) who developed the concept of social capital from Bourdieu (1984). Unlike Bourdieu, however, Coleman's view of social capital is rooted in the family, with peers and friendship growing out of a strong patriarchal family base. While this may be true for some families, for people like Alex and Sara their family could not provide the knowledge and opportunities they needed to progress into HE. Coleman's lack of attention to difference and class position in his use of social capital is a serious flaw in his theories – as these accounts show, it was friendships more than families which offered support.

Bourdieu (1984) argued that the middle classes use a variety of 'capital' – economic, cultural and social – to reproduce their privileged position. The life stories in this study found pervasive cultures across the home, community, school and university which affected decision-making and success for the participants. This is not to argue that such cultures determine or fix students' life chances completely, as we have seen from George's story; rather that other factors have to intervene to challenge traditional trajectories for particular groups.

In the previous chapter I discussed why parental support and encouragement were vital to enable children to see the possibility for them to go on to higher education. The accounts showed that it was those who grew up in first generation middle-class families, such as Tom and Henrietta, who had strong support to go on to higher education even though no one in their family had been to university: 'I went to uni because my dad said it would be a great opportunity. He hadn't gone but he knew I needed to go' (Henrietta, who started in 1999); 'Uni was always a goal for us kids. Mom and dad always said it was the path to a decent career' (Tom). Tom's father understood that the route he had taken into the middle classes now required a degree in order to begin a professional career. The support networks for these young people were powerful. Their parents may have been unable to help with homework, but their economic resources could be used to enable success at school for their children: 'I was rubbish at Maths, even thought I would fail GCSE so my mum arranged for me to have extra lessons so I got through' (Henrietta).

Amongst the working-class respondents, however, there were few such support mechanisms, but their accounts record a strong sense of personal determination: 'I always believed I should strive to do my best' (Kelly), and 'I always studied hard, had goals and high aims' (Jack), 'The single most important thing that keeps me studying is my own personal determination' (Sara).

This sense of personal determination is common across all the accounts of those from working-class backgrounds in this book, but perhaps one of the most striking descriptions of persistence comes from this generation, from a young man called TJ.

Defying expectations

Born in south east London to parents from Bengal, TJ went to university and studied genetics: 'I went to the local school and sixth form college, and went to a university which was only half an hour from where I live in London. I did a year of mathematics then changed to study biomedical as I want to get into medicine later.' TJ recounted that the expectations of his teachers and community had been extremely negative about his decision to continue into HE as there were high expectations from his family, school teachers and peers to get a job straight after school. TJ therefore felt that going to university was 'selfish':

> Where I'm from, it's just really drug excessive and loads of crime. I found the situation where I lived, it's mostly Bengali, hardly anyone goes to university from my area, I mean no one in my family have been to university before. I'm the only son as well in the family so there's pressure there. University seemed like a kind of selfish choice really, because it's taking years out of your life and the fact that you don't earn any money until then...

TJ's aspirations to go to university were also explicitly discouraged by his careers teacher:

> I do remember when I was in year 9, we had a careers interview, where a careers advisor came into class and some of us could volunteer to speak with them. I said maybe university. But he was really unenthusiastic. He said it's very difficult to get into, considering where you live, and the school is not very good. He said I should think about something else.

As Reay *et al* point out, 'choice for the majority of [working-class] students involves either a process of finding out what you cannot have, what is not open to negotiation and the looking at a few options left or a process of self-exclusion' (2005:85).

For TJ, however, this lack of support at school set an early precedent for coping alone and working independently. He described how he felt unsupported by his peers and teachers who did not share his interest in school work:

> I was really like no one else at school. I felt distant definitely. Most kids there were just into football and mucking around ... I just used to sit in the library just reading books. So yeah, I was kind of lonely I suppose if

anything looking back. I would stay after school and I would come early just to get extra work done.

Teachers never asked me to do any of this stuff but I was just coming in and hanging around after hours, reading extra books ... Yeah. I was a little bit of a geek.

The teachers were very passive, to be honest that's the best way to describe them. They were there and doing their thing; then they'd leave exactly on time at the end of the day. They wouldn't stick around after school unless you were there hassling them, which is what I had to do to a certain extent. After 3 or 3.30pm they were rushing to leave, almost as badly as the other kids. I was the kid pestering them to hang around after class had finished.

TJ was a reader. He developed his love of learning despite the attitude of the teachers and his school. He remembers when he 'dropped off the radar' at a critical time in his education. During his A levels he became ill. He describes how his absence at a time when he should have been revising went unnoticed:

I was out of college for two and a half weeks due to illness and it was just before exams. No one noticed really, the teachers took the register but no one really cared. And when I got back we just started exams. I think they just thought I was studying at home, maybe, because I didn't go to any classes. And unfortunately no one from my house contacted them to say I was ill. I was unable to revise, that was the main thing. Up until then I'd always got good grades, I was predicted 3 A's, but I ended up with 3 C's. ... I remember my teachers were very disappointed, shaking their heads at me when we got our results. I was like, 'This is not my fault, I was doing well until the illness'. And they just didn't believe me really. I was really upset about that.

As with other accounts in this book, such as Paula's in chapter 3, TJ expressed a desire to 'prove people wrong' and felt it was a significant motivating factor: 'I think [my background] will be there always, to some extent. I don't think I will get away from it. But then that kind of pushes me to study harder to some extent, it kind of pushes me on.' TJ developed a strong academic identity, his own sense of belonging in an academic world. He got a place at university but disliked the course he chose and transferred at the end of the first year.

TJ is an example of someone who would have benefited from the widening participation initiatives that were developing in the later part of his schooling, but he coped alone despite his initial incorrect decision as to which course to study. Once at university, he enjoyed his time there and made friends: 'There were many more people like me at uni, wanting to work hard.'

By the end of his degree TJ had developed a new network of support through the students' union. He went on to take up office as a sabbatical officer and decided to continue in student union politics, saying: 'A year of doing this to support students like me is really worth it. The union helped me so I want to help others.'

The self-determination and persistence described by TJ illustrates Beck's view of our individualised society where people bear social risks personally:

> In the individualised society the individual must therefore learn, on pain of permanent disadvantage, to conceive of himself or herself as the centre of action. ... Under these conditions of a reflexive biography 'society' must be individually manipulated as a 'variable.' ... What does that mean for forging my own fate, which nobody else can do for me? (1992:135)

Beck goes on to point out that the individual risks for working-class people are more extensive than for middle-class groups. Personal determination is essential if students from working-class backgrounds are going to succeed. Working-class students have to rely on their own capabilities as they lack the additional resources that middle-class students can fall back on. Although their families were close, many working-class students encountered difficulty because their parents, especially their fathers, did not understand their interest in study. The hostility from family discussed in the previous chapter is found again in this generation: Alex's father did not believe she was capable of doing well in her A levels; Kayleigh wrote: 'My parents discouraged it [going to university]; I was stubborn and wanted to prove them wrong'; while Claire attributed her decision to the influence of her peers, not her parents: 'I did ... feel that it was the best thing to do, despite what they [her parents] said, as most people in my year applied...'

In the picture that emerges from this group of students, friendships and personal determination feature much more significantly than any other factor in their academic decision making and practice. The role of friendship as a form of 'bridging' social capital (Field, 2005: 111) for students from working-class backgrounds is significant and carries the potential to mitigate against the lack of other forms of capital. It suggests that social ties and support can help people overcome perceived barriers to continuing in education. In the absence of academic support working-class students seemed to draw on their friendships for the support and knowledge they need, as well as on their own determination to succeed. With teachers and tutors failing to fill this gap, friendship groups become the primary influence in these students' educational trajectories.

Alex's father's reaction to her success at school highlights families' lack of aspiration and their belief that 'people like us can't do well academically' (Cath). While her personal determination and self-belief were necessary to counter her father's attitude, Cath also needed support and proper information to enable her to progress into HE. Alex's account echoes several of the life histories discussed in the previous chapter, where parental attitude prevented their children from going into HE straight from school. Those like Jenny, who went back to study as a mature student, illustrate how negative attitudes can influence the course of a life.

While the respondents in the book all went on to study in higher education, some recall their peers 'giving up.' They also recognised that those who did so came from working-class backgrounds. Alex's insightful comments on her working-class peers point starkly to the issues of class that need further attention. Her insights are borne out by research from Forsyth and Furlong (2003), Willis (2003) and Wyn and White (1997):

> Although education is potentially liberating, the evidence is clear that schooling plays a significant role in the systematic marginalisation of young people who are poor ... (Wyn and White, 149)

The role of young people's friendship has emerged as a powerful influencing factor in creating success for first generation students, particularly for those who cannot access other forms of cultural or economic power. Friendship groups can also operate to confirm students' perceptions of learning and can drive students away from study. But equally, they can offer a bridge for students who lack any other resources to support their educational aspirations. Alex, like others in previous generations, effectively made a decision to become friends with middle-class peers so she could continue successfully in her studies. This is not a cold hearted decision but one that changed the social capital available to her (Field, 2005). She was able to use her friends and their families to gain access to vital information to help her enter HE. Friendships located the youngsters as 'academic' or 'hardworking', 'sporty' or 'hard.' These locations had serious consequences for their future and greater attention needs to be paid to the social hierarchies developed in playgrounds, since these have so much power.

However, self-determination is also an important element in these accounts. TJ's story details how personal resolve, almost in spite of the difficulties he faced, can enable success. In his account and in those of many others, we see that having a strong reading culture provides a framework for success in study. TJ wrote: 'Some people found it odd the way I was always reading, even at uni, cause most of my mates are studying science they don't get novels, but it is a sort of solace really, a way to imagine other worlds.' This theme of books offering a view on to other worlds is explored further in the next chapter.

All 28 participants have now gained employment in HE, whether teaching on BA courses, on a research contract, working in the students' union or providing learning support for others. For most, their desire to work in HE is based on their own belief that education can transform lives. The next chapter draws out the key elements from all these life histories, discussing the themes that positively influence upward mobility.

7
Gateways and gatekeepers: Mobility and class revisited

The second half of the twentieth century saw immense change in the shape of British society, with working-class employment shrinking to around a quarter of all jobs by the 1970s and significant growth in the middle classes. The growth of middle-class employment is also reflected in the massification of higher education, creating many more professional jobs in the sector. Looking across the generations recorded in the life histories in this book, two themes emerge which detail how individuals were able to 'move class.' The first is the role of significant others in supporting or hindering social mobility. The second is the development of an aspirant identity, often supported by the increasingly mobile society. This chapter explores these two themes which support widening participation and social mobility, focusing on how individual experience and social process affected the possibilities for upward social mobility.

The life stories reveal that employment in the HE sector has provided opportunity for people who were the first in their families to go into higher education. Accordingly, the chapter begins with a discussion about the changes in staffing in the higher education sector.

Employment in higher education and social mobility
Higher education has greatly expanded over the last 70 years, moving from about 20,000 full-time academic posts in the 1950s to more than 100,000 by the beginning of the twenty-first century (Universities UK,

2007, 2011a and b). Employment in the professional services in HE also increased steadily to nearly 205,000 by 2009 (HESA, 2010). Of the 139 authors featured in this book, just over half, 73, were in academic posts and the others in administrative roles.

The male respondents who studied in the 1950s and 1960s found gaining employment in the sector 'easy': 'I had three job offers waiting for me' (Peter, who went to Hull University in 1963). For women the story was very different as they faced prejudice about their role in the workplace. However, all the authors from the 1950s and 1960s cohorts, male and female, are now at the peak of their careers, holding senior positions, mostly academic, in the sector as principals, pro vice chancellors, heads of faculty or schools or professors.

Beyond the 1970s, the accounts of employment suggest that working in HE became more fractured. Many of the authors started in teacher education or further education and found their way into HE later. Others came into the sector from industrial backgrounds as the economic landscape of the UK changed. Starting your career in another part of the economy before coming to work in higher education is quite common. In 2001, 'Academic employees were recruited from two main sources: students 34 per cent and employees from other sectors in the UK 42 per cent' (Universities UK, 2007:4). There are more recruits into HE jobs from outside the sector than there are of people who go straight into employment in the sector directly after completing their studies.

As higher education became more professionalised in the 1980s, developing a career in administration increased in popularity. This route is detailed in many of the life histories. Administrative roles in HE continued to grow throughout the rest of the century with an increasing number of authors finding their way into jobs in student administration, the careers service, widening participation activities and student unions.

During the 1980s, as the unit of resource decreased in the sector, opportunities for employment in academic posts became more competitive. Many of the accounts from this period highlight a route from part-time, insecure employment into full-time, permanent posts later. This remains a common route for academic careers in the twenty-first century. Maria, who went to university in 1986, said: 'I was offered part-time hours to teach while I was studying for my PhD. Once I completed that

I looked for jobs. Firstly a year-long contract before I got my first real lecturing post.'

While success in higher education does not provide an automatic right to upward social mobility, Elias and Purcell (2004) found that gaining a degree delivered graduate outcomes in employment. However, Purcell and Elias (2008) also indicate that women graduates, while earning more than their non-graduate counterparts, still earn less than male graduates and encounter greater difficulty in gaining employment than men. Kim, who started her PhD in 1998, said:

> It was not easy at all to get employment. Throughout my PhD I believed the heads of departments when they insisted that you needed teaching experience to get work as a lecturer so I took on part-time teaching whenever it was going. I found making the leap to full-time difficult as you also now need publications so that took some time but in the end I got there after five years of insecure part-time work after completing my PhD. I got a couple of publications and got this lecturing job ... phew!

In 1975, 11 per cent of academics were women, moving to 13 per cent in 1980, and while female students increased and overtook male students in the HE student population, changes in employment were slower and women still remain less secure, lower paid and in less senior positions across the sector (Halvorsen, 2002; Goode, 2000). The proportion of black academics is even more unequal and some argue that HE remains an unfriendly environment for ethnic minority staff (Pilkington, 2011).

It is difficult to know what impact changes in policy in higher education may have on the progress of social mobility. This topic is explored in the next chapter. But while higher education acted as an engine for social mobility in these life histories, insecurity in employment becomes increasingly prevalent over time in these accounts. It is difficult to evaluate the importance of this insecurity as the time lag in gaining permanent employment may be due to the fact that careers develop gradually. However, since a growing body of evidence (*Times Higher Education*, 5 April, 2012) suggests a surplus of qualified graduates applying for academic posts, it may be that the time when higher education played a role in providing significant employment opportunities, especially for academic posts, is over.

Whitchurch (2008) found that university administrator roles were becoming more diverse and more hybridised. Administrative roles can work closely with students, frequently offering academic support or taking on what would have been the role of academic tutors in the past. The sector is being reshaped in the twenty-first century and, while employment opportunities will continue in HE, they may look different to the jobs of previous decades.

Employment in higher education is predominantly middle-class and the authors of these life histories were extremely conscious that their class identity had changed. The next section examines their reflections on their class position.

Class and identity

> ... those with a university education were more confident in reflecting on the use of class labels ... they were more comfortable in reflecting on class than were those without cultural capital. (Savage, 2000:114)

The authors' thoughts on their class position were often ambiguous. Their reflections can be divided into two categories: those who had embraced a middle-class identity and those who still felt 'working-class', despite being aware that they were now middle-class in occupational terms. For some participants issues of class were important simply because 'it is so powerful' (Ben, who went to university in 1967). Ben is typical of a number of authors who see class in relation to wider social inequalities. He went on to say: 'it sounds like I've got a real 'working-class hero' chip on my shoulder, maybe I have, but there are a lot of very bright people who have not had the benefit.' Ben's position as a senior lecturer in the social sciences suggests that his reflections are informed by social theory. This is also true for Peter, a political scientist, who argued that class divisions continued to matter at the social level:

> ... the issue of class is extremely important. In spite of the fact that politicians and social commentators deny the existence of class it remains the single most important factor in the determination of an individual's lifestyle, health, education and opportunities. (Peter, who went to university in 1963)

Many authors regarded class as intrinsic to their life history and identity. Susan who went to university in 1970, claimed that she was:

... still the only person in my family to have passed an O or A level and am still the only one to have gone to university. I consider myself to be of working-class origin because of my parent's family backgrounds occupational status, income and education backgrounds.

For Jane the emphasis was primarily on the family income. She stated that she came from a working-class background where her family were 'poor – little in the way of material wealth, owned nothing of value – overcrowded, rented accommodation...' She went on to say that class mattered to her because it is 'symbolic of inequalities within our society – unacceptable differences between groups of people in terms of material wealth and opportunities.' Jane had internalised class and saw it as central to her identity but she also regarded it as part of wider social inequality. For all the authors, class relates to their personal identity or, as Savage puts it:

> ... class operates as a benchmark by which people can measure their own life histories ... class is salient in terms of constructing an idea of difference not in terms of defining a class which one belongs to ... with a collective identity. (2000:113)

This is very clear in Dave's comments. Despite his current occupation he feels strongly that he remains working-class: class is part of his personal identity based on his childhood experiences and sense of self. Dave's father was a miner and participated in the miners' strikes in the 1970s and 1980s. Dave went to university at the height of the latter and was very influenced by these events. He talked about his perceptions of his current position as a careers adviser at a university now, starting by examining the changing society in the UK in the twenty-first century:

> ... despite it being a so-called classless society this is not the case. Many jobs are still issued along class lines I think, depending upon your accent, cultural capital, how you present yourself (confidence, assertiveness etc) and education ... I will always be working-class, despite my salary or job type. My philosophy is that socio-economic status is a useful tool, but crude. I believe you will always remain the class that, culturally, you grew up in. For example, if I won the lottery tomorrow it would not automatically make me middle-class or especially upper class. Would I be accepted within these social circles? Would I be automatically offered a job in the Foreign Office? No.

Many recent graduates felt that 'the edges of class distinctions are blurred now' (Abi, who went to university in 2000). This dilution of class boundaries came up in the data for several participants, particularly in the life accounts of women and those who grew up in the 1980s and 1990s. Jill went so far as to say: 'I consider myself to be partly declassed.' Judy, who went to university in 1988, rejected a class identity entirely: 'Everyone is just an individual with different values/ideas/back-grounds.' Kelly, meanwhile, who went to university in 2004, said: 'I don't feel any need to belong to or be labelled as a member of any particular class.'

While most participants appreciate their current middle-class position many were reluctant to accept it and expressed ambivalence about their status. Mark described himself as 'working-class with middle-class children' and Peter said 'middle-class by day, working-class by night.' He explained that it 'depends on the circumstances, middle-class by other people's criteria, but family roots/experiences are always with you, so yes – working-class.' Barbara, who went to university as a mature student in 1988, also felt 'by definition I am probably middle-class, certainly in income bracket terms but my roots are working-class and I work hard for my money so I consider myself to be working-class.' In his study of class identity Savage highlights the use of 'working-class identity as a means of announcing your independence' (2000:116). This theme is strong throughout this group of life histories.

The authors' second major response to class focused on a conscious desire to change their class background. Mark reflected on the irony of his young perceptions of the differences between a middle and working-class lifestyle. He said:

> I suppose [I am] middle-class ... when I was a child I had every intention of getting out of the working-classes – not that they were bad – just thought I could do better and procure a better financial deal. I remember dad going out to work at 07.15 on his pushbike – I could hear the gate close from my bed and thinking I don't want to do that ... but I leave for work now at 07.00 and would love to ride my bike to work!

Becoming middle-class was an early goal for some of the participants. Education was seen as 'the way out' (June, who went to university in the 1990s), or the route away from home: 'I wanted friends who thought like me, not the dead boring dull life my parents lived and wanted me to live' (Jack, who went to university in 1966).

For others, being middle-class is a badge of pride: 'I feel I have made something of myself, against the odds. No one thought I could do it' (Sue, who attended university in the 1970s). Pat, who went to university in 1964, said: 'for my family I was the 'hope', I couldn't let them down. They wanted me to be someone who 'mattered'. That was just the way they saw it.' These authors while asserting their movement into the middle class, are still conscious of that change. They are aware that within their own lifetime they have altered their social status.

Class, then, from whichever perspective, is a key feature of most of the authors' personal identities, but whether they see themselves as middle or working-class, these identities are divided, never quite one or the other, memories of their backgrounds continuing to contrast with their present situation. Those who still see themselves as working-class do so against an understanding of the social science definitions; they prefer to identify as somehow counter-cultural, keeping a distance from the 'middle.' Mark's description of himself as 'working-class with middle-class children' or Joanne's comment that she is 'middle-class at work and working-class at home' encapsulate this position.

For all authors, the awareness of their family backgrounds creates a sense of being 'in-between' (Bhabha, 1994:4) or as John, who went to university in 1998, explained it: 'Students from working-class back-grounds are consciously or unconsciously stepping out from a comfort zone into a different world, for me, never feeling I belong in either.'

The language used in this statement both emphasises the notion of 'in-betweeness' and highlights a further aspect of social mobility that is often passed over in theoretical debates: social mobility is first and fore-most about movement, from one class to another. Urry refers to this as 'vertical' mobility (2007:8). While this is true, in these accounts the ex-perience of upwards social mobility is often described in the language of movement, real or imagined. The participants present a complex picture of mobility. As well as upward, vertical mobility, many describe moving geographically, virtually and imaginatively, and explicitly con-nect such movement to the development of their aspirations. This provides an alternative way of looking at social mobility and draws on the mobilities' theory set out by Urry. The next section explains the theoretical base for this analysis.

Class as a place, real or imagined

As we saw in chapter 1, conventional debates around social mobility centre on a vertical movement of people up or down a clear hierarchy. Most of these studies used quantitative data which fixes people at certain points on a scale, of either occupation or income at a particular age. This locates the individual at one point in time and cannot provide the rich detail offered by a life history approach. When working with the qualitative data, as I did in this study, movement emerged as an important theme in the data. Any form of mobility requires a passing from one place to another, even social mobility. Place and movement were therefore important in all the accounts. Urry highlights the significance of place, saying:

> In a simple sense almost all mobilities entail movement between specific places and there is something about places that are complicit within that movement. (2007:253)

The authors consistently identify class position by reference to place, whether surroundings be middle or working-class. Explanations of class position include reference to particular spaces, as in the case of Joe who described his class background in this way:

> I was born in Haddington Scotland, about 20 miles east of Edinburgh. I was born into the working-class ... We lived in a rented council house in a small town where the main industries were mining and agriculture.

Linking class and place, as Joe does here, is common amongst the life stories and points to how individuals experience class, through social and cultural positioning along with physical location. Pete, who went to university in 1987, justified his definition of coming from a working-class background by saying 'I grew up on a council estate.' Brian talks about his class background in the same way: 'I was born into the working-class ... we lived in a rented council house in a small town – main industries were mining and agriculture.' Jane, who went to university as a mature student in 1988, talked about her sense of class also in relation to place:

> Very quiet post war seaside town ... there were two sides to the place I lived in – both on opposite sides of the tracks and with the gasworks situated where the housing estates were. We lived in a house with my mother's parents until I was 13. We always lived in rented accommodation.

She later talks about going to the grammar school where she discovered 'different class backgrounds'. This is again described with reference to place:

> There were three streets I can remember, one was terrace – no front gardens (where rough people lived), the next still terrace with back yards and alleyways between and little front gardens and the next was an 'avenue' with semi-detached houses and gardens all round. Those three streets which I passed from the working class to the middle class every day to get to the grammar school were a sort of microcosm of the class system...

The middle-class space is also located. Jack, who went to university in 1966 and is now a professor at a university, commented on the university as a middle-class space:

> So I am middle-class – as I sit at my desk in front of this screen; as I write to you, I look out across the campus, see attractive landscaping, trees and so on. I can walk across the grass; take lunch (not dinner!) in the university restaurant – yes middle-class.

So, while class is experienced in terms of culture and lifestyle as many theorists argue (Bennett *et al*, 2010), from these accounts it is also experienced as a location. For these authors, class is rooted in geography.

Informing the importance of place, the life histories further reveal how movement from one place to another, whether real or virtual, affected the chances of social mobility. The histories draw out other forms of mobility which had an influence on the authors, helping them move beyond their family backgrounds into a middle-class lifestyle. It is possible to tell part of the story of social mobility through the lens of movement.

Since the late 1990s, social theorists have explored the idea of mobility as part of a new set of analytical tools to understand society. Writing about this new analysis, Urry argues that our understanding of society and the people within it would be greatly enhanced by examining; 'movement, mobility and contingent ordering, rather than [focusing] upon stasis, structure and social order.' (2007:46). Urry's suggestion is that society is more fluid than static and more incomplete and transitory than fixed and settled supports the idea that the one shot approach to measuring mobility discussed in chapter 1 cannot account for the range of movement taking place in our society (Sorensen, 1986). This range of mobilities – physical, imagined and virtual – Urry argues, will affect both identities and social interaction.

I argued in chapter 2 that class is inscribed into identity and it is through the lived experience of individuals that class is felt. Just as class is experienced between different people in society as well as between different cultural practices (Bennett *et al*, 2010), so too is it experienced in localities and places (Urry, 2007). Class and place are intrinsically linked in many of the life histories in this book and the next section discusses how geographical movement influenced the authors' possibility for social mobility.

Gateways to the future: moving place, entering new worlds

Along with the changes in how people live, the life histories also chart the story of the rapid expansion of a mobile society. Accounts in this book from the 1950s mention families who relied almost entirely on a 'foot economy': parents walked to work, children walked to school and any shopping was also conducted on foot. Such accounts are very much bound within limited geographical communities linked to class position. Helen, who went to university in 1955, talked about the movements of her early life in Glasgow:

> The dancing classes were held in a converted corner shop a couple of blocks away. Our church was further away and we walked on Sundays. Primary school was closer.

As British society became more affluent as a whole during the 1960s, working-class families began to acquire other 'mobility technologies' bicycles for the children and second-hand cars for the family. As Urry points out: 'footpower came to be challenged by the mobility systems of cycling and automobility...' (2007:64).

Part of the growing affluence is reflected in some accounts where parents became upwardly mobile themselves as a result of better employment and rising income. Many of these families chose to move out of the inner cities as the children grew up. Scott, who went to university in 1969, talked about the difference between his childhood in London and his teenage experiences living in a leafy suburb of Harlow:

> It was a bunch of old cockneys that had escaped from the east-end to the new towns so it was pretty much all working-class people, although some had made a bit of money along the line and probably thought they were something special.

The authors in these accounts highlight how travel to school, especially as they moved into secondary education, took them out of their working-class communities. Jack, who went to Oxford University in 1968, talked about his movements as a child in this way: 'I went to infants, junior and grammar school locally (on foot – primary – or by bicycle for grammar which was further away).' Charles, who went to university in 1977, said: 'my primary was 200 yards away from home, the grammar a 20 minute bus ride to another part of Nottingham.' Riddell argues that to support working-class learners into higher education, mixing more widely than within their immediate community is important:

> [The young people] meet a wider group ... from ... different backgrounds from a wider geographical area and with cognate developing aspirations and plans. (2010:79)

Journalists such as Luckhurst (2005) have argued that grammar schools are more likely to encourage continuing on into higher education. While many of the life histories recall positive experiences of their grammar school, there are also accounts of good comprehensive schools:

> I passed the 11+ but did not go to grammar school. My primary head was a staunch socialist as was my father and we all agreed the comprehensive was the thing. It was the other side of town. I got the bus there – I met my best friend Jackie that way, we both took the bus. She got on later than me – from a more affluent neighbourhood – I would keep her a seat. I had a great English teacher at secondary school. Introduced us to the theatre. She encouraged me to apply to Cambridge though I didn't get in, also Jackie. She was highly academic and much more middle-class. We were quite competitive with each other (Margaret, who went to Sussex in 1976).

In their 2011 study Boliver and Swift found that grammar schools produced better mobility results in absolute terms than comprehensives.

However, as the authors clearly show, different school types did not necessarily determine the amount of social mobility. They conclude:

> Since grammar schools, unlike comprehensives, were selecting those judged more able one would expect any such advantage to be reduced when we control for children's attributes, and so it is. (2011:101)

Opening up horizons at school was a shared theme in the life histories. However, it was not only a feature of school but also of the mobility itself: as the authors cycled or got the bus to school, they moved beyond their local community, seeing other ways of living, different lifestyles and encountering different people. Moving outside the community seems to have contributed to developing an aspirant identity.

Remaining within the community of the family created a particular set of horizons but moving out of their local community, even to a different part of town, to attend a grammar or comprehensive school had an impact on the authors' sense of self. Many of the accounts describe the move to the grammar or comprehensive as 'moving out of my community.' Judy, who went to university in 1966, talked about it this way:

> In primary school all my friends were local; I didn't know anyone from outside. From age 11 I knew girls from all over Sheffield – a big difference for me! We wore uniform – we all looked the same at school, but most girls were well off, as school was on the posh side of town.

As these young people moved into their teenage years, the bonds with their communities loosened. Relationships between their school, families and home communities were 'distant' and several describe the move to the grammar or comprehensive as 'moving to a different world.' The physical movement from a local environment to a different part of town symbolised a change for many of the participants. Peter recalled meeting an old junior school friend when he was 15 and talking excitedly about what he was doing at the time and being told:

> 'my you don't half talk posh now', so I had soaked up a different accent and way of speaking very quickly and had to 'unlearn' it whenever I was with family. But I realised I had moved on.

Activities also provided travel away from their local communities, such as being involved in the scouts, guides or Sunday school. 'Scouts always took us away, it was great to be out with other lads your own age trying things you would never do at home' (John, who went to university in 1965). Early holidays to the seaside also feature prominently, offering a glimpse at a different set of possibilities. David, who went to university in 1966, talked about going on holiday from Glasgow:

> For holidays we rented a room for a week in Mrs Lamb's guesthouse on the west coast. It always felt like another world that week. Dad was easier on holiday. It made me think I didn't want the drudgery and worry he lived with – it got him down always worried about the job.

Geographical movement seems to have been important in enabling social mobility, as it offered a chance to experience a different life, meet other people outside the local community and provide recognition that there were other possibilities: 'I just felt that our life at home was so closed. I wanted something different and I noticed there were other ways of being I guess' (Sarah).

The move to university was a final rite of passage away from the family home to another life. Ruth, like several others, referred to moving to university as 'an escape.' Frank, who went to Hull University in 1968, described his journey on his first day:

> I have vivid memories of the train journey to Hull from Kings Cross. All a bit like Harry Potter going off to the wizard school. While waiting for the train I got into discussion with a very nice German woman who was on her way back to Germany. The train was a specially chartered train full of student union people. They were handing out leaflets and such so lots of talk as we rattled through the countryside. I had never been that far north before and didn't know what to expect but it seemed to go so quickly from A to B which amazed me. And then arriving in Hull being bussed to my student house and meeting my roommate Pat for the first time.

Physical movement also symbolised the transition into a world that was much more middle-class. It provided the opportunity to develop different horizons and allowed 'gateways' into different lives. As Elliot and Urry put it: 'Everyday mobilisation is intricately interwoven with what people feel, desire and think about their lives' (2010:155). As well as physical movement, Urry (2007) also describes other forms of mobility such as imagined or virtual mobility. The next section reflects on the role of imagined mobility in these accounts – travelling through reading.

Imagined mobilities: books as gateways to other worlds

Perhaps the most significant feature the respondents talked about in their life histories was a love of books. Ninety-six per cent of the authors were strong readers: 'I was an avid reader' (Mike, who went to university 1968); 'I loved books from an early age' (Jenny, who went to university 1955); 'We didn't have many books in the house but we did have a few travel books and an encyclopaedia, my love of 'knowing' started as a 5 year old pouring over that book' (John, who attended university 1986). Books feature in nearly all accounts of those who started university in the 1950s through to those who went in 2007. However as time went on different media came to dominate, particularly music radio in the 1960s, films in the 1970s and, from the 1970s onwards, TV became important to the experiences of these young people.

The 70 years which cover the life stories of the participants in this research coincides with the development of youth culture, the rise of popular music and youth rebellion. The radio played an important part in many authors' accounts when they were young. Pat talked about her contact with youth culture in the early 1960s:

> Music, television, reading, loads of teenage mags (my dad was a news-agent, remember, so we read them and put them back). Radio Luxembourg, wonderful imagined place Radio Luxembourg coming out at you from the ether.

These outlets provided a form of imagined mobility, an opportunity to travel to different worlds while staying in their own family homes. Urry points out that 'people travel elsewhere through memories, texts [books] ... radio and film' (2007:169). This process 'abolishes remoteness' (*ibid*), enabling the readers, listeners and viewers to imagine a different world.

Anderson (1991) maintains that the development of the printing press and the mass publication of books created the possibility of imagining nations. People might not have known each other but they were able to feel part of something bigger through sharing text and news. Books gave these authors the sense of academic entitlement that enabled them to imagine being at university. This imagining permitted empathy with different social groups, cultures and experiences and created the possibility of living differently themselves.

While most were avid readers, books were not common in the authors' homes and most went to the public library. As Kev, who went to university in 1985, said, there were very few books in his home 'but I had good access to the local library. I used to go there to escape. I would read all afternoon.' Jon, who went to university in 2000, said:

> ... my parents did not have books and still don't but I would go to the library. I suppose I did read a lot but I always read at a very fast pace. I did not read children's books but mainly history books. I learned a lot.

Others had parents who took them to the library: 'We joined when I was 7 and went every Wednesday, I always remembered the library' (Carole, who returned to HE as a mature student).

The library was a gateway in itself, opening the door to countless possibilities and many different ideas. Others recognised the power of the book itself as a source of imagined mobility. Jane commented that 'books were a window on other worlds. It took me out of myself gave me a different perspective. It also made me different to others at school who didn't read. I was sort of marked out.'

The connection with books was a particular beacon for many of the authors. For those who were unable to get to university as young people, reading kept their interest and love of learning alive, encouraging them to come back to study at a later stage. Margaret is an example of such mature students:

> As a child I would stop by the library on my way home from school. It gave me some solace from the family home. I always remembered this and am still an avid reader. It helped me believe I could be somebody. I did not have to become my mother – her slaving for my father – I could develop my own life.

As well as offering windows onto other worlds and securing a sense of their own academic abilities, books also provided an intrinsic understanding of what learning in higher education is about: a focus on text, appreciating a body of knowledge, whether numerical or word based, and developing the skills of assimilating and interpreting information. As Brian stated: 'Books were an important route to ideas and thought.' Understanding the process of education whilst gaining a window on the world offered these authors a further vital skill that helped them succeed in their academic careers. Whether real or imagined, these forms of travel provided aspiration, imagination and an understanding that a different life to that of their parents and community existed, one that supported their social mobility. As Urry argues:

> Social research typically focused upon one of these separate mobilities and its underlying infrastructure ... this new paradigm ... emphasises the complex assemblage between these different mobilities that may make ... and ... maintain social connections. (2007:48)

The next section moves from gateways to the gatekeepers: those who supported and those who hampered the upward mobility of the authors in this book.

Gatekeepers – social capital and influence

Over the years research into widening participation in higher education has emphasised the importance of a family's cultural capital (Thomas, 2002; Reay *et al*, 2005; Bourdieu, 1984). Being in a family who have successfully engaged with higher education provides the next generation with the knowledge and understanding that reproduce further success. Alongside cultural capital, Bourdieu (1977) identified the value of 'social capital' the networks available to the middle-classes which enable them to reproduce their position in society. Field puts it this way:

> By pursuing appropriate 'cultural investment strategies' within the family, some social groups were able to ensure that their children optimised the yield from education. (2008:18)

American sociologists Putman (2000) and Coleman (1994) developed the idea of social capital showing how it can be used in different community settings, although they focused mostly on the importance of the family environment. Working in the UK, Field (2008) expanded on the value of strong positive social networks for educational development in families and communities.

Where these networks are weak it is harder for the younger generation to gain a purchase on their future development. While parents and other family members have a significant influence on children's engagement with education and study, it is possible to draw on others who can provide the social resources needed to be successful in higher education and to be socially mobile. Writing about social capital Field says:

> People may sometimes find that options are constrained by the nature of the resources that they can get hold of through their connections. At other times, they will use these networks to liberate them from other constraints. (2008:3)

Bourdieu and Wacquant highlighted this issue in talking about the re-production of class positions in France. They explained social capital as:

> ... the sum of resources, actual and virtual, that accrue to an individual or a group by virtue of possessing a durable network of more or less institutionalised relationships of mutual acquaintance and recognition. (1992:119)

The network powerful individuals possess can be described as in effect the gatekeepers of the gateways discussed earlier and there are many possible gatekeepers who hold keys to young people's futures. The authors' accounts in the book demonstrate that while individual ability is a precursor for social mobility, support in some form is crucial to success. While parents are potentially the most profound gatekeepers for their children, others can also be important. As Coleman points out 'social capital exists within the family, but also outside the family, in the community' (1994, 334). The next section looks at the role of parents and teachers as gatekeepers to social mobility discussed through the authors' accounts.

The role of significant others in social mobility

Across the generations, parents and carers were important to the authors' development of self-belief. Parents needed to believe in their children's potential to 'better themselves': 'I think my mother probably influenced me ... not because she had much concept of university so much but [because] she believed I was capable of doing something with my life ... my father was too...' (Kevin, who went to university in 1969). The life histories also indicate that parents did not need to understand or provide academic support: others, such as teachers, could do that. What was essential, however, was that parents provided emotional and aspirational support, believing that 'bettering oneself' was an impor-tant goal that was achievable for their children. As we have seen, some parents did not see this as important and wanted their children to re-main within their local community. Paula spoke in chapter 3 about how her parents felt that travelling to university eight miles away was 'too far' and encouraged her to attend the local teacher training college.

Barbara (see chapter 5) was expected to work in her father's bakery and not continue beyond school despite her teachers' support:

> I had lots of pressure at home, working in the bakery the whole time. Mum said I was getting above myself and I was never allowed to bring friends home. I didn't do as well as I would have liked at school and didn't do as well as those others who had not shown the same ability as me at junior school because of being forced to take time off school to work at home. I was treated far more fairly at school than at home. I often had to hide my homework as my parents didn't like me doing it. Later I would try and stay at school to do it but if I got home late dad would beat me.

Barbara's parents acted as gatekeeper, keeping her aspirations firmly under lock and key until she was an adult and was able to go to university as a mature student. Although Barbara's story is extreme, several other accounts describe parents belittling their children's efforts: Alex (see chapter 6) said her father could not believe she had done so well in her A levels and recalled him asking if she was lying; Frances, said her mother would not believe she was studying in her room and forced her to take time off school to look after her siblings; while Shelley, whose parents discounted the importance of school and learning entirely, said she was forced to go to secondary modern school despite passing the 11 plus. While all these authors went back into higher education as mature students, their stories illustrate the power parents have to restrict their children's potential.

Although some show parents stifling their children's ambitions, the majority of the accounts highlight the extent to which parents believed in education and were supportive emotionally if not academically. June's experience was typical of this group. She emphasises that with the support of her father she carried on, but that her peers who did not have this emotional support left school:

> My father was keen for me to go. He always believed in me, that was what mattered really. None of my friends went to university at the same time as me but some went later as mature students. (June)

Like parents, teachers too are gatekeepers. They could either provide opportunities and open doors for their students or act as barriers to success. As the accounts of Claire and Kelvin show, teachers could deliver the additional impetus to help a young person make the decision to go on to university if parents were less keen:

> I feel the relationship between my school and family was an uneasy one. My parents were conscientious and attended all the parents' evenings but didn't really buy into the idea of education. In their view it should end at 16 and you then get on with the serious business of learning a craft and earning a living so that caused awkward silences when, for example, teachers broached the possibilities of sixth form studies. (Claire)

> Some teachers were very supportive. One called Mr Dodds encouraged me to stay on at school and go to university. My parents were less keen but Mr Dodds inspired me. We played chess most lunchtimes. (Kelvin)

These accounts illustrate how teachers provided the esteem necessary to succeed through the validation of ability and gave their students a sense of academic entitlement.

Equally important in the accounts across the generations is the role teachers can play beyond the classroom – playing chess during the lunch hour with Kelvin, taking students like Margaret on trips to the theatre discussed earlier in the chapter and so on. The level of commitment provides two important elements that enhance aspiration and self-belief. Teachers support the development of middle-class cultural capital that these young people could otherwise not access and they are remembered and valued many years later. They exercised their influence by taking an interest in the authors' lives and providing encouragement. As Riddell points out, middle-class lives 'produce the complete and complex cultural congruity between family life, leisure activities and expectations' (2010:121). These teachers, by working with the authors beyond the classroom, offered some of the additional cultural frameworks that supported the authors' future success.

Because of their power to validate ability teachers can also be negative influences. Many of the authors who went into HE as mature students felt their school had failed them (see chapter 5). In schools like Anna's which 'did not expect people like me to carry on', teachers often had low aspirations for their students. Accounts from earlier generations also highlight gender prejudice and in the life stories of black and ethnic minority students, racial prejudice. The school environment also deterred some of the authors like Janet, who said: 'I was always fairly confident and talkative and this was not acceptable in school in the seventies.' Perhaps the school environment and teachers would respond differently to pupils now.

The final set of gatekeepers frequently mentioned in the life histories are friends and peers. Friends provided considerable support for many of the authors, as in the accounts of John and Claire, where friendship assisted them in making the leap into the middle-class world, show:

> I was part of an academic and arty set ... we were also lucky with many of our teachers particularly in the later years and I certainly remember being enthused by them and also being treated as an adult quite early on. They made me believe I could achieve so I went to university. A lot of what I liked was to do with developing a self-image and fitting in. so I went down the ultra academic and arts route – English, Ancient History, Greek, and Latin were my A levels and also did lots of sports. It's hard to tell the difference between what you might have been and what you decided to become isn't it? I always had a fairly clear idea of what I wanted to be and I have turned out pretty much like that. Has it made me happy? An interesting question. It hasn't made me unhappy that's for sure and I don't dig the roads or come home soaking wet after a day in the open like my father and grandfather did and that is a real plus. (John)

Claire reflected that as her abilities developed her friends changed: 'As I went up through the school and was placed in the higher sets I became aware that my classmates were not the same social mix as on entry. More of my friends were from middle-class households in the 4th and 5th year.'

Seeing themselves in relation to their peers, these young people developed a self-identity that provided them with an academic entitlement to higher level study. However, peers could also create a sense of alienation from school and school work, as Karen who went to Kingston University as a mature student, describes below:

> Loved primary school, teachers, lessons and play. My memories of the term I spent in the London Grammar school are mainly negative. Of the 3 girls from my junior school who passed the 11+ we then had to take an entrance test for the grammar ... I was put in the A stream and my 2 school friends into the C stream so saw little of them the school day. The school was in Highgate and the other girls in my class came from Highgate, Hampstead

etc. (only four miles from my home but foreign territory – big houses, rich posh people). I was acutely aware I was different...

George, discussed in the previous chapter, had very good friendships but his friends were not interested in school work and, although he was an avid reader, he ignored his studies and left school with no qualifications.

This book demonstrates that enabling mobility is complex. It is as much about desire and imagination and aspiration as it is real hard work (Riddell, 2010). Saunders is of course right to point out that:

> Throughout business, the professions and the public services we find examples of individuals who have made good as a result of their own abilities and their own efforts. (2010:123)

However, these life histories demonstrate that alongside hard work and determination certain other conditions are required. Success in upward mobility is conditional on the availability of a range of opportunities, resources and supporters before the individual can make that leap into a different class. Gatekeepers can open up or limit potential. Urry argues that it is the intersections between being mobile and the social networks people can access which create or restrict opportunity. Life in twenty-first century requires that 'people have to access networks if they are to participate in a complex multiply networked society' (2007:193).

Stories told here of the working-class heroes in HE are stories of determination and vision for a different life, but they are also accounts of ambivalence for lost community and a desire to hold onto their roots. The authors in this book are success stories. They are people who have been able to transform themselves, now working in the sector that seemed to their families an impossible achievement.

Higher education has greatly expanded since the 1950s, providing opportunities for many. But the issues of relative social mobility are not yet resolved, despite the considerable progress made over the last few years (HEFCE, 2010). Globally HE is still expanding, but since 2010 student numbers in the UK have flat-lined at 47 per cent entrants. The next chapter looks at changing HE policy, examining its potential impact on social mobility in the future. It draws on the lessons learned from the life histories to suggest possible policy implications.

8

Social mobility and higher education in the future

> The upsurge in professional employment in the middle of the last century created an unparalleled wave of social mobility in Britain. It created unprecedented opportunities for millions of women and men. (Milburn, 2012a:1)

In his role as independent assessor for social mobility, Alan Milburn places considerable weight on the role of higher education to deliver upward social mobility. His report on higher education and social mobility (2012b) highlights the importance of widening participation and fair access in creating the possibility for social mobility but it also emphasises the importance of universities supporting graduates into professional employment (Milburn, 2012a and b).

The personal accounts presented in this book offer three different perspectives in evaluating social mobility: the individual, the institutional and the view across wider society. This concluding chapter considers these perspectives in the context of current developments in HE, and assesses their impact on social mobility in the future.

In each of the nations of the UK, different policy environments are affecting HE: in England, a change from a supply side form of higher education to demand led education; in Scotland, there is still state support for teaching but also direct institutional widening participation targets (Mullen, 2010). In Wales, a much greater controlled HE landscape with significant direct interventions in the supply of provision. Each set of policies has different effects on the sector's ability to create upward social mobility. The changes taking place in the UK also need to be seen in the context of a far more globalised economy than in the last century. The chapter begins by exploring the impact of devolution in the UK on widening participation policies.

Different nations and different policies

So, in essence, the challenge is to cope with all of this … preparing for the implementation of what are radically new funding arrangements from 2012 onwards. And all the while, …we have to remember that our real task through this period is to try and maintain excellence in learning and teaching, to ensure that our research continues to be internationally competitive, to think hard about issues of social mobility, widening participation, fair access, on a wider basis to secure the interest of students and, certainly at this time in our economic history, to be playing our part in growth and economic development. Higher education can mount a strong argument that it performs well against these overarching objectives, but performing well and continuing to perform well whilst dealing with …this longer term prospect of change is the challenge we all face… (Langlands, 2011:1).

While many policy analysts are examining the significant changes in the higher education landscape in England set out above by the chief executive of the English funding council, higher education across Britain has undergone a transformation in all four nations in the UK since the turn of the century. The changes have affected all aspects of HE but this chapter draws out those that affect students and widening participation.

As devolution for Scotland, Wales and Northern Ireland has developed, each nation's education policy has begun to diverge from the others. Higher education in Scotland had already achieved the 50 per cent HE participation rate set out by the labour government as its goal in 2000, but widening participation activities continue to be seen as integral to HE policy in Scotland. Since 1999 the further education sector in Scotland has continued to play a significant part in providing higher education. More than 18 per cent of HE students in Scotland studied in the FE sector, whereas less than 5 per cent did so in England (Scottish Government, 2011).

While the HE Act to increase fees in England was going through parliament in 2003/4, the Scottish government set itself against an increase in fees. A range of widening participation activities was funded. The Scottish government established a new university in 2011, the University of the Highlands and Islands, demonstrating its commitment to offering higher education for all who could benefit across the whole country.

In 2007 the Scottish National Party (SNP) won the election from the Labour party. The SNP provided additional funding for widening participation in a contested fund called 'New Horizons'. Institutions bid for funds against a set of criteria established by the government. Creating a bidding round in this way gave the government more control over institutional priorities. Once re-elected, the Scottish government established a review of higher education. The review focused on governance in the sector, highlighting the importance the government placed on universities serving their communities stating: 'We would like to see universities becoming more involved in community planning partnerships and to consider more effective ways of community engagement.' (Scottish Government, 2012:2). In terms of widening participation itself, through the Scottish Funding Council the government committed to both first and second chance education, flexible routes into HE – including support for further articulation from HNDs offered in further education colleges – and the possibility of a new statutory duty around institutions agreeing 'Widening Access Outcome Agreements', with penalties if they are not achieved. The determination to ensure fair access is further emphasised in funded projects to encourage disadvantaged young people into the professions. Such projects taking on board the issues of social mobility and widening participation to HE.

In Wales the funding council established specific targets: a 10 per cent rise in the proportion of all Welsh domiciled students studying higher education courses who lived in areas of high deprivation called Welsh Communities First areas (HEFCW, 2009). Alongside such interventions, the Welsh government has also focused on degree completion rates for students from disadvantaged backgrounds.

Like England and Scotland, Wales has also had a specific programme to support widening participation. This project has developed an integrated approach to activities for disadvantaged young people, with a range of other services including schools (HEFCW, 2009). In 2012, the Welsh government reshaped its student number control, offering institutions the chance to bid back for places based on government-established criteria including widening access and lower fee criteria. This development provided the government with significantly more control over the type of HE provision offered by Welsh institutions.

In England the government had introduced the Aimhigher programme in 2004. Aimhigher drew together schools and further and higher education institutions to target and support aspiration and attainment-raising for students from lower socio-economic backgrounds. The principles of the programme were based on initiatives, successfully developed in the USA in the 1970s and 1980s, to encourage black and minority students to aspire to HE. The programmes focused on raising the aspirations and attainment of individual young people.

To ensure students from lower socio-economic groups could access HE once their aspirations were raised, the government also set up the Office for Fair Access (OFFA), partly as a compromise to gain enough parliamentary support for the increase in fee levels. OFFA required HEIs to develop Access Agreements that focused on developing their admission processes to encourage working-class students into their institution.

Recognising that the school leaving age of 16 did not encourage young people to stay on to gain HE entry level qualification, the government also introduced the Education Maintenance Allowance (EMA) which gave a financial reward to students who stayed in full-time education beyond 16.

Following the election in 2010, a new coalition government between the Conservatives and the Liberal Democrats was created. In 2011, the new government abandoned the Aimhigher programme and stopped EMAs, placing further emphasis on the OFFA to monitor HEIs to ensure widening access and retention. Institutions were now required to provide annual Access Agreements with clearer targets for both access and retention. Within schools a pupil premium was introduced to provide some resource for teaching students from deprived backgrounds and a new financial support programme was introduced targeted at disadvantaged 16 and 17-year-olds was also implemented.

These developments need to be set in the context of legislation which increased the undergraduate home student fees from just over £3,000 per year to a possible £9,000 per year. The government had earlier cut the funding for undergraduate courses by 80 per cent and the fee increase was designed to replace the funding for institutions, essentially funding students not institutions. The system of loans paid back after graduation continued and the threshold earnings for graduates which triggered contributions was raised to £21,000 from £15,000.

In any environment widening participation activities take time to produce outcomes, but with a programme like Aimhigher that focused on young people in their early years in secondary school, reflecting any impact on HE admissions took some years. Just before the Aimhigher programme was abandoned in 2011, the higher education funding council for England evaluated progress towards widening participation in the sector and concluded that despite the increase in fee levels in 2006 in England:

> ...there is no indication that from the national-level trends that changes to HE tuition fees or student support arrangements have been associated with material reductions in the overall HE participation rate (HEFCE, 2010:4)

HEFCE also noted an on-going rise in overall participation in HE, with a further 43,000 entrants from the 2009-2010 cohort (HEFCE, 2010).

Of particular relevance to widening participation, HEFCE found that: '...young people from the 09/10 cohort living in the most disadvantaged areas are around ... 30 per cent more likely to enter higher education than they were five years previously' (2010:6).

These improvements were further highlighted by analysis which showed that the gap between middle and working-class participation had narrowed:

> Since the mid-2000s the difference in the participation rates of advantaged and disadvantaged neighbourhoods, whether measured as a percentage point gap or the proportional difference, have declined (HEFCE, 2010:6).

This change showed real progress in the sector, offering greater opportunity for young people from working-class backgrounds. In his review of social mobility and higher education, Milburn (2012b) also noted this progress. There are many variables which affect participation rates in HE. However, not only did the gap between those attending HE from disadvantaged and advantaged backgrounds decrease from 2004 it did so specifically year on year:

> Around …15 per cent for the 04/05 cohort of young people living in dis-
> advantaged areas entered higher education … the participation rate increas-
> ing by around one percentage point a year, taking it to (an estimated) 19 per
> cent for the 09/10 cohort. (HEFCE, 2010:21)

It is interesting to note that the year on year progress coincides with the period of Aimhigher activities. However, while the relative gap between middle and working-class participation had narrowed significantly in the overall HE population, there was concern that the more selective institutions had not made progress. Martin Harris, chief executive of OFFA found that:

> …we know that although participation has widened significantly across the
> sector in the first 5 years [since OFFA was established]; this has not been the
> case at the most selective universities. … Participation of the least advan-
> taged 40 per cent of young people has remained almost flat at such [highly
> selective] institutions since the mid-1990s. (2011:6)

This offers a number of possible explanations for the disparity between overall improvements and a lack of progress in particular parts of the sector. Either certain institutions were discriminating against working-class students or working-class applicants were not meeting their academic admissions criteria for these institutions. There is a difference between achieving the level three qualifications threshold for entry into HE and the particular requirements of different institutions in the UK. It is also possible that working-class applicants were choosing to study at other institutions.

The issue of choosing a HEI is itself problematic. Students' choices are shaped by their social position, education, familial and social experiences and economic conditions. What we perceive as simply being our choice is therefore made up of a range of factors related to our background and current conditions. As Reay et al., argue:

> Choice is rooted in fine discriminations and classificatory judgements of
> places for us and places for others … A sociological view of choice must re-
> cognise both obviousness (what people like us do) and necessity (the limita-
> tions of social and spatial horizons) and the complex and sophisticated
> nature of individual and familial decision making. (2005:160)

Questions of preferences are thus developed socially, through experience and engagement with family, school, peers and seeing one's place in society. Choice and preference grow out of individuals' life experiences, which vary according to their access to economic, social and cultural capital. Students and their parents are making choices based on the cultural capital they have acquired over their lives and their choices are sometimes constrained by personal circumstances, such as institutional locality or a feeling of how well an individual will 'fit in' at a particular institution. Students may well feel uncomfortable in certain institutional environments, and as Thomas (2002) argues an institutional 'habitus' or set of taken-for-granted practices can affect a student's decision to study in a particular environment. All of these points may have implications for social mobility. As Milburn points out in his report on social mobility and higher education, many employers only value degrees from particular types of institutions (2012b).

It is ironic, however, that the highly selective institutions which are the subject of current concern were once seen as the widening participation institutions of their day:

> The division between Oxbridge and Redbrick ... is essentially a class one. While 50 per cent of Oxbridge undergraduates come from public schools, less than 10 per cent of Redbrick do: many public school boys would ... prefer no degree to a Redbrick degree. (Sampson, 1962:206)

As the massification of higher education has grown, so too has the number of selecting institutions and all, increasingly, have some elements of selectivity in particular disciplines. In the 1960s only Oxbridge were perceived as 'high class' universities, but now a larger group of institutions are regarded as the leading establishments in the country. Taking the long view, the class hierarchy in the British HE system is not as fixed or static as some would imagine.

The major concern in English higher education policy since the new coalition government took office has been the increases in fees for home undergraduate students from 2012. Just as there had been concern about the impact on widening participation students when the fees were increased in 2006, the 2012 reforms have also raised questions about the effect the changes might have on potential students from lower socio-economic groups: '...many speculate that even with the fee waivers in place such significantly higher fees will deter disadvantaged students from going to university' (Harris, 2011:7).

The policy context in UK HE has shifted significantly since the turn of the century and continues to change. The next section reflects on how the current government's HE policy might affect working-class students in the future. It draws out lessons from the life histories in the book to evaluate some of these policies.

Current government policy for England

The life histories discussed in this book offer some explanations for personal success in higher education. From an individual perspective they draw out four elements that enable persistence and success in social mobility that spring from the possible gateways and gatekeepers discussed in the previous chapter.

Firstly, there is a need to create the opportunity to go on to higher education. This includes imagining the possibility of moving beyond your family background and circumstances – raising aspirations, opening up gateways. Secondly, there is also a need for the young person to develop a passion for learning and knowledge. Many of the life stories make mention of a love of books and reading. Books will always be important to higher level learning. As technology changes over time, the way text is accessed and used will evolve but success in education will always require an engagement with text as well as a thirst for further knowledge and an understanding of theories. In their different forms texts will remain central to the development of the scientific method in the future. Creating an early interest in knowledge provides the right framework for continuing in education.

Thirdly, individuals need to develop a self-belief which fosters an academic entitlement. Some of the authors in the book describe this as choosing to be middle-class, others as recognising they were a swot, or intellectual. In middle-class families, where higher education study is taken for granted, this academic entitlement is automatic (Riddell, 2010). For people from working-class backgrounds it is often hard-won against wider social perceptions of ability and position.

Self-belief grows out of the interaction with others, people who have an important influence on the young person – family, teachers or peers – who recognise their potential and encourage them to persist with learning. Selfhood is created within a social context (Mead, 1934) and the life histories demonstrate how important such gatekeepers are from child-hood through to adulthood.

All these elements found in the life histories can be replicated in activities and programmes targeted at working-class youngsters. The current government, through the OFFA, has suggested that HEIs should take on this work individually rather than through large-scale programmes such as Aimhigher:

> ...encouraging universities and colleges to concentrate more on the out-comes of their work, to increase the long term targeted outreach ...to set themselves stretching targets including retention where relevant, and to target financial support more clearly to the most disadvantaged. (Harris, 2011:6)

This explains why raising aspirations within their working-class com-munities is even more important for universities to provide future opportunities for people from disadvantaged backgrounds.

The removal of the educational maintenance allowances evoked con-siderable anger from young people in England when it was announced. But a more limited targeted scheme was none the less introduced by the coalition government, and it is too soon to tell whether this policy has had any effect on staying on rates in education. The government has decided to raise the school leaving age to 17 in 2013 and 18 in 2015. This in itself is expected to provide a larger pool of possible applicants for higher education in the future as currently a significant number of qualified young people currently still leave education at 16. Changes to GCSEs and A levels in the future will potentially also have a significant impact on future widening participation in HE.

Some proposals for widening participation in higher education are more contentious. Although there is considerable support to improve the criteria and entry process for higher education (UCAS, 2012b) there re-mains concern about what are the most appropriate criteria to achieve this. Tariff points are seen as problematic although clear and through the OFFA, the government is increasingly encouraging institutions to use 'contextual data' about applicants to try to adjust for schooling dis-advantage:

> Where education provided by universities is of a high quality and tailored to students' needs, it can overcome the disadvantages of attending a less

academic school. Universities will want to consider this and other evidence taking a wider range of factors into account as they decide which students have the greatest potential to succeed on their courses. (HMG, 2011:50)

This approach is particularly targeted at institutions with very high entrance requirements. Such institutions have matched the success of the rest of sector at attracting people from working-class backgrounds. Raising attainment in schools continues to be vital in enabling widening participation and future upward social mobility. The argument for using contextual data is based on research which suggests that bright young people with lower entry tariffs who attended poor schools do as well or better at university than young people with higher scores who went through private education:

State educated pupils do a lot better [than those having been privately educated] given their A level results – the gap in the proportion getting good degrees is between 3 and 10 per cent depending on what A levels the students achieved. (Springford, 2012:1)

However, contextual data can also provide useful information for any institution. Understanding students' educational backgrounds can enable HE establishments to deliver appropriate individualised support for their new entrants.

Limited access in the context of the market

Perhaps the most significant policy development, initially introduced by the Labour government and continued under the coalition government, that could affect working-class students going into HE was the establishment of the student number control. The policy restricts the number of overall places available in higher education. Its rationale for was simple: demand for HE continues to grow and the cost has become increasingly burdensome on the public purse. With the increase in fees in 2012 in England, the situation is considered even more unsustainable. The supply of HE places continues to be tightly controlled, creating limited access – as the applications service, UCAS, points out:

The indications are that demand for HE will continue to outstrip the number of places available in 2012. Applications are already 50,000 ahead of the number of acceptances in 2011 and last year UCAS received over 100,000 further applications between January and the close of the cycle. (2012a:2)

The outcome of the admissions cycle for 2012 indicates that there has been a reduction in the number of students taking up places in HE. The reasons behind this decline are complex but they do seem to suggest that the increase in fees has had some effect on student choice. Recent research by the Sutton Trust indicates that young people from poorer backgrounds are being put off study by a fear of debt (*THE*, 2012c). The coalition government is committed to creating more of a market for HE, however, and allowing growth if affordable. In the white paper, *Students at the Heart of the System* (DBIS, 2011), the ambition to encourage new providers into HE was announced. The paper also set out the development of more accessible information for potential applicants in the hope that this will drive up quality in the sector. Removing funding from the supply side – ie institutions – and courses and providing funding for the demand side – ie students – is also part of this market-driven philosophy.

In attempting to free up the strict controls on student numbers, the government has agreed to remove all very high tariff applicants from the number control, allowing institutions to recruit as many of these students as they can. The government intends to continue to remove applicants from the number control and reduce the threshold for removal incrementally to increase the market element in HE. This may also give these applicants greater buying-power, as they can seek to attend any institution of their choice. Milburn (2012b) worries about this policy.

He argues that the policy could have unintended consequences for both students and institutions, consequences which could affect the possibility for upward social mobility. Milburn's concern is based on evidence that many working-class applicants, although meeting HE entry tariff thresholds, often do not gain the high level tariff required for exclusion from the number control. What institutions choose to do, or will be able to do, for high tariff applicants, however, is still to be proved.

Along with the policy on very high tariff applicants, the government also established a core and margin policy within the number control. This policy was designed to permit new HE providers into the sector to increase choice of provision. Intended to alleviate the problem of spiralling costs, the policy encouraged HE institutions which charged less than £7,500 per annum for their courses to bid for places that had been removed from current HE providers. It therefore reduced places at typically selective institutions that were well placed in the HE admissions market which had set fees higher than £7,500.

The redistribution of limited student numbers particularly benefited further education colleges that wanted to offer higher education provision. Further education colleges in England have historically provided local HE opportunities but have also faced had difficulties in filling their quotas of student numbers. A further small margin of places for 2013 is also being redistributed.

Applicant behaviour in changing circumstances is always difficult to predict. There is concern that the new fee regime would put off working-class applicants. However, applicant figures for 2012 suggest that the new regime has not affected working-class aspirations:

> Our analysis shows that decreases in demand are slightly larger for more advantaged groups than in the disadvantaged groups. Widely expressed concerns about recent changes in H.E. funding arrangements having a disproportionate effect on more disadvantaged groups are not borne out by these data. (UCAS, 2012a:3).

There is also evidence from the 2012 admissions cycle to suggest that some middle class students have stayed away, whether to take a gap year or deciding to study abroad. The number of mature students, already dwindling for some years, have significantly declined in 2012. The research by the Sutton Trust indicating that younger people are put off HE by higher debt is also worrying (*THE*, 2012c). It is still too early to understand the full implications of attempts to create a more market-based economy in higher education in England. But there are concerns that doing so in the context of restricted supply will affect widening participation in the sector and consequently social mobility.

The history of higher education told through the accounts in this book is a story of the sector's expansion and massification. As student numbers grew so too did the opportunities for the authors to participate in HE. While it is true that massification did not proportionately increase working-class participation in HE, it did increase the overall raw numbers of working-class students, and in the last few years proportional differences has been addressed. Growth also served the needs of aspirational women coming into the sector, many of whom had missed out on education the first time round. The accounts of men documented in the book often describe the women who encouraged them to study, as in Donald's, Mike's and Eugene's stories discussed in chapter 5. However as Archer *et al* (2003) point out successful engagement in education is sometimes difficult for young men. To succeed in higher education both men and women need confidence in their abilities and they must develop an academic identity. If the student number control, which restricts growth, continues it is highly unlikely that middle-class parents will be prepared to lose their advantage to enable other people's children to capitalise on their academic entitlement (Wolf, 2002). In this context the use of contextual data by institutions becomes politically charged.

Contextual data presents the opportunity to look beyond the A level entry level examination at a wider set of factors that indicate a candidate's ability to succeed in HE. If contextual data is to be used it needs to be agreed across all parts of the UK and transparent for applicants and the information must be handled sensitively. If supply of student numbers within the number control is limited, it is likely to be open to challenge, particularly if one set of applicants is chosen over another who may have done better in their A levels. Institutions can develop aspirational activities for working-class youngsters and help raise their attainment to meet entry-level thresholds. However, they might not be able to admit them onto their courses without abolition of the student number control.

Each of these changes may dramatically alter the HE sector in England in the future. However, in terms of social mobility within society, perhaps the most significant issue is the changing shape of the UK economy in the twenty-first century.

The hourglass society

In the post-war decades technological changes...prompted job displacement from lower to higher skilled jobs. The overall effect of technology was to push the labour market upwards. Jobs were removed from the lower end ... and replaced at the top. (Hackett, Shutt, and MacLachlan, 2012:9)

Chapter 1 explored how this re-shaping of British society created absolute social mobility which moved a significant number of people out of the working-class into the middle classes. It also pointed out that although more opportunities were created, relatively:

> ...poorer children are ... less successful than the law of averages would lead us to expect and richer children are more adept at avoiding downward mobility than would be expected by chance. (Saunders, 2010:38)

Recent research has suggested that British society became more unequal in the 1980s and 1990s (Dorling, 2010). The all-party parliamentary group on social mobility (2012) point to the importance of social mobility in creating economic wealth and social justice (2012:5). In the current economic crisis Schleicher has pointed out that: 'the increase in the number of knowledge workers has not led to a decrease in their pay ... which is what has happened to low-skilled workers' (2011: 25).

Across the developed nations society is seeing growth at the top and bottom ends of the social spectrum. In the twenty-first century, rather than taking jobs from the lower strata of society – as happened in the last half century – in advanced economies such as the UK the new trend is for contracting middle wage, routine jobs (Sissons, 2011). Unlike earlier economic revolutions, where technologies automated low-skilled jobs, many of the routine, automatable jobs are now clustered in the middle of the earnings distribution (Goos and Manning, 2007). Growth in employment has been at the top and bottom ends of society creating a squeezed middle (CEDEFOP, 2011) or what Sissons (2011) calls an hourglass economy. Nearly three quarters of growth in employment since 2000 has been at the top and bottom of the occupational ladder, with more people in the UK now in managerial, professional and technical occupations as well as elementary and personal service employment (Labour Force Survey, 2010). If the middle is squeezed and no longer resembles a ladder with equal rungs up or down, the way to upward mobility is more precarious and more advanced technological know-how required to literally jump from the lower into the upper end of employment.

In advanced societies such as the UK technology is again changing the shape of employment, but other changes in demography and globalisation are also significant. As our society grows older, the pattern of employment has shifted to accommodate an ageing population, increasing the number of personal care service jobs by about 20 per cent in the last 10 years (Labour Force Survey, 2010). Such work is largely low-paid and low-skilled.

The previous chapter explored the development of mobile societies in the latter half of the twentieth century. In the twenty-first, mobilities and globalisation are entwined (Urry, 2007). As markets, goods, services and jobs move around the world more freely (Giddens, 1991) nation states can no longer contain capitalism, as it moves relentlessly across the globe seeking profit. This continues to reshape of employment structures within nations as jobs move. In advanced societies, automated routinised activities can be, and are being, outsourced to developing nations where wages are lower. As Urry argues: 'multiple mobilities become central to the structuring of inequality within contemporary 'disorganised' societies' (2007, 186). Just as different forms of mobility, real or imagined, affect an individual's chances for upward mobility, within national economies, movement of capital affects a nation's opportunities for social mobility.

The role of higher education in reshaping employment

The composition of the global talent pool has changed from 39 million who attained tertiary level of the 55-64 year-old population to 81 million people who attained tertiary level of the 25-34 year-old population. (Schleicher, 2011:20)

Many countries across the globe now see the need to invest in their higher education systems. Nations are investing in developing the knowledge and skills of their workforce. Nations such as Australia and the USA that have been concerned with social mobility and widening participation in the past have seen significant changes in recent times. In Australia *The Bradley Review* (Australian government, 2008) concluded that the proportion of graduates in the country needed to increase to 40 per cent amongst the 25 to 34 year old age population by 2025 (Birrell and Edwards, 2009). The review indicated a clear commitment to ensuring that people from lower socio-economic groups were well represented in HE.

As capital moves across the globe, the emerging powers like China and India are also investing in education with the latter pledging to increase the proportion of graduates from 10 per cent of the population to 30 per cent in a decade (Altback and Salmi, 2011). This suggests that to foster increases in social mobility in a shifting, fluid employment environment, Britain should develop its education provision and in particular, look to increase the number of graduates ready for this changing employment market. As Holmes (2011) points out, when workers are displaced from routine occupations, gaining higher level qualifications makes the difference between falling down or moving up.

Going beyond HE graduate outcomes

Chapter 1 highlighted concerns about differential graduate outcomes for the following groups of people: women, working-class graduates, ethnic minority groups, disabled graduates (Purcell and Elias, 2008, Purcell *et al*, 2007, Elias and Purcell, 2004). While many of these concerns relate to practices amongst employers, including the use of filters for A level or even GCSE grades, and the type of higher education institution, HE still has a role to play in enabling its graduates to transfer successfully into the world of work. In the accounts in this book, where many were transferring into higher education itself, knowing what was required to gain employment was essential. Recent research (Stuart *et al*, 2012) suggests that understanding what employers are looking for and ensuring students are given this information is vital, particularly if those students are the first in their family to go into HE. Milburn observes in his report on access to the professions (2012a) that students from working-class backgrounds are often disadvantaged in the labour market. He argues that Universities need to play their part in equipping all their graduates with the tools to succeed in their careers (2012b).

Across the generations the life histories revealed a growing level of insecurity about employment in higher education that continued into the 1980s and 1990s. Today there is concern that this is increasing and many see employment within HE becoming more difficult. In the hourglass economy ensuring equal opportunity for graduates is even more important.

There is considerable debate about the future possibilities for upward social mobility in Britain. Goldthorpe and Jackson argue that:

> There is no policy route back to the structural conditions of the mid-twentieth century; the very substantial growth in demand for professional and managerial personnel that then occurred was created by a historic shift in the

148

scale of the public administration of health, education and social welfare provision or of industrial and commercial organisation that could scarcely be repeated. (2007, 541)

If the 'hourglass' theory is correct however, there will be an increased need for a different type of graduates to those in the middle of the last century. Recently, the Higher Education Careers Services Unit explored the changing nature of graduate employment in a number of different categories: traditional – solicitors, doctors, etc – modern – teachers, nurses, software programmers etc and new – designers, therapists, etc. As our employment profile changes in society, so too do graduate jobs.

The new graduates can fulfil the new graduate roles in the changing shape of the twenty-first century's global economy. Goldthorpe and Jackson (2007) are right that the type of upward mobility that occurred in the second half of the twentieth century, chartered through personal accounts in this book, may not happen again. Urry points out that our societies have been shaken by the way communications have altered time and geography and technology has reshaped economies and societies:

> ...the elaborate interconnections of physical movement and communication, the development of mobility domains that by-pass national societies ... an increased importance on multiple mobilities for peoples' social and emotional lives... (2007:195)

Such profound change does not eradicate the need for more graduates nor does it mean that there is no further space at the top for people from working-class backgrounds. Far from being fixed the shape of society is much far more fluid than has previously been understood. Britain, like other countries, is now part of a global network and if it is to compete globally it must re-focus the Academy to meet the future needs of society. The World Bank highlighted the changing nature of global economies in the following description:

> ...well-articulated network of firms' research centres, universities and think tanks that work together to take advantage of global knowledge – assimilating and adapting it to local needs, thus creating new technology. Tertiary education systems figure prominently in such systems, serving not only as the backbone for high-level skills, but as centres of basic and applied research. (Salmi, 2009:38)

In its strategy for social mobility, the British government argues for a focus on relative social mobility to ensure those from working-class backgrounds with talent are able to develop careers suited to their abilities (HMG, 2011). Ensuring access to higher education for more working-class students is important. Despite progress in bridging the gap between middle and working-class entrants, there is more to do (Milburn, 2012a and b) Raising aspirations, providing gateways into a new life and creating the right supportive environment for youngsters to succeed are all vital. However, as demand continues to outstrip supply, failure to increase the overall supply of HE, jeopardises continued progress in widening participation.

Higher education is a major motor of innovation in society and the skills it provides become even more important as the hourglass economy develops in the UK. The sector needs to continue to develop new ideas, to innovate and to drive technological change in our society. This will continue to ensure absolute social mobility is still possible in the future.

Looking back to look forward

> Some young people from working-class backgrounds have always done it [gone to University] … there will be some movement between social classes over the next generation as there always has been… [but] this is a fragile process. (Riddell, 2010:84)

The personal accounts of the respondents in this book set out the different routes taken from working-class communities into middle-class lives. The expectations of middle-class families that their children will simply follow into successful careers may not be present in working-class family environments. It is, as Riddell points out, 'a fragile process' (2010:84) to change class.

The life stories demonstrate that raising aspirations and attainment is vital for widening participation, but that achieving this is complex. However the accounts do reveal a number of possible policy implications – at an individual level the need to create an environment where people's self-belief includes an academic entitlement, where horizons are opened up, where the individual's sense of themselves is nurtured, guided and supported by significant others. All these ideas can be implemented in schools, in partnership with HE institutions.

The life histories chart the massification of HE. They demonstrate that qualified applicants should be able to access higher education. If places are limited and if further cuts to HE budgets are implemented, it is the middle classes who will fill the spaces in Universities. They will not give up their academic entitlement.

As our society responds to the further challenges of globalisation and as technology hollows out middle tier employment, there is a greater need to develop high level skills. Without them the possibilities for upward social mobility are bleak as soon there will be no middle ground.

While it is true that some working-class young people have always made it through to university, as demonstrated by the authors in this book, the changing shape of our economy may make this more difficult in the future. It is as though some of the treads on the escalator are being removed. The leap from the lower end of the hourglass will increasingly be achieved only with high level skills. The need for an open, opportunity-focused, higher education system has never been more important.

References

Abbott, J (1971) *Student Life in a Class Society.* Oxford: Pergamon

Altbach, P and Salmi, J (eds) (2011) *The Road to Academic Excellence: The Making of World-Class Research Universities.* Washington DC: World Bank

All Party Parliamentary Group on Social Mobility (2012) 7 key truths about social mobility. The interim report of the all party parliamentary group on social mobility May, 2012 www.appg-socialmobility.org (May, 2012)

Anderson, B (1991) *Imagined Communities: reflections on the origin and spread of nationalism.* London: Verso

Archer, L (2003) Social class and higher education. In Archer, L, Hutchings, M and Ross, A (2003) (eds) *Higher Education and Social Class.* London: RoutledgeFarmer

Archer, L, Hutchings, M and Ross, A (2003) (eds) *Higher Education and Social Class.* London: RoutledgeFarmer

Armstrong, P (1987) *Qualitative Strategies in Social and Educational Research – the life history method in theory and practice.* Hull: University of Hull Press

Association of Commonwealth Universities (ACU) (2001) *Engagement as a Core Value for the University.* London: ACU

Arnot, M, David, M and Weiner, G (1999) *Closing the Gender Gap: postwar education and social change.* Cambridge: Polity Press

Australian Government (The Bradley Review) (2008) Review of Australian Higher Education Final Report December, 2008 www.deewr.gov.au/HigherEducation/Review/Documents/pdf/Higher%20Education%20Review_one%20document_02.pdf (July, 2011)

Beck, U (1992) *The Risk Society.* London: Sage

Becker, H (1970) *Sociological Work.* Chicago: Aldine

Beddie, F (2010) Diversity and excellence: prompts from the history of the tertiary education sector *Australian Policy and History* http://www.aph.org.au/files/articles/deversityexcellence.htm (March, 2012)

Bennett, T, Savage, M, Silva, E, Wade, A, Gayo-Cal, M and Wright, D (2010) *Culture, Class, Distinction.* London: Routledge

Bentley, R, Earls, M and O'Brien, M (2011) *'I'll Have What She's Having' – mapping social behavior.* Cambridge Mass: MIT press

Bhabha, H (1994) *The Location of Culture.* London: Routledge

Birrell, B and Edwards, D (2009) The Bradley review and access to higher education in Australia. *Australian Universities Review* 51 (1) www.unversityworldnews.com/filemgnt_data/files/AUR_51-01_birrell_edwards.pdf (August, 2011)

Blair, M and Bourne, J (1998) *Making the Difference: teaching and learning strategies in successful multiethnic schools. Research Report.* London: DfES

Blanden, J and Gregg, P (2004) *Family Income and Educational Attainment: a review of approaches and evidence for Britain.* Centre for Market and Public Organisation (CMPO), working paper series NO 04/101 Bristol: CMPO

Blanden, J, Gregg, P and Machin, S (2005) *Social Mobility in Britain: low and falling.* http://cep.lse.ac.uk/centrepiece/v101/blanden.pdf (December, 2010)

Blanden, J, Gregg, P and MacMillan, L (2007) *Accounting for Intergenerational Income Persistence: noncognitive skills, ability and education IZA DP No 2554.* Bonn: Institute for the Study of Labour

Blanden, J, Gregg, P and Macmillan, L (2010) *Intergenerational Persistence in Income and Social Class: the impact of within-group inequality.* Centre for Market and Public Organisation working paper No 10/230 Bristol: CMPO

Blasko, Z (2002) *Access to What? Analysis of Factors Determining Graduate Employability.* Bristol: HEFCE

Bourdieu, P (1977) *Outline of a Theory.* Cambridge: Cambridge University Press

Bourdieu, P (1984) *Distinction: a social critique of the judgement of taste.* London: Routledge

Bourdieu, P (1985) The Genesis of the Concepts of Habitus and of Field. *Sociocriticism* (2) p11-24

Bourdieu, P and Wacquant, L (1992) *An Invitation to Reflexive Sociology.* Cambridge: Polity Press

Boliver, V and Swift, A (2011) Do comprehensive schools reduce social mobility? *The British Journal of Sociology* 62 (1) p89-110

Breen, R and Luijkx, R (2004) Social mobility in Europe between 1970 and 2000. In Breen, R (ed) *Social Mobility in Europe.* Oxford: Oxford University Press

Brennan, J and Shah, T (2003) *Access to What? Converting educational opportunity into employment opportunity.* London: CHERI Open University Press

Brennan, J (2004) Graduate Employment: issues for debate and enquiry. *International Higher Education* (34) p12-20

Broeke, S and Nicholls, T (2007) *Ethnicity and Degree Attainment: Research Report: RW92.* London: DfES

Brooks, R (2003) Discussing higher education choices: differences and difficulties. *Research Papers in Education* 18 (3) p237-58

CEDEFOP (2011) (European Centre for the Development of Vocational Training) Labour-market polarisation and elementary occupations in Europe http://www. cedefop.europa.eu/EN/Files/5509_en.pdf (December, 2011)

Chapman, B and Ryan, C (2003) *The Access Implications of Income Contingent Charges for Higher Education: Lessons from Australia. Discussion paper 436.* Canberra: Centre for Economic Policy Research

Chevalier, A. (2004) *Motivation, expectations and the gender pay gap for UK graduates. Discussion paper no. 1101.* Bonn: Institute for the study of Labour http://www.ucd.ie/ economic/staff/achevalier/web/dp1101.pdf (June, 2009)

Christie, H, Munro, M and Fisher, T (2004) Leaving university early: exploring the differences between continuing and non-continuing students. *Studies in Higher Education* 29 (5) p617-31

Clegg, N (2011) Forward. In *Opening Doors, Breaking Barriers: A strategy for social mobility.* London: Cabinet Office

Coard, B (1971) *How the West Indian Child is made Educationally Subnormal in the British School System.* London: New Beacon Books (reprinted in Richardson, B *op.cit*)

Coleman, J S (1994) *Foundations of Social Theory.* Cambridge, MA: Belknap Press

Committee on Higher Education (1963) *Report.* London: HMSO

Connor, H, Tyers, C, Modood, T and Hillage, J (2004) *Why the Difference? A closer look at higher education minority ethnic students and graduates research. Report No. 552.* London: DfES

Cotgrove, S (1958) *Technical Education and Social Change.* London: Allen and Unwin

Delors, J (1997) *International Commission on Education for the 21st Century.* Paris: UNESCO

Department for Education and Science (DfES) (1978) *Higher Education into the 1990s: A discussion document.* London: HMSO

DfES (1985) *The Swann Report: Education for All.* London: HMSO

Department for Business Innovation and Skills (DBIS) (2011) *Students at the heart of the system* http://c561635.r.35.cf2.rackcdn.com/11-944-WP-students-at-heart.pdf (June, 2011)

Dorling, D (2010) *Injustice: Why social inequality persists.* Bristol: Polity Press

Dyhouse, C (2006) *Students: a gendered history.* Abingdon: Routledge

Dyhouse, C (2008) *Going to University: funding, costs, benefits.* http://www.historyand policy.org/papers/policy-paper-61.html (February, 2011)

Eggleston, J, Dunn, D K, and Anjali, M (1986) *Education for Some: the educational and vocational experiences of 15-18 year old members of ethnic minority groups.* Stoke on Trent: Trentham Books

Elias, P and Purcell, K P (2004) Mass higher education working? Evidence from the labour market experiences of recent graduates. *National Institute Economic Review* (190) p60-74

Elias, P and Jones, P (2006) *Representation of ethnic groups in chemistry and physics.* London: Royal Society of Chemistry and Institute of Physics

Elliot, A and Urry, J (2010) *Mobile Lives.* Abingdon: Routledge

Erikson, R and Goldthorpe, J H (2010) Has social mobility in Britain decreased? Reconciling divergent findings on income and class mobility. *British Journal of Sociology* 61 (2) p211-30

Field, J (2005) *Social Capital and Lifelong Learning.* Bristol: The Policy Press

Field, J (2008) *Social Capital.* Abingdon: Routledge

Forsyth, A and Furlong, A (2003) *Losing Out? Socioeconomic disadvantage and experience in further and higher education.* Bristol: The Policy Press

Foster, L and Harper, S (2010) *British Culture and Society in the 1970s the lost decade.* Newcastle: Cambridge Scholars Publishing

Furneaux, W (1961) The two few chosen and the many who could be called. In Halmos, P (ed) *The Sociological Review Monograph* 7, Sociological Studies in British University Education Keele: University of Keele

Gaine, C (1987) *No Problem Here: a practical approach to education and race in white schools.* London: Hutchinson

Gazeley, I (2003) *Poverty in Britain, 1900-1965.* Basingstoke: Palgrave Macmillan

Giddens, A (1991) *The Consequences of Modernity.* Cambridge: Polity Press

Gillborn, D (1990) *'Race', Ethnicity and Education: Teaching and learning in multi-ethnic schools.* London, Unwin Hyman

Gillborn, D and Gipps, C (1996) *Recent Research into the Achievement of Ethnic Minority Pupils.* London: Ofsted

Goldthorpe, J H with Llewellyn, C and Payne, C (1987) *Social Mobility and the Class Structure in Modern Britain.* Oxford: Clarendon

Goldthorpe, J H, Llewellyn, C and Payne, C (2003) *Social Mobility and Class Structure in Modern Britain, revised edition.* Oxford: Clarendon Press

Goldthorpe, J H and Jackson, M (2007) Intergenerational Class Mobility in contemporary Britain: political concerns and empirical findings. *The Journal of Sociology* (58) p526-46

Goldthorpe, J H (2010) Class analysis and the reorientation of class theory: the case of persisting differentials in educational attainment. *British Journal of Sociology* (45) p481-505

Goode, J (2000) Is the position of women in higher education changing? In Tight M (ed) *Academic Work and Life: What it is to be an Academic and How it is Changing.* Oxford: Elsevier Press

Goos, M and Manning, A (2007) *Lousy and lovely jobs: the rising polarisation of work in Britain.* http://ideas.repec.org/p/cep/cepdps/dp0604.html (May, 2012)

Gorard, S (2008) A re-consideration of rates of social mobility in Britain or why research impact is not always a good thing. *British Journal of Sociology of Education* (29) p317-24

Guardian (2010) Nick Clegg to announce Alan Milburn appointment as social mobility tsar 15 August, 2010 www.guardian.co.uk/society/2010/aug15/alan-milburn-appointed-social-mobility-tsar (August, 2010)

Hackett, L, Shutt, L and Maclachlan, N (2012) *The Way We'll Work: labour market trends and preparing for the hourglass.* London: University Alliance

Hall, P (1999) Social capital in Britain in *British Journal of Political Science* 29 (3) p417-61

Halvorsen, E (2002) Gender Audit. In Howie, G and Tauchert, A (eds) *Gender, Teaching and Research in Higher Education: challenges for the 21st century.* Aldershot: Ashgate

Harris, M (2011) Forward. *Office for Fair Access Annual Report and Accounts 2010-2011.* London: The Stationery Office

Harris, M (2010) *What more can be done to widen access to highly selective universities?* London: Office for Fair Access.

Her Majesty's Government (HMG) (2011) *Opening Doors, Breaking Barriers: A Strategy for Social Mobility.* London: Cabinet Office

Higher Education Careers Service Unit (HECSU) (2004) *Seven years on: graduate careers in a changing labour market.* http://www.hecsu.ac.uk/assets/assets/documents/seven_years_on.pdf (March, 2011)

Higher Education Funding Council for England (HEFCE) (2005) *Young Participation in Higher Education* 05/03 Bristol: HEFCE

HEFCE (2010) *Trends in young participation in higher education: core results for England 2010/03.* Bristol: HEFCE

Higher Education Funding Council for Wales (HEFCW) (2009) *HEFCW's strategic approach and plan for widening access to higher education.* 2010/11 to 2012/13 http://www.hefcw.ac.uk/documents/publications/circulars/circulars_2011/W11%2009 HE%20Annex%20A%20Strategic%20Approach%20%20Plan%20for%20WA%20to %20HE.pdf (February, 2012)

Higher Education Statistics Agency HESA (2007) *Students in higher education institutions 2005/06.* Cheltenham: HESA

HESA (2010) Staff data record accessed at www.hesa.ac.uk (January, 2012)

Holmes,C (2011) *The route out of the routine: Where do displaced workers go?* www.skope.ox.ac.uk/sites/default/files/WP100.pdf (January, 2012)

Institute for Public Policy Research (IPPR) (2008) *Social Mobility a background review.* London: ippr www.socialmobilitycommission.org/ippr-social-mobility.pdf (June, 2009)

Iannelli, C and Paterson, L (2005) *Education and social mobility in Scotland Working Paper 5.* http://www.ces.ed.ac.uk/research/SocMobility/papers/WP5.pdf (August, 2011)

Johnston, R and Merrill, B (2005) From Old to New Learning Identities: Charting the Change for Non-Traditional Adult Students in Higher Education. In Bron, A, Kurantowicz, E, Salling Olesen, H and West, L (eds) *'Old' and 'New' Worlds of Adult Learning,* (Wroclaw, Wydawnictwo Naukowe)

Kahlenberg, R D (ed) (2004) *America's Untapped Resource: low income students in higher education*. New York: Century Foundation Press

Kintrea K, St Clair R and Houston M (2011) *The influence of parents, places and poverty on educational attitudes and aspirations*, Joseph Rowntree Foundation October, 2011 http://www.jrf.org.uk/sites/files/jrf/young-people-education-attitudes-full.pdf (May, 2012)

Labour Force Survey (2010) www.esds.ac.uk/government/ofs/ (June, 2011)

Layard, R, King, J and Moser, C (1969) *The Impact of Robbins*. Harmondsworth: Penguin

Langlands, A (2011) Higher education in an age of austerity HEPI seminar, 17 Feb 2011 http://www.hepi.ac.uk/484-1930/Higher-Education-in-an-Age-of-Austerity.html (February, 2012)

Leslie, D. (2005) Why people from the UK's minority ethnic communities achieve weaker degree results than whites. *Applied economics* (37) p619-32.

Little, B. (2006) The student experience and the impact of social capital. In McNay, I (ed) (2006) *Beyond Mass Higher Education*. Maidenhead: SRHE Open University Press

Luckhurst, T (2005) writing in *The Times*, 9 August, 2005

Macpherson, W (1999) *The Stephen Lawrence Inquiry, the report of an inquiry by Sir William Macpherson*. London: The Stationery Office

Mayers, J (2011) Why support students? Continuity and change in forms of student support in English higher education Unpublished PhD thesis, UCL

Mead, GH (1934) Mind, self and society. In Thompson, K and Tunstall, J (eds) (1979) *Sociological Perspectives*. Penguin: London

Meehan, D (1999) The under-representation of women managers in higher education: are their issues other than style? In Whitehead, S and Moodley, R (eds) *Transforming Managers: gendering change in the public sector*. London: UCL press

Merrill, B, Gallacher, J, Crossan, B and Field, J (2002) Learning careers and the social space: exploring the fragile identities of adult returners in the new further education. *International Journal of Lifelong Education*, 21 (6) November/December p33-50

Milburn, A (2009) *Unleashing Aspiration: The Final Report on the Panel on Fair Access to the Professions*. London: Cabinet Office

Milburn, A (2011) Speech to the Universities UK Annual Conference 7 September, 2011

Milburn, A (2012a) Forward and Summary. In *Fair access to professional careers: a progress report by the independent reviewer on social mobility and child poverty*. London: Cabinet Office

Milburn, A (2012b) Report on Social Mobility and Higher Education. London: Cabinet Office (in press)

Miles, S (2000) *Youth Lifestyles in a Changing World*. Milton Keynes: Open University Press

Mullen, F (2010) *Widening Access to Higher Education: Policy in Scotland 10/09.* http://dera.ioe.ac.uk/1271/1/SB10-09.pdf (February, 2012)

National Committee of Inquiry into Higher Education (NCIHE) (1997) *The Report of the National Committee of Inquiry into Higher Education.* London: HMSO

National Union of Teachers (1979) *In Black and White.* London: NUT

National Union of Teachers (1989) *Combating Racism in Schools.* London: NUT

Naylor, R and Smith A (2004) Determinants of educational success on higher education. In Johnes, G and Johnes, J (eds) *International Handbook on the Economics of Education.* Cheltenham: Edward Elgar

Newby, H (2005) Doing widening participation: social inequality and access to higher education. In Layer, G (2005) *Closing the Equity Gap: the impact of widening participation strategies in the UK and the USA.* Leicester: NIACE

Office for Fair Access (OFFA) (2011) *Annual Report and Accounts 2010-2011.* London: The Stationery Office

Osborne, M (2003) Policy and Practice in widening participation: a six country comparative study of access as flexibility in the *International Journal of Lifelong Education* 22 (1) January-February p43-59

Owen, D, Green, A, Pitcher, J and Maguire, M (2000) *Minority ethnic participation and achievements in education, training and the labour market. Research Report No. 225.* London: DfES

Paterson, L and Iannelli, C (2007) Patterns of absolute and relative social mobility: a comparative study of England, Wales and Scotland. *Sociological Research Online*, 12, (6) 15 http://www.socresonline.org.uk/12/6/15.html (August, 2011)

Payne, G Payne, J and Hyde, M (1996) 'Refuse of all classes'? social indicators and social deprivation *Sociological Research Online*, 1 http://www.socresonline.org.uk/1/1/3.html (November, 2000)

Pilkington, A (2011) *Institutional Racism in the Academy: a case study.* Stoke on Trent: Trentham Books

Platt, J (1981) Whatever happened to the case study? Or from Znanaiecki to Lazansfeld in one generation Unpublished paper, University of Sussex

Plummer, K (1975) *Sexual Stigma: an interactionist account.* London: Routledge and Kegan Paul

Plummer, K (1983) *Documents of Life.* London: Routledge and Keegan Paul

Purcell, K P and Elias, P (2008) Women and employment: changing lives and new challenges – achieving Eequality in the knowledge economy. In Scott, J, Dex, S and Joshi, H (eds) *Women and Employment, changing lives and new challenges.* Cheltenham: Edward Elgar Publishing

Purcell, K P, Wilton, N and Elias, P (2007) Hard lessons for lifelong learners? Age and experience in the graduate labour market. *Higher Education Quarterly* 61 (1) p57-82

Purcell, KP, Elias, P, Davies, R and Wilton, N (2005) *The Class of '99: A study of the early labour market experience of recent graduate.* Research Report No. RR691 RTP01-03 London: DfES

Putman, R (2000) *Bowling Alone: the collapse and revival of American community.* New York: Simon and Schuster

Ross, A (2003) Access to higher education: inclusion of the masses? In Archer, L, Hutchings, M and Ross, A (2003) *Higher Education and Social Class Issues of exclusion and inclusion.* London: RoutledgeFalmer

Reay, D, David, M and Ball, S (2005) *Degrees of Choice: Social class, race and gender in higher education.* Stoke on Trent: Trentham

Richardson, B (ed) (2005) *Tell It Like It Is: how our schools fail Black children.* London: Bookmarks

Richardson, T E (2008a) The attainment of ethnic minority students in UK higher education. *Studies in Higher Education*, 33 (1) p33-48

Richardson, T E (2008b) *Degree attainment, ethnicity and gender: A literature review.* Report for the Equality Challenge Unit and the Higher Education Academy http://www.heacademy.ac.uk/assets/York/documents/ourwork/research/J_Richardson_literature_review_Jan08.pdf (June, 2008)

Richardson, T E and Woodley, A (2003) Another look at the role of age, gender and subject as predictors of academic attainment in higher education. *Studies in Higher Education* (28), p475-93

Riddell, R (2010) *Aspiration, Identity and Self-Belief: snapshots of social structure at work.* Stoke on Trent: Trentham Books

Rudd, E (1984) A comparison between the results achieved by women and men studying for first degrees in British universities. *Studies in Higher Education* (9) p47-57

Rose, D and Pevalin, D J with Karen O'Reilly (2005) *The national statistics socio-economic classification: origins, development and use.* http://www.statistics.gov.uk/methods_quality/ns_sec/downloads/NS-SEC_Origins.pdf (August, 2011)

Rowntree, B S (1902) *Poverty: a study of town life.* London: Macmillan

Rustin, M (2000) The biographical turn. In Chamberlayne, P, Bornat, J and Waengraf, T (eds) *The Turn to Biographical Methods in the Social Sciences.* London: Routledge

Salmi J (2009) *The challenge of establishing world-class universities.* Washington DC: World Bank

Sampson, A (1962) *Anatomy of Britain.* London: Hodden and Stoughton

Saunders, P (2010) *Social Mobility Myths.* London: Civitas

Savage, M (2000) *Class Analysis and Social Transformation.* Buckingham: OUP

Sayer, A (2002) What are you worth? Why class is an embarrassing subject. *Sociological Review Online* 7, 3, p1-24 www.socresonline.org.uk7/3/sayer.htm (December, 2002)

Scheff, T (1990) *Microsociology: discourse, emotion and the social structure.* Chicago: University of Chicago Press

Schleicher, A (2011) Organisation for Economic Co-operation and Development (OECD) (2011) Global trends in higher education. Unpublished presentation to Universities UK 6 September, 2011

Scottish Government (2011) *Putting learners at the centre: delivering our ambitions for post 16 education* http://www.scotland.gov.uk/Publications/2011/09/15103949/4 (April, 2012)

Scottish Government (2012) *Report of the Review of Higher Education Governance in Scotland.* http://www.scotland.gov.uk/Publications/2012/02/3646/2 (March, 2012)

Shattock, M (2003) *Managing Successful Universities.* Maidenhead: OUP

Shaw, C (1966) *The Jackroller: A delinquent boy's own story.* University of Chicago Press: Chicago

Sheriden, D (1993) Writing to the archive: mass-observation as autobiography. *Sociology* February 1993, 27 (1) p27-40

Sissons, P (2011) *The hourglass and the escalator.* The Work Foundation http://www.theworkfoundation.com/DownloadPublication/Report/292_hourglass_escalator1 20711%20(2)%20(3).pdf (April, 2012)

Sizer, J (1988) British universities response to events leading to grant reductions announced in July 1981. *Financial Accountability and Management* 4 (2) p79-97

Smith, J and Naylor, R (2001) Determinants of degree performance in UK universities: a statistical analysis of the 1993 student cohort. *Oxford Bulletin of Economics and Statistics* (63) p29-60

Smith, J, McKnight, A and Naylor, R (2000) Graduate employability: policy and performance in HE in the UK. *Economic Journal* (110) p382-411

Sorenson, A (1986) Theory and methodology in social stratification In Himmelstrand U (ed) *Sociology from crisis to science?* London: Sage

Springford J (2012) *University Access: Dumbing up?* www.smf.co.uk/marketsquare/john-springford/university-access-dumbing-up/ (March, 2012)

Stuart, M, Lido, C and Morgan J (2012) Choosing a student lifestyle? Questions of taste, cultural capital and gaining a graduate job. In Hinton-Smith T (ed) *Widening Participation in Higher Education: casting the net wide?* London: Palgrave

Stone, (1981) *The Education of the Black Child in Britain: the myth of multiracial education.* London, Collins Fontana

Sunderland, M (1985) *Women Who Teach in Universities.* Stoke on Trent: Trentham Books

Thomas, L (2002) Student retention in higher education and the role of institutional habitus. *Journal of Education Policy* 17 (4) p423-42

Thompson, E P (1964) *The Making of the English Working Class.* Harmondsworth: Penguin Books

Thompson, P (2000) *The Voice of the Past.* Oxford: OUP

Tight, M (2009) *The Development of Higher Education in the United Kingdom since 1945.* Maidenhead: OUP/SRHE

Times Higher Education (THE) (2012a) University participation rate stalls 28 March, 2012 http://www.timeshighereducation.co.uk/story.asp?sectioncode=26&storycode=419496(April, 2012)

Times Higher Education (THE) (2012b) Junior researchers led a merry dance as up to 300 circle each post 5 April, 2012 http://www.timeshighereducation.co.uk/story.asp?sectioncode=26&storycode=419602&c=1(April, 2012)

Times Higher Education (THE) (2012c) Poll suggests fear of debt is deterring poorest applicants 28 September 2012 http.//www.timeshighereducation.co.uk/story.asp?sectioncode=26&storycode=421331&c=1

Troyna, B (1993) *Racism and Education.* Milton Keynes: Open University Press

Troyna, B and Williams, J (1986) *Racism, Education and the State: the racialisation of educational policy.* London: Croom Helm

Universities and Colleges' Admissions Service (UCAS) (2012a) *UCAS comment on January application statistics.* http://www.ucas.com/about_us/media_enquiries/media_releases/2012/20120130a (March, 2012)

UCAS (2012b) *Qualifications information review: findings and recommendations.* http:// www.ucas.ac.uk/documents/qireview/qirfindings_english.pdf (July, 2012)

Universities UK (UUK) (2007) *Talent Wars: The international market for academic staff.* London: UUK

UUK (2011a) *Patterns and Trends in UK Higher Education.* London: UUK

UUK (2011b) *Driving Economic Growth.* London: UUK

UUK (2012) *Futures for Higher Education: analysing trends.* London: UUK

Urry, J (2007) *Mobilities.* Cambridge: Polity Press

West, L (1996) *Beyond Fragments: adults, motivation and learning; a biographical analysis.* London: Taylor and Francis

Whitchurch, C (2008) Beyond administration and management: changing professional identities in UK higher education. In Barnett, R and di Napoli, R (eds) *Changing Identities in Higher Education: voicing perspectives.* London: Routledge

Willis, P (2003) Foot soldiers of modernity: the dialectics of cultural consumption and the 21st century school. *Harvard Educational Review* 73 (3) p390-415

Wyn, J and White, R (1997) *Rethinking Youth.* London: Sage

Wolf, A (2002) *Does Education Matter? Myths about education and economic growth.* London: Penguin Books

Woodruff, W (2002) *The Road to Nab End.* London: Abacus Books

Woodruff, W (2003) *Beyond Nab End.* London: Abacus Books

Index

academic entitlement 72-75

access
    courses 71, 75-84
    fair access 3, 14-16,136-138, 145
    widening access 4-8, 101, 136

aspiration 43, 71-75, 100, 122

books 42, 57, 124-126

community 39-41, 56-57, 124

Dearing 92-93

ethnicity 15-16, 85-90, 98-99, 105-106

friends and friendship 74, 96-105, 108, 130-131

gender 44-45, 48-50, 64-68, 71, 75-85

graduate employment 15-17, 109, 111-114, 148-150

HE policy
    after the second world war 36-38, 50
    in different countries 4-6, 51-52,133-134, 147-148
    in the 1960s and 1970s 52-55
    in the 1980s and 1990s 69-71

in the twenty-first century 91-94; 140-142

hourglass economy 146-148

inequality 12-13, 25, 112-114

libraries 57, 74, 124-125

Life History method 27-31, 150

massification 53-54, 68-71, 131

mature students 55, 64-65, 71, 75, 93, 97-99, 144

Milburn, A 4, 133, 139, 143

mobilities 41, 61-62, 120-126

parents 39-42, 57-59, 73-75, 79-80, 99-100, 127-129

polytechnics 52, 63

reading 73, 124-126 *see also* books

Robbins 51-52, 66, 92

schooling
    and class 39-43, 59-61, 76-78, 129-130
    comprehensive schooling 55, 121-122
    the eleven plus 42, 55, 60, 121
    grammar schools 42, 59-60, 121-122

social and cultural capital 96, 126-131

social class
    and other social divisions 23-24, 64-67, 89-90
    as a place 118-122
    definitions 11-12, 20-22, 95-96, 114-116
    identity 23-25, 27, 60-61, 114-118, 150-151
    middle class 9, 12-13; 17, 59, 96, 116-117
    working class 9, 24-26, 38, 59, 73-74, 107

teachers 42-43, 58-60, 75, 129-130

universities
    and funding 38-39, 52-53, 66, 136-137, 141-142
    and staff 48-50, 67-68, 111-114
    and students 46-48, 62-64
    and women 37, 48-50

widening participation 17-18, 136-137, 150-151

INNOVATIVE SIMULATIONS FOR ASSESSING PROFESSIONAL COMPETENCE

From Paper-and-Pencil
to
Virtual Reality

Ara Tekian
Christine H. McGuire
William C. McGaghie
and Associates

UIC
University of Illinois at Chicago
Department of Medical Education

Address for Orders, Editorial correspondence and copyright permission:

Ara Tekian, PhD, MHPE
University of Illinois at Chicago
Department of Medical Education (MC 591)
College of Medicine
808 S. Wood St.
Chicago, IL 60612-7309

Phone: (312) 996-8438
Fax: (312) 413-2048
E-mail: Tekian@uic.edu

Library of Congress Cataloging-in-Publication Data

Tekian, Ara
Innovative simulations for assessing professional competence: from paper-and-pencil to virtual reality / Ara Tekian, Christine H. McGuire, William C. McGaghie, and Associates.

  Includes bibliographical references and index.
  Library of Congress Catalog Card Number: 99-93267
  ISBN 0-9671689-0-2
  1. Competence Assessment   2. Innovative Simulations-Assessment
I. Tekian, Ara   II. McGuire, Christine H.   III. McGaghie, William C.

FIRST EDITION

Production Manager   Niambi Jaha
            Design   Mary Eagan Badinger
          Printing   United Graphics

Contents

Preface   *Christine H. McGuire, Ara Tekian, William C. McGaghie* . . . . *iii*

Part One: Overview

Introduction   *William C. McGaghie* *1*

Chapter 1   Simulation: Its Essential Nature and Characteristics
Christine H. McGuire *3*

Chapter 2   Simulation in Professional Competence Assessment:
Basic Considerations
William C. McGaghie *7*

Part Two: Prototypic Simulations from the Professions

Introduction   *Ara Tekian* *24*

Section A   **Assessing Cognitive Skills: Can They Think Like a Professional?**

Introduction   *Christine H. McGuire* *27*

Chapter 3   Computer-Based Case Simulations from Medicine:
Assessing Skills in Patient Management
Stephen G. Clyman, Donald E. Melnick, Brian E. Clauser *29*

Chapter 4   Computerized Design Problems in Architecture:
The New Licensure Examination
Jeffrey F. Kenney *43*

Chapter 5   Simulated Work Sample in Law: A Multistate Performance Test
Jane Peterson Smith *59*

Section B   **Assessing Communication, Technical and Affective Responses:
Can They Relate Like a Professional?**

Introduction   *Ara Tekian* *73*

Chapter 6   Data Collection and Interpersonal Skills:
The Standardized Patient Encounter
Robyn Tamblyn, Howard Barrows *77*

Chapter 7   The Objective Structured Clinical Examination (OSCE) of
Technical Skills: The Canadian Experience In Licensure
*Richard Reznick, David E. Blackmore, Dale Dauphinee,
Sydney M. Smee, Arthur I. Rothman* *105*

Chapter 8   Handling Critical Incidents: Sweaty Palms and
                 Post Traumatic Stress Syndrome
                 Christine H. McGuire *113*

Section C   **Assessing Integration of Performance Skills and Knowledge:**
                 Can They Behave Like a Professional?

Introduction   *Ara Tekian, William C. McGaghie* *123*

Chapter 9   Assessing Knowledge and Skills in the Health Professions:
                 A Continuum of Simulation Fidelity
                 S. Barry Issenberg, William C. McGaghie *125*

Chapter 10   The Individual as a Member of a Working Group:
                 Evaluating Team Performance in Aviation and Medicine
                 Robert L. Helmreich *147*

Chapter 11   Military Mission Rehearsal: From Sandtable to Virtual Reality
                 Eugene K. Ressler, James E. Armstrong, George B. Forsythe *157*

                 Part Three: Challenges and Opportunities

Introduction   *Ara Tekian* *177*

Chapter 12   The Future Is Now: Virtual Reality Technologies
                 Richard M. Satava, Shaun B. Jones *179*

Chapter 13   Measurement Issues in the Use of Simulation for Testing Professionals:
                 Test Development, Test Scoring, Standard Setting
                 John Norcini *195*

Chapter 14   Philosophical and Ethical Concerns:
                 Benefits, Limitations and Unexpected Consequences
                 of Simulation in Professional Assessment
                 Ara Tekian *213*

Chapter 15   Conclusions and Recommendations: A Suggested Strategy
                 Christine H. McGuire, Ara Tekian *233*

                 Author Biosketches *243*

                 Subject Index *251*

Preface

Until 1889, occupational and professional practice in the United States was viewed as a Constitutionally guaranteed individual property right. It was generally thought that the right to earn a living—an essential precondition for the "pursuit of happiness,"—presupposed freedom to pursue any career, with or without training.

But in 1889, in the landmark *Dent vs West Virginia* decision, the Supreme Court upheld a state licensing board's requirement that completion of specified training was an essential credential for medical licensure. In so doing the Court affirmed sovereignty in the regulation of the professions as a Constitutionally guaranteed *state* right. Over the next one hundred years one or more states came to require licenses for practitioners in more than eleven hundred occupations and professions, ranging from cosmetology and barbering to lawyering and doctoring.

Writing in 1992, Morrison and Carter observed that "Early political science theories were divided as to whether regulation was caused by the desire of legislators to increase social welfare, or purchased by interest groups seeking personal gain." They concluded that "the accumulated evidence squarely supports the latter." Following World War II, enormous pressures for licensure were brought by many new groups, especially behavioral scientists such as psychologists and social workers. This proliferation of demands for regulatory action strongly suggested that licensure had become a prize sought by practitioners themselves for economic advantage, prestige and social status. Whether designed to protect the public welfare or to defend a privileged private monopoly, examinations for certification and licensure had become big business, defended on the ground that performance on such tests has a clear and direct relation to professional competence, and that decisions based on them would help to identify persons not qualified to practice.

Selection of professionals by examination can be traced to dynastic China where, some 3,000 years ago, the Ch'in, in order to avoid the necessity of relying exclusively on hereditary local power, initiated the practice of recruiting some officials by examination—a system later credited as an important means of holding the country together and called "one of the most successful political devices ever invented by man" (Latourette, 1929).

As far as we now know, the oldest application of testing for licensure in the Western World was in the field of medicine. In the early 700s, following a physician error that had resulted in the death of a member of the Court, the Caliph of Baghdad decreed that physicians practicing in his Court be examined regularly. In the mid 900s King Roger of Sicily instituted a similar practice, and from there the requirement spread slowly through Europe for physicians attending powerful people.

However, such examinations have not been uniformly successful in eliminating unqualified professionals. At least until the middle of this century, most licensure and certification examinations in all jurisdictions, for all professions, violated practically every accepted principle of educational measurement. In medicine, for example, as late as the 1950s, examinations by agencies at all levels (medical school, state licensing authorities, residency programs and specialty boards) were conducted for the most part by senior physicians who were themselves uncontaminated by any understanding of measurement theory. Commonly, the required examination included totally unstandardized oral interviews in which an established eminence grilled a nervous candidate about anything in the field of the examiner's interest, and judged the examinee's responses by standards that were all too often idiosyncratic, arbitrary and frequently frivolous. Some jurisdictions supplemented the oral encounter with a practical; others combined it with, or even replaced it by, written examinations of dubious merit.

Rapidly escalating resort to litigation by those denied the right to practice as a result of failure on what they argued were flawed examinations, together with the growth of the testing industry, brought about mounting demands for reform during the late 50s and early 60s. It was in this climate, one congenial to change, that one of our Associates was introduced to the opportunities and frustrations of assessment for licensure. Convinced that the best predictor of future performance is current performance on the same task in a similar situation she, in collaboration with members of the medical profession, introduced the concept of simulation for the summative evaluation of some undergraduate medical students and the certification procedures of a few specialty boards (McGuire, 1967).

Compared to today's capabilities, those early simulations were indeed primitive. At the most simple level, they included such devices as basing multiple choice and short answer questions on a variety of specific, individual patient data, presented in as nearly realistic form as possible—photomicrographs of slides; reproductions of X-rays and tracings; videotapes of patient interviews; movies of physical examinations; heart, lung and abdominal sounds played through individual stethophones, and the like. In the exercises based on these stimuli, examinees were required to interpret the data, speculate about the probable cause of the reported condition, describe other findings that might be associated, predict what might exacerbate the symptoms and make other judgments about the meaning and significance of the data presented. The technique which created the greatest interest, however, was the paper-and-pencil simulation of patient management problems (PMPs). These exercises were introduced with a brief verbal description (or film) displaying the presenting complaint of a patient, followed by long lists of possible strategies(e.g., hospitalize the patient, take a history, etc.), data-gathering inquiries (e.g., Where does it hurt? When did it start? What makes it worse?, etc.), laboratory orders (e.g., CBC, SGOT, etc.) and other possible interventions (e.g., start an IV, prepare for urgent surgery, prescribe X, etc.). Examinees recorded their decisions on a specially treated answer sheet in a manner that revealed the patient's response to each inquiry and action or that provided instructions directing respondents to the next stage of the problem appropriate to their respective choices. In this way a simulation could be carried through many stages in the work-up and management of a life-like situation. Depending on the unique set of decisions each individual had made, the complications to be handled and the ultimate patient outcomes differed, as they do in the real life office and clinic.

Today's highly sophisticated computer-based simulations of clinical problems and the meticulously designed live interviews of laymen who have been carefully scripted to simulate a real patient can be claimed as direct descendants of those pioneer PMPs. With the advent of PCs and robotics the range of competencies that can be simulated with a high degree of fidelity has increased many-fold. Today, applications of simulation technology from paper-and-pencil to virtual reality are popular in the training and testing of personnel from Hamburger University (the School for aspiring McDonald's employees) to NASA.

Our studies of the wondrously diverse types of simulation now being increasingly introduced for various purposes in the assessment of professionals convinces us that those of us involved in testing for licensure and certification could learn much from each other. We therefore asked outstanding experts working in widely different professional arenas to prepare an essay for publication, describing the innovative applications of simulation technology in licensure and certification in their respective disciplines. Not surprisingly, many of the leaders in the field come from aviation, the military and medicine—professions long noted for the dangerous nature of their practice, the gravity of individual decisions and the limitations of conventional methods for assessing professional competence. However, it is important to observe that traditionally low-tech fields among the "learned professions," (such as teaching, law and the ministry) have also been pioneers in introducing innovative types of simulation exercises that are applicable even in professions using the most advanced technology.

The scholarly chapters contributed by our invited Associates are not only interesting, stimulating and informative, but also immediately useful in areas generally considered far afield. The reader will find that the perceived relevance of experience in one profession to other superficially very different types of work is often quite startling. Anyone involved in assessing professional competence-—whether as a member of a policy board, an agency staff, a professional school faculty, a commercial testing agency, a research and development institute—will find this volume of brilliant essays by those on the cutting edge, interesting, informative, and deeply challenging, in short – indispensable.

References

Latourette, K.S.L. 1929. "China: History." In *Encyclopedia Britannica,* 14h ed., vol 5, New York: Enc. Brit., p. 535.

McGuire, C. 1967. Simulation Techniques in the Measurement of Problem-Solving Skills. *Journal of Educational Measurement* 4(1): 1-10.

Morrison, R. H. and Carter, E. A.: "Licensure, Certification, and Registration:" In Marvin C. Alken 1992, Editor-in-Chief, *Encyclopedia of Ed. Research*, 6th ed, New York: MacMillan Pub. Co., p. 746.

Chicago, Illinois   Christine H. McGuire
May 1999   Ara Tekian
                                                                        William C. McGaghie

Acknowledgements

We are indebted to Andrew J. Krainik and Michael Jalovecky for proofreading and technical assistance, Vivian Johnson for secretarial support, Mary Egan Badinger for cover design and book layout, and Lisa Harris for typesetting. Leslie Sandlow, M.D., provided the administrative and financial support needed for publication of this volume.

Ara Tekian
Christine H. McGuire
William C. McGaghie

Part One: Overview

Part One: Overview

Introduction

The use of simulation technology is now widespread in professional education and evaluation. Flight simulators in aviation, standardized patients in medicine and nursing, computer-based design examinations in architecture, and high and low technology combat simulations in the military are only a few examples of how such representations of reality are being used for the training and assessment of professional personnel.

This Part of the volume, which contains two chapters, aims, in broad terms, frame to the scope and utility of simulations in professional education.

Chapter One, authored by Christine McGuire, briefly presents the limits and the benefits of simulation technology in professional education. The *primary* limits are readily acknowledged: no simulation of professional practice can be isomorphic with the rich complexity of the work that aviators, doctors and nurses, architects, and military officers perform everyday. Thus teaching and testing simulations represent a narrow focus of professional practice. They can rarely capture even the most routine challenges of professional work, much less the extraordinary professional responses required in "crisis" situations such as a surgical procedure gone wrong, an aircraft equipment malfunction, or a nuclear "core meltdown."

However despite these limits, McGuire also describes the clear-cut *benefits* of professional simulations, especially their ability to *standardize* the presentation of professional problems for teaching and testing. This is in sharp contrast to the "rumpled reality" of professional education that occurs in real life settings (e.g., practicums, internships) where professional problems are complex, indistinct, and have more than one right approach or answer. McGuire points out that simulations approximate, but can never duplicate, the true conditions of professional practice.

Chapter Two, authored by William C. McGaghie, amplifies McGuire's orienting work. Here the author (a) gives an historical perspective about the educational use of simulations, (b) provides a framework for understanding the educational role of simulations, (c) illustrates the use of educational simulation technology in the nuclear power industry, (d) addresses the issue of evaluating simulation technology as an educational intervention, and (d) talks about

1

several unresolved issues in the realm of educational simulations.

These two chapters frame the use of simulation technology in professional education generally. Their presentation is intended to prepare readers for the detailed accounts about the use of simulations in specific professions which follow.

William C. McGaghie

1

Simulation: Its Essential Nature and Characteristics

Christine H. McGuire

*Educational simulations are, in many respects, analogous to the play of the young of any species. Both share three essential attributes: (a) they **imitate** but do not **duplicate** reality; (b) they offer almost limitless opportunity to "go wrong;" (c) they provide corrective feedback as a guide to future action. Systematically designed simulations embodying these features are not new; they have been employed since ancient times in those pursuits where training and testing in the real world are too dangerous (e.g., war games), too expensive, (e.g., aviation) or simply unfeasible. (e.g., space exploration). Characteristics which make simulations so valuable in those settings explain their utility for assessment of professional competence.*

From game arcades to NASA, sophisticated simulations have become so nearly ubiquitous in tests of skill and cunning that we tend to think of them as offspring of the post-robotics, post-computer age. But that is a serious misconception. Simulation is not new: it has constituted a fundamental educational tool for both teaching and testing at least since the days when the human race developed the capacity for play.

Indeed, some would argue that simulation as a means of facilitating learning is even more ancient; it has been around ever since the young of the first mammalian species could afford to take time off from foraging for food and, instead, indulge in the luxury of "pretend." Have you ever watched a kitten "stalk" a feather in the grass, and seen her try to pounce on that elusive intruder? Have you ever observed juvenile primates in mock battle, though never to the point of wounding each other seriously? Witnessing such delightful scenes, it is hard not to believe that the kitten is practicing to become the hunter for her pride, and that the primate is gearing up to vie for the position of alpha male in his adult family group.

Images of such animal antics are vivid reminders of three essential attributes of simulation which, together, define its essence. First, simulation *imitates*, it does not *duplicate* reality; that is both its greatest strength and greatest potential weakness. Second, well designed simulations provide maximum opportunity for the player to go wrong in all, or most all, of the ways that life itself offers in similar situations. Third, in true simulations, the respondent's ploys elicit substantive, life-like consequences that direct subsequent action. As applied in the assessment of professional competence, each of these essential characteristics has implications for the design of test situations and for the inferences that can legitimately be made about the examinee's responses to them.

That simulation imitates but does not duplicate life implies that any test situation is fully controllable. Authors are able to focus on what they think to be the salient elements of the relevant reality, without being distracted and/or possibly misled by the trivial irrelevancies and random variations which life necessarily entails. Further, simulation provides the freedom to design potentially dangerous situations without exposing respondents to the full penalties that life inevitably extracts for mistakes.

On the other hand, the luxury of being able to avoid duplicating life in all its complexities is also a source of potential weakness, in that we cannot always be certain whether and to what universe we can safely generalize from performance in a sanitized situation. In avoiding the infinitely more variable and complex conditions reality embraces we risk inadvertently missing critical factors which may be fundamental in dictating responses in the real world.

For example, when standardized patients (i.e., situations in which examinees are required to interact with actors playing scripted parts) were first introduced in the testing of health professionals, they were enthusiastically hailed as "high fidelity" simulations of patient care problems, presumably in contrast with the allegedly "low fidelity" of then popular "paper patients." What was not clearly recognized was that, while live simulations did indeed have the potential for faithfully reproducing the verbal interaction characteristic of **some** types of patient-provider encounters, it was virtually impossible to structure such exercises to present the challenges of patient management over time and in response to changing conditions. For this purpose the "fidelity" of a well designed computer or paper patient clearly exceeds that of a one-shot interview with a human being, however well coached. Thus, in escaping the demands of duplicating life in its infinite variability, the simulation author must be rigorous in selecting the critical features of a situation essential to imitate. In short, for testing purposes, *imitations of reality are superior to reality itself so long as the salient variables are accurately identified, carefully defined and faithfully mimicked.*

With respect to the second attribute of well designed test simulations—i.e., freedom for the respondent to err in multiple ways—"answers" are not constrained to "correct" vs. "incorrect;" rather, they can diverge from an optimum path in wondrously diverse directions, each of which may have different implications for diagnosis and counseling. The kitten, for example, can pounce too soon, not soon enough, or not sufficiently on target, and thus be doomed to watch its feather prey swirl frustratingly out of reach; the juvenile primate can be too timid, too aggressive or, to his sorrow, can misjudge his opponent's strength, agility and/or determination, and can compound that error by a dubious choice between flight and fight. Each path requires different remedial measures.

Finally, the freedom which a genuine simulation provides for the respondent to choose among a theoretically infinite number of patterns of action, is responsible for what many regard as the most attractive feature of the technique: namely, the opportunity to obtain, as a guide to subsequent action, feedback suggestive of possible mid-course corrections. Thus, a well designed simulation can (in my view, should) provide realistic, though not devastating, information about the consequences of the choices the respondent is making—advice that is incomparably more valuable than a simple 1/0 denoting correct/incorrect. Thus, as she "plays," the kitten can learn from her misjudgments of timing and direction; however, if she awkwardly persists in indulging in what clearly prove to be inept maneuvers, she will exhaust herself without catching her "prey." Fortunately, however, she will be able to learn the consequences of her mistakes in a safe environment; neither she nor her future kits will starve as a price of her current failure. Similarly, the juvenile primate who misjudges his opponent's capabilities and hits him ineffectually, learns that his blow will be painfully returned and that he will temporarily lose his dominance, but he will not be permanently ostracized, nor will he be driven from his family. In short, Gertrude Stein and her roses notwithstanding, in my view (not shared by all my colleagues), a simulation is not a simulation, is not a simulation unless *it triggers relevant feedback that guides further action and that contributes to learning.*

To illustrate the essential attributes of simulation, I have chosen to use a couple of cases of spontaneous simulation from the animal world because such incidents are so easy to dissect. Historically, however, systematically chosen and consciously designed simulations have been used for generations, wherever training and/or testing in the real world are too dangerous (war games), too expensive (flight simulators), or simply not feasible (space exploration). Today, purposely devised simulations range from "low tech" (e.g., paper and pencil, role playing) to "high tech" (e.g., virtual reality) and from low to near perfect fidelity in their replication of life (e.g., sand tables vs. battle practice with live ammunition). Today, as in the times of the colorful medieval tournaments, simulations embrace both individual and group exercises, ranging from those designed to test small flight crews and surgical teams to those developed to evaluate readiness of army battalions and more. Such varied simulations are already being employed in numerous fields for purposes both of developing and of assessing many elements of behavior, including cognitive problem solving, technical and communication skills, interpersonal interactions, and affective responses.

Close analysis suggests that, in essence, even the most elaborate such exercises share many of the basic features that distinguish child and animal play from other instructional and assessment methodologies. However, it must be noted that the same characteristics—imitation of life, freedom to "go wrong" and realistic corrective feedback—which make simulation so appealing to both the creator and the respondent, also raise fundamental problems that must be considered before adopting so powerful a tool for use in high stakes testing—i.e., testing used for such purposes as admission to professional schools, hiring, promotion, licensure, and certification. The issues posed in those circumstances range from broad, general philosophic and ethical concerns, including cost/benefit, unintended consequences and the like, to highly technical psychometric questions. Thoughtful attention to these matters and on-going data collection about them will enable us to embrace the benefits of a truly potent and intriguing tool, while minimizing the risk of allowing it to degenerate into a tiresome fad, worthy only of relegation to gaudy, neon-lit arcades.

2

Simulation in Professional Competence Assessment: Basic Considerations

William C. McGaghie

This chapter presents a broad overview of the uses of simulations in professional education and evaluation, setting the stage for consideration of the specific illustrations of simulation technology presented in Part Two. The chapter reviews the literature on the use of simulation in professions ranging from architecture, law and medicine to management, the military, and nuclear power plant operation. Various applications of simulation technology are described from an historical perspective, alternate frameworks or typologies for their classification are suggested and criteria for their application in the assessment of professional competence are suggested.

S imulations are widely used to evaluate and train professional persons. Simulations are approximations to reality that require trainees to react to problems or conditions as they would under genuine circumstances. They range in complexity from high technology flight simulators used to evaluate and train pilots and astronauts to inert football tackling dummies. To illustrate:

- In April 1997 former U.S. President George Bush voluntarily parachuted to safety from an airplane 12,500 feet above the Arizona desert. This replicated an experience 50 years earlier when Navy pilot Bush was forced to bail out when his torpedo bomber was shot down by Japanese fire during World War II. Commenting on the recent experience septuagenarian Bush declared, "I'm a new man. I go home exhilarated" (Seligman, 1997). This was not a chance event. Bush trained for the 1997 parachute jump using a virtual reality parachute flight training simulator which was originally designed to prepare smoke jumpers to fight forest fires ("Simulator Trained Bush," 1997).

- Medical students at the University of Michigan learn to provide counsel about smoking cessation from work with simulated patient instructors (SPIs). The SPIs are simulated patients who play the role of genuine patients who are basically healthy yet smoke cigarettes habitually. The SPIs give the medical students detailed feedback about the substance and style of the stop smoking message and evaluate student performance rigorously (Eyler et al. 1997).

- Assessment Centers are widely used in business and industry to educate and evaluate managers and executives. However, Spencer and Spencer (1993) report that an Assessment Center has been used to evaluate intelligence officers' capacity to withstand stress under dangerous circumstances, which are simulated with much realism.

  ".... in a well-known assessment center where spies were selected for work behind enemy lines, candidates were locked in a small room with one naked light bulb, then slipped a note that told them they had been captured in the middle of the night photographing documents in the enemy's headquarters. A few minutes later, the door was broken down by men dressed as enemy soldiers, who then forcefully interrogated the subject. These exercises test for self-control and influence skills under stress" (p. 251).

In their recent book *Engines for Education* (1995) Schank and Cleary make a strong case for "Simulation-Based Learning By Doing." Schank and Cleary argue that simulations, especially computer-based high-fidelity varieties like flight simulators, place students in realistic learning situations unlike those of the customary classroom or laboratory. These authors write with passion and conviction about the educational advantages of simulation-based learning. Contributors to this volume present examples and argue for the utility of simulations for personnel evaluation, especially evaluation of the competence of professional persons.

But what do evaluators mean by the term *simulation?* What's the definition? In broad, simple terms a simulation is a person, device, or set of conditions which attempts to present evaluation problems authentically. The student or trainee is required to respond to the problems as he or she would under natural circumstances. Frequently the trainee receives performance feedback as if he or she were in the real situation.

Simulation procedures for evaluation and teaching have several common characteristics:

- Trainees see cues and consequences very much like those in the real environment.

- Trainees can be placed in complex situations.

- Trainees act as they would in the real environment.

- The fidelity (exactness of duplication) of a simulation is never completely isomorphic with the "real thing." The reasons are obvious: cost, avoidance of danger, ethics, psychometric requirements, time constraints.

- Simulations can take many forms. For example, they can be static, as in an anatomical model. Simulations can be automated, using advanced computer technology. Some are individual, prompting solitary performance while others are interactive, involving groups of people. Simulations can be playful or deadly serious. In personnel evaluation settings they can be used for high-stakes, low stakes, or no stakes decisions.

This volume is strong testimony to the widespread use of simulations in professional education and evaluation. Witness the variety of professions represented here: architecture, aviation, law, medicine, and the military. Various chapters of this book demonstrate the utility of "approximations to reality" in these fields for the purpose of candidate or practitioner evaluation. Many other professions where simulations are in use or under development for education and especially personnel evaluation are *not* represented in this book. Examples include business and industrial management (Eldredge & Watson, 1996; Motowidio & Tippins, 1993, Streufert, Pogash & Piasecki, 1998), the clergy (Hunt, Hinkle & Malony, 1990), clinical psychology and psychiatry (Jachna et al. 1993) where consultation skills can be practiced and evaluated by computer, nuclear power plant operation (American Nuclear Society, 1993), teaching (Haertel, 1990; Klein & Stecher, 1991; Vanlehn, Ohisson & Nason, 1994), dentistry (Houlihan, Finklestein & Johnson, 1992), nursing (Henry & Waltmire, 1992), and even commercial sex workers (Fisher & Fisher, 1992), i.e., female and male prostitutes, especially in Third World countries where the AIDS pandemic is being addressed, in part, through simulated encounters among professionals and their patrons (Elkins et al. 1996; Maticka-Tyndale, 1997).

The purpose of this chapter is to set forth some basic considerations about the use of simulations in professional competence assessment. The chapter has five sections.

- The *first* section traces the history of using simulations for professional education and evaluation. Simulations have been around for quite some time and it's informative to understand them in historical perspective.

- Section *two* considers typologies now in use to classify simulations according to their features and aims. This is an important intellectual exercise, an activity that will help us ask better questions about applications of simulation technology.

- Section *three* reviews selected applications of simulation-technology in professional competence evaluation with special attention to a profession not isolated in this book: i.e., nuclear power plant simulators for use in professional operator training and evaluation.

- Comments about technology evaluation account for the *fourth* section. The focus here is on selected published studies that rigorously evaluate the utility of simulations for professional assessment. This section also addresses another question: "Why bother with formal technology evaluation when it's obvious, in cases like flight simulators, that the simulations are much better than other alternatives for professional assessment?"

- The *fifth* section raises a series of issues—call it agenda setting—that need to be addressed to bring coherence to this rapidly growing field. Throughout, evaluators need to be mindful of another key distinction raised by Schank and Cleary (1995), the difference between simulations as *objects* of study (which is the academic imperative) versus simulations as *means* of study (the practical or engineering response). Closing remarks speak to reconciliation, i.e., trying to figure out if these two cultures can live and prosper together.

Historical Perspective

Writing in the *Journal of Management*, Keys and Wolfe (1990) sketch a short history of the use of simulations for professional education and evaluation.

> "The first use of games for education and development were the war game simulations of Wei-Hai, which originated in China about 3,000 B.C. and the Hindu game of Chaturanga (Wilson, 1968). These games bore a vague similarity to the early 17th century warfare game, chess. Soon these parlor exercises became 'serious' games as observed in the development of the King's Game by Weikhmann at Ulm in 1664, War Chess by Helwig in 1780 at the Court of Brunswick in Germany (Sayre, 1912; Young, 1959) and the most elaborate came, the 'New Kriegspeil' created by George Venturini at Schleswig in 1798 (Thomas, 1957). War games have also been used extensively in this century to test plans for military operations (Fuchida & Okumiya, 1955; Hausrath, 1971)."

This short passage teaches that simulations, especially military gaming, have been in use—chiefly for training—for thousands of years. The principal idea, i.e., place trainees in lifelike problem situations, gauge their responses, provide performance feedback, and judge their performance is not new. What's contemporary, of course, is that today's simulations can operate in high-speed and high-capacity computer environments that become more powerful almost by the month. The historical bottom line is that personnel evaluators who use simulations are working with an old idea in new and breathtaking ways whose possibilities are just beginning to be understood.

Framework or Typology

Mature sciences, and perhaps mature technologies as well, have schemes where current knowledge can be organized or classified (Bailey, 1994). These are conceptual typologies or empirical taxonomies that give scholars and researchers leads about important yet untouched territory and that allow for incorporation of new knowledge as data and experience accumulate. For example, we owe huge intellectual debts in the natural sciences to Linneaus in botany and zoology for his pioneering 18th Century organization of plant and animal species, and to Mendeleev in chemistry for the Periodic Table of the Elements first developed in the 19th Century. Each of these methods of scientific classification provides intellectual organization to natural science research. John Dewey's decimal system, a cornerstone of library science, has worked as a similar intellectual tool in that field.

Typologies and taxonomies that organize knowledge in botany, zoology, chemistry, and library science are both important and rare in intellectual life. Few fields of science or technology can match their elegance or comprehensiveness because classification or taxonomy is demanding and often unheralded work (Altman, 1968). The human genome project, now underway, is the latest large-scale manifestation of a scientific classification project (Schuler et al., 1996).

An attempt to find a consistent and coherent typology to better understand and classify work on simulations for professional education and personnel evaluation leads to the conclusion that the cupboard is indeed very bare (Kryukov & Kryuova, 1986; Cecchini & Frisenna, 1987). Several contributors to this volume, led by Eugene Ressler and colleagues (Chapter 11), will illustrate a three dimensional conceptual framework for military combat simulations. The model organizes military simulations by their *purpose* (training, assessment, analysis), *scope* (individual, team/crew, unit), and *type* (live, virtual, constructive). However, Colonel Ressler would be among the first to acknowledge that this framework is woefully inadequate as a typology to capture rich and rapidly changing military challenges and response patterns, especially in dangerous situations. The same criticism could be made of an even broader conceptual framework for military modeling and simulation (M & S) recently published on the World Wide Web by the United States Department of Defense (Under secretary of Defense for Acquisition and Technology, 1995). This broad scheme classifies military simulations by *scope* (range from subsystem/component to theater/campaign), *sponsoring component* (Army, Navy, Air Force, Marine Corps, etc.), and *functional area* (training, analysis, acquisition).

These military typologies provide tacit recognition of the need to improve ways to classify simulations (and their features) for professional training and evaluation. A practical classification scheme for simulations and their features will go a long way toward helping us use them intelligently. For example, without better classification methods *at the design stage, as the simulations are created*, even the most sophisticated simulations of professional challenges may be engineering marvels, yet leave us at a loss to explain such scientifically important principles as human performance generalization. Psychometrician John Norcini addresses this and other key scientific measurement issues in Chapter 13.

A Selected Application

Most North American adults recall the close call that occurred at the Three Mile Island Nuclear Power plant in Central Pennsylvania in 1979. Here, a combination of operator error and miscommunication nearly resulted in a meltdown of a reactor core which could have had disastrous consequences for Pennsylvania and other regions of the Northeastern and Midwestern United States. And who can forget the "real thing," the actual disaster that occurred at the Russian nuclear power plant at Chernobyl in 1986? The core meltdown and subsequent loss of containment of nuclear material resulted in an immediate loss of human life in the hundreds, perhaps thousands as the timetable stretches; devastation to nearby air, soil, and water supplies; untold losses of domestic and wild plant and animal life; and long-term consequences that are the subject of speculation and worldwide scientific scrutiny.

It is obvious that factors including power plant design and location and the *selection, training, certification, and monitoring* of persons responsible for power plant operation are very high-stakes issues. So how is this done in the United States, not only to insure the availability of electrical power for commercial, industrial, and private consumption but also to insure protection of the public from the horror of possible nuclear contamination?

One of the most ambitious uses of *high fidelity simulations* for professional training and evaluation exists in the nuclear power industry. Power plant operators must be certified by industry and licensed by the U.S. Nuclear Regulatory Commission. In addition, the power plant simulators used for training and personnel evaluation must also be certified before use and recertified annually. The simulators are *site specific* and every power plant in the United States is required to have a simulated control room for operator training and evaluation. There is no presumption that training, certification, and licensure obtained for one power plant can be generalized to another power facility (American Nuclear Society, 1993).

Nuclear power plant simulators are required to have minimum capabilities. The 1993 operating *Standards* state, "The scope of simulation shall be such that the operator is required to take the same action on the simulator to conduct an evolution as on the reference unit using the reference unit operating procedures. The scope of simulation shall permit conduct of all of the evolutions required until a stable condition is obtained. Simulator performance validation testing, as well as configuration management capabilities, shall be provided." The *Standards* continue, "The response of the simulator resulting from [a] operator action, [b] no operator action, [c] improper operator action, [d] automatic reference unit controls, and [e] indirect operating characteristics shall be realistic and shall not violate the physical laws of nature, such as conservation of mass, momentum, and energy, within the limits of the performance validation criteria" (American Nuclear Society, 1993, p.2).

The simulator performance criteria are complicated. They include steady-state operations, transient operations such as start-up and minor malfunctions and alarms, and major disasters. Given the potential consequences of real-life nuclear power plant malfunctions, it is reassuring that competence evaluations of plant operators and plant simulators are done with great rigor.

Nuclear power plant operator training exercises on a control room simulator and operator evaluations are not only hard nosed but also involve individual and team performance. Selected illustrations include:

- Control rooms for nuclear power plants are managed with military efficiency. The chain of command is established clearly, orders are repeated and verified, the interpersonal environment is businesslike and efficient. Simulated and actual control rooms are carefully demarcated. For example, a red carpet in front of the control panels is operator only territory. No one else, not even supervisory personnel, may set foot there, just like in a real power plant.

- Entry-level operators spend a minimum of 18 months in focused training after undergoing a rigorous screening and selection procedure. Early training involves classroom study and practical work in simulated and real control rooms. The washout rate in initial training is about 40%.

- Following certification and licensure, individual operators and operator crews at most nuclear facilities work and train in 5:1 weekly rotations. That is, after every five weeks of regular work, individuals and crews undergo one week of training and evaluation throughout their careers, without exception. All control room operations are done "by the book" according to a procedural manual. Individual judgment is exercised only under extraordinary circumstances, conditions that can be introduced routinely in this environment.

- Individual operators must be relicensed annually after passing written and operator (i.e., simulated control room) examinations each year. The passing standards for these examinations are set very high: 80% overall on the written component, flawless performance on the operator evaluation. Failures result in remediation and retesting. Washouts are rare at this stage, but they do happen. Of course, operators are subject to mandatory blood and urine toxicology screening which is done on a random basis.

Despite such rigorous training, evaluation, and retraining using sophisticated power plant simulators, operational errors still occur. A news report published in The *Chicago Tribune* describes a breakdown that occurred at the Zion nuclear facility operated by Commonwealth Edison north of Chicago.

"With his bosses and a federal regulator standing nearby, an operator at the Zion Nuclear Power Station was recently ratcheting down the reactor to 40 percent power when he held the switch down too long, shutting it off altogether.

Then he made an even more remarkable mistake: He pushed the switch back up and held it there. The operator was single-handedly trying to respark the nuclear reaction, violating the most fundamental tenets of operation.

No reactor should even be started without making sure safety systems are in place.

Why, officials are wondering, would a worker with almost a decade of experience do something so contrary to all his training, especially with his bosses looking over his shoulder?" (Kendall, 1997).

Flaws in human judgment, even under highly controlled conditions and in the presence of supervisors, can counteract professional training, and evaluation protocols in surprising ways. Hammond (1996) reminds us that human judgement inevitably involves uncertainty and introduces a margin of error even among skilled and experienced professionals.

Technology Evaluation

Technology evaluation is an important activity regarding the use of simulations in professional competence assessment if for no other reason than to grant assurance that the measurements taken in evaluation settings are reliable and valid (Mayer, 1997). We simply cannot make accurate judgments about the competence of professional people without trustworthy data.

However, the broader issue of technology evaluation beyond psychometric fine points also warrants attention. This is in spite of the point raised earlier that in some circumstances it would be foolish to use anything other than a simulator to evaluate professional competence. For example, in her recent book, *Choosing the Right Stuff: The Psychological Selection of Astronauts and Cosmonauts*, psychiatrist Patricia Santy (1994) notes that a number of psychological traits comprise aptitude for the job of astronaut. They include:

- Intelligence and Technical Aptitude

- Being a Team Player

- Stress or Discomfort Tolerance

- *Ability to Function Despite Imminent Catastrophe or Personal Danger*

- Ability to Tolerate Separation from Loved Ones

- Ability to Tolerate Isolation

There is *no way* that traditional paper and pencil measures can be used to evaluate such personal traits. The brief description of nuclear power plant simulators and chapters later in this book by Ressler and colleagues (military combat), Helmreich (aviation), Satava (virtual surgery) and others will make it plain that different types of simulators are the only way to evaluate these and other features of professional performance with safety and accuracy.

Returning to the distinction made earlier, these examples underscore the utility of simulations as a means of study or evaluation. But what about simulations as an object of study or evaluation? Do they work?

Evidence is accumulating that with careful construction and pilot testing, simulations can be used for training and professional assessment with great effectiveness. This presumes that the *efficacy* of simulations for education and evaluation is established under controlled laboratory conditions (Alpha testing), followed by tests of their *effectiveness* under less controlled field settings (Beta testing) (Fletcher, Fletcher, & Wagner, 1996). Studies cited throughout this volume demonstrate the growing reliance that many professions are placing on simulations as a component of their competence assessment schemes. Of course, all applications of simulation technology for professional assessment need to meet basic psychometric quality standards as articulated by John Norcini in Chapter 13.

Here are three illustrations of good outcomes studies from the simulations literature.

First, Harless and his colleagues present convincing data about the TIME interactive patient simulation model, developed under auspices of the Lister Hill National Center for Biomedical Communications of the National Library of Medicine (Harless et al. 1990). This research shows that medical students interacting with a videodisc patient simulation model "became individually committed to the care and management of the simulated patient" (p. 327). Second, outcomes research reported by Schwid and O'Donnell (1992) using an anesthesia simulator, deserves praise for reporting the finding that, " . . . anesthesiologists should review the management of emergency situations such as cardiac arrest, anaphylaxis, myocardial ischemia, and malignant hyperthermia *every 6 months to maintain the appropriate skill level*" (p. 495, emphasis added). Third, a recently reported meta-analysis of outcomes of computer-based instruction in health professions education, published by Cohen and Dacanay (1992) is a useful quantitative synthesis of research involving simulations and other computer-based modalities.

There are some circumstances where simulators are the only way to evaluate rare but potentially catastrophic events, reoccurrence of serious events, training goals that require frequent repetition and overlearning, or professional errors. When a surgeon blunders the adverse outcome can be the loss of a single life. Airline pilot errors can kill hundreds. Mistakes by a nuclear power plant operator or crew can potentially affect the population of an entire metropolitan area or geographic region. One's choices about methods of professional competence evaluation are clearly limited under such conditions.

Unresolved Issues

In summary, there are at least six unresolved issues that need intellectual and research attention to advance the field of competence assessment using simulations.

- There is a pressing need for framework or typology development to improve the classification of simulations and their features. Several obvious dimensions include degree of fidelity, individual vs. group, profession of application, and severity of problem or issue. Application of facet theory (Shye, Elizur & Hoffman, 1994) and its technology may be a useful approach to this problem.

- Criteria should be specified for judging the applicability of a simulation, a standardized patient, for example for professional assessment. What is the value added or *incremental validity* (Sechrest, 1963) of a simulation, beyond use of standard assessment tools like multiple-choice questions?

- What are the tradeoffs between high and low fidelity simulations? This is not an either/or question but an inquiry about what aspects of reality can best be simulated and how the purpose of a simulation influences the decision.

- Simulation planning and design should be more explicit and public. This is a matter of public engineering. What objectives does the simulation aim to accomplish and how do its features address the objectives?

- Tradeoffs between costs and benefits need explicit treatment. In instances like flight and spacecraft simulators this issue may be transparent. However, with many simulated professional tasks, teaching for example, the calculus may not be obvious.

- Finally, in the area of professional competence evaluation, measurement problems just won't go away. Work on basic psychometric problems will receive research attention well into the future.

Coda

Educator Gene Glass (1978) had it right when he noted nearly 20 years ago that, "A common expression of wishful thinking is to base a grand scheme on a fundamental, unsolved problem" (p. 237). This is *not* to assert that simulation technology is built on a foundation of sand, just that our ability to use it intelligently for professional competence assessment is slow to mature. Simulations are inventions, not discoveries, and the science of assessment needs to catch up with the technology of their use.

References

Altman, Irwin. 1968. "Choicepoints in the Classification of Scientific Knowledge." In *People, Groups, and Origanizations*, edited by B. P. Indik and F. K. Berrien, pp. 47-69. New York: Teachers College Press.

American Nuclear Society. 1993. *Nuclear Powerplant Simulators for Use in Operator Training and Examination: An American Natural Standard.* La Grange Park, IL: Author. (ANS/ANS-3.5-1993).

Bailey, Kenneth D. 1994. *Typologies and Taxonoimies: An Introduction to Classification Techniques.* Sage University Press Series on Quantitative Applications in the Social Sciences, 07-102. Thousands Oaks, CA: Sage

Cecchini, Arnaldo, and Frisenna, Adriana. 1987. Gaming simulation. A general classification. *Simulation/Games for Learning* 17:60-73.

Cohen, Peter A., and Dacanay, Lakshmi S. 1992. Computer-based instruction and health professions education: A meta-analysis of outcomes. *Evaluation and the Health Professions* 15:259-281.

Eldredge, David L., and Watson, Hugh J. 1996. An ongoing study of the practice of simulation in industry. *Simulation & Gaming* 27:375-386.

Elkins, David B., Kuyyakanond, Thicumporn, Maticka-Tyndale, Eleanor, Rujkorakorn, Darunee, and Haswell-Elkins, Melissa. 1996. Multisectorial strategy for AIDS prevention at community level. *World Health Forum* 17:70-74.

Eyler, A. E. et al. 1997. Teaching smoking-cessation counseling to medical students using simulated patients. *American Journal of Preventive Medicine*, 13, 153-158.

Fisher, Jeffrey D., and Fisher, William A. 1992. Changing AIDS-risk behavior. *Psychological Bulletin* 111:455-474.

Fletcher, Robert H., Fletcher, Suzanne W., and Wagner, Edward H. 1996. *Clinical Epidemiology: The Essentials*, Baltimore: Williams & Wilkins.

Fuchida, M., and Okumiya, M. 1955. *Midway: The Battle That Doomed Japan.* Annapolis, MD: United States Naval Institute.

Glass, Gene V. 1978. Standards and Criteria. *Journal of Educational Measurement* 15: 237-261.

Haertel, Edward H. 1990. "Performance Tests, Simulations, and Other Methods." In *The New Handbook of Teacher Evaluation*, edited by Jason Millman and Linda Darling-Hammond, pp. 278-294. Newbury Park, CA: Sage Publications.

Hammond, K. R. 1996. *Human Judgment and Social Policy*. New York: Oxford University Press.

Harless, William G. et al. 1990. A field test of the TIME patient simulation model. *Academic Medicine* 65:327-333.

Hausrath, A. M. 1971. *Ventures Simulation in War, Business, and Politics*. New York: McGraw-Hill.

Henry, Suzanne B., and Waltmire, Don. 1992. Computerized clinical simulations: A strategy for staff development in critical care. *American Journal of Critical Care* 1:99-107.

Houlihan, Paunpimon A., Finklestein, Michael W., and Johnson, Lynnea A. 1992. Adaptive instructional use of the DDx & Tx system. *Journal of Computer-Based Instruction* 19:125-130.

Hunt, Richard A., Hinkle, John E., Jr., and Malony, H. Newton, editors 1990. *Clergy Assessment and Career Development*. Nashville, TN: Abingdon Press.

Jachna, John S., Powsner, Seth M., McIntyre, Patrick J., and Byck, Robert. 1993. Teaching consultation psychiatry through computerized case simulation. *Academic Psychiatry* 17:36-42.

Kendall, Peter. 1997, March 9. Machines safer but there's still a human element: Error at Edison nuclear plant underscores new risk factors. *The Chicago Tribune*, p.C 1.

Keys, Bernard, and Wolfe, Joseph. 1990. The role of management games and simulations in education and research. *Journal of Management* 16:307-336.

Klein, Stephen P. and Stecher, Brian. 1991. Developing a prototype licensing examination for secondary school teachers. *Journal of Personnel Evaluation in Education* 5: 169-190.

Kryukov, M. M., and Kryukova, L. I. 1986. Toward a simulation games classification and game dialogue types. *Simulation and Games* 17:393-402.

Maticka-Tyndale, Eleanor, Elkins, David, Haswell-Elkins, Melissa, Rujkarakorn, Darunee, Kuyyakanond, Thicumporn, and Stam, Kathryn. 1997. Contexts and patterns of men's commercial sexual partnerships in northeastern Thailand: Implications for AIDS prevention. *Social Science and Medicine* 44:199-213.

Mayer, Richard E. 1997. Multimedia learning: Are we asking the right questions? *Educational Psychologist* 32(l):1-19.

Motowidlo, Stephen J., and Tippins, Nancy. 1993. Further studies of the low-fidelity simulation in the form of a situational inventory. *Journal of Occupational and Organizational Psychology* 66:337-44.

Santy, Patricia A. 1994. *Choosing the Right Stuff: The Psychological Selection of Astronauts and Cosmonauts.* Westport, CT: Praeger.

Sayre, Farrand. 1912. *Map Maneuvers and Tactical Rides,* 5th ed. Springfield, MA: Springfield Printing & Binding Co.

Schank, Roger C., and Cleary, C. 1995. *Engines for Education.* Hillsdale, N.J.: Lawrence Erlbaum Associates.

Schuler, G.D. et al. 1996. A gene map of the human genome. *Science* 274:540-546.

Schwid, Howard A., and O'Donnell, Daniel. 1992. Anesthesiologists' management of simulated critical incidents. *Anesthesiolgy* 76:495-501.

Sechrest, L. 1963. Incremental validity: A recommendation. *Educational and Psychological Measurement* 23:153-158.

Seligman, J. 1997, April 7. Presidential high: More than 50 years after a tragic wartime jump, George Bush has a happier landing. *Newsweek,* 129, 68.

Shye, Samuel, Elizur, Dov, and Hoffman, Michael. 1994. *Introduction to Facet Theory: Content Design and Intrinsic Data Analysis in Behavioral Research.* Applied Social Research Methods Series Vol. 35. Thousand Oaks, CA: Sage Publications.

Simulator trained Bush for voluntary jump. 1997, April 28. *Aviation Week & Space Technology,* 146, 62.

Spencer, L. M. and Spencer, S. M. 1993. *Competence at Work: Models for Superior Performance.* New York: John Wiley & Sons.

Streufert, Siegfried, Pogash, Rosanne, and Piasecki, Mary. 1988. Simulation-based assessment of managerial competence: Reliability and validity. *Personnel Psychology* 41:537-557.

Swanson, David B., Norman, Geoffrey R., and Linn, Robert L. 1995. Performance-based assessment: Lessons from the health professions. *Educational Researcher* 24(5):5-11,35.

Thomas, C. J. 1957. "The Genesis and Practice of Operational Gaming." In *Proceedings of the First International Conference on Operational Research*, 65-78. Baltimore: Operations Research Society of America.

Under Secretary of Defense for Acquisition and Technology, U.S. Department of Defense. 1995. *Modeling and Simulation (M&S) Master Plan*, DoD5000.59-P. Alexandria, VA: Author. (Available at http:www.dmso.mil).

Vanlehn, Kurt, Ohisson, Stellan, and Nason, Rod. 1994. Applications of simulated students: An exploration. *Journal of Artificial Intelligence in Education* 5:135-175.

Wilson, A. 1968. *The Bomb and the Computer: Wargaming From Ancient Chinese Mapboard to Atomic Computer*. New York: Delacorte.

Young, J. P. 1959. *A Survey of Historical Developments in War Games*. ORO-SP-9B (AD210865). Bethesda, MD: Johns Hopkins University, Operations Research Office.

Part Two: Prototypic Simulations from the Professions

Part Two: Prototypic Simulations from the Professions

Introduction

Part Two of this book explores various issues concerning the appropriateness, utility, and limitations of simulation for assessment of professional competence in licensure and certification. It addresses the following question: How can simulations help examiners to properly evaluate whether examinees actually think like professionals, relate to others like professionals, and behave like professionals?

Section A provides examples and discusses the advantages and disadvantages of simulation in the evaluation of various cognitive and problem-solving skills. Section B illustrates and evaluates the use of simulation in assessing communication and technical skills, and affective behavior. Section C explores the utility of simulations in assessing procedural skills and team performance.

Overall, Part Two describes the use of simulation for assessing all aspects of competency, ranging from purely intellectual skills to purely affective behavior. It offers a broad range of examples using a variety of techniques, across diverse professional settings, including law, medicine, aviation, architecture, and the military. Interestingly, the techniques and methodology utilized in simulations developed for one profession seem appropriate to many others. Although the specific content will be modified, depending on the nature of the simulation, the technology available, and the professional setting within which the evaluation is being conducted, simulations appear generally applicable and highly efficacious in professional assessment across the spectrum.

Ara Tekian

Section A: Assessing Cognitive Skills: Can They Think Like a Professional?

Section A

Assessing Cognitive Skills: Can They Think Like a Professional?

Introduction

Over the years licensure and certifying agencies have, under the guidance of measurement experts, increasingly shifted from the once almost ubiquitous unstructured oral and/or vague essay ("Discuss X") examinations widely employed in the first half of this century, to "objective" written examinations, consisting primarily of questions posed in variants of true-false and multiple choice formats.

In situations where examinations are adequately vetted by both subject matter and measurement experts, the move from "subjective" to "objective" questions has resulted in the elimination of some of the most egregious defects in certifying procedures employed in earlier times. Certainly, today's certifying examinations are more likely than their forerunners to meet reasonable psychometric standards, particularly those relating to the *reliability* of measurement. And so, we have often been lulled into believing that "we do a pretty good job" of assessing a candidate's fund of knowledge and his or her problem-solving skills.

Unfortunately, however, enhanced reproducibility (i.e., reliability) of examination results has not been accompanied by comparable increases in their *validity*. For that we must look to more basic reform—reform of the type occurring in medicine, architecture and law, as described in this Section. The examples from medicine and architecture make use of the most advanced computer technology currently available; the example from law requires nothing more high tech than a few sheets of paper and a pen. But all share a common characteristic which makes them fundamentally different from more conventional certifying examinations.

Specifically, each chapter describes a sample exercise in which the candidate is confronted with a unique, concrete situation of the type that the aspiring professional could expect to see and would need to be able to cope with in everyday practice. The example from medicine is especially useful for the kinds of situations in which the professional must make a series of sequential decisions as the problem evolves. The example from architecture is generally applicable to those cases (especially ones involving graphics) in which the professional must be able to create a unique solution that will achieve a defined goal, given specified limitations. The example from law is particularly valuable for all those situations in which the professional must perform an ordinary task that entails using specific data culled from multiple resources.

All the examples are generally useful, not only in the assessment of professional competence at the certification and licensure levels, but also in training and testing (including formative evaluation) at every level of education and experience. Their use will not tell us all we need to know about the competence of professionals, but they will tell us much more than we have known heretofore about their ability "to think like a professional" when they are trying their best to make a good impression.

Christine H. McGuire

3

Computer-Based Case Simulations from Medicine: Assessing Skills in Patient Management*

Stephen G. Clyman, Donald E. Melnick, Brian E. Clauser

The National Board of Medical Examiners (NBME) has approved a strategic plan calling for computer administration of the licensing examinations beginning in late 1999. A key element of this plan is the introduction of computer-based case simulations. In these simulations, the physician-candidate obtains information by requesting a history and/or physical examination, ordering laboratory studies, performing procedures, and requesting consultants. The examinee must combine clinical information with judgments about the acuity of the problems and responsiveness of the patient to interventions in ordering and modifying treatments. Progression of the disease and the effects of treatments must be monitored, using information about the simulated patient previously requested by the candidate. The central features of the system are the availability of thousands of patient care options, free-text entry of management plans, simulation of time, a dynamic patient response to examinee interventions, limited cuing and an automated scoring system emulating expert ratings. *The chapter describes the process of developing the system, presents specific case illustrations, discusses alternative approaches to scoring and interpreting candidate performance and identifies areas of professional competence not currently assessed by conventional licensure examinations.*

W hat is computer-based case simulation (CCS)? Primum™ CCS is a computer program, developed by the National Board of Medical Examiners of the United States, that simulates a patient with an unknown problem or health care request, and allows an examinee to care for the patient. The computer records each step in the care of the patient and scores the performance.

The physician obtains information by requesting a history and/or physical examination, ordering laboratory studies, procedures, and consultants. The doctor must balance the clinical information available with evidence of the acuity of the clinical problem in deciding what treatments to begin and when. Progression of the disease and the effects of treatments must be monitored, again using history, physical examination, and laboratory studies. Complications of the disease or treatment must be recognized and treated appropriately.

The computer simulates an environment familiar to all physicians. Orders for tests, treatments, hospitalization, etc., are written on an order sheet. The system accepts orders for thousands of different tests and treatments. A "clerk" verifies the accuracy of the orders. The patient can be seen in the office or the emergency department and/or admitted to the hospital, either to a ward or intensive care environment. The patient's chart contains the expected records as they are accumulated by the examinee: vital signs and medication records, notes describing history, physical examination, and procedures, nurses' notes, and results of tests.

A major feature of *Primum* CCS is the simulation of time. The physician controls the movement of time. The clock moves forward (and the patient's condition changes) only when the physician initiates the movement of time. Although time cannot be reversed, the movement of time can be suspended while the doctor considers the next steps. As a result, Primum CCS records physician decision-making through time in an unfolding clinical situation.

After the physician completes the care of a group of patients, the computer system compares the strategies employed with those defined by expert panels and tested with many physicians. Physicians score higher when their actions are closer to those defined as ideal. This scoring system avoids rewarding thoroughness at the expense of efficiency. Risky, dangerous, or otherwise unindicated commissions and dangerous omissions are tracked and may have a substantial impact on the final scores.

Why is the CCS format useful?

Primum CCS allows evaluation of patient care strategies. These strategies are captured in a realistic context, without artificial cues or segregation of the component tasks that make up patient management. For educational purposes, the care of patients is often segregated into individual tasks: differential diagnosis, laboratory studies, diagnosis, and treatment. However, this is a highly artificial representation of the actual sequence of events in caring for real patients.

In real life, diagnosis unfolds, often as a result of observed responses to treatment. Differential diagnosis changes from hour to hour or day to day as the available clinical information changes. Diagnosis is not an endpoint; rather, it is a tentative step in total care of the patient. Effective monitoring of changes in the patient's condition because of the disease and/or its treatment is as important as accurate diagnosis is to the outcome of the patient.

The totality of patient care is more than the simple sum of its constituent parts. The complex interplay of clinical information about the patient with time and physician action cannot be accurately and comprehensively represented and evaluated by the separation of patient care into many individual parts. Furthermore, testing methods that reduce patient care to a series of questions necessarily provide artificial cues, which become unnatural clues. These clues affect examinee responses. *Primum* CCS is designed to avoid unnatural cuing by providing only those cues that would occur in the real world.

CCS is useful, therefore, because it allows the evaluation of important patient care skills in a more realistic and integrated manner than other available testing methods.

What does Primum CCS *not* do?

Primum CCS is designed to maximize information about physician decision-making while caring for specific patients. It does not gather information regarding the adequacy of history-taking or physical examination skills. In order to simplify the computer program and scoring and because it is less germane to the objective of CCS testing, doctors are not asked to specify doses or dosing frequency when ordering drugs. The examinee is not asked to make a diagnosis currently; rather, comprehensive care of the patient is emphasized. An enhancement under review will require entry of a diagnosis at key points.

The patient in CCS responds to treatment as defined by the author of the case. *Primum* CCS does not apply a probabilistic algorithm in deciding how the patient responds to a given intervention. This feature, while unlike the real world, assures that the stimulus presented to each examinee who cares for the patient in the same manner is identical.

Because of the high cost and limited availability of image and sound delivery technology, *Primum* CCS does not currently present visual images or sounds. Early versions successfully incorporated the presentation of images for common examination and test results. These features can be activated again when they are deemed useful and cost effective, and the test administration infrastructure makes it feasible. Use of a short motion video is under investigation for display at the beginning of the case to convey the patient's overall condition, body habitus, and comfort level.

How does a *Primum* case work?

A *Primum* case begins with a brief statement of the patient's presenting complaint. The examinee then must specify what kind of information is to be obtained next: history, physical examination, tests, or treatments. When the examinee initiates some actions that require simulated time to complete, such as physical examination or history, time automatically advances by the amount required to complete the action and the findings are displayed. For other actions, such as most diagnostic studies, the examinee is notified of the time when results will be available. The examinee then advances the clock to or past that time, and the results of the test are displayed. When a treatment is ordered, no additional information is provided automatically. As in real life, the examinee must initiate appropriate monitoring.

The examinee can move the patient from location to location as desired. Each location presents the patient care opportunities and limitations that would be present in real life. Sometimes, clock advances are interrupted by realistic messages regarding the patient's condition: nurses' notification of patient status if the patient is hospitalized, calls from the patient or patient's family if the patient is an outpatient.

As the physician indicates choices in caring for the patient, the computer recomputes test results and selects appropriate text for reports based on the untreated disease, as programmed by the case author, and the cumulative effects of actions taken. Whenever the examinee asks for information by talking to or examining the patient or ordering additional tests, these dynamically updated results are displayed.

The doctor continues to care for the patient, ordering tests and examinations to monitor the patient's evolving condition and initiating treatments to intervene. At a time preselected by the case author, the examinee is thanked for caring for this patient, and another patient is presented. Throughout this process, the examinee's actions have been recorded and time-stamped. When the examination is scored, this list of examinee transactions is compared with various care strategies considered effective by experts. Credit is assigned based on the relative acceptability of the strategies employed.

How does CCS compare with other testing methods?

CCS complements simulations using standardized patients (SPs). Whereas SPs gather information about conversational, behavioral, and psychomotor elements of the physician-patient interaction, *Primum* CCS gathers information about patient care that follows that encounter: the interpretation of history and physical examination information, synthesis into a working diagnosis, use of laboratory studies in a timely, efficient, logical, and sequential fashion, initiation of treatment at the appropriate point, and understanding of the evolving disease course through monitoring and other appropriate intervention.

SP simulations do not effectively assess care of the patient over time, and they are relatively inefficient at gathering information regarding diagnosis and treatment. On the other hand, the SP method has the unique capacity to effectively assess   history-taking, physical examination, and patient communication skills. CCS largely ignores the latter skills, but assesses patient care over time effectively. Preliminary study comparing performance on SPs and CCS show low to moderate correlation.

Multiple-choice questions (MCQs) are highly efficient at assessing application of information in a constrained situation. They allow efficient sampling of broad domains, producing highly reproducible measures. However, no matter how clinically oriented they are, MCQs do not allow the presentation of dynamically unfolding clinical case presentations without artificially cuing the examinee. Studies comparing student performance on CCS and MCQs are described below. Of particular note is the finding that some students who would pass MCQ examinations do poorly on CCS examinations and would likely fail. The converse is also true. Thus, each method seems to provide unique information about the examinee and contributes to the mastery/non-mastery decision.

How is *Primum* CCS scored?

Scoring refers to the application of patient care criteria defined by experts to examinee actions, producing a measure of examinee performance. *Primum* scoring is expert based; details of processes used in optimal patient care are elicited from content specialists and serve as the basis for the scoring key. This approach was adopted after consideration of and experimentation with other scoring methods, such as analyses of examinee progress at key points or case end, or approaches measuring efficiency of information-obtaining behavior.

Expert opinion is used prospectively rather than retrospectively. This means that experts define criteria for performance before examinees care for the *Primum* patient. In the ideal setting, perfectly reliable content experts would review each examinee's patient management actions and classify performance as passing or failing. In practice, this would require huge numbers of physicians that would be prohibitively expensive and impractical; great efficiencies are introduced if the computer can perform this review instead of humans. In fact, experts' performance criteria are entered into the computer, compared with examinee performance, and the computer produces mechanically accurate results, thus removing one source of rater unreliability.

The goal of *Primum* scoring is for the computer to rate performance with a result that resembles that produced by expert physician judges, but with reasonable cost and score reporting times. The next section describes the processes by which the computer emulates expert physician scoring.

Input to scoring

CCS provides a rich source of physician performance information, including carefully considered sequencing and ranking of patient care decisions. A record of these decisions is maintained as the *Primum* transaction list. When the case is completed, the Primum transaction list represents an accurate, detailed audit trail of the step-by-step decisions made by the physician managing the patient.

An example of a transaction list is shown below. The left column lists the simulated time at which the examinee initiated the action. The far right column lists the simulated time at which a result was seen by the examinee. For example, the CBC with differential was ordered at day 1 at 10:35am. The examinee did not see the result until day 2 at 10:35am. Sequential decision making is revealed by noting actions ordered based on results of other actions already seen by that time.

The transaction list, representing a physician's decision making in a complex, uncued simulation, is reduced to a score by comparison with the scoring key.

CASE TRANSACTION LIST

Examinee ID: 123-45-6789   Case ID:77   Date: 11/10/93

Ordered Day Hour	Action	Seen Day Hour
1 @ 10:00	History, comprehensive	1 @ 10:20
1 @ 10:20	Physical exam, complete	1 @ 10:35
1 @ 10:35	Cholesterol, serum	1 @ 18:35
1 @ 10:35	Electrocardiography, 12 lead	1 @ 11:05
1 @ 10:35	Chemistry profile 12	1 @ 13:05
1 @ 10:35	CBC with differential	2 @ 10:35
1 @ 10:35	Chemistry profile 6	1 @ 13:05
1 @ 10:35	Skin test, tuberculin	Case ended before result seen
1 @ 10:35	Abstain from alcohol	
1 @ 10:35	No smoking	
1 @ 11:05	Location change to Home	
1 @ 11:05	Consult, psychiatry	2 @ 11:05
2 @ 10:35		
2 @ 19:00	History, interval/follow up	2 @ 19:05
2 @ 19:05	Location change to Inpatient Ward	
2 @ 19:05	Cardiac monitor	2 @ 19:05
2 @ 19:05	Pacemaker, permanent	
2 @ 19:05	History, interval/follow up	2 @ 19:18
2 @ 19:05	Temperature	2 @ 19:18
2 @ 19:05	General appearance	2 @ 19:18
2 @ 19:05	Cardiac examination	2 @ 19:18
2 @ 19:05	Extremities examination	2 @ 19:18
2 @ 19:05	Neurologic/psych examination	2 @ 19:18
2 @ 19:05	Vital signs (MD recorded)	2 @ 19:18
2 @ 19:05	Cardiac monitor	Case ended before result seen
2 @ 21:05	Case end	

Scoring key

The scoring key contains criteria for performance on a *Primum* case. It reduces the transaction list to a string of numbers representing the examinee's observed response to the test "questions;" this reduction is the first step in scoring.

A scoring key is produced by a group of expert physicians who manage the case as an unknown without any prior knowledge of the case. They manage the patient as if they were examinees. The content experts represent the range of primary care, generalist medicine. In interdisciplinary groups of three or four, they discuss the patient's problem and alternate approaches to care of the patient. When they reach consensus, their actions are recorded by NBME staff and classified as follows:

Benefit:	- three levels (most, more and least important)
	- appropriate for patient care
	- distinguishes better examinees from less effective examinees
Inappropriate:	- three levels (nonharmful, risky, and extremely dangerous)
	- not indicated in the care of the patient
	- ranges from extraneous testing to missing the measurement objective of the case

Scoring items are defined by action logic, which is based on relative merit, sequence, and relative timing of actions. For example, an item might simply require that the examinee order an action (if an abdominal ultrasound ordered, score +1). Or, it might award credit based on the type of abdominal imaging study ordered (if an abdominal CT ordered, score +2; if an abdominal ultrasound ordered, score +1). Action combinations (if abdominal ultrasound and chest x-ray ordered, score +1), sequence (if blood cultures ordered before antibiotics, score +1), and timing (if abdominal ultrasound ordered in the first hour, score +2; if ordered after the first hour, score +1) can be defined, also. More complex items are possible by combining different action logic.

Actions classified in this way represent the "items" on a *Primum* test. The approach to aggregating these item responses to produce a score that validly represents the examinee's performance has undergone considerable evolution. Early efforts to score CCS demonstrated that a reasonable score could be produced by simply summing the beneficial actions ordered and subtracting from this sum the total number of non-indicated actions. This approach was improved by accounting for the variation in item difficulty by calibrating items using the Rasch (item response theory) model and by allowing for partial credit (based on the timing of the action of other item related considerations).

Although this score had demonstrated validity, it had the limitation that it disregarded the relative importance of the various item types. The most critical and most trivial actions had the same weight. Subsequently, two approaches to scoring have been developed in an explicit attempt to capture the judgment policy used by experts in rating examinee performance. The first of these used a regression-based policy capturing procedure. Weights for the various item types were estimated by using expert ratings of transaction lists as the dependent measure and the number of items in each category (i.e., inappropriates, risks, benefits, etc.) as the independent measures in a regression equation. The estimated regression weights were then used to weight items to compute scores. The resulting score was shown to be both more highly correlated with the actual ratings than were the previously used scores and to be superior in discriminating between examinees displaying passing and failing performance based on independent judgment of the performance.

This line of research demonstrated that a more valid score could be produced by weighting items based on the relative importance of the actions that they represented. However, this approach failed to account fully for the possible interaction of actions in the process of managing a case. Two diagnostic procedures in combination may not provide the same degree of benefit as two other diagnostic procedures of equal beneficial weight. This statistical or actuarial approach to scoring could result, in theory, in some examinees receiving inflated scores. To respond to this limitation, a second approach was studied which attempted to relate scores directly to patterns of behavior. Again, the intention was to capture the policy used by experts in judging (rating) transaction lists. This approach avoids the need to base scores on a sum of items, weighted or otherwise.

This second approach to scoring also has other important advantages. Because the approach is substantive (i.e., based on the structure of the case) rather than actuarial (i.e., based on estimates of characteristics of a population) it is largely independent of the sample of examinees who completed the test. This results in a scoring system that should be invariant across potential populations of examinees. It also means that the scoring algorithm can be developed prior to test administration. This could be a substantial advantage in allowing for rapid score reporting.

Research on the performance of this "substantive" approach to scoring shows that (as with the regression-based procedure) it is more highly correlated to the actual ratings than were earlier scoring methods and that it is substantially more useful than the earlier scores in discriminating between performance independently judged by experts. Currently, a combination of approaches is being investigated for operational use.

Is CCS valid?

The "validity" of the information derived from any examination is dependent on its intended use. Informed evaluative judgments are made based on theoretical rationales and empirical evidence. *Primum* CCS measure validity can be evaluated by examining test content, construct related evidence, score characteristics and consequences.

Test Content: Content expertise

The foundation for any validity claims for *Primum* scores is the expertise of case, scoring key, and standard setting committee members. Physicians—committee members of the National Board of Medical Examiners not completely satisfied with multiple choice questions or with alternate performance assessment methods—designed *Primum* CCS. Their desire was to observe performance in a realistic setting, bypassing the limitations and problems of oral examinations, bedside observation, and other patient management problems. The result of this desire, after twenty-five years of research with physicians and educators, is *Primum* CCS.

Content experts refine the features of individual case simulations; they specify the competencies, problems, and diagnoses tested; they select sets of patient problems that best meet defined test objectives; they define how patient problems will unfold based on examinee intervention; their patient management strategies are used to build scoring criteria; they interpret examinee performance as part of key validation; their judgment policies are used to determine item weighting and ultimately the rank ordering of examinees; and their judgment is emulated in setting pass-fail standards at both case and examination levels.

Construct related evidence: Training level performance/Comparisons with other measures

Comparisons of performance at different levels of training have shown that physicians more advanced in training achieve higher scores than physicians not as advanced in training.

Comparison with reliable measures like MCQs shows correlations (corrected for unreliability) between .35 and .55. This could be interpreted in many ways. It likely suggests that *Primum* CCS and MCQs measure related constructs.

Comparisons of those identified as failing by the two formats yield groups that differ; CCS and MCQs identify many different examinees as failing.

Score characteristics: Emulating physician rating/Other factors

By far, the strongest argument for the meaning of CCS measures is the fact that *Primum* scoring emulates physician ratings of examinee transaction lists. If the simulation is a faithful depiction of a clinical scenario, and if physicians behave with it as they do with real patients, then the score is a meaningful reproduction of how expert physicians would rate other physicians in that patient care setting. Reliability is discussed under "Are *Primum* scores reliable?"

CCS research has been conducted to ensure that factors extraneous to the examinee's patient management skills do not affect performance. While research continues, studies to date have shown that computer experience, computer anxiety, gender, and field dependence do not influence the performance measures obtained from CCS in any systematic manner. Research has shown the need for examinees to practice with *Primum* cases before being tested. Many examinees require managing three to four CCS patients before their scores stabilize.

Consequential validity

Increasingly, validity theorists are arguing that the consequences, intended or unintended, of an examination must be taken into account in evaluating the validity of the scores derived from its use. This argument often pertains to evaluating performance assessment formats that require more testing time of more complex items. Not that performance assessments should be held to lower standards for validation, but rather that the consequences of their use be used equally in evaluating their merits. *Primum* CCS, with its problem-oriented and patient-oriented format, might have salutary implications for instruction and self learning. Evidence of consequential validity has to await effects observed after *Primum* CCS is used in a setting where the scores have consequences.

Are Primum scores reliable?

Examination results should be reproducible so that the measures are a stable estimate of a person's ability. More importantly, it is vital that the margin of error in the score is as small as possible at the point dividing passing from failing performance. Performance assessments inherently require more time for administration than traditional written tests. The measure of reliability or accuracy at the pass-fail point for any test is dependent in large part on the number of problems encountered by the examinee. Because each problem is complex (compared with an MCQ), it requires more time on an item by item basis. To approach the reliability of MCQ tests, CCS requires more time. To achieve acceptable accuracy, a CCS examination may require from 8 to 16 simulations depending on the content area assessed and the intended use of the measures. This represents 4-8 hours of testing time. Reliability issues are discussed in more detail elsewhere (Clauser, Swanson, Clyman, 1996).

Is nationwide administration feasible?

NBME has seven years of experience with computer-based testing in medical schools in the United States and Canada. About half the schools have used sets of cases in a nontesting setting. A subset of those schools has used CCS to assess students in clinical clerkships. Some schools have the available resources to administer CCS; others do not. While facilities within schools are commonly adequate for testing, the lack of standardization of facilities across schools raises questions of comparability of test environments and security of test materials. Greater standardization of facilities will likely be required for *Primum* CCS use in licensure assessment. Standardized facilities have been developed by commercial vendors and are already being used by organizations administering licensing and aptitude examinations. In these facilities, careful attention has been paid to security of the testing system.

What is the plan for use of CCS?

The National Board of Medical Examiners and the Federation of State Medical Boards, the parent organizations of the United States Medical Licensing Examinations, plan to administer the examinations through a commercial vendor solely by computer beginning as early as late 1998. As part of that plan, *Primum* CCS will be administered in USMLE Step 3 as a complement to MCQs. In keeping with current procedures, USMLE Steps 1 and 2 will be administered at sites worldwide; USMLE Step 3 will be administered in the United States. Planning for those administrations is underway, and final approval by USMLE governance is pending.

Use of CCS for evaluation of medical students as part of intramural assessment is also under development. Implementation in USMLE will be followed by use in medical schools for evaluating student performance at the completion of clinical clerkships or at other milestones at the school's discretion.

Additionally, other members of the medical and allied health professions have expressed interest in using *Primum* CCS or modifying it for related purposes. Two NBME client organizations are researching *Primum* CCS or an adaptation of it for use in their respective certification and licensure examinations.

References

Clauser, B. E., Swanson, D. B., and Clyman, S. G. 1996. The generalizability of scores from a performance assessment of physicians' patient management skills. *Academic Medicine* 71(10 Suppl): S109-S111.

Suggested Readings

Clauser, B. E., and Clyman, S. G. 1994. A contrasting group approach to standard setting for performance assessments of clinical skills. Proceedings of the Thirty-third Annual Conference of Research in Medical Education. *Academic Medicine* 69(10):S42-S44.

Clauser, B.E., Clyman, S. G., Swanson, D. B. 1999. Components of rater error in a complex performance assessment. *Journal of Educational Measurement* 36(1): 29-45.

Clauser, B. E., Ross, L. P., Clyman, S. G. et al. 1997. Development of a scoring algorithm to replace expert rating for scoring a complex performance-based assessment. *Applied Measurement in Education* 10(4): 345-358.

Clauser, B. E., Subhiyah, R., Nungester, R. J., Ripkey, D. R., Clyman, S. G., and McKinley, D. 1995. Scoring a performance-based assessment by modeling the judgments of experts. *Journal of Educational Measurement* 32(4): 397-415.

Messick, S. 1992. The Interplay of Evidence and Consequences in the Validation of Performance Assessment. Research Report RR-92-39 *Educational Testing Service*, Princeton, NJ.

Moss, P. A. 1992. Shifting Conceptions of Validity in Educational Measurement. *Review of Educational Research* 62(3): 229-258.

National Board of Medical Examiners' Computer-Based Examination Clinical Simulation (CBX). Spring 1991. *National Board of Medical Examiners*, Philadelphia, PA.

Swanson, D. B., Norcini, J. J. and Grosso, L. 1987. Assessment of clinical competence: written and computer-based simulations. *Assessment and Evaluation in Higher Education* 12(3): 220-246.

Note: This article represents the state of the project in 1997. More recent publications (see Clauser 1999 above) are available. Also, *Primum* is now a registered trademark of NBME.

41

4

Computerized Design Problems in Architecture: The New Licensure Examination

Jeffrey F. Kenney

This chapter describes the nature, development and scoring of the Architect Registration Examination now required for licensure in the United States and Canada. Introduced in February, 1997, this new test is one of the most complex ever administered and scored on a computer platform. It consists, in effect, of presenting the examinee with a series of simulated "commissions" to design various types of buildings for specified uses, together with all the accoutrement (e.g., roads, driveways, parking, appropriate support facilities and amenities, etc.) on a site with defined characteristics (and problems). Using computer graphics, the candidate creates a design and a set of specifications for each of the required structures, locates them on the site in appropriate relation to each other and performs other tasks relevant to the particular problems posed. The chapter describes and illustrates specific examination tasks presenting varied challenges, describes the current approach to scoring candidate responses, and demonstrates how standards of acceptable performance are set.

Licensure Process for Architects

In order to talk about the licensure examination for architects, it is important to understand the process through which architects proceed to become licensed. Since the licensure of professionals is left to the states in the United States and to provinces in Canada, there is no single process that applies to all jurisdictions. Currently, 32 states, the District of Columbia, Puerto Rico, the Commonwealth of the Northern Mariana Islands and all Canadian provinces require architects to hold an accredited degree in architecture,[1] but the states with the largest numbers of architects—California and New York-do not require formal education beyond a high school diploma. The next step in the process required by most states is completion of an internship period. In the states that require a professional degree and in Canada, this is usually a three-year requirement fulfilled by working for a registered architect. During these three years, interns are expected to develop the skills they will need to practice architecture without supervision once they are licensed. In the states where no professional degree is required, longer internships are required for those individuals who do not have a formal education in architecture (8 years in California and 12 in New York, for example). Finally, all U.S. states and territories as well as the Canadian provinces[2] require the successful completion of the Architect Registration Examination (A.R.E.). The A.R.E. is composed of nine separate divisions, each of which can be passed independently. Six of these divisions are administered using a Computerized Mastery Test format and the remaining three divisions are administered using graphic simulations of parts of the architectural design process. This chapter will discuss the system used to administer the three graphic divisions of the A.R.E.

---

[1] As of July 1, 1996   [2] Except Quebec

Research and Development Project

In 1985, the National Council of Architectural Registration Boards (NCARB) began a research project to determine whether it would be possible to administer a paper-and-pencil graphic simulation examination on a computer. At that time the profession of architecture was beginning to see the movement of architectural drawings from the hand-drawn method used for centuries to a computer-assisted drawing method. In 1985, only the largest architectural firms in North America were using CAD (Computer Assisted Drafting) software in their offices. The biggest barrier to widespread use of CAD was the cost of the hardware. The limited amount of software that was available was fairly sophisticated for the time, but few firms could afford to purchase the hardware needed to use CAD.

NCARB began this project by discussing a research plan with the Research Department at ETS. The two organizations first looked at the commercial CAD programs that were then available. It was quickly determined that existing CAD programs would probably not serve the examination very well. These programs were designed to assist architects in the preparation of construction documents (drawings and specifications) but were not well suited for measuring an individual's abilities related to the NCARB and the registration board's licensure decision. CAD systems allow architects to create building drawings from a series of lines and notes, but these systems can't intelligently determine what the lines represent. It takes a human reading the drawings to interpret the meaning of the lines and notes. If commercially available CAD systems had been used, it would have meant the continuation of NCARB's traditional process of assembling architects every year and training them to grade examinations.

While reviewing CAD programs, researchers also reviewed the status of research being conducted in other professions that were trying to develop computer-administered free-response examinations. NCARB was fortunate to be greatly assisted in this review by the National Board of Medical Examiners (NBME). The NBME shared their work with NCARB's Research Committee and consultants from Educational Testing Service (ETS). The Committee was impressed with the work the NBME had done on their medical licensure examination, but knew that their mostly text-based delivery of scenarios would not work well for an architectural examination—a very visual test.

In 1987 and 1988, ETS developed new concepts for the exam and presented the first prototype to NCARB's Board of Directors. The Board approved the ETS prototype and agreed to proceed with development of the computer-based test.

Initially the test evaluated not only the candidates' solutions, but also the way they arrived at their decisions. The first computer interface used two monitors. On one monitor the candidate created a solution to the problem and on the second monitor the candidate had access to a library of reference materials that might be found in a typical architect's office. In this design a candidate's movement through the supplied references was tracked to see if he or she took an appropriate path in arriving at a decision. For example, if a problem required a candidate to select a steel beam for a particular span, the scoring system would check to see that the candidate performed a calculation (candidates were provided with an on-screen calculator) and then looked at beam selection tables. After a year of pilot testing this delivery system, it was determined that tracking the decision path a candidate took would be impossible, since the scoring system couldn't evaluate the things a candidate knew and therefore never looked for in reference materials. In this example, it was entirely possible that a candidate didn't need to look in the beam selection charts because the candidate already knew, from his or her professional experiences, a correct beam to select. In the early model it had been assumed that the scoring system would not only reward candidates who went directly to the correct reference but would also penalize candidates who looked at references that should be useless in solving the problem they were solving. In the beam selection example, it was entirely possible that a candidate who knew which beam to select would use the extra time to browse the references supplied simply to become more familiar with them for later sections of the test. NCARB didn't want to penalize a candidate who just happened to be browsing through the materials that they knew they didn't need. That led NCARB's Research Committee to determine that the scoring system would not evaluate the path used by a candidate to arrive at a solution, but only the correctness of the final solution.

In this first draft of a test design, the NCARB Research Committee members and ETS staff envisioned a test that encompassed "a day in the life of an architect." They anticipated a test where one problem would start, a phone would ring, taking the candidate to a higher priority task that required the candidate to juggle priorities. The Committee quickly determined that while this type of test might have great face validity, it did not test the knowledge, skills and abilities that were important in the licensing of architects. Architects practice their profession with different time pressures than other professions, such as those in the medical fields. Architects have the luxury of making a design decision and thinking it over for days before committing it to paper and even then they usually have many months in which to refine that initial decision. So the Committee determined that to test candidates in a one-day test on decisions that in reality they would have months to refine was not a fair representation of architectural practice. The ability to prioritize one's work day is important in an employment decision, but it is not important in the decision of whether or not to issue that individual a license. This decision led to the design of a series of vignettes, or small design problems, targeted at specific skills and abilities.

The design of the vignettes proved to be a fairly easy task for the architects on the Research Committee to accomplish. By 1990, a large battery of vignettes was available and the ETS staff had been able to implement most of these vignettes on a computer-delivery system. Since NCARB had just completed a practice analysis in 1988, the Research Committee took a break from designing the test in 1990 and looked at what had been created and what needed to be created based on the results of the practice analysis. This led to dropping a few vignettes and identifying other areas where the Committee needed to create new vignettes (See Figure 1).

Comparison to Practice Analysis

	Vignette 1	Vignette 2	Vignette 3	Vignette 4	Vignette 5
Task 1	■	■	■		□
Task 2		■		■	
Task 3	□	□	■	□	
Task 4			□	□	■
Task 5		□		□	■

Key to Symbols:
■ The task is dealt with in a major way in the vignette
□ The task is dealt with in a minor way in the vignette
(blank) The task is not dealt with in the vignette

Figure 1

Concurrently with the review of the vignettes for content, a subcommittee focused on developing scoring systems for the automated vignettes. Early studies (Bejar, 1991 and Oltman, Bejar & Kim, 1993) into what was already being done with paper-and-pencil vignette-based testing helped the Research Committee focus on how to score computer-administered vignettes. Combining both the better understanding of the paper-and-pencil vignettes that came from early work at ETS and NCARB's typical grading process for these exams, the Research Committee determined that it could break each candidate's solution into distinct parts, or features.

Test Design

The computer-delivered Architect Registration Examination's three graphic divisions all use a similar interface, designed and tested over many years. The interface was designed to be as intuitive as possible, requiring candidates to invest only a small amount of time learning the interface. NCARB's goal, as is the case with almost all examinations, was to test the knowledge, skills and abilities of the candidates in architecture and not to test interface use. Figure 2 shows the first screen that a candidate sees when a vignette starts. On this screen candidates can move the mouse pointer to one of the items highlighted with bold text and move to that information. Figure 3 shows a program for the block diagram vignette. Candidates use this programmatic information to create their solutions.

Reference Screen

NCARB A.R.E.

| Index | Task Information |

Block Diagram Vignette

All of the information you will need to develop your solution can be accessed through this Index screen.

Click on one of the following to select:

Vignette Directions
Program
Tree Diagrams
Tips

To access this screen while you are working, simply press the space bar. When this screen appears, click on the topic you wish to view.

To return to the Index from one of the topics, click on the Index button that appears at the top of the screen.

To go to the work screen, press the space bar.

Review the General Test Directions

Figure 2

Block Diagram program

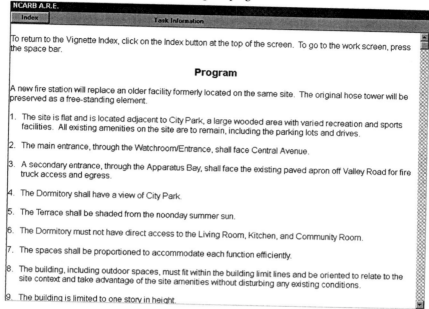

Figure 3

The only keyboard entry possible with this system is using the space bar to toggle between the reference screens (Figures 2 and 3) and the work screen (Figure 4). Figure 4 shows a blank work screen with only background drawings displayed. The work screen has multiple areas, each designed for a different purpose. The majority of the screen is reserved for the candidate's solution. The icons along the left edge of the screen allow candidates to draw items, manipulate items, increase the magnification of the work area, etc. The icons along the upper left portion of the screen are designed specifically for the vignette being worked on, in this case, the block diagram vignette. The icons along the bottom left portion of the screen are tools that work the same in all vignettes. The two bars along the bottom of the screen supply the candidate with specific information related to the item they are working on (top bar) and help information specific to the tool they are using (bottom bar).

Figure 5 shows a completed block diagram vignette[3]. In early trials, some candidates worked exclusively on the screen using all of the tools provided to create their solutions. Other candidates used the scratch paper that was provided to them and then transferred their solution to the screen. Either method is acceptable, as long as the candidate completes his or her solution on screen so that it can be scored.

[3] All screens shown here are black and white, however, the actual computer monitor use colors and therefore it is easier to distinguish between the background drawings and the candidate's solution.

Block Diagram work screen

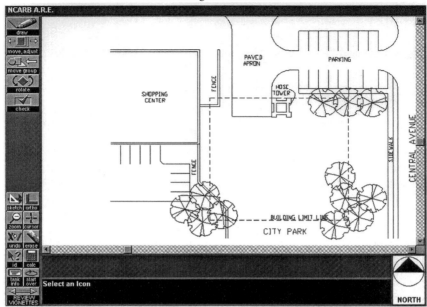

Figure 4

Block Diagram work screen with completed solution

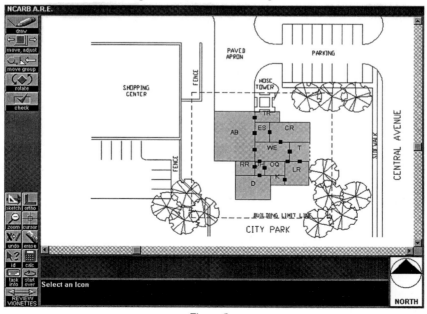

Figure 5

Scoring Methodology

An easy way to discuss the NCARB scoring system is to explain the terms used in this process.

A.R.E. Division

There are three graphic divisions of the Architect Registration Examination. They are: Site Planning, Building Planning, and Building Technology. Candidates receive either a "Pass" or "Fail" score for each division, along with diagnostic information that identifies the vignettes within the division where they could benefit most from additional study.

Vignette

Each of the three divisions is made up of a series of vignettes. All candidates take all of the vignettes within a division. The Site Planning division is composed of six vignettes. The Building Planning division is composed of three vignettes. The Building Technology division is composed of six vignettes.

Division Score

Each of the three graphic divisions is scored pass or fail. To arrive at the score for the division the scores on the various vignettes that make up that division are accumulated. The vignettes are given weights that relate to the specific importance of each vignette's tasks.

Script

In order to offer the exam on multiple days of the year, there is a large library of various versions of each vignette. For example, in the Block Diagram vignette, within the Building Planning division, candidates lay out a schematic floor plan for a one-story building. One script for this vignette might describe the plans for a small community library. Another script might be for a bank or a post office.

Isomorph

To add to the number of variations of a vignette, minor changes are made to each script so that the time and effort involved in setting up a script is used to its maximum advantage. In the previous example, the library script for the Block Diagram vignette can be modified to include a rare books room in one isomorph or a drive-through book drop in another. Additionally, the site plan for the building can be rotated 90 degrees to come up with three additional isomorphs. The site-plan changes, in combination with changes in the number or names of rooms, can produce a large library of isomorphs with relatively little additional effort. It is important to create isomorphs that result in solutions that look different and seem different to the candidates, but that require the same amount of work on the part of the candidates and are of equal difficulty levels.

Weight

Everything scored is assigned a weight based on relative importance. At the highest level of scoring, the individual vignettes are assigned a weight relative to all other vignettes in that division. NCARB only uses whole numbers for these weights and they rarely exceed four. Therefore, in a division with six vignettes, one of the vignettes may be assigned a weight of three, three of the vignettes assigned a weight of two and the remaining two vignettes assigned a weight of one. This results in eleven scoring points that have to be accumulated into the pass/fail decision. At lower levels of scoring, there may be only two features being studied and both may have a weight of one, resulting in only two scoring points.

Vignette Score

Each vignette is assigned a score of acceptable, unacceptable or indeterminate. (Bejar and Braun, 1994) The first two scores mean that the candidate has demonstrated either an acceptable or unacceptable level of performance on the vignette. The indeterminate score means that the candidate's level of performance on the vignette is neither clearly acceptable or unacceptable. This score allows the scoring system to avoid severely penalizing candidates who demonstrate marginal, but not acceptable levels of performance. The vignette score is arrived at by combining the scores on a number of major task groupings. Each one of these major groupings has a score assigned to it—again, acceptable, indeterminate and unacceptable are used. The scoring system also uses weights for each grouping, just as is done at the higher level of scoring— the division score.

Feature

The lowest level of scoring is the feature (Bejar and Braun, 1994). Each feature covers a topic that the vignette is designed to address. In some cases the feature is for something easy to quantify such as, "did the candidate provide all nine rooms in the building?" In other cases, the feature may look at whether a patio receives noon day sunlight. Some features deal with the relationships of objects that the candidate draws or places in his or her solution, such as the ability for building users to get from the lobby to each space in the building. One important life-safety feature of scoring these solutions might be a check on whether the candidate provided a fire-resistant wall assembly between a corridor and an occupied room. In each case, the architects on NCARB committees developed rules for how to score the feature and the programmers at ETS implemented the rules.

Feature Tree

For every vignette, a map of the scoring features is created using branches starting with the vignette score at the top and breaking down into major task groupings, then breaking each of these groupings into smaller and smaller branches (Bejar and Braun, 1994). Each vignette is unique in its number of branches and the depth of these branches. A sample tree is shown here where "F_x" is the number of a feature and "M_x" is the number of a matrix. Each feature "F" and matrix "M" is assigned a score of either acceptable "A," indeterminate "I," or unacceptable "U."

Feature Tree

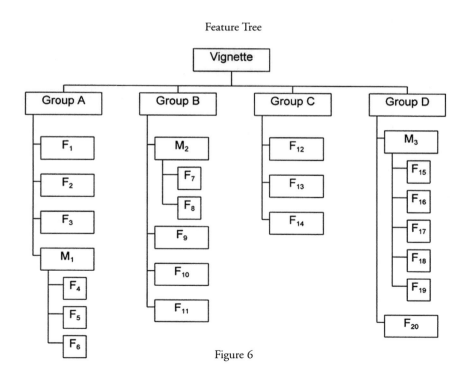

Figure 6

Feature Cluster

Features are clustered into logical groupings to allow for a simplified discussion of the importance of one feature against another. While it is possible for the computer to analyze all of the features in a very short time period, the humans who have to program the scoring rules need to break the task down into smaller manageable pieces (Bejar and Braun, 1994). Every feature cluster results in a matrix to assign a score to the accumulated features within the cluster.

Matrix

At all levels of the feature tree, a matrix is used to map out a group of features into a sub-score or vignette score (Bejar and Braun, 1994; Bejar, 1995). The matrix shown in figure 7 maps the number of unacceptable scores assigned across the top row and the number of indeterminate scores assigned along the left column. Since each feature mapped through the matrix has a weight, the number of unacceptable or indeterminate from each feature is multiplied by the weight assigned to that feature. In this example, three features from the feature tree are being analyzed in Matrix number 1 (M_1). Feature number 4 (F_4) is assigned a weight of one, F_5 is assigned a weight of 2 and F_6 is assigned a weight of 2. The decision on which features are assigned which weights is made in committee where the architects working on the project debate the relative importance of each feature in relation to the other features within the feature cluster being studied and arrive at a consensus. In this example, F_5 has only two possible scores—acceptable (A) and unacceptable (U). At the lowest level of scoring there is not always an indeterminate score. For example, if one of the features being scored is, "Did the candidate draw a parking lot?" the only two possible scores are "A" for yes she did or "U" for no she didn't.

To fill out the cells of the matrix, the Research Committee members discuss the features to be evaluated and the weight assigned to each. They then debate the score for each cell in the matrix and arrive at consensus. The first cell in all matrixes represents 0 unacceptable scores and 0 indeterminate scores. Since this means that a candidate did not have any errors, a score of "A" (acceptable) is always assigned. Moving down one cell, a solution that receives 0 unacceptable scores and 1 indeterminate score is discussed. Since only one feature (F_4) in this example is assigned a weight of one, the only possible combination of scores is an indeterminate score on F_4 and acceptable scores on F_5 and F_6. In this example, the Research Committee members assigned a score of acceptable. Again moving down, the cell that represents 0 unacceptable scores and 2 indeterminate scores is evaluated. Here, F_6 received an indeterminate score and F_5 received an acceptable score (the reverse cannot be true since F_5 can only receive acceptable or unacceptable scores). In addition, F_4 received an acceptable score. In this case the members of the Research Committee assigned a score of indeterminate to the matrix cell. This process continues until the matrix is complete. In some cases, scores are not possible in a given cell. In the 1 unacceptable, 1 indeterminate, cell no score is possible, since there is only one feature (F_4) with a weight of one, and that feature must have a score of either acceptable, indeterminate, or unacceptable. It can't have two scores.

Scoring Matrix M₁

Feature	Weight	Possible Scores		
F_4	1	A	I	U
F_5	2	A		U
F_6	2	A	I	U

		Number of Unacceptables					
		0	1	2	3	4	5
Number	0	A	I	I	U	U	U
of	1	A		I		U	
Indeterminates	2	I	I	U	U		
	3	I		U			

Cells that are blank represent combinations of indeterminates and unacceptables that are not possilbe

Figure 7

Scoring Summary

All of the parts of the scoring system are organized in a hierarchical fashion. The lowest level piece of information—the feature—has rules that are specified by NCARB committees and implemented by the computer programmers. Scores on each feature (acceptable, indeterminate or unacceptable) are accumulated in feature clusters, through the use of a matrix. Clusters of features and other individual features are grouped together on the feature tree to arrive at a score for each of the major groups of features. These scores are then combined, again using a matrix to arrive at a score for the vignette. Finally, all of the vignettes within a division of the A.R.E. are given weights, and the scores on each are reviewed with a pass or fail score assigned to each of the possible scoring profiles.

The scoring system created by NCARB and ETS has proven to be an easy system for new committee members and the members of the state boards of architecture to understand. This is important, since NCARB needs to have its membership support it in any testing system it develops. If the members of the boards of architecture didn't feel comfortable that the scoring system was fair and equitable, the test would not be administered to candidates.

In February 1996, NCARB administered these vignettes to approximately 250 candidates in seven U.S. and Canadian jurisdictions. Following the test administration, a team of architects was assembled to develop holistic grading criteria. This group was not given access to the computer scoring programs, so they developed grading criteria that were similar to the criteria used in the past for paper-and-pencil grading. The criteria developed by this committee were used to train another group of architect-graders using a computer interface developed by ETS. The architects were trained to grade individual vignettes by assigning a score of 0 (for a totally blank vignette), 1, 2, 3, or 4, where 4 is the highest score. This scoring system had been used for many years by NCARB to grade paper-and-pencil examinations. Concurrently, the vignette solutions that the candidates had completed were run through the automated scoring system. After this grading session, the Research Committee reviewed the results of the automated scoring system and the architect-assigned grades. The Committee focused on those vignettes that received discrepant scores (e.g. an unacceptable score was assigned by computer and a 3 or 4 assigned by the architect-graders.) By reviewing the detailed scoring information at the feature level, a cause for the discrepancy could almost always be found. The results of this process led to refinements of both scoring rules and the weights assigned to the features. Re-running the vignettes through the scoring programs after the revisions led to higher correlations. Almost all of the remaining discrepancies could be attributed to differences in the grading criteria used for the architect-assigned scores versus the automated scoring programs. These remaining discrepancies were considered acceptable by the Research Committee given the two different sets of grading criteria used in this process. Candidates received pass or fail scores on the field test examination based on the scores assigned by the architect graders.

Aside from comparing the results of the two scoring systems, the field test allowed NCARB and ETS to determine the success of the scripting and isomorphing process. Data were collected that showed the time spent and the pass rate on each script and isomorph. The Research Committee analyzed these data to determine the aspects of particular scripts and/or isomorphs that might cause a candidate to take more time or have a higher or lower pass rate. The Committee then recommended ways to revise the scripts and isomorphs from the data, and NCARB hired a group of architects to work during the summer of 1996 to implement these changes.

In March and April 1997, NCARB and ETS will once again analyze data from the early weeks of test administration using a group of architects who will assign holistic scores to the computer-administered vignettes. Then, once again, the Research Committee will review the results of the two scoring systems, recommend revisions to the scoring programs, if necessary, and the vignettes will be re-run through the automated scoring system. Candidates will now receive scores derived from the automated scoring system. With the current program, the timing data for individual scripts and isomorphs is constantly monitored along with pass rate data, to determine if there is a problem with a particular script or isomorph's difficulty level.

Conclusion

The development of this scoring system has required extensive effort to refine all aspects of the system for developing tests. NCARB found the process of designing the vignettes to test specific aspects of architectural knowledge to be an iterative one with many passes over the same material. The changes made to the way an object is delivered affect the scoring system through changes in the feature or arrangements of features on the scoring tree or though changes in the weights assigned to features. These changes to scoring often then initiate new changes to the delivery system. One of the basic principles that NCARB's Research Committee members worked with is that they would not ask a candidate to do anything that was not being scored. Therefore, if they couldn't find a way to score something, they dropped that item from the delivery of the vignette.

Over time the vignettes are bound to change in an evolutionary process. These changes won't be as easy to implement as simply printing a different test every year. The changes need to be carefully studied and implemented over time to allow for adequate understanding of how one change affects the larger delivery and scoring system.

Finally, the rigors of the automated scoring system have led to improvements in the design of the test for architectural licensure. As careful as NCARB was in the past to closely align what was being tested with what was being scored, the new system requires extreme coordination. This has led to better tests of entry-level architectural knowledge and skills and provides candidates with a more level playing field, where all tests are equal in their content and difficulty level.

NCARB could not have completed a project as complicated as this without the invaluable assistance of ETS researchers and test developers. NCARB looks forward to finalizing this examination scoring system and to the day to day use of the new test by thousands of architectural-licensing candidates each year.

References

Bejar, I. I. 1991. A methodology for scoring open-ended architectural design problems. *Journal of Applied Psychology* 76(4): 522-532.

Bejar, I. I., and Braun, H. 1994. On the synergy between assessment and instruction: Early lessons from computer-based simulations. *Machine-Mediated Learning* 4(1): 5-25.

Bejar, I. I. 1995. From adaptive testing to automated scoring of architectural simulations. In *Assessing Clinical Reasoning: The oral examination and alternative methods*, edited by E. L. Mancall and P. G. Bashook. Evanston, Illinois: American Board of Medical Specialties.

Oltman, P. K., Bejar, I. I., and Kim, S. H. 1993. An approach to automated scoring of architectural designs. *CADD Futures 93*, edited by U. Flemming and S. Van Wyk, pp. 215-224. Pittsburgh, PA: Elsevier Science Publishers B. V.

5

Simulated Work Sample in Law: A Multistate Performance Test

Jane Peterson Smith

Traditionally, bar examinations have been limited to essay and multiple choice responses to factual questions. In 1997, the National Conference of Bar Examiners began offering a Multistate Performance Test incorporating simulations of various types of tasks lawyers must be competent to perform. For example, the candidate for licensure may be required to demonstrate the ability to handle a select number of legal authorities in the context of a factual problem involving a client. In these exercises, the candidate is presented with a description of the Court structure in a fictitious state, a "File" containing factual information about a case, a memorandum of instructions for the task to be performed, and a "Library" containing the legal authorities needed to complete the task. The "Memorandum" will describe a specific situation and a defined task, for example, one in which a personal injury action for negligence is being brought by a client. The examinee is instructed to prepare a motion for summary judgment on the theory of assumption of the risk, in accord with the standard for summary judgment in the district of the fictitious court. Candidates are allowed up to ninety minutes to complete each task; the resulting essays are scored by examiner teams who apply a series of criteria, including ethical, as well as competency, standards. This chapter presents sample exercises illustrating simulated work samples, summarizes research conducted in California in the 1980s and nationally in 1993, recounts the evolution of specifications for a national examination, describes the developmental procedures for the new test, and reports the results of the first administration.

Bar examinations have historically included state-developed essay questions. Since 1972, a nationally developed and graded multiple-choice examination, called the Multistate Bar Examination, has been the centerpiece of bar examinations. The National Conference inaugurated a Multistate Essay Examination in 1988, and it is currently used in thirteen states. In addition to these two components of what is usually a two- or three-day test, most states require applicants to pass a multiple-choice test of ethics (the Multistate Professional Responsibility Examination) as a separate requirement for admission to practice.

During the last fifteen years, a few states have added written simulations—called performance tests—to their bar examinations. Unlike multiple-choice and essay questions, bar examination performance tests are designed to test an applicant's ability to use fundamental lawyering skills in a realistic situation. Each test evaluates an applicant's ability to complete a task that a beginning lawyer should be able to accomplish, and the test materials simulate the sorts of documents with which lawyers work. Applicants receive instructions for the task they are to complete in a memorandum from a supervisor, which is the first document in a File that also contains other source documents such as interview notes, letters, police reports, news articles, motions filed with court, etc. Legal source materials, such as statutes and cases from fictional jurisdictions, are contained in a simulated Library. Applicants complete a written assignment using the facts in the File and the statutes and cases in the Library. Examples of the kinds of tasks an applicant might be assigned include: writing a brief in support of motions for summary judgment, memoranda of points and authorities, an appellate brief, a closing argument, a position paper, a declaration, office memos, a letter to a client, or an investigation plan. An applicant might be asked to outline a deposition, draft or review provisions for a contract or a will, or critique an interview plan or trust instruments.

Applying George Miller's hierarchical pyramid of physician behaviors in terms that describe a lawyer's behavior, we might say that multiple-choice questions test what an applicant "knows" in that he selects the right answer to an item; essay questions demonstrate that he "knows how" in that he responds to an essay question by writing about how a case should be resolved; and performance tests create the opportunity for the candidate to "show how" in that he must produce an actual document, designed for a specific purpose, to be read by a particular audience.

The first national performance tests were administered on February 25, 1997, to applicants in four states (Georgia, Hawaii, Iowa, and Missouri), joining candidates in three other states that administered tests they had developed themselves (Alaska, California, and Colorado). The launch of the Multistate Performance Test (MPT) follows almost fifteen years' experience with simulations in California and several other states.

California Research

Performance testing as it exists on bar examinations in the United States is an outgrowth of a major research project conducted in California in 1980. The goal of the research was to determine whether it is feasible to measure a broader range of lawyering skills in a bar examination and whether alternative testing instruments would narrow the difference in passing rates between minority and majority candidates.

Several experimental tests were administered to the 8,000 candidates who took the July 1980 exam in California, including a Trial Practice Test that used videotape, and a Research Test, designed to see how well applicants worked with a given set of materials—a file of memoranda and a library of cases. In addition to the experiments conducted during the Special Session, 500 candidates were selected to participate in a two-day Assessment Center where they completed several written and oral tasks each day. Actors played the parts of clients, witnesses, and judges, and oral tasks were videotaped for subsequent evaluation.

The results of the California experiments indicated that those who did well on the traditional MBE and essay exam tended to do well on the alternative testing instruments and that none of the experimental models narrowed the gaps in performance levels among racial groups (Klein, 1993). Nevertheless, the California Committee of Bar Examiners concluded that the new test model more closely approximated the actual practice of attorneys, and some addition to the exam was deemed appropriate.

However, even though California liked the more authentic tests developed for the research project, there are limitations on what the bar examiners concluded they could do. It was not feasible to take 12,000 candidates a year through a two-day assessment center, and the time and costs associated with videotaping oral presentations made that form of testing impractical. The Committee determined that written tasks like the Research Test and the written components of the Assessment Center could be given to all applicants, and, despite strong correlations between scores on these tests and scores on essay and multiple-choice tests, two three-hour written tests of practical skills became a mandatory part of the California bar examination in July of 1983 (Menocal et al. 1983; Smith, 1984).

NCBE Research

The National Conference has been studying performance testing since 1980, when it sponsored the California experiments. A series of grants was made to California during the 1980s, and the Conference proposed a version of the California model in 1990. In the Conference test, applicants answered two sequential tasks during a three-hour period. In discussions during the Spring of 1992, bar examiners asked whether ninety-minute tests could be created, so that they would have the flexibility of using one or two tests rather than a single three-hour examination. In light of these discussions with examiners, the Conference commissioned a study designed to determine whether a three-hour, two-task version of the California performance test could be administered and graded reliably as two ninety-minute performance tests.

At about the same time the Conference decided to conduct further performance test experiments, in 1992, the American Bar Association released the report of the Task Force on Law Schools and the Profession chaired by Robert MacCrate, whose goal was to identify ways of narrowing the gap between legal education and the practice of law, with special emphasis on professional skills. The MacCrate Task Force's Statement of Fundamental Lawyering Skills and Fundamental Values identifies ten skills and four values. The ten fundamental lawyering skills are:

- Problem Solving
- Legal Analysis and Reasoning
- Legal Research
- Factual Investigation

- Communication
- Counseling
- Negotiation
- Litigation and Alternative Dispute-Resolution Procedures
- Organization and Management of Legal Work
- Recognizing and Resolving Ethical Dilemmas

The four fundamental values are:

- Provision of Competent Representation
- Striving to Promote Justice, Fairness, and Morality
- Striving to Improve the Profession
- Professional Self-Development

Specifications for the performance tests the National Conference developed for its 1993 research incorporated the California model and the new MacCrate list of fundamental skills. The NCBE test was designed to test three of these skills areas: Legal Analysis, Fact Analysis, and Problem Solving.

A number of problems were identified during the development stage of the 1993 project. First, the test drafters believed it was much easier to create unique ninety-minute problems than it was to create a single factual setting that would work for two tests (Smith, 1994). Second, the items did not sample the full range of tasks. They were heavily weighted to litigation, rather than law office work. Furthermore, the items were criticized for focussing more strongly on legal analysis and fact analysis than on problem solving. Third, the items were of varying level of difficulty (and one item was extremely difficult), and applicants uniformly reported that they did not have enough time to complete the problems.

As a result of the July 1993 Research Project, we concluded that we should develop a menu of tasks to be used in items, just as we identify various topics for essay examinations, and use other methods—such as scaling written scores to the mean and standard deviation of equated multiple-choice scores—in order to insure fairness across examinations.

Applicants in the four states that participated in the research were assigned one three-hour test or a random pair of the four ninety-minute tests. The fourteen possible combinations of test items allowed ACT, the Conference's test contractor, to examine the effect of time limits and the order in which applicants answered the items. Applicants also completed a questionnaire that solicited background information and their opinions of the tests they took (Kunce et al. 1995).

The answers of the applicants were graded over the course of a weekend by six teams of graders recruited from ten states. About 25% of the answers were scored twice for purposes of the research.

Finally, a panel of content experts gathered to review the items and evaluate how successful they were in testing what they were designed to test (Kuechenmeister, 1995).

The technical research drew several conclusions: Not unexpectedly, the four tasks were not equivalent to one another, and scores from the ninety-minute PT were not equivalent to scores from the three-hour PT. Some tasks were harder than others; graders' scores correlated higher on some than others; it mattered what order the applicants took them in. Similarly, as might be expected, scores on two tests provided better information than a score on one, and two gradings of two tests was better than one grading. Interestingly, virtually all test takers' scores were higher on the second PT they answered than they were on the first, indicating that some learning was going on and/or that applicants became more comfortable with the format as they approached the second problem. A complete report of the technical research was presented at the annual meeting of the National Council on Measurement in Education (Gamache et al. 1994).

In order to answer questions regarding the performance test's *overall* impact, the Conference asked Stephen P. Klein, a psychometric consultant who works with the bar examiners in over 25 states, to review data gathered by ACT as well as score data from the participating jurisdictions. Dr. Klein was able to compare how applicants did on the PT to their performance on the essay portions of the state exams as well as the MBE, and his report provides a context for judging the relative reliability and value of a performance test component. His study found that:

- The correlation between PT tasks was higher than the correlation among essay questions in the states participating in the experiment.

- While the scores of attorneys already licensed to practice were not uniformly higher than the scores of non-attorney applicants, their scores were statistically significantly higher on the PT than would be expected on the basis of their scores on the other two parts of the exam, the MBE, and essay.

Dr. Klein concluded that the performance test is measuring an important ability that is related to, but not fully measured by essay examinations or the

MBE, and that "a PT section would be a useful addition to most state bar exams" (Klein, 1994).

Development of a Multistate Performance Test

Based upon the results of the 1993 research and meetings with states held in the fall of 1994, the National Conference decided to add two ninety-minute performance tests to its battery of multistate examinations, giving states the choice of administering one or both in conjunction with the other components of their exams.

The test specifications were revised to test six of the ten fundamental lawyering skills identified by the MacCrate Task Force:

- Problem solving
- Legal analysis and reasoning
- Factual analysis
- Communication
- Organization and management of a legal task
- Recognizing and resolving ethical dilemmas

The MacCrate statement of fundamental skills and values was a seminal event in defining the legal profession—and thereby defining what the profession would test for in deciding whether one is minimally competent to practice law. Because the work of lawyers is largely word-based, it is appropriate for a paper and pencil test to be the basic component of testing for competency. However, some lawyering skills—such as the ability to negotiate or interview a client—lend themselves to in-person, oral tests, which bar examiners have so far been unwilling to engage in. The expense of such tests is one significant obstacle, but the perception that such tests would be unfairly subjective, and/or would result in a rater's bias by a candidate's gender or ethnicity have prevented serious attempts at expanding its scope or format.

Moreover, a paper and pencil test is limited in testing for fundamental values. We can deduce that an applicant who completes a written task satisfactorily will also "provide competent representation," and by testing whether an applicant will identify and resolve an ethical dilemma in a case simulation, we can make assumptions about whether he will "strive to promote justice, fairness, and morality." But a demonstration of values like "striving to improve the profession" and "professional self-development" can come only after an attorney has been admitted to practice.

Development of the Multistate Performance Test began shortly following the Conference's decision to add it, and a drafting committee, drawn from the pool of experienced PT writers and editors, was appointed in 1995.

Procedures for developing and grading MPT items include the following steps:

- **Commission new item:** a member of the drafting committee writes a problem.

- **Edit new item, draft grading guidelines:** the committee meets to review the problem and preliminary grading guidelines are created.

- **Pretest edited item:** recently admitted attorneys complete the task under test conditions, respond to a questionnaire, and provide suggestions for change.

- **Conduct independent expert review of item and guidelines:** two independent experts, one an academic and the other a practitioner, critique the item and the proposed guidelines.

- **Edit item second time, revise grading guidelines:** the committee grades the pretest responses, reviews the expert reviews, and edits the item to respond to problems raised.

- **Conduct state review:** states that are administering the MPT review and critique the proposed items and grading guidelines.

- **Edit item third time, revise grading guidelines:** the committee revises the item and guidelines based on comments from the states.

- **Administer:** states administer one or two items in conjunction with their bar examinations.

- **Conduct grading workshop, revise grading guidelines:** states send graders to a grading workshop where copies of actual answers are reviewed to identify potential problems in grading; grading guidelines are modified as necessary.

- **Assign scores:** each state grades the answers written by its applicants, determines the relative weight to be assigned to the tests, and establishes pass/fail standards.

As with development procedures for other tests, feedback from pretesters and independent reviewers has been particularly helpful, both in identifying ways to improve the tests and in reinforcing our belief that the format is appropriate for licensing attorneys. Among the comments reported by pretesters are the following: "I like this much better than the MBE or traditional essay. It makes you synthesize more information." "This is exactly the type of work I am currently doing every day, and it's what practitioners must confront with each new case." "I think the test is fair and tests real skills." "It tests analytical skills more effectively than does a 'closed-book' exam where you have to memorize points of law for an essay or multiple-choice test."

The first two MPT items were administered on February 25, 1997, about two years after the decision was made to implement the new test. The first MPT, *Alexander v. BTI and Bell,* placed applicants in the setting of a law firm representing the defendants in a personal injury suit brought by a tennis player who was injured while playing with the pro at a tennis club. Applicants were asked to write a persuasive brief in support of a motion for summary judgment, on the ground that the plaintiff had assumed the risk of injury when she agreed to play a match with the defendant. The simulated File included the memo from the supervising attorney, a physician's report of plaintiff's injuries, and excerpts from the depositions of the defendant pro and the plaintiff player. Using the cases in the Library, applicants are expected to argue that Alexander and Bell were co-participants rather than instructor/student and that Alexander's assumption of the risk of being injured is a complete defense to an action against the pro and the tennis club.

A key document in the file is an office policy memo that describes what is expected in writing persuasive briefs. This memo establishes the expectations for form. The brief should include a statement of facts and argumentative subject headings, examples of which are given. On the other hand, the memo establishes that the applicant need not prepare a table of contents, summary of argument, etc. These kinds of office instruction memos have been especially valuable in developing items: they allow us to instruct applicants on the specifics of an assignment and put everyone on a level playing field. If the candidate has never actually done the task called for before, or if he has questions about what the graders of this test item will be looking for, the office memo gives him the instruction he needs.

The second February 1997 item, *In re Hayworth and Wexler,* involves a premarital agreement between the client, Hank Hayworth, and his intended, Wendy Wexler, who is not represented by counsel. Hank wants to protect all his assets and has requested a premarital agreement that asks Wendy to waive her rights to an equitable share of all property acquired during the marriage, increases in the value of property brought into the marriage, and alimony or maintenance to which she might be entitled because of the disparity in their incomes. The wedding is scheduled to take place in two weeks. Using the rules of professional conduct and a case from the fictional state of Franklin, applicants are expected to advise the supervising attorney that she is treading on very thin ice: that the drafted agreement is unenforceable because it is patently unfair to Wendy, and that the attorney may actually be subject to a malpractice suit if she doesn't take every step to insure that Wendy realizes and knowingly waives her rights to independent counsel.

A grading workshop was conducted the first weekend in March, with participants from all the states that administered the tests. Copies of randomly selected answers were used to calibrate graders (although each state ultimately applies its own standards and assigns its own scores to answers). Answers to the *Alexander* item ran the gamut from those whose statement of facts in support of defendants' motion focussed on the pain and suffering of the plaintiff to those who characterized one of the cases in the Library as being about an "insufficient horse." Similarly, the *Hayworth* answers included some who said the premarital agreement as drafted was fair on its face to one who suggested that the supervising attorney should "get Wendy alone" to discuss her rights.

Conclusion

The Multistate Performance Test is a classic pencil-and-paper, free response test. It differs from essay testing for law in that the foundational materials are included, so that the would-be lawyer need not rely upon memory, as he or she is asked to do when answering traditional multiple-choice or essay questions. One of the ironies of implementing this simulation of a lawyer's task is that, in psychometric terms, it takes us full circle from the days when only essay questions were used, to the days when a standardized, objectively graded multiple-choice exam was added for the sake of reliability, to the new day when a new, possibly even more subjective, free response test is added to the battery.

During a panel discussion about performance testing in 1983, shortly after the administration of the first tests in California, I stated that we could not understand what the performance test meant to the profession by asking whether it was a success or a waste of time; that it had to be viewed as a profound change in our perception of licensure. I believe that remains true today. In the 1980s, I predicted that the 21st century will see the testing of professional skills on bar examinations across the country; that small states would experiment with Assessment Centers; that some might try portfolio evaluation; that some might investigate computer simulations. I stated that interest in new testing forms—and pressure from the public to insure that licensed attorneys have the *skills* as well as the knowledge to be competent to practice—would continue to grow (Smith, 1989).

There is a natural competition for time on a bar examination. Examiners and applicants alike want to spend as little time in the process as possible but want to insure the fairness and reliability of the scores that are earned. The goal is to find a test that will provide as much information as possible about an applicant in as little time as possible, for the least amount of money.

It goes without saying that a two-day multiple-choice test would probably be the most efficient and reliable method of making licensure decisions. But, in the practice of law, virtually all skills require a command of language. There is no "right answer," only a series of competing arguments. Thorough research, rather than memorized "law bites," is the hallmark of conscientious practice.

The essay test ostensibly adds to the validity of the bar examination by presenting the applicant with an open-ended inquiry. However, the essay form of testing misses the essence of legal practice. The real world never offers facts coherently, and it is the lawyer's job to sift through seemingly contradictory facts to find those that are essential, to find those that bolster the legal argument. Performance testing adds an important, authentic dimension to licensure testing for lawyers. It tests skills not tested by other exams in a format which more closely simulates the actual practice of law.

Ultimately, the decision to substitute performance test items for essay questions or to add performance test items to bar examinations will be made by weighing the authenticity of the test against its relative reliability and its relative cost. Bar Examiners must weigh the costs in test reliability, money, and applicant time against a number of competing perspectives—the desire of the applicant to feel that the test is authentic, the criticism of judges who find attorneys' work incompetent, the concerns of law schools who claim they cannot afford to provide practical skills training to all their students, and the perception of the public that a license means an attorney is competent to practice law.

It's gratifying to see that predictions have come true, at least in part. Four states used the first multistate performance tests, and a total of thirteen will be using the test by February of 1998. We have every reason to believe that our colleagues are agreeing that performance testing adds a valuable new dimension to testing for competency to practice law.

References

Gamache, L.M. and R.L. Brennan. 1994. Issues of Generalizability: Tasks, Raters, and Contexts for a Performance Test for Lawyers. *Performance Assessment: Evaluating Competing Perspectives for Use in High Stakes Testing.* Symposium conducted at the annual meeting of the National Council on Measurement in Education, New Orleans.

Klein, S.P. 1993. *Summary of Research on the Multistate Bar Examination.* GANSK & Associates.

Klein, S.P. 1994. Relationships Among MBE, Essay, and July 1993 Performance Test Scores. Report prepared for NCBE.

Kuechenmeister, M.A. 1995. A Performance Test of Lawyering Skills: A Study of Content Validity. 64 *The Bar Examiner* 2 (May 1995), p. 23.

Kunce, C.S., and S.E. Arbet. 1995. A Performance Test of Lawyering Skills: Candidate Perceptions. 64 *The Bar Examiner* 2 (May 1995), p. 43.

MacCrate, R. et al. 1992. *Legal Education and Professional Development— An Educational Continuum.* Report of the Task Force on Law Schools and the Profession: Narrowing the Gap. American Bar Association Section of Legal Education and Admissions to the Bar.

Menocal, A. et al. 1983. Performance Testing: A Valuable New Dimension or a Waste of Time and Money? 52 *The Bar Examiner* 4 (November 1983), p. 12.

Smith, J.P. 1984. Preparing and Grading the California Performance Test. 54 *The Bar Examiner* 1 (February 1984), p. 16.

Smith, J.P. 1989. Performance Testing in California, 1983-1989. 58 *The Bar Examiner* 3 (August 1989), p. 17.

Smith, J.P. 1994. Issues in Development of a Performance Test for Lawyers. *Performance Assessment: Evaluating Competing Perspectives for Use in High Stakes Testing.* Symposium conducted at the annual meeting of the National Council on Measurement in Education, New Orleans.

Section B: Assessing Communication, Technical, and Affective Responses: Can they Relate Like a Professional?

Section B

Assessing Communication, Technical, and Affective Responses: Can They Relate Like a Professional?

Introduction

The previous section of this book discussed the utility of simulations for evaluating thinking skills, the following section addresses the integration of knowledge, skills and affect. This section will address the emotional and technical components of competence.

The examples of the effectiveness of simulations for evaluating the cognitive competencies of professionals provided in Section A make clear that simulation offers educators and evaluators a reliable means of determining whether or not the student/trainee can think like a professional. However, failing to exploit evaluative simulations for information about other types of competency would be an inefficient use of the total amount of information available from simulations. The value of simulation is its ability to reproduce "real" situations in a "non-real," non-dangerous context. Simulation allows us to recreate the climate within which the professional is expected to perform, with all of its inherent stresses, annoyances, perceived dangers, obstacles, and frustrations, yet free of actual danger.

Performance on conventional tests can demostrate accurately whether an individual has the knowledge to think like a professional. But tests cannot reveal whether the individual can apply that knowledge under stress. Will this physician suffer a mental block when confronted by an aggressive patient? Will this police officer be able to think rationally when pursuing an armed suspect? Will this pilot panic if his aircraft goes into a spin? In other words, will the professional "choke" when placed in a real pressure situation? Simulations can provide answers about an individual's ability to integrate communication and technical skills, as well as appropriate affect, in responding to professional demands.

In some professions, the attitude or disposition of the professional is as important as the cognitive and/or psychomotor ability. Consider a hypothetical example. The physician who prescribes correct treatment nearly all of the time and is very rarely affected by on-the-job pressures may appear to be the ideal doctor. The patients of this physician, however, may find him uncompassionate, condescending, difficult to get along with, and lacking in compassion. As a result, his patients may have an abnormally high rate of non-compliance, thus limiting his effectiveness at least as much as that of physicians with analogous cognitive or psychomotor deficiencies. It follows that, given a choice between licensing/certifying a professional with appropriate attitudes vs. one who is lacking, the answer would be the former. This section explores various methods of using simulation to assess these affective responses.

"Data Collection and Interpersonal Skills: The Standardized Patient Encounter" by Robyn Tamblyn and Howard Barrows presents an overview of the standardized patient form of simulation in which an actor is trained to present actual medical problems in a realistic way. The medical student interacts with the simulated patient as a basis for decisions about the next steps in the management of the patient. Tamblyn and Barrows discuss some of the difficulties involved in measuring attitudes in the standardized patient-physician encounter, as well as some of the new and emerging techniques of evaluating this elusive quality.

In "The Objective Structured Clinical Examination (OSCE) of Technical Skills: The Canadian Experience in Licensure," Reznick and Associates detail the start of a new system of certification based in part on standardized patient simulation. Their chapter is among the first to document the trend of using simulation to appraise affective components of professional competence.

In her essay, "Handling Critical Incidents: Sweaty Palms and Post Traumatic Stress Syndrome," Christine McGuire examines the challenges facing evaluators in using current methods to assess affective responses. She notes differences in what should be measured in knowledge and skills evaluation versus attitude/values evaluation. For instance, in testing skills, the evaluator is concerned with measuring peak performance which is representative of what the examinee *can* do. In testing attitudes, however, McGuire proposes that evaluators should be concerned with how the examinee *habitually* performs. However, typical performance also involves motivations and values, which are unlikely to be elucidated by peak performance scores. Complicating matters further, McGuire discusses the difficulties inherent in evoking an accurate response from subjects who are more than likely unwilling to display their real attitudes, values and emotions. She reports on some of the advantages and disadvantages of several evolving low-tech, low-cost simulations that may prove useful in addressing the problems she describes.

Evaluating the affective responses of professionals is a dimension of simulation that has often been neglected. Inadequate technology may partially account for the paucity of measures of affect. Only today are we beginning to breach the technological barrier that has prevented us from examining the emotional component of professional ability. For example, though airplanes have existed for almost a century, only recently has the flight simulator become feasible as a means of evaluation. The Boeing 777 simulator that McGuire describes could not have existed much earlier because computers capable of running such high-fidelity simulations are only now available.

Other barriers also exist. For instance, the standardized patient has been employed as an assessment tool for only thirty years, yet the technology required to support it (mainly acting and personal communication) has existed since the time of Hippocrates. The explanation for this long delay may lie in the changing professional environment. The patient-physician relationship has recently been altered in such a way that examining the communication skills and empathy of the physician has become a priority for credentialing authorities. Forty years ago, a patient would seek out physicians they found agreeable, and refuse to see those they did not personally get along with. With the increasingly detailed regulations of insurance companies and HMOs, there has been a steady deterioration in the personal relationship between patients and physicians, and patients have increasingly found themselves without the freedom to choose a physician they like. In other words, the consumer is less able to promote doctors competent in patient interaction skills. Consequently, in the last thirty years, the burden of identifying physician skills in this area has fallen increasingly on licensure and certifying authorities, who have gravitated toward simulation.

Regardless of what might have slowed or masked progress in evaluating professional emotional competence, simulation now offers us the opportunity to gather data about this dimension of professional behavior. Though pinning down all the details of this elusive quality will take much study, we now have a useful basic approach.

Ara Tekian

6

Data Collection and Interpersonal Skills: the Standardized Patient Encounter

Robyn Tamblyn
Howard Barrows

Over the last decade, numerous undergraduate institutions and certifying boards in health professions have incorporated role playing exercises in their certifying procedures to assess interviewing and data-gathering skills. In these exercises, the candidate is required to interview laymen trained as simulated patients who present with various health communications problems. The candidate is judged both competency to elicit relevant information and on sensitivity to patient needs and concerns. This chapter describes typical exercises, delineates methods of training the role players, explains various scoring systems now employed and reports the results of extensive research on the reliability, validity, transportability and feasibility of using such exercises in large group testing programs.

T he rapid growth of standardized patient assessment in health professional training programs (Stillman et al. 1990) and in licensing and certifying examinations (Grand'Maison et al. 1992) is testimony to the widely held belief that an individual's ability to collect data from history and physical examination, and establish an effective therapeutic relationship with the patient needs to be assessed. These two aspects of clinical competence are required for the effective delivery of health care, and it is known that not only are these abilities not tested by paper-and-pencil methods, but problems in practice are arising precisely because of deficiencies in these areas (Entman et al. 1994; Adamson et al. 1989; Lambrew et al. 1996).

The Standardized Patient Method-An Overview

A standardized patient (SP) is an individual who is trained to provide an accurate and reproducible presentation of a real patient's problem, a problem that the SP may or may not have had in the past. The SP method was first developed by Barrows in 1968 (Barrows, 1971), and has since been used for teaching, evaluation and research (Barrows, 1993). There are several unique advantages of the SP method that contribute to its popularity.

For teaching, SPs can be used to provide students with an opportunity to acquire skills that may be difficult to learn in the clinical environment, such as learning how to break bad news to patients, managing the dying patient, the rape victim, or sexual counseling. Typically, SPs in this context are trained to present a 'real-life' problem, and also to provide feedback, and in some instances instruction to the student about their approach. Course and workshop designers have also used SPs to provide learning opportunities with a specific set of problems, 'real-life course material,' that can be readily reproduced and scheduled to suit their educational objectives (Sachdeva et al. 1997; Pololi & Potter, 1996; Kay, Johnson, & Kopp, 1994; Robinson & McGaghie, 1996; Lockyer et al. 1996). Examples span the spectrum from teaching how to counsel patients in changing high-risk health behaviors to the assessment of trauma patients (Pololi & Potter, 1996).

Researchers have used SPs so that they can select problems to test certain hypotheses about practice patterns, risk factors or interventions (Ali et al. 1996; Wenrich et al, 1995; Howard, Garman, & McCann, 1995; Kokotailo et al. 1995; Carney et al. 1995; Shahabudin et al. 1994; Badger et al. 1994; Solomon et al. 1994; Haydon et al. 1994; Day et al. 1993; Carney et al. 1993; Rethans, Martin,

& Metsemakers, 1994; Roter et al. 1990; Norman, Tugwell, & Feightner, 1982; Renaud et al. 1980). SPs provide a method to control for differences in the population of patients seen by different providers (Badger et al. 1995), and to conduct blinded evaluation in the practice setting (Carney et al. 1993; Rethans et al. 1991; Rethans et al. 1991; Norman et al. 1985; Gordon et al. 1992; Day et al. 1992; Woodward et al. 1985; Tamblyn et al. 1992; Tamblyn et al. 1997). For example, Renaud used SPs to determine if differences existed in the quality of care provided by salaried and fee-for-service physicians. Tamblyn et al. (1997) used SPs to determine how often drug-related illness was misdiagnosed and mismanaged, and Ali used SPs to evaluate the effectiveness of an advanced trauma life support program for physicians in Trinidad and Tobago (Ali et al. 1996).

Growth in the use of SPs has been most dramatic in the area of assessment (Barrows 1993; Norman, Tugwell, & Freightner, 1982; Swartz & Colliver, 1996; Van Der Vleuten & Swanson, 1990; Stillman et al. 1991; Johnson, Kopp, & Williams, 1990; Vu, 1979; Tamblyn et al. 1991; Petrusa, Blackwell, & Ainsworth, 1990; Cohen et al. 1990; Newble & Swanson, 1988). The objective structured clinical examination, developed by Harden and Gleeson (1979) to test technical skills (e.g., examination of the knee, interpretation of an x-ray) (Newble, 1988), was adapted to provide more comprehensive assessment of data collection, diagnostic and management abilities (e.g., assessment and management of a patient presenting with low back pain) (Williams et al. 1987; Stillman et al. 1990; Petrusa et al. 1987; Barrows, Williams & Moy, 1987). SPs were used to present a series of 'real-life' cases. Typically, case-specific checklists are used to assess a student's ability to collect relevant information from history and physical examination. Interpersonal and communication skills are usually assessed by a standardized checklist that is common to all cases presented. Diagnosis and management is assessed in a follow-up 'station' where students provide a written response to open-ended questions about the case. This methodology has been used to assess clinical competence in specific clinical disciplines and specialty areas, at different levels of training, and in a variety of health professional groups including medicine, nursing, physiotherapy, occupational therapy, dentistry, and chiropractic medicine (Lewis & Tamblyn, 1987; Johnson, Kopp, & Williams, 1990; Jain et al. 1997; Robb et al. 1996; Traina et al. 1996; Hodges et al. 1996; Sutnick et al. 1994; Jain, DeLisa, & Campagnolo, 1994; Norman et al. 1993; Stillman et al. 1986; Stillman, Regan, & Swanson, 1987; Boudreau, Tamblyn & Dufresne, 1994) . More recently, this method of assessment has been incorporated into licensing and certifying examinations (Grand'Maison et al. 1992; Grand'Maison et al. 1997; Wothington, Willis & Boyett, 1994; Sutnick et al. 1993; Grand'Maison, Lescop & Brailovsky, 1993).

What Needs to be Assessed, How and Why?

There is consensus that SP methods are particularly useful for assessing an individual's ability to collect information from history and physical examination, and to establish a relationship with the patient. While these two domains of competence are commonly lumped together and labeled as interviewing skills, they are really two separate domains (Maxim & Dielman, 1987) that have different objectives in the process and outcome of care.

Data Collection

The ability to collect relevant data from history and physical examination is considered to be essential for accurate diagnosis and for follow-up management. Three components of data collection can be assessed with SP methodology: 1) decisions about relevant information to collect, 2) collection of information from history and physical examination, and 3) interpretation of the information collected.

Decisions about relevant information to collect

Decisions about relevant data collection is probably the one of the most difficult and critical skills health professionals need to acquire. An individual must determine which items, from the hundreds that could be obtained, are most relevant to determine the likely diagnosis, the most appropriate therapy, and the effectiveness of therapy once established. Paper-and-pencil methods systematically overestimate an individual's ability to collect relevant data. This is likely because the summary of the patient problem presented or the optional actions cue the examinee to choose items on history and physical examination that might not normally have been considered.

Accurate assessment of this ability is essential because there is evidence that failure to collect relevant information from history and physical exam increases the risk of misdiagnosis and mismanagement (Tamblyn et al. 1997), which in turn increases the risk of avoidable morbidity (Leape et al. 1991; Hiatt et al. 1989). This is particularly true in settings such as the emergency room or in ambulatory practice where visits are short and follow-up opportunities are more limited. In light of these observations, several issues need to be considered in the selection and development of SP cases.

Case Selection: Priority needs to be placed on the selection of SP cases where the adequacy of information collected from history and physical examination has an impact on diagnosis, treatment, and patient outcome. While there may be agreement that the collection of relevant health information is important for all patients, it is particularly critical for certain types of problems. These include situations where:

1) History and physical examination are the only means by which the diagnosis is made (i.e., there is no diagnostic test), and further, where failure to make an accurate diagnosis may have short term adverse consequences for the patient (i.e., delays in diagnosis and the institution of treatment make a difference) (e.g., syncopal episodes, nocturnal asthma, and epiglottitis)

2) Decisions about the pace of intervention are determined by a patient's clinical status, and where the failure to act expeditiously may result in avoidable adverse outcomes (e.g., respiratory failure, pulmonary embolus, fetal distress, crescendo angina, and acute appendicitis)

3) The adequacy of treatment and its side effects are judged by information collected from history and physical examination, and where a failure to collect information on relevant side effects or treatment response may result in temporary or permanent deterioration in health status (e.g., theophylline toxicity, hearing loss with aminoglycosides, tardive dyskinesia with anti-psychotic drugs, and post-operative infection)

4) Students and practicing physicians commonly experience difficulty in determining what information is relevant to collect (e.g., vague complaints such as dizziness, headache and fatigue, and neurological problems) (Shahabudin et al. 1994; Haydon et al. 1994).

Context of Assessment: To test these abilities, the initial information provided about the problem and the time available for assessment should closely match the reality of the practice environment. There is a debate about the pros and cons of using short (5 minute) versus long (10 to 20 minute) SP encounter times to assess data collection skills. Typically, short encounter times are accompanied by more structured directives on the focus that should be taken by the examinee in the assessment of the problem. For example, the information given to the examinee before a 5 minute SP encounter might say "A 67-year-old female has been brought into the emergency room because she developed sudden confusion. Carry out a focused mental status examination." As only 5 minutes is available for the encounter, the examiners have to provide a structure and focus for the student's assessment. In this situation, the student's ability to conduct a condensed mental status examination can be assessed, but not their ability to decide what should be assessed in this situation. To assess the latter, a longer encounter time would, in general, be required where introductory pre-encounter material is limited to the patient's presenting problem and the setting.

The Checklist: In order to judge a student's ability to collect relevant information, judgements have to be made *a priori* about what information is relevant to collect—what history should be obtained and what physical examination should be done. These judgements are usually made by the examiner who selects and develops the SP case, typically an academic faculty member with expertise in the field. In high stakes examinations, these case specific decisions about relevant data collection are usually reviewed by colleagues, who may or may not have expertise in the specific content area. Identified items are listed in a standardized checklist format, usually with a dichotomous scale (done/not done). The checklist is used to score the performance of each student (proportion of relevant data collected). There are two limitations in this process. The first is the poverty of empirical evidence and lack of consensus on what data are relevant for specific patient problems. When we asked a panel of 10 experts to rate (scale of 1–18) the clinical relevance of 22 items they had independently identified as important in the initial assessment of a case of chronic recurrent hip pain in a patient with co-existing diabetes and hypertension, we found considerable variation in their opinion (See Figure 1).

In this instance, we used the average rating of experts to classify items as essential and important. We also used average ratings as a weight in the generation of a continuous quality of care score. Of interest, the two items that were classified as important (hypertension history) and essential (past peptic ulcer disease history) by average expert rating were the only significant predictors of contra-indicated NSAID prescribing (not obtaining the information was a risk for mismanagement) (Haydon et al. 1994). If the purpose of assessment is to determine whether an individual is competent to practice, then better methods of defining clinically important omissions in data collection need to be developed.

The second limitation relates to the inferences that can be drawn about an individual's ability to make decisions about relevant data collection on the basis of what they do in the SP encounter. Just by the nature of their training, students will develop a 'routine' list of questions they ask on medical history and do on physical examination—for every patient whether it is relevant or not.

Clinical History Item	Rating of clinical Relevance* (*n*=10 experts)		Classification of Clinical Relevance		
	Mean	Range	Essential	Important	If Time Available
Chronic Hip Pain History					
* location of pain	14.4	6 to 18	X		
* duration of symptoms	12.5	6 to 18		X	
* quality of pain	9.6	4 to18		X	
* aggravating factors	11.8	10 to 18		X	
* pain-related functional limitations	12.1	6 to 18		X	
* present and past medication	13.9	10 to 18	X		
* past physiotherapy for pain	8.6	3 to 15		X	
* presence of systemic symptoms (fatigue, fever, weight loss)	7.5	1 to 15		X	
* patient's belief about cause of pain	6.4	3 to 10			X
* patient's expectations of the visit	6.0	3 to 10			X
Other Health Problems					
Determined status of:					
*hypertension	9.6	4 to 15		X	
* diabetes	9.9	4 to 15		X	
* past ulcer history	14.3	10 to 18	X		
Medications					
*amount of acetaminophen taken	15.5	14 to 18	X		
* use of other drugs for pain	15.6	14 to 18	X		
* how patient is taking hypertension meds (amount/method)	10.1	4 to 15		X	
* how patient is taking diabetic meds (amount/method)	10.1	4 to 15		X	
* side-effects hypertensive meds	9.3	14 to 15		X	
* side effects diabetic meds	8.6	4 to 15		X	
Patient Understanding					
* of his/her health problems	8.3	4 to 12		X	
* current drugs and side effects	8.4	2 to 15		X	

Figure 1, Performance Checklist

There appear to be important differences in the use of information when it is collected as part of a 'routine' inquiry, as opposed to a 'selected' inquiry. For example, Starfield (1972) showed that when blood counts were ordered as a routine, without documented reasons for the choice, that physicians were far less likely to take action on abnormal results than when there was a documented reason for the investigation (e.g., to confirm or reject a hypothesis of anemia). This implies that individuals who ask or examine as part of a routine will be scored as having a higher level of ability than they actually possess with respect to decision-making about relevant information. Vu proposed one method of circumventing this problem. After the encounter, she asked students to justify their reasons for the data collected during the encounter, and incorporated the quality of the rationale for their choices into the score obtained on data collection. The utility of this method needs further evaluation. It is possible that post-encounter justification of data collected would not only improve the reliability of assessment by increasing the variation between students, but also may provide a more valid assessment of an individual's capability to collect relevant information in a patient encounter.

The Raters: There has been some debate over the type of rater that should be used to document student performance during a SP encounter. Basically the task of the rater, when measuring relevant data collection, is to document what questions were asked and what examinations done according to the items listed on the case-specific checklist. Three types of raters are generally used: 1) a physician examiner who observes the performance of the student during the encounter, 2) the SP who presents the case recalls and documents actions taken by the student at the end of the encounter, or 3) a second SP who acts as an observer and records actions taken during the encounter. For documenting actions taken, SPs and physician examiners appear to be equally accurate (Day et al. 1993; Kopp & Johnson, 1995; Tamblyn et al. 1991; Vu, 1992) . The main problems, when present, appear to arise because of differences in the accuracy of documentation when one is based on 'recall' and the other is based on 'direct observation'. In this situation, longer checklists (more items to remember) tend to lower the concordance between SP documentation by recall and documentation by direct observation (Tamblyn et al. 1997; Vu, 1992). When problems occur in recalling student actions, there will be a systematic tendency for SPs to record that the action was done, even when it might not have been (Tamblyn et al. 1997; Nieman et al. 1988). This results in an overestimation of student performance.

The collection of information from history and physical examination

The second component of data collection is the ability to actually acquire information from history and physical examination. Paper and pencil methods do not allow an examiner to assess whether or not an individual is capable of adequately collecting information or carrying out a physical examination even if they know what is important to assess. For example, it may be considered relevant to examine a college student complaining of fatigue for splenomegaly to rule out the possibility of infectious mononucleosis. Using the SP method, examiners can determine whether or not the student a) knows whether splenomegaly is important to assess, and b) can actually conduct an adequate examination to determine if splenomegaly is present. When there is an interest in knowing not only whether the student knows what data to collect (component 1) but also how well they are able carry out relevant history and physical examination (component 2), then additional issues need to be considered in case selection and development.

Case selection: Cases are often selected to provide representative sampling of the relevant clinical disciplines and types of assessment that are most commonly required. In addition to these considerations, emphasis is placed on measuring an individual's ability to collect information in situations in which data collection is more difficult, or in situations where the interpretation of abnormal findings is particularly relevant to diagnosis, prognosis, and treatment.

For the medical history, these situations include:

- A language or cultural barrier exists which makes it difficult to collect information from the patient

- The patient is confused or unable to respond and a family member/friend must be used to obtain the relevant history

- The situation is one in which 'highly emotionally-charged' information needs to be obtained to adequately assess the problem (e.g., cases of abuse or rape)

- The patient is aggressive, delusional, withdrawn, inebriated or seductive: behaviors that must be managed to obtain an adequate history of the presenting problem (Hodges et al. 1996)

- The patient presents multiple problems and past treatments that need to be sorted out to address the current problem

For the physical examination, situations include:

- Patients who have a physical barrier to adequate examination (e.g., obesity, severe pain)

- Examinations where there is typically poor agreement among clinicians because of differences in the technical expertise (palpation, auscultation, percussion, opthalmological examination,) or that are poorly done by clinicians (musculo-skeletal examination, neurological examination) (Connell et al. 1993)

- Abnormal findings that have implications for diagnosis, prognosis, and treatment (carotid bruit)

For most cases, SPs can be trained to accurately reproduce the patient problem selected (Tamblyn et al. 1991; Tamblyn et al. 1990). In fact, in many situations, such as those involving difficult medical history assessment, SPs may be the only means by which such capabilities could be systematically assessed. However, in the case of abnormal findings, examiners are often faced with the prospect of having to recruit actual patients who have stable but abnormal physical examination findings (Bryans & Crothers, 1979). The challenge in these situations is to train actual patients to be reproducible in their presentation (even if it is their own health problem), and to debrief them in relationship to misguided or erroneous statements made to them during the course of the examination.

Context of Assessment: The assessment of the ability to collect information from history and physical examination is often measured by short, 5 minute encounters. The student is provided with explicit instructions about the nature of the data to be collected, or aspect of the physical examination to carry out. For the 5-minute encounter, training requirements for SPs are considerably condensed. SPs are trained to provide a reproducible response to a fairly narrowly defined set of questions and examinations. To assess a student's ability to handle difficult challenges in the history or on physical examination, longer encounter times are generally required as well as more in-depth SP training. While longer encounters provide the opportunity to test a student's ability in more complex tasks, there is a trade-off. Longer encounter times mean that the number of situations in which a student's performance ability can be tested are fewer than with shorter encounter times for a given test time. While this tends to lower reliability because a smaller number of situations are sampled and a broader domain of abilities are tested (Shatzer et al. 1993), it would theoretically improve the validity of inferences that could be drawn about an individual's data collection abilities.

The Checklist: The objective in assessing this component of data collection is not only to determine if the student collects information from history and physical examination (i.e., they ask the question or carry out the physical examination procedure) but how well they are able to do it. For the physical examination, this means that the examiners would assess whether the examination was performed with sufficient skill to detect an abnormal finding if it were present. For the history, it means did they ask questions in a such a way that they were likely to obtain an accurate account from the patient. Two methods have been used to assess 'how well' a student is able to collect data. The first method asks the observer to rate the adequacy of the student's technique for each checklist item for the history and physical examination (McRae et al. 1995). This generally takes the form of a three category scale—not done, done partially (technique suboptimal or exam incomplete), done adequately. The second method uses the findings reported by the student at the end of the encounter to draw inferences about the adequacy of their examination technique. If the student was able to retrieve the relevant data from history and physical examination, then it is assumed her their technique must have been adequate. Both methods have problems. Raters will vary in the qualitative judgements they make about the adequacy of examination technique (Newble, Hoare & Sheldrake, 1980). This will add to random errors in measurement and lower reliability. Rater training and/or more detailed specification of what constitutes optimal technique for each item of history and physical examination are ways of minimizing this problem (Ferrell & Thompson, 1993). The second method is problematic if the vast majority of SPs have no physical findings (negative findings attributable to poor technique cannot be identified), and when the SPs have not been adequately trained about the conditions for providing information about their health problem. It is common to find that SPs either provide the student with all the information about their problem, regardless of the skill with which the question was asked, or they play the 'no win' game with the student, where no matter what the student does, the SP fails to respond. In both situations, the examiner is unable to measure the quality of a student's history and examination technique, because the SP fails to respond as actual patients would in relationship to the student's history-taking technique (Dawson-Saunders et al. 1987). Methods of overcoming these problems by effective training having been outlined by Tamblyn (1997).

The Raters: When the rater is asked to judge how well the history was taken or the examination done, rather than just record whether it was done or not, more extensive rater training is generally required. For judging the adequacy of the physical examination, it is more efficient to use physicians or other knowledgeable health professionals. While Van der Vleuten et al. (1989) demonstrated that lay persons could be trained to accurately rate the adequacy of the physical examination, they were still no better than untrained medical faculty. The only exception to this rule is when SPs have also been trained as 'teaching associates'. In some schools, lay persons (or patients) are trained to instruct students on examination technique, such as the gynecological or the musculoskeletal examination (Behrens et al. 1979; Anderson & Meyer, 1979). Extensive training is generally provided, and a standard set of criteria are used to instruct and rate students on optimal technique. An added bonus of the teaching associate is that they can provide feedback on the degree of discomfort associated with the student's examination. When available, teaching associates who are trained as SPs are ideal candidates for rating the quality of the examination. For history-taking skill, there are benefits to using both the SP and physician rater. As the recipient of the student's ministrations, the SP is in the best situation to rate empathy and non-verbal skills, while physician raters are in the best position to judge the adequacy of the student's ability to obtain and refine clinically useful information from the history.

The Interpretation of the Information Collected

In SP methods of assessment, the student's interpretation of the information collected from history and physical examination is usually judged by their responses to follow-up questions about the problem. Written open-ended response formats are generally used, although in some settings, assessment is conducted by semi-structured oral examination. The student may be asked to summarize significant positive and negative findings, and/or list likely diagnoses justified by significant positive and negative findings from the history and examination (Solomon et al. 1994). In this respect, the SP method of assessing data interpretation is not distinctive from paper-and-pencil methods of testing; the only difference is the route by which the data were obtained.

To increase the number of cases used to sample performance in data collection (components 1 and 2), some centers have abandoned the post-SP encounter assessment of data interpretation, diagnosis and management, believing that this might be more efficiently done with standard written test formats. This appears to produce a very interesting paradox. When students realize that the examination score is based on the proportion of relevant items collected on history and physical examination, some adopt the bulldozer strategy—ask as many questions and do as many physical examination procedures as possible in the 5 or 10 minutes available. The answers provided by the patient, in fact, are irrelevant, because only the data requested is being judged, not its interpretation. Others have concerns about the validity of assessment when components of performance are fragmented and tested as component parts, rather than as a whole, as is done with the SP method. The optimal method is important in test development, yet there are no data to definitively address the issue.

Interpersonal Skills

One of the greatest challenges in the evaluation of clinical competence is the measurement of the student's ability to communicate effectively with patients. A positive therapeutic relationship with a patient has been shown to improve patient compliance and health outcomes (Hulka et al. 1975; Greenfield et al. 1988; Kaplan, Greenfield & Ware, 1989), and reduce the risk of malpractice litigation (Entman et al. 1994; Adamson et al. 1989). The effective delivery of primary and secondary preventive care has been shown to be highly influenced by the presence of a regular provider (Shea et al. 1992). However, patients without a regular provider, those who doctor shop and use the emergency room and walk-in clinics for episodic care (Lambrew et al. 1996; Shea et al. 1992; Kasteler et al. 1976), claim dissatisfaction with their physician as one of the most important reasons for seeking alternate sources of care. Perceived deficiencies in physician communication skills, including a lack of patient involvement in decision-making and communication about their health problems, are common complaints (Lambrew et al. 1996; Francis, Korsch & Morris, 1969; Tamblyn et al. 1994; Duffy, Hamerman & Cohen, 1980; Savage & Armstrong, 1990), and physician training and evaluation is seen as the root of—and solution to—these problems (Tamblyn et al. 1994; Simpson et al. 1991; Stewart, 1995; Tamblyn et al. 1994).

Clinical supervisors' ratings have been the most common method of evaluating patient communication skills. However neither supervisor's ratings nor self-evaluation have proven to be valid predictors of real patient responses (Woolliscroft et al. 1989; Merkel, 1984; Klessig et al. 1989). As a consequence, efforts have been made to use real patients to assess an individual's communication abilities (Tamblyn et al. 1994). An extensive feasibility study, conducted by the American Board of Internal Medicine, found that while reliable estimates of communication abilities could be obtained from real patient ratings, differences in the characteristics of patients seen in different clinics biased performance estimates. The standardized patient provides a method of overcoming problems with real patient rating because the same (or equivalent) patient can be used to test all students, and, unlike supervisors' rating, SP ratings are strongly correlated with real patient responses (Tamblyn et al. 1994).

Case Selection: To assess interpersonal skills, priority needs to be placed on the selection of cases where the establishment of an effective relationship has an impact on patient compliance, disease status, quality of life, and likelihood of establishing an on-going relationship with a health care provider. In this respect, cases should provide representation of:

- Patients with chronic disease whose compliance with recommended treatment (e.g., medication, diet, lifestyle change) has an impact on their disease status (e.g., diabetes, asthma, chronic renal failure, ischemic cardiac disease, hypertension)

- Patients who are typically 'hard to reach' in terms of primary and secondary preventive care (e.g., adolescents, unemployed, lower education and income, mentally ill)

- Patients who are experiencing a 'critical event' in their health status where the initial response of health providers may have an immediate impact on anxiety related to the situation and possibly long-term impacts on their continuing relationship with the health care system (e.g., diagnosis of a serious illness such as breast cancer, AIDs), a change in illness status (e.g., need for dialysis), or in prognosis (e.g., recovery from head injury)

Context of Assessment: There are two approaches that can be used to test interpersonal and communication skills. In the first approach, interpersonal skills are assessed in all SP encounters, regardless of the problem presented or the amount of time planned for the encounter. This approach should improve the reliability of assessment, as it increases the number of times a student's behavior is sampled. Approximately 20 to 30 ratings of student performance are required to obtain a reliability of 0.7-0.8 for SP rating of interpersonal and communication skills (Swanson & Norcini, 1989). The second approach bases the assessment of interpersonal and communication skills on a subset of SP cases specifically designed to test these abilities. Generally, encounter times for these types of cases are longer (10-30 minutes), and the emphasis is on communication with the patient, rather than the relevance and quality of data collection. For example, in a study of consultation skills of respiratory residents, Boudreau (1994) selected a case of a poorly controlled asthma that was referred for education and management. The case was selected as an example of a chronic disease, where 'patient education' and 'shared decision-making' (patient and physician) were key to effective control of disease status.

Case Description:

A 25-year-old male, an asthmatic since childhood, is referred by an internist to a recently opened clinic specializing in the management of asthma.

The patient is atopic (i.e., hay fever, allergies to cats and shellfish) and asthmatic, but otherwise has no other significant past medical history. He has been admitted to the hospital on 6 occasions in the past 2 years, twice in the past month. He was also admitted on numerous occasions as a child but then there was a period of stability during his teens. He has also been to the emergency room on many occasions in the past few years. During the last admission, he required ICU admission for about three days. He has never been intubated. His present medications are: Berotec ii puffs q4h prn, Beclofort iii puffs tid, Uniphyl 400 mg.qhs and Seldane prn for hay fever. He has also been on prednisone, always on tapering doses, approximately one dozen times in the past two years.

The patient attacks are usually provoked by allergies and although his worst season is the Spring, he has attacks year-round. He also has attacks precipitated by physical exertion, especially in the cold air. He has been unable to cross-country ski for the past two years and is concerned that he may not be able to even skate next Winter. The last attack was the worst ever; it appears to have been brought on by exposure to a cat at a friends place.

Since his last discharge, from St.Jude's Hospital, he has been feeling fairly well, although he is often awoken with dyspnea and wheezing and still using the Berotec at night-time. He uses it about 10 times per day and recently a canister lasts less than 2 weeks. He also has a vague constriction feeling in the chest on awakening in the mornings. There is no cough, unless he is having an attack, and no sputum.

There is a positive family history of allergies but no asthma in the immediate family. The patient is employed in an office-type setting. He does not smoke. No pets at home.

The patient is concerned about his illness and the fact that it appears to be getting worse. He has read alarming things in the newspaper such as "commonly used puffers in asthma management are linked to death" and wants to know what to do. He also read about this new asthma clinic and about "taking control of your own asthma" and wished more details about this. He also wants to have a medical opinion regarding natural herbs and acupuncture in the management of asthma.

Case Protocol:

The SP will not have any abnormal findings on physical examination except wheezing on a forced expiratory manoeuvre.

The SP will have with him a letter from the referring physician outlining briefly the problem and including reports of recent pulmonary function tests and a histamine challenge dating back about 3 years. There will also be the report of a recent chest x-ray.

The SP will also have the results of a routine spirometry done several minutes before.

The evaluation for this case will consist of two check-lists: one to be completed by the SP and one to be completed on the basis of the content and construction of the dictated consult.

Excerpts from the Checklist:

This doctor:	Did it well	Did it	Didn't do it
Spent some time teaching me about asthma:	☐	☐	☐
Asked me to show him how I use the puffer:	☐	☐	☐
Showed me how to use the puffer properly:	☐	☐	☐
Taught me the difference between the two types of puffers I'm using:	☐	☐	☐
Told me to use the Bertotec only when I feel I need it:	☐	☐	☐
Created an 'action plan' for me which will allow me to change the dose of my medications myself; or told me he would do this in the near future:	☐	☐	☐
Discussed what I should do in an emergency:	☐	☐	☐
Gave me an open prescription for steroids:	☐	☐	☐
Answered my questions re: herbs/acupuncture:	☐	☐	☐
Addressed my concern re: newspaper article:	☐	☐	☐

This second approach to the measurement of interpersonal skills may optimize the validity of inferences that can be drawn about a student's ability, but may suffer from lower reliability because of reduced sampling opportunities. Optimally, both approaches could be combined to enhance reliability of assessment as well as validity.

One variant of these approaches is to use a two-step patient encounter. In the first step, the student's ability to collect relevant information in relationship to the patient's presenting complaint is assessed. The student then receives the results of investigations and consultations requested. In the second stage of the encounter, the student returns to discuss diagnosis, prognosis and management plans with the patient. The advantage of this approach is that it closely matches the sequence of events that occur in the practice setting. It seems less artificial to students and may provide a more valid assessment of their abilities. The disadvantage is that it lengthens the test time for one case, and thus reduces the total number of cases that can be evaluated.

The Checklist: The chief challenge in constructing a checklist to measure interpersonal and communication skills is to identify the aspects of the patient-provider encounter that are relevant to the patient. In an interaction analysis of resident-patient interviews, Wooliscroft (1989) found that the attributes of the interview that were associated with thorough data collection were different from those associated with patient satisfaction. Patient perceptions of satisfaction with the encounter were influenced by the amount of time spent discussing concerns about the socio-emotional aspects of their health problems (Klessig et al. 1989). In contrast, the adequacy of data collection was influenced by the use of narrowly focused questions to probe medical problems and psycho-social circumstances. Considerable efforts have been made by well-established researchers to develop and evaluate questionnaires/checklists that provide a valid assessment of patient perceptions (Klessig et al. 1989; Ware & Hays, 1988; Roberts & Tugwell, 1987). The short form ABIM questionnaire (Figure 1) is an example of such an instrument (PSQ Project Co-Investigators, 1989). It has been used for assessment of performance by both real patients and standardized patients. To draw inferences about a student's capability to establish an effective relationship with the patient, examiners should select from the available validated instruments. The limitation of these instruments is that they have been designed to evaluate the perceptions of patients in general, not those that may particularly pertain to a specific type of problem. To overcome this problem, general assessment instruments are often augmented by case-specific checklists that are designed to assess aspects of the patient interaction that are specific to the situation. The checklist presented in Figure 1 is an example of this type of instrument.

The Raters: Although academic faculty may often be used to rate the quality of a student's interpersonal and patient communication skills, there is no substantive rationale for this choice. In fact, most studies have shown weak and even negative correlations between faculty ratings of patient communication skills with ratings provided by the actual recipients of care; the patients. The reason for these findings may be related to the finding that faculty ratings of student communication skills are strongly influenced by the student's competence in technical skills (Klessig et al. 1989), whereas the patient's focus is on socio-emotional aspects of the interaction (Woolliscroft et al. 1989). Ratings by SPs, by contrast, appear to provide a more accurate measure of real patient rating (Tamblyn et al. 1994). The validity of SP ratings is likely influenced by the extent to which they represent key characteristics of the real patient population (Tamblyn et al. 1994; Woolliscroft, 1989). For example, both age and education influence the satisfaction patients will have with the care they receive. SPs are commonly middle-aged and well educated. While their ratings of communication and interpersonal skills may reflect the expectations of this segment of the real patient population, they are probably not valid for others. Broader representation of educational levels, age, sex, and cultural groups among SPs recruited for training would likely enhance the validity of assessment.

Conclusions

It is generally accepted that SP methods of assessment provide unique and important advantages particularly in the evaluation of data collection and interpersonal skills. However, it is also acknowledged that SP methods of assessment: 1) cost more than paper-and-pencil examinations, 2) require longer testing time to obtain reliable measures of an individual's performance, and 3) require specialized expertise to develop the examination and administer it on a large scale (Carpenter, 1995; Cusimano et al. 1994; Battles et al. 1994). To maximize the benefits of SP assessment, examiners need to specify what is being assessed and why. In this chapter, the components of data collection and interpersonal skills that could be assessed with the SP method were outlined, as well as the issues that need to be considered in case selection, checklist development, and rater selection and training. Ultimately, health professional faculty make an investment in training and evaluating students so that they are capable of delivering optimal care to the patients they serve. The challenge for assessment will always be not whether it can be assessed, but whether we are measuring what we actually should measure.

References

Adamson, T. E., Tschann, J. M., Gullion, D. S., and Oppenberg, A. A. 1989. Physician Communication Skills and Malpractice Claims. A Complex Relationship. *The Western Journal of Medicine* 150:356-360.

Ali, J., Cohen, R., Adam, R., Gana, T. J., Pierre, I., Bedaysie, H. et al. 1996. Teaching effectiveness of the advanced trauma life support program as demonstrated by an objective structured clinical examination for practicing physicians. *World Journal of Surgery* 20(8):1121-1125.

Anderson, K. K., and Meyer, T. C. 1979. The Use of Instructor-Patients to Teach Physical Examination Techniques. *Journal of Medical Education* 54:897-899.

Badger, L. W., deGruy, F. V., Hartman, J., Plant, M. A., Leeper, J., Ficken, R. et al. 1995. Stability of standardized patients' performance in a study of clinical decision making. *Family Medicine* 27(2):126-131.

Badger, L. W., deGruy, F. V., Hartman, J., Plant, M. A., Leeper, J., Ficken, R. et al. 1994. Psychosocial interest, medical interviews, and the recognition of depression. *Archives of Family Medicine* 3(10):899-907.

Barrows, H. S., Williams, R. G., and Moy, R. H. 1987. A Comprehensive Performance-Based Assessment of Fourth-Year Students' Clinical Skills. *Journal of Medical Education* 62:805-809.

Barrows, H. S. 1971. *Simulated Patients (Programmed Patients) The Development and Use of a New Technique in Medical Education.* Springfield, Illinois: Charles C. Thomas.

Barrows, H. S. 1993. An overview of the uses of standardized patients for teaching and evaluating clinical skills. AAMC. *Academic Medicine* 68(6):443-453.

Battles, J. B., Carpenter, J. L., McIntire, D. D., and Wagner, J. M. 1994. Analyzing and adjusting for variables in a large-scale standardized-patient examination. *Academic Medicine* 69(5):370-376.

Behrens, A., Barnes, H. V., Gerber, W. L., Albanese, M., Matthes, S., and Cangelosi, A. 1979. A Model for Teaching Sophomore Medical Students the Essentials of the Male Genital-Rectal Examination. *Journal of Medical Education* 54:585-587.

Boudreau, D., Tamblyn, R. M., and Dufresne, L. 1994. Evaluation of Consultative Skills in Respiratory Medicine Using a Structured Medical Consultation. *American Review of Respiratory Diseases* 150:1298-1304.

Bryans, A. M., and Crothers, K. 1979. The Volunteer Patient as an Educational Resource. *Journal of Medical Education* 54:932-937.

Carney, P. A., Dietrich, A. J., Freeman, D. H., and Mott, L. A. 1993. The Periodic Health Examination Provided to Asymptomatic Older Women: An Assessment Using Standardized Patients. *Annals of Internal Medicine* 119(2):129-135.

Carney, P. A., Dietrich, A. J., Freeman, D. H. J., and Mott, L. A. 1993. The periodic health examination provided to asymptomatic older women: an assessment using standardized patients. *Annals of Internal Medicine* 119(2):129-135.

Carney, P. A., Dietrich, A. J., Freeman, D. H. J., and Mott, L. A. 1995. A standardized-patient assessment of a continuing medical education program to improve physicians' cancer-control clinical skills. *Academic Medicine* 70(1):52-58.

Carpenter, J. M. 1995. Cost analysis of objective structured clinical examinations. *Academic Medicine* 70(9):828-833.

Cohen, R., Reznick, R. K., Taylor, B. R., Provan, J., and Rothman, A. 1990. Reliability and Validity of the Objective Structured Clinical Examination in Assessing Surgical Residents. *The American Journal of Surgery* 160:302-305.

Connell, K. J., Sinacore, J. M., Schmid, F. R., Chang, R. W., and Perlman, S. G. 1993. Assessment of clinical competence of medical students by using standardized patients with musculoskeletal problems. *Arthritis & Rheumatism* 36(3):394-400.

Cusimano, M. D., Cohen, R., Tucker, W., Murnaghan, J., Kodama, R., and Reznick, R. 1994. A comparative analysis of the costs of administration of an OSCE (objective structured clinical examination). *Academic Medicine* 69(7):571-576.

Dawson-Saunders, B., Verhulst, S. J., Marcy, M., and Steward, D. E. 1987. Variability in Standardized Patients and its Effect on Student Performance. In *Further Developments in Assessing Clinical Competence*, edited by I. R. Hart and R. M. Harden, pp. 451-458. Montreal, Quebec: Can-Heal Publications Inc.

Day, R. P., Hewson, M. G., Kindy, P. J., and Van Kirk, J. 1993. Evaluation of resident performance in an outpatient internal medicine clinic using standardized patients. *Journal of General Internal Medicine* 8(4):193-198.

Duffy, D. L., Hamerman, D., and Cohen, M. A.. 1980. Communication skills of house officers : a study in a medical clinic. *Annals of Internal Medicine* 93:354-357.

Entman, S. S., Glass, C. A., Hickson, G. B., Githens, P. B., Whetten-Goldstein, K., and Sloan, F. A. 1994. The Relationship Between Malpractice Claims History and Subsequent Obstetric Care. *Journal of the American Medical Association* 272:1588-1591.

Ferrell, B. G., and Thompson, B. L. Standardized patients: a long-station clinical examination format. *Journal of Medical Education* 1993; 27(4):376-381.

Gordon, J. J., Saunders, N. A., Hennrikus, D., and Sanson-Fisher, R. W. 1992. Interns' Performances with Simulated Patients at the Beginning and the End of the Intern Year. *Journal of General Internal Medicine* 7:57-62.

Grand'Maison, P., Brailovsky, C., Lescop, J., and Rainsberry, P. 1997. Using standardized patients in licensing/certification examination: comparison of two tests in Canada. *Family Medicine* 29(1):27-32.

Grand'Maison, P., Lescop, J., and Brailovsky, C. 1993. Canadian experience with structured clinical examinations. *Canadian Medical Association Journal* 148(9): 1573-1576.

Grand'Maison, P., Lescop, J., Rainsberry, P., and Brailovsky, C. A. 1992. Large-scale use of an objective, structured clinical examination for licensing family physicians. *Canadian Medical Association Journal* 146(10):1735-1740.

Greenfield, S., Kaplan, S. H., Ware, J. E., Yano, E. M., and Frank, H. J. L. 1988. Patients' Participation in Medical Care: Effects on Blood Sugar Control and Quality of Life in Diabetes. *Journal of General Internal Medicine* 3:448-457.

Harden, R. M., and Gleeson, F. A. 1979. Assessment of clinical competence using an objective structured clinical examination. *Journal of Medical Education* 13:41-54.

Haydon, R., Donnelly, M., Schwartz, R., Strodel, W., and Jones, R. 1994. Use of standardized patients to identify deficits in student performance and curriculum effectiveness. *American Journal of Surgery* 168(1):57-65.

Hiatt, H. H., Barnes, B. A., Brennan, T. A., Laird, N. M., Lawthers, A. G., Leape, L. L. et al. 1989. A study of medical injury and medical malpractice. *New England Journal of Medicine* 321:480-484.

Hodges, B., Turnbull, J., Cohen, R., Bienenstock, A., and Norman, G. 1996. Evaluating communication skills in the OSCE format: reliability and generalizability. *Journal of Medical Education* 30(1):38-43.

Howard, L. W., Garman, K. A., and McCann, R. E. 1995. Another go at the experiment. *Public Health Reports* 110(6):668-673.

Hulka, B. S., Kupper, L. L., Cassel, J. C., and Mayo, F. 1975. Doctor-Patient Communication and Outcomes Among Diabetic Patients. *Journal of Community Health* 1(1):15-27.

Jain, S. S., DeLisa, J. A., and Campagnolo, D. I. 1994. Methods used in the evaluation of clinical competency of physical medicine and rehabilitation residents. *American Journal of Physical Medicine & Rehabilitation* 73(4):234-239.

Jain, S. S., Nadler, S., Eyles, M., Kirshblum, S., DeLisa, J. A., and Smith, A. 1997. Development of an objective structured clinical examination (OSCE). *American Journal of Physical Medicine & Rehabilitation* 76(2):102-106.

Johnson, J. A., Kopp, K. C., and Williams, R. G. 1990. Standardized Patients for the Assessment of Dental Students' Clinical Skills. *Journal of Dental Education* 54:331-333.

Kaplan, S. H., Greenfield, S., and Ware, J. E. 1989. Assessing the effects of physician-patient interactions on the outcomes of chronic disease. *Medical Care* 27 (suppl.):S110-S127

Kasteler, J., Kane, R. L., Olsen, D. M., and Thetford, C. 1976. Issues Underlying Prevalence of "Doctor-Shopping" Behavior. *Journal of Health and Social Behavior* 17:328-339.

Kay, C. J., Johnson, J. A., and Kopp, K. C. 1994. Standardized patients for teaching geriatric dentistry. *Special Care in Dentistry* 14(6):229-232.

Klessig, J., Robbins, A. S., Wieland, D., and Rubenstein, L. 1989. Evaluating Humanistic Attributes of Internal Medicine Residents. *Journal of General Internal Medicine* 4:514-521.

Kokotailo, P. K., Langhough, R., Neary, E. J., Matson, S. C., and Fleming, M. F. 1995. Improving pediatric residents' alcohol and other drug use clinical skills: use of an experimental curriculum. *Pediatrics* 96(1):99-104.

Kopp, K. C., and Johnson, J. A. 1995. Checklist agreement between standardized patients and faculty. *Journal of Dental Education* 59(8):824-829.

Lambrew, J. M., DeFriese, G. H., Carey, T. S., Ricketts, T. C., and Biddle, A. K. 1996. The Effects of Having a Regular Doctor on Access to Primary Care. *Medical Care* 34:138-154.

Leape, L. L., Brennan, T. A., Laird, N., Lawthers, A. G., Logalio, A. R. et al. 1991. The Nature of Adverse Events in Hospitalized Patients: Results of the Harvard Medical Practice Study II. *New England Journal of Medicine* 324(6): 377-384.

Lockyer, J., El-Guebaly, N., Simpson, E., Gromoff, B., Toews, J., and Juschka, B. 1996. Standardized patients as a measure of change in the ability of family physicians to detect and manage alcohol abuse. *Academic Medicine* 71(1 suppl): S1-S3

MacRae, H. M., Vu, N. V., Graham, B., Word-Sims, M., Colliver, J. A., and Robbs, R. S. 1995. Comparing checklists and databases with physicians' ratings as measures of students' history and physical-examination skills. *Academic Medicine* 70(4): 313-317.

Maxim, B. R., and Dielman, T. E. 1987. Dimensionality, internal consistency and interrater reliability of clinical performance ratings. *Journal of Medical Education* 21:130-137.

Merkel, W. T. 1984. Physician Perception of Patient Satisfaction Do Doctors Know Which Patients Are Satisfied? *Medical Care* 22 No. 5:453-459.

Newble, D. I., Hoare, J., and Sheldrake, P. F. 1980. The Selection and Training of Examiners for Clinical Examinations. *Journal of Medical Education* 14:345-349.

Newble, D. I., and Swanson, D. B. 1988. Psychometric Characteristics of the Objective Structured Clinical Examination. *Journal of Medical Education* 22:325-334.

Newble, D. I. 1988. Eight years' Experience with a Structured Clinical Examination. *Journal of Medical Education* 22:200-204.

Nieman, L. Z., Vernon, M. S., Holbert, D., and Boyett, L. 1988. Training and Validating the Use of Geriatric Simulated Patients. *Research in Medical Education* 27:154-159.

Norman, G. R., Davis, D. A., Lamb, S., Hanna, E., Caulford, P., and Kaigas, T. 1993. Competency assessment of primary care physicians as part of a peer review program. *Journal of the American Medical Association* 270(9): 1046-1051.

Norman, G. R., Neufeld, V. R., Walsh, A., Woodward, C. A., and McConvey, G. A. 1985. Measuring Physicians' Performances by Using Simulated Patients. *Journal of Medical Education* 60:925-934.

Norman, G. R., Tugwell, P., and Feightner, J. W. 1982. A Comparison of Resident Performance on Real and Simulated Patients. *Journal of Medical Education* 57:708-715.

Petrusa, E. R., Blackwell, T. A., and Ainsworth, M. A. 1990. Reliability and Validity of an Objective Structured Clinical Examination for Assessing the Clinical Performance of Residents. *Archives of Internal Medicine* 150:573-577.

Petrusa, E. R., Blackwell, T. A., Rogers, L. P., Saydjari, C., Parcel, S., and Guckian, J. C. 1987. An Ojective Measure of Clinical Performance. *The American Journal of Medicine* 83:34-42.

Pololi, L. H., and Potter, S. 1996. Behavioral change in preventive medicine. An efficacy assessment of a physician education module. *Journal of General Internal Medicine* 11(9):545-547.

Renaud, M., Beuchemin, J., Lalonde, C., Poirier, H., and Berthiaume, S. 1980. Practice Settings and Prescribing Profiles: The Simulation of Tension Headaches to General Practioners Working in Different Practice Settings in the Montreal Area. *American Journal of Public Health* 70:1068-1073.

Rethans, J., Drop, R., Sturmans, F., and Van der Vleuten, C. 1991. A method for introducing standardized (simulated) patients into general practice consultations. *British Journal of General Practice* 41:94-96.

Rethans, J., Martin, E., Metsemakers, J. 1994. To what extent do clinical notes by general practioners reflect actual medical performance? A study using simulated patients. *British Journal of General Practice* 44:153-156.

Rethans, J., Sturmans, F., Drop, R., and Van der Vleuten, C. 1991. Assessment of the performance of general practitioners by the use of standardized (simulated) patients. *British Journal of General Practice* 47:97-99.

Robb, A., Cohen, A., Norman, G., and Turnbull, J. 1996. Performance-based assessment of clinical ethics using an objective structured clinical examination. *Academic Medicine* 71(5):495-498.

Roberts, J. G., and Tugwell, P. 1987. Comparison of Questionnaires Determining Patient Satisfaction with Medical Care. *Health Services and Resources* 22(5):637-654.

Robinson, J. K., and McGaghie, W. C. 1996. Skin cancer detection in a clinical practice examination with standardized patients. *Journal of the American Academy of Dermatology* 34(4):709-711.

Roter, D. L., Cole, K. A., Kern, D. E., Barker, L. R., and Grayson, M. 1990. An Evaluation of Residency Training in Interviewing Skills and the Psychosocial Domain of Medical Practice. *Journal of General Internal Medicine* 5:347-354.

Sachdeva, A. K., Wolfson, P. J., Blair, P. G., Gillum, D. R., Gracely, E. J., and Friedman, M. 1997. Impact of a standardized patient intervention to teach breast and abdominal examination skills to third-year medical students at two institutions. *American Journal of Surgery* 173(4):320-325.

Savage, R., and Armstrong, D. 1990. Effect of a general practitioner's consulting style on patients' satisfaction: a controlled study. *British Medical Journal* 301:968-970.

Shahabudin, S. H., Almashoor, S. H., Edariah, A. B., and Khairuddin, Y. 1994. Assessing the competence of general practitioners in diagnosing generalized anxiety disorder using standardized patients. *Journal of Medical Education* 28(5): 432-440.

Shatzer, J. H., Darosa, D., Colliver, J. A., and Barkmeier, L. 1993. Station-length requirements for reliable performance-based examination scores. *Academic Medicine* 68(3): 224-229.

Shea, S., Misra, D., Ehrlich, M. H., Field, L., and Francis, C. K. 1992. Correlates of Nonadherence to Hypertension Treatment in an Inner-City Minority Population. *American Journal of Public Health* 82:1607-1612.

Shea, S., Misra, D., Ehrlich, M. H., Field, L., and Francis, C. K. 1992. Predisposing Factors for Severe, Uncontrolled Hypertension in an Inner-City Minority Population. *New England Journal of Medicine* 327:776-781.

Simpson, M., Buckman, R., Stewart, M., Maguire, P., Lipkin, M., Novack, D. et al. 1991. Doctor-patient communication: the Toronto consensus statement. *British Medical Journal* 303:1385-1387.

Solomon, D. J., Speer, A. J., Perkowski, L. C., and DiPette, D. J. 1994. Evaluating problem solving based on the use of history findings in a standardized-patient examination. *Academic Medicine* 69(9): 754-757.

Starfield, B., and Scheff, D. 1972. Effectiveness of Pediatric Care: The Relationship Between Processes and Outcome. *Pediatrics* 49:547-552.

Stewart, M. A. 1995. Effective Physician-Patient Communication and Health Outcomes: A Review. *Canadian Medical Association Journal* 152 (9):1423-1433.

Stillman, P., Swanson, D., Regan, M. B., Philbin, M. M., Nelson, V. et al. 1991. Assessment of Clinical Skills of Residents Utilizing Standardized Patients. *Annals of Internal Medicine* 114:393-401.

Stillman, P. L., Regan, M. B., Philbin, M., and Haley, H. 1990. Results of a Survey on the Use of Standardized Patients to Teach and Evaluate Clinical Skills. *Academic Medicine* 65:298-292.

Stillman, P. L., Regan, M. B., and Swanson, D. B. 1987. Fourth-Year Performance Assessment Task Force Group. A Diagnostic Fourth-Year Performance Assessment. *Archives of Internal Medicine* 147:1981-1985.

Stillman, P. L., Regan, M. B., Swanson, D. B., Case, S., McCahan, J. et al. 1990. An Assessment of the Clinical Skills of Fourth-Year Students at Four New England Medical Schools. *Academic Medicine* 65:320-326.

Stillman, P. L., Swanson, D. B., Smee, S., Stillman, A. E., Ebert, T. H. et al. 1986. Assessing Clinical Skills of Residents with Standardized Patients. *Annals of Internal Medicine* 105:762-771.

Sutnick, A. I., Stillman, P. L., Norcini, J. J., Friedman, M., Regan, M. B., Williams, R. G. et al. 1993. ECFMG assessment of clinical competence of graduates of foreign medical schools. Educational Commission for Foreign Medical Graduates. *Journal of the American Medical Association* 270(9): 1041-1045.

Sutnick, A. I., Stillman, P. L., Norcini, J. J., Friedman, M., Williams, R. G., Trace, D. A. et al. 1994. Pilot study of the use of the ECFMG clinical competence assessment to provide profiles of clinical competencies of graduates of foreign medical schools for residency directors Educational Commission for Foreign Medical Graduates. *Academic Medicine* 69(1): 65-67.

Swanson, D. B., and Norcini, J. J. 1989. Factors Influencing Reproducibility of Tests Using Standardized Patients. *Teaching and Learning in Medicine* 1:158-166.

Swartz, M. H., and Colliver, J. A. 1996. Using standardized patients for assessing clinical performance: an overview. *Mount Sinai Journal of Medicine* 63(3-4): 241-249.

Tamblyn, R., Berkson, L., Dauphinee, W. D., Gayton, D., Grad, R., Huang, A. et al. 1997. Unnecessary Prescribing of NSAIDs and the Management of NSAID-Related Gastrophy in Medical Practice. *Annals of Internal Medicine* 127(6): 429-438.

Tamblyn, R. M., Abrahamowicz, M., Berkson, L., Dauphinee, W. D., Gayton, D. C., Grad, R. M. et al. 1992. First-Visit Bias in the Measurement of Clinical Competence with Standardized Patients. *Academic Medicine* 67(10): S22-S24

Tamblyn, R. M., Abrahamowicz, M., Schnarch, B., Colliver, J., Benaroya, S., and Snell, L. 1994. Can Standardized Patients Predict Real-Patient Satisfaction with the Doctor-Patient Relationship? *Teaching and Learning in Medicine* 6 (1): 36-44.

Tamblyn, R. M., Benaroya, S., Snell, L., McLeod, P., Schnarch, B., and Abrahamowicz, M. 1994. The Feasibility and Value of Using Patient Satisfaction Ratings to Evaluate Internal Medicine Residents. *Journal of General Internal Medicine* 9:146-152.

Tamblyn, R. M., Grad, R., Gayton, D., Petrella, L., and Reid, T. 1997. Impact of Inaccuracies in Standardized Patient Portrayal and Recording on Physician Performance during Blinded Clinic Visits. *Teaching and Learning in Medicine* 9:25-38.

Tamblyn, R. M., Klass, D. J., Schnabl, G., and Kopelow, M. 1990. Factors Associated with the Accuracy of Standardized Patient Presentation. *Academic Medicine* 65(9): S55-S56

Tamblyn, R. M., Klass, D. J., Schnabl, G., and Kopelow, M. 1991. Sources of Unreliability and Bias in Standardized Patient Rating. *Teaching and Learning in Medicine* 3(2): 74-85.

Tamblyn, R. M., Klass, D. J., Schnabl, G., and Kopelow, M. 1991. The use of standardized patients in the evaluation of clinical competence: The accuracy of patient problem presentation. *Journal of Medical Education* 25:100-109.

Traina, A. D., Goubran, E., Gourf, N. J., Scaringe, J. G., Talmage, D. M., and Wells, K. 1996. Description of integrated competency examination: tools to assess the chiropractic curriculum effectiveness and students' competency levels. *Journal of Manipulative & Physiological Therapeutics* 19(7): 463-468.

Van der Vleuten, C. P., Van Luyk, S. J., Van Ballegooijen, A. M., and Swanson, D. B. 1989. Training and experience of examiners. *Journal of Medical Education* 23(3): 290-296.

Van Der Vleuten, C. P. M., and Swanson, D. B. 1990. Assessment of clinical skills with standardized patients: State of the Art. *Teaching and Learning in Medicine* 2(2): 58-76.

Vu, N. V. 1979. Medical Problem-Solving Assessment: A Review of Methods and Instruments. *Evaluation & The Health Professions* 2:281-307.

Vu, N. V. 1992. Standardized Patients' Accuracy in Recording Clinical Performance Checklist Items. *Journal of Medical Education* 26:99-104.

Ware, J. E., and Hays, R. D. 1988. Methods for measuring patient satisfaction with specific medical encounters. *Medical Care* 26:393-402.

Wenrich, M. D., Paauw, D. S., Carline, J. D., Curtis, J. R., and Ramsey, P. G. 1995. Do primary care physicians screen patients about alcohol intake using the CAGE questions? *Journal of General Internal Medicine* 10(11): 631-634.

Williams, R. G., Barrows, H. S., Vu, N. V., Verhulst, S. J., Colliver, J. A. et al. 1987. Direct, Standardized Assessment of Clinical Competence. *Journal of Medical Education* 21:482-489.

Woodward, C. A., McConvey, G. A., Neufeld, V., and Norman, G. R. 1985. Measurement of Physician Performance by Standardized Patients. *Medical Care* 23:1019-1027.

Woolliscroft, J. O., Calhoun, J. G., Billiu, G. A., Stross, J. K., MacDonald, M., and Templeton, B. 1989. House officer interviewing techniques: impact on data elicitation and patient perceptions. *Journal of General Internal Medicine* 4:108-114.

Worthington, R. C., Willis, S. E., and Boyett, R. L. 1994. Standardized patients and licensing examinations. *Academic Medicine* 69(10): 821-822.

7

The Objective Structured Clinical Examination (OSCE) of Technical Skills: the Canadian Experience in Licensure

Richard Reznick, David E. Blackmore,
Dale Dauphinee, Sydney M. Smee, Arthur I. Rothman

In 1989, the Medical Council of Canada initiated a program to incorporate in its licensing examination a clinical skills component using an OSCE. The examination consists of twenty ten-minute "stations," all standardized-patient based. At each station the candidate is instructed to perform a specific task (e.g., ascultate the abdomen, examine the knee, elicit the simulated patient's chief complaint, instruct the patient, etc.). The examinee's performance at each station is observed and scored by physician examiners, and a criterion-referenced approach is used to set performance standards. This chapter describes the nature and development of the examination, and reports the results of three large-scale administrations in which a total of almost 5,000 candidates were tested. Reliability estimates, dependability indices at the cut score and generalizability analyses were calculated for each of the three administrations. The authors conclude that the Canadian experience has demonstrated the feasibility of testing clinical competence using an OSCE at the licensure level. Present efforts are focused on sequential testing and validity studies.

Throughout the world, the Objective Structured Clinical Examination (OSCE) has emerged as the best method we have of formally assessing the clinical skills of undergraduate medical students and residents. The OSCE has many strengths. It relies on witnessed observations of actual clinical performance. It employs a highly structured marking scheme in an attempt to be as objective as possible. It is capable of assessing a broad range of clinical skills including history taking, physical examination and patient-doctor communication. Its major drawback is that it is expensive, logistically challenging, and requires a large team of dedicated and knowledgeable individuals to make it work well.

The Medical Council of Canada (MCC) is charged with the task of administering an examination to prospective licensees throughout Canada. In the mid to late 1980s, there was a growing dissatisfaction amongst Provincial Licensing Authorities that the MCC examination, which at that time was strictly a paper and pencil based examination, was not assessing all of the competencies that were thought to be important for aspiring practitioners. A decision was made at that time to examine the possibility of adding a component to the licensing exam that would assess clinical skills in a performance based manner. In 1989, a committee was struck to conceptualize and pilot test an examination format that might be appropriate for licensure.

The committee decided on a 20 station, 200, minute OSCE format. In 1991, a pilot project was run to address several research issues that were essential considerations prior to full scale testing. The details of the MCC examination and pilot tests have been reported previously (Reznick, et al. 1992). The results of the pilot test prompted adoption of a performance based component to the MCC's licensing examination. This was first run on a small scale in 1992, testing 400 candidates at two centers. Three large scale administrations have now been run, in 1993, 1994, and 1995. The purpose of this report is to present data from these three administrations and to discuss future directions that the MCC is taking with this examination.

Structure of the Examination

The examination is a 200-minute OSCE that is divided into two components. There are 10 couplet stations, which are 5-minute patient encounters followed by a 5-minute post encounter probe (PEP). These probes are paper and pencil based exercises that question the candidates about aspects of the patient they had just seen. The second component of the examination is ten 10-minute patient encounters. All patient encounters are standardized patient based. Marking is accomplished through a structured check-list approach. Additionally, a 6 point global rating score is completed by the examiner. All examiners are qualified physicians.

The examination is delivered at multiple sites (11 in 1995) over a period of two days. The MCC has felt that it is important to give different examinations on each of these two days and, as such, in any given year there is a Form A and a Form B of the examination. These forms are specifically designed to be as equivalent as possible. The attempt at equivalence goes back to station creation. During the station creation phase, we asked authors to create two stations that test similar competencies in similar domains of knowledge of similar difficulty. We then populate the Form A and Form B in any given year with one of a pair of stations.

Data Analysis

Means and standard deviations of total test scores for the two forms of the examination have been calculated for each center. Reliability has been calculated using Cronbach's coefficient alpha. Alpha coefficients have been computed for the entire examination, for each 10 station component of the examination, and separately for all test takers and Group I candidates defined as first time takers who are graduates of Canadian medical schools. Generalizability coefficients are also reported as an index of reliability, as are dependability coefficients at the cut score. Generalizability analyses have been done to determine the variance attributable to centers, sessions within a center, items, and examinees. Corrected item total test score correlations were calculated as indices of station stability.

Standard Setting

A criterion referenced approach has been used to set the passing score for all three administrations. In 1993, a modified Angoff approach was used (Angoff, 1971). In that year, an initial *a priori* cut score was established for each station, by a panel of physicians. In addition, physician examiners were asked to make pass/fail determinations for each candidate that they saw. This determined a "new" cut score for each station which was averaged with the *a priori* determination to formulate a station passing score. The number of stations required to pass the examination was set by a central committee. In 1994 and 1995, the cut score for each station was determined differently. Building on a positive experience with the use of global ratings by physician examiners, we expanded the global rating form from a pass/fall decision to a 6-point global rating scale where candidates were identified in each station as superior, good, borderline pass, borderline fail, poor, or inferior. We then took the average score of the two borderline groups, that is borderline pass and borderline fail, and used that as a cut score for each station. Again, the number of stations required to pass the examination was set by a central committee. Pass/fall rates are reported for the total examinee pool and for Group I candidates.

Results

Three large scale administrations of the MCCQE Part II tested 1352, 1672, and 1737 candidates in 1993, 1994, and 1995 respectively. In each year, over 1000 SPs and over 1000 physician examiners were recruited.

Scores are reported as percentages with each 10-minute unit of the examination receiving equal weighting and accounting for 1/20th of an examinee's total score. In 1993, means ($\pm$SD) for the 7 centers ranged from 65% $\pm$4.4 to 69.6% $\pm$4.0 for Form A, and from 65% $\pm$6.4 to 69.4% $\pm$5.3 for Form B. In 1994 the scores for the 10 centers ranged from 67.13% $\pm$5.9 to 69.9% $\pm$5.0 for Form A and from 63.8% $\pm$5.1 to 69.2% $\pm$4.6 for Form B. For 1995, across 11 centers, mean scores varied from 65.6% $\pm$5.9 to 69.7% $\pm$4.4 for Form A and from 65.3% $\pm$4.9 to 70.1% $\pm$5.2 for Form B. Mean scores for Group I candidates have been consistently higher than mean scores for the total examinee pool. Group I candidates constitute approximately 85% of the examinee pool.

Reliability indices are reported for 1993 to 1995 on Table 1. Corrected item total test score correlations range from .27 to .46 and from .24 to .51 for Forms A and B of 1993 respectively, from .12 to .40 and from .18 to .46 for Forms A and B of 1994 respectively, and from .16 to .38 and from .20 to .42 for Forms A and B of 1995 respectively. Generalizability analyses are reported in Table 2.

Table 1:

Reliability Estimates for the Two Forms of the MCCQE Part II Given in 1993,1994 and 1995

	# of Test Takers		20 Stations		10-Minute Pt. Encounters		10 Couplet Stations		Generalizability Coefficient	Dependability Index
	All	GpI	All	GpI	All	GpI	All	GpI	All	All
93 Form A	744	581	.80	.64	.69	.52	.71	.55	.74	.99
93 Form B	607	398	.81	.65	.70	.55	.69	.58	.78	.99
94 Form A	970	797	.72	.62	.55	.39	.59	.51	.61	.99
94 Form B	702	501	.76	.64	.62	.36	.65	.58	.65	.99
95 Form A	966	799	.74	.59	.63	.45	.51	.42	.76	.99
95 Form B	771	618	.74	.65	.54	.41	.64	.56	.74	.99

Table 2:

Generalizability Analyses of Forms A and B for the 1993, 1994, and 1995 Administration of the MCCQE Part II for All Test Takers

	1993 Form A		Form B		1994 Form A		Form B		1995 Form A		Form B	
	Variance	%	Variance	%	Variance	%	Variance	%	Variance	%	Variance	%
	1.65	.69	0.00	0.00	.09	0.03	0.58	0.20	1.28	.51	2.23	1.07
C	0.00	0.00	0.24	0.11	.14	0.05	2.73	0.97	0.02	.01	0.00	0.00
S:C	26.34	11.0	28.2	13.3	20.94	7.50	21.99	7.82	22.47	10.40	18.84	9.10
	58.48	24.75	33.38	15.43	78.65	28.33	82.52	29.70	24.34	11.33	33.86	16.30
I	10.22	4.32	6.56	3.03	9.91	3.56	8.91	3.16	11.15	5.16	10.37	5.01
I:C	13.59	5.75	14.34	6.63	16.95	6.10	21.98	7.81	18.55	8.59	14.53	7.02
I:S:C	125.93	55.31	133.56	61.75	150.93	54.36	141.48	50.31	131.99	63.93	127.11	61.42

Centers, S=Sessions, E=Examinees, I-Items (Stations)

The failure rates for the total examinee pool were 17%, 13%, and 9% in 1993, 1994, and 1995 respectively. Failure rates for first time takers who are graduates of Canadian medical schools (Group I) were 7%, 6%, and 3% for 1993, 1994, and 1995 respectively.

Discussion

Any testing body, particularly those responsible for setting examinations used for certification and licensure, must ensure that the examinations they give are relevant, accurate and continuously improving. The relevancy of paper and pencil based tests as the sole method of ensuring competency in any professional domain, has been appropriately challenged over the last few decades. In 1989, the MCC took up the challenge of incorporating a performance based test into its examination process. That challenge has proved difficult but doable, and costly but rewarding. In the last three years, the MCC has administered a nation-wide OSCE for licensure to over 5,500 examinees in eleven cities across Canada, deploying the effort of thousands of SPs and physician examiners. The principal reason for mounting this extensive program has been to use an examination format that we believe complements the other elements of the MCC qualifying examination (MCCQE) and in so doing test competencies that previously went largely untested.

The three pillars of any examination process are reliability, validity and feasibility. Which of these three basic considerations addressed in examination creation should predominate? Some would argue feasibility. If an examination is not logistically doable, then all other issues pale in comparison. While seemingly trite, the issue of feasibility is generally perceived to be the major barrier to running any OSCE, particularly so for large scale OSCEs that require multiple sites and examine a large pool of candidates. Over the last three years, the MCC has worked hard at systematizing the process of delivering the OSCE across the country. It has developed structured teams of personnel for each center, produced several manuals for running a center, streamlined the process of data collection and data entry, developed protocols for station creation and review, and put into place procedures for handling anticipated problems in the elaboration of a large scale operation. It has worked co-operatively, with Canadian medical schools using a process of central control and peripheral delivery. The result has been an examination that has proved costly, but a system that is working well and efficiently. The cost of the examination to each candidate is approximately $1,200 Canadian. This figure takes into account all direct costs of creating and administering the examination, but does not include proportional costs of the MCC infrastructure.

Reliability has been a focus of many studies examining the properties of OSCEs for several reasons (Van der Vleuten, Norman & DeGraaff, 1991). First, if reliability is inordinately low, several critical problems arise jeopardizing the entire examination. The lower the reliability, the less confident one can be in drawing inferences from examination results. A low reliability renders the standard setting process extremely difficult. If the reliability of an examination is very low, individuals who fail the examination and are allowed to repeat, may well pass in repeat examinations by chance alone, even though they may have remained incompetent. Second, reliability estimates are easy to measure. Any single iteration of an examination can provide an estimate of internal consistency. As such, "reliability data" have become a focus for OSCE researchers and a barometer of the quality of the examination. Reliability estimates for the 20 station examination for all takers have, for the last three years, ranged from .72 to .81. What is perhaps more important than interstation reliability focusing on the total examinee pool is the dependability index at the cut score (Colliver et al. 1989). For all of the six iterations over the last three years this index has been .99, indicating that scores around the cut point can likely be interpreted with confidence.

Many would argue that the most important pillar of any examination is the extent to which it is a valid measure of what it intends to measure. However, accruing evidence for the validity of an examination is as difficult as it is important. Of the three classic elements of validity, content, criterion and construct, we have examined the first two to a limited degree. The major focus on issues of content validation has come from a rigorous station review process. Prior to administration of a station, it is reviewed in a five step process by a cumulative total of seventeen physicians. In addition, after each iteration, every station is reviewed in light of candidate performance on each item of a checklist, candidate performance on the station as a whole, and feedback from the roughly twenty-five physicians who would have served as examiners at that station nationwide. Criterion related validity has been addressed only to a limited degree. We have no data about the predictive validity of the examination. In terms of concurrent validity, we have looked at the correlation of the Part II examination with the other elements of the MCCQE, which consist of a multiple choice examination and a key features (Bordage & Page, 1987) component. The correlations between the OSCE and the MCQ components of the examinations for the years 1993 and 1994 range from .32 to .47 and when corrected for attenuation, from .38 to .58. The correlations between the OSCE and the key features component of the examination for 1993 and 1994 range from .39 to .56 and when corrected for attenuation, from .53 to .75. Our interpretation of these data is that they lend support for the criterion related validity of this examination. The correlations are in the moderate range, which can be viewed as appropriate from two vantage points. The first is that very low correlations would be problematic when one considers that, generally speaking, very good candidates should do very well on most elements of an examination, and very poor candidates do poorly on all elements. The second is that very high correlations would be problematic when one considers that the major impetus for the development of the Part II examination was to test competencies that are fundamentally different from the Part I examination.

To date, we have not made a formal attempt to gauge the examination's construct validity. There is a general feeling amongst examiners, examinees, and test creators that the OSCE is an appropriate vehicle for assessing clinical skills. However to date there have been no studies with respect to the MCCQE designed to corroborate this impression.

The MCCQE Part II is a logistically challenging form of assessment that is costly to each candidate. In an effort to reduce costs and streamline the examination process, the MCC is engaged in a research effort to embark upon a process of sequential testing. It is estimated that a 100-minute, 10 station screening examination could be used to accurately predict a large proportion of examinees, who in all probability would pass the full twenty station examination. Full testing would then be done for the remaining examinee pool, currently estimated to be about 40% of the candidates. If successful, this effort will reduce costs and streamline the process.

The challenges for the future include validity studies, continuously improving the quality of existing stations, creation of new stations that will break the mold of the traditional OSCE stations, and streamlining the process. The MCCQE Part II has been a product of the commitment of hundreds of individuals dedicated to the ideal that the more closely a test simulates a real world experience, the more valid are the inferences that can be drawn from the test.

References

Angoff, V. M. 1971. Norms scales and equivalent scores. In *Educational Measurement,* edited by R. L. Thomdike. Washington, D.C.: American Council on Measurement.

Bordage, G., and Page G. 1987. An alternative approach to PMPs: The "key features" concept. In *Further developments in assessing clinical competence*, edited by I. R. Hart and R. M. Harden, pp. 59-75. Montreal: Heal Publications.

Colliver, J. A., Verhulst, S. J., Williams, R. G., and Norcini, J. J. 1989. Reliability of performance on standardized patient cases: A comparison of consistency measures based on generalizabilltv theory. *Teaching and Learning in Medicine* 1: 31-7.

Reznick, R. K., Smee, S., Rothman, A. et. al. 1992. An objective structured clinical examination for the Licentiate: Report of the pilot project of the Medical Council of Canada. *Academic Medicine* 67: 487-94.

Van der Vleuten, C. P. M., Norman, G. R., and DeGraaff, E. D. 1991. Pitfalls in the pursuit of objectivity: Issues of reliability. *Medical Education* 25: 119-26.

8

Handling Critical Incidents: Sweaty Palms And Post Traumatic Stress Syndrome

Christine H. McGuire

Challenges involved in the assessment of affective responses differ from those inherent in the assessment of cognitive, technical and/or communication skills, in numerous respects. One of the most important of these entails the distinction between determining what an individual **can do** *vs. what he or she* **habitually does.** *In the case of skills assessment we are concerned with documenting what the examinee is capable of doing, i.e., his or her maximum performance under strictly controlled and highly standardized conditions. In the case of affective responses, however, we are concerned with observing how the examinee* **habitually** *behaves, i.e. what motivations, values, and stress management techniques drive his or her actions when nobody is looking. In the nature of the case, neither typical tests nor conventional assessment centers can reveal that; hence, the popularity of portfolio assessment and other means of collecting longitudinal data. To supplement and/or replace such laborious, potentially biased and frequently unreliable data sources, three types of* *low-tech simulations have been evolved and are currently being utilized in special circumstances. These include what can best be described as: (1) the impossible dilemma, (2) the role play for which there is no wholly satisfactory resolution, and (3) the "stealth" stimulus. Simple examples of each of these techniques are described, the limited data available about them are reported, their impacts on examinees are noted and their uses and limitations discussed.*

S kill—cognitive, technical and interpersonal—though absolutely essential, is not sufficient to assure effective action as a professional. What is also required is a predisposition (or tendency) to respond appropriately to critical situations that may range from mildly annoying to exceedly dangerous. Consequently, in making personnel decisions—admission, hiring, promotion, licensure and certification—it would be exceedingly helpful to be able to assess attitudes and to predict probable affective responses to stressful situations in order to identify those people who are not only capable of behaving in a technically "correct" way, but who are also predisposed to display the "right" attitudes, and whose actions promote the "proper" values.

For far too long we have depended on so called "direct" measures of attitudes —opinion surveys and other forms of self report—which we know to be totally inadequate and even misleading, both because the accuracy of a respondent's self image is questionable and because the more astute examinees will deliberately try to disguise attitudes they know to be socially unacceptable, even in situations where nothing important is at stake.

In an effort to protect themselves from inflated positive findings on direct attitudinal measures, those responsible for personnel decisions have always attempted to supplement data from such sources with testimonials from persons who have known and presumably observed the subject in a variety of situations over a long period of time. More recently, with the rise in popularity of Portfolio Assessment, subjects have been increasingly required to submit a collection of documents, video tapes and other evidence of performance over time.

But these are also subject to bias and distortion that make inferences about attitudes based on them exceedingly suspect. It is not surprising therefore that psychologists urge us to turn to indirect methods of assessing affective characteristics. It seems that if we are to have any hope of success we must disguise the purpose of our tests by camouflaging attitudinal assessment as a test of skill directly related to a clearly relevant task. In accord with this principle, I propose in this brief survey to call to your attention different types of simulation that have proved useful for assessment in the affective domain. Several are illustrations of high-tech simulations that can be used to assess simultaneously both skill and stress management in genuinely dangerous situations. To find examples of these it seemed logical to look to organizations that prepare people for dangerous occupations. So we informally surveyed some non-military institutions such as police departments, fire departments, the FBI and others. All readily identified complex disaster scenarios in which trainees are required to act quickly, often using sophisticated equipment to contain damage, to rescue people, to undertake triage, and the like. However, these agencies almost uniformly insisted that these were *training*, not *evaluation*, exercises and that, while they served to provide a kind of quality assurance to assess company readiness, they were not used to eliminate unsuitable individuals but, at most, only to counsel them.

My first personal encounter with such simulations was in the late thirties at the Chicago World's Fair, where there was a booth with what was then regarded as cutting edge technology for testing driving skill. Having just obtained my learners permit I was eager to prove myself. I walked into the darkened booth, hopped up into what appeared to be the driver's seat of a typical car, with all the usual controls. I was instructed to operate the simulated vehicle in the usual way in response to a challenge presented in a movie that unrolled in front of me. It gave the impression that I was driving down a quiet neighborhood street. In the course of which I was required to turn corners, park, back up and perform other increasingly complex but perfectly normal maneuvers, when suddenly, from behind a parked car, a child seemed to dash into the middle of the street chasing a ball. I still remember the muscle aches from jumping on the brakes and the sickening feeling that the car was about to roll over as a consequence of my jerking the wheels around uncontrollably. It was so real I completely forgot it was a movie. Frankly, I simply panicked, I couldn't control my response to do what I had been taught. I was literally shaking when I climbed out. Though that was 60 years ago, I still have a vivid memory of that child and the terror I felt. Compared to today's capabilities my experience was certainly based on primitive technology; nonetheless is had the power to override my training and provoke a purely emotional response that I couldn't possibly disguise for the examiner.

Similarly, flight simulators of today can be programmed to test both skill and stress management simultaneously. Ask any pilot to describe his/her response when the simulator stalls, goes into an uncontrolled roll or dive, and you will hear tales of sweaty palms and racing heart. For a mere $425/hour you can try it for yourself on a giant 747 simulator at Northwest's Aerospace Training facility outside Minneapolis, or if you wish really to frighten yourself you can go for a luxury two hours at $2,550/session playing Walter Mitty to your heart's content on the Boeing 777 simulator in Denver. I defy you to be able to disguise your emotional response to the challenge it presents.

Among the most highly successful simulations capable of simultaneously assessing both skill and affect in critical situations were those employed by the OSS in training and testing special forces to undertake dangerous missions behind enemy lines during World War II. The complex scenarios the OSS used required trainees to traverse uncompromising terrain and to perform various sensitive jobs under difficult circumstances, where even a barking dog in the back yard of an obviously friendly US farmer often proved so unnerving as to cause the candidate to fail in performing specific tasks for which he had already demonstrated adequate technical skill.

As recently as February 1997 you, personally, could have witnessed on the CBS evening news a simulated Coast Guard rescue juxtaposed with clips of the real thing in which three crewmen had been washed overboard and lost when their rescue craft was rolled over in high seas. It was impossible to distinguish between the actual rescue and the simulation except for the fact that a crewman survived the latter to describe in trembling voice his emotional reaction to what all on board were convinced was a life threatening situation none expected to survive. The fact that the "body" they picked up was clearly a dummy was irrelevant to the emotion the experience had obviously engendered. Incidentally, I contacted CBS and the Coast Guard in an effort to get pictures from the tape of that news story to demonstrate how impossible it would have been for any respondent to dissimulate in that situation. CBS who claimed proprietorship, firmly refused to release it.

I present these examples of high-tech simulations for one purpose: namely, to demonstrate that it is possible to obtain accurate data about affective reactions to critical situations in what, to the examinee, appears to be a straight forward test of skill. But those of us who do not have access to such technology are not doomed to failure. In the second set of illustrations I wish to call to your attention, you will not be overwhelmed either by their sophistication or by the amount of research data available about their psychometric properties. But I do hope you will be impressed by their level of creative deceit.

Specifically, I wish to describe and illustrate three types of low tech simulations, all of which are inexpensive and quite feasible for any of us to develop, and demonstrably useful for assessment of specific attitudes. I have labeled these three types, respectively, as "the impossible dilemmas," role plays with no acceptable solution, and the case of the stealth stimuli.

The first set—"impossible dilemmas"—consists of confronting the examinee with a realistic and relevant task that poses mutually exclusive alternatives, representative of different value positions that are more or less equally politically correct. For example, the examinee may be told that he is a member of the admissions committee of his/her professional school. The entering class is almost filled; there are only X places left and there are 3X or 5X or 10X applicants to consider. The respondent is provided with demographic and other data about the qualifications of each of the applicants (age, gender, ethnic group, admissions test scores, preprofessional major and GPA, recommendations from teachers and supervisors, etc.). The examinee's task is to prioritize the applicants and select the few he/she would recommend for acceptance. Since the characteristics of the applicants have been systematically varied, the examinees cannot avoid revealing their value positions by their choices.

Similarly, the examinee may be told to imagine himself to be a member of the House Budget Committee whose task is to find $200 billion in some combination of cuts in expenditures and/or enhancement of revenues in order to meet an agreed budget target. Again the choices of examinees will necessarily make crystal clear their economic beliefs and social values in ways that cannot be disguised or denied.

An aspiring physician can be told that he/she is a member of the hospital transplant committee. The health condition and personal situation of three patients currently awaiting a liver transplant are described. The committee has been notified of an available liver that is compatible with all three patients. The examinee's task is to assign priorities among the three patients.

The impossible dilemma technique is applicable in a broad range of fields; it is particularly suitable in situations where it is realistic to assume limited resources and the existence of reasonable alternatives representative of a wide variety of equally salient and acceptable values. In creating such situations one is limited only by one's own imagination.

The second type of low-tech simulation that has been frequently employed, especially in the health professions, consists of role plays with no universally acceptable resolution. The following are examples of brief 5-10 minute simulations:

- You are an obstetrician who has been asked by the young, healthy, stable, married couple now sitting in your waiting room to advise them what to do about an unintended pregnancy, now in its second month, which they think they want to terminate.

- You are an oncology consultant to whom a 35-year old female patient has been referred. It is your task to tell her she has an inoperable brain tumor.

- You are the orthopedic surgeon who has examined a 55-year old steel worker complaining of back pain. You think he is suffering from a ruptured disc, but you are not completely sure and you want him to come into the hospital for a few days for a complete work-up. He is obviously very reluctant; it is your task to try to gain his cooperation in your proposed plan of management.

- You are the cardiac surgeon who is completing open heart surgery on a 58-year old man whose wife is waiting outside. Suddenly, as you are closing, something unexpectedly goes wrong and the patient dies on the operating table. It is your task to explain what happened to the new widow.

In the 1960's the very courageous American Board of Orthopedic Surgery, soon followed by the child psychiatrists, led the way in introducing such role plays into their certifying exams. I, personally, can testify about two very interesting findings from them: First, even in high stakes testing they have succeeded in identifying the real outliers. For example, in the simulation of the reluctant 55 year old steel worker, one examinee drew himself up at the first sign of resistance, rose from his chair and said calmly but firmly: I'm sorry, but if you don't want to take my advice I would be glad to refer you to my colleague down the street." In the case of the operating room tragedy, one candidate hesitated a moment and then put his arm around the woman playing the role of the patient's wife, and said: "You poor woman, that damned anesthetist."

The second result I can report is the finding of much higher correlations between performances in widely different role play situations than characterize the correlations between performances on simulations of management problems where differences in required knowledge seem to influence success. Apparently style and values are relatively more consistent across the role plays.

As an aside, I am told that even Hamburger University, an institution some twenty miles west of Chicago, also uses analogous role plays in training and testing employees for the Golden Arches. Presumably they use similar techniques in trying to assure that even notoriously rude Russian workers learn how to deal courteously with abusive customers.

Finally, now to low-tech simulations I've called "stealth stimuli." These are fake clients, customers, patients and other standardized performers who are secretly introduced, without notice, into a professional's normal place of business. Some years ago Gordon Page and his associates employed the technique to evaluate a Continuing Medical Education course designed to train pharmacists in giving advice to customers. Not surprisingly performance varied enormously depending on circumstances prevailing in the pharmacy at the time the stealth customer appeared; but even under relaxed conditions the pharmacist's performance rarely reached the level achieved during the education program.

Similarly, stores and other businesses have for many years successfully used stealth shoppers to evaluate how employees deal with demanding customers and outright trouble makers. After the many complaints the Internal Revenue Service received about so-called customer service, it used stealth callers to assess employee courtesy and the accuracy of their advice.

There is, to my knowledge, a medical school that is seriously considering introducing stealth patients into the fourth year clerkships to assess students' humaneness, empathy and skill in dealing with anxious, depressed and otherwise difficult patients. In a bow to the requirements of informed consent they plan to get signed waivers from the students at time of admission.

In closing I should warn you not to make your simulations too real unless you are prepared to deal with some unexpectedly hostile responses. I tell you this because in early 1997 the *Washington Post* headlined a story of a suit being brought by a group of female employees against a local corporation. It seems that some of the workers were regularly employed on the night shift and that the company was concerned about their ability to handle possible emergencies. The company therefore offered a training program on dealing with various kinds of emergencies. To test the efficacy of the training program and the employees' skill in responding to unexpected situations, the company hired a couple of characters to stage a fake break-in and robbery, complete with toy guns and all the proper props. The act was so convincing that the women claimed to have been severely traumatized. They now allege that they suffer from post-traumatic stress syndrome, and they are suing for both compensatory and punitive damages.

Section C: Assessing Integration of
Performance Skills and Knowledge:
Can They Behave Like a Professional?

Section C

Assessing Integration of Performance Skills and Knowledge: Can They Behave Like a Professional?

Introduction

Recent technological developments have made man-machine boundaries difficult to discern. While advanced technology in the early 20th Century (e.g., the locomotive) was easy to separate from the human condition, contemporary work in, say, artificial intelligence (AI) blurs the distinction between human and machine functions.

Important professional problems are complex and unpredictable, they often defy uniform responses. Competent professional behavior requires that an individual be able to integrate acquired skills [including sentiments and values] and knowledge in addressing problems of professional practice. Consequently, an individual's capacity to handle such situations needs to be shaped and tested in equally rigorous circumstances.

This Section on assessing the integration of performance skills and knowledge includes examples from health professions, aviation, and the military.

In "Assessing Knowledge and Skills in the Health Professions: A Continuum of Simulation Fidelity," (Chapter 9) S. Barry Issenberg and William C. McGaghie describe a progression from low technology to very high technology ranging from very basic simulators (e.g., simple anatomical models), through surgical apparatus, to an advanced cardiology simulator——"Harvey"——that today involves a lifelike mannequin coupled to a sophisticated computer-based instruction and assessment system. The authors focus throughout this chapter not only on the features of low and high technology simulations in health professions education, but also on data from empirical studies that establish the simulations' educational efficacy.

In Chapter 10, "The Individual as a Member of a Working Group: Evaluating Team Performance in Aviation and Medicine," Robert Helmreich provides an overview of the role of simulation technology in these fields and examines the growing use of simulation to enhance and to evaluate team performance and communication. The need for improved communication in aviation is already well-established: 70% of airline crashes are related to human error, usually manifested as a breakdown in communication between crewmembers. Similarly, in medicine, poor communication among operating room personnel can result in loss of life. Helmreich argues that simulation, at present, is not being employed to its maximum capability. He asserts that, if we are to use this tool to its fullest potential, we must shift the focus of simulation to include team-oriented, as well as individually-oriented, training and assessment.

"Military Mission Rehearsal: From Sandtable to Virtual Reality," (Chapter 11) by Lieutenant Colonels Eugene Ressler and James Armstrong and Colonel George Forsythe, examines the interface between knowledge and performance in the context of training soldiers for combat. The United States Army uses three general types of simulation to develop mission skills, both on the individual and unit level. The *Live Simulation* provides a situation which is acted upon by real actors, using real systems. *Virtual Simulation* uses real actors and simulated systems to recreate a military scenario. *Constructive Simulation* uses both simulated actors and simulated systems. The authors provide numerous examples of each type, and demonstrate how various simulations are being used together to enhance military training and prevent losses in combat situations.

Together these three chapters highlight the challenges and the opportunities of using simulations to assess the integration of professional skills and knowledge in individual and group situations.

Ara Tekian
William C. McGaghie

9

Assessing Knowledge and Skills in the Health Professions: A Continuum of Simulation Fidelity

S. Barry Issenberg
William C. McGaghie

Simulations used for education and assessment in the health professions vary in their fidelity with "real life" objects and circumstances. This chapter describes the use of such simulators along a continuum of fidelity. The continuum ranges from basic simulators including inert anatomical models and devices used to practice laparoscopic surgery to the sophisticated "Harvey" cardiology patient simulator and its companion UMedic computer-assisted instruction system. Evidence is cited throughout the chapter which supports the educational efficacy of simulation technology in health professions education.

Threadde use of simulation technology including multimedia computers is now widespread in medical education and medical skills assessment. The major forces driving this trend have been expanding educational needs and improving technology. Medical practice changes that reduce physician teaching time, the decreased availability of patients for education, and the "information explosion" boost the need for new methods of instruction and assessment.

Mastery of "hands on" physical examination skills has suffered from these changes. To illustrate, survey research shows the cardiac bedside examination, an icon of general physical examination skills (Roldan, Shivley & Crawford, 1996), is being taught less frequently (Mangione, Nieman, Gracely & Kaye, 1993). Controlled clinical research shows that medical students and residents have difficulty identifying common cardiac findings (Mangione & Nieman, 1997). Educational research has also uncovered clinical skill deficits among trainees in other medical specialties. Among anesthesia residents, for example, management of [simulated] common emergency situations is often poor, sometimes leading to catastrophic results (Byrne & Jones, 1997; DeAnda & Gaba, 1990; Gaba & DeAnda, 1989; Schwid & O'Donnell, 1992). The strongest predictor of proper management of a simulated cardiac arrest is the time duration (short is best) since a trainee's last episode of Advanced Cardiac Life Support training (Schwid & O' Donnell, 1992).

Similar problems in other fields have been solved by using simulation techniques. Illustrations include flight simulators for pilots and astronauts (Garrison, 1986; Goodman, 1978; Rolfe & Staples, 1980), war games and training exercises for the military (Ressler, Armstrong, & Forsythe, 1999, Chapter 11), management games for business executives (Keys & Wolfe, 1990; Strufert, Pogash, & Piasecki, 1988), and technical operation of nuclear power plants (Wachtel, 1985). Simulations are not identical to "real life" events. Instead, simulations place trainees in lifelike situations where they receive feedback about the results of questions, decisions, and actions. There is no doubt that simulation techniques are valuable for teaching. Airlines are convinced of the value of the flight simulator for pilot training because these sophisticated devices closely approximate in-flight situations. Working on a flight simulator has been shown to greatly improve pilot skills (Office of Naval Research, 1973; Society of Photo-Optical Engineers, 1975).

Medical patient simulation (standardized patients) can reproduce a wide variety of complicated conditions (Barrows, 1993). The conditions range from aphasia and hearing loss to joint restrictions and seizures. Simulators are not intended to replace real patients. However, they can address the disadvantages inherent in a totally patient-dependent curriculum (Collins & Harden, 1998). The disadvantages include:

- Unavailability of patients demonstrating known diseases at specific times in the curriculum schedule

- Embarrassment and stress to patients and beginning students

- Reluctance among patients to participate in an examination where they are exposed to large number of learners

- Unpredictable patient behavior because their physical signs of disease may change and their overall condition may deteriorate

- Nonstandardized patients without stable disease with the result that students assessed on one patient may have a very different experience on others

- Skills to be learned and tested may be inappropriate or dangerous for real patients. Examples include cardiopulmonary resuscitation (intubation, chest compressions), intravenous access, and administration of medications.

The value of simulators to complement clinical teaching and assessment has long been recognized. Such simulators have a place in the assessment of clinical skills such as physical examination techniques, practical procedures, cardiopulmonary resuscitation and anesthesia. Evidence from studies using simulations indicates they are effective aids for teaching skills and are reliable and valid methods for assessing students' clinical skills. Penta and Koffman (1973) showed that simulators can be used effectively to supplement instruction of the physical examination if students practice with them frequently. These investigators randomly formed an experimental group that used a heart sound simulator. The experimental group scored significantly higher on objective tests than a control group that did not use the simulator. Sajid, Magero and Feinzimer (1977) confirmed the hypothesis that skills learned on a heart sound simulator generalize to examinations of real patients. These results establish the instructional effectiveness of a limited simulation device and demonstrate that patients feel equally comfortable when examined by students regardless of whether the students were trained on a simulator or on human subjects.

Simulators used in medical education vary in complexity and in their fidelity with real patients. Some models are static, permitting examination and manipulation by the student, but do not respond or provide feedback about what the learner is doing. Others are more interactive, responding in some way to student manipulations. The simplest use of a simulator is one that provides a "body" to substitute for a real person during training. The only requirement is that the simulator resembles a body in size and weight, much like a department store mannequin. Such simulators are used extensively in Emergency Medical Skills Training (EMST).

This chapter describes simulators that vary in fidelity (i.e., realism) which are used to assess knowledge and skills in the health professions. There are two sections. First, we begin with basic simulators, devices that are simple, static, and inert. These simulators, including anatomical models, have been used for decades to teach and test basic clinical skills. Second, the chapter continues with a description of an advanced form of simulation technology in the health professions: the "Harvey" cardiology patient simulator and its companion UMedic multimedia computer system. Evidence is presented throughout the discussion to support the use of simulation technology in health professions education.

BASIC SIMULATORS

Simple Body Simulators

Since 1982, over 40,000 course registrants have been trained at the University of Miami School of Medicine Center for Research in Medical Education (CRME) in EMST. The EMST programs have grown from Advanced Cardiac Life Support to include Trauma, Pediatrics, Advanced Airway, Hazardous Materials Management, Acute Myocardial Infarction, and Acute Stroke. The Center's facilities include a simulated fully equipped rescue vehicle and an automobile for extricating "accident" victims. There is also a large hazardous materials decontamination shower and a mock-up emergency room that includes an electrocardiogram (ECG) receiving based station. Simple mannequins are used in Trauma cases as automobile accident victims. Learners use these simulators to practice techniques of stabilizing accident victims and the best methods to remove them from an automobile. These simulators typically have "built-in" injuries: head lacerations, contusions, dilated and "blown" pupils, compound leg fractures. Simple simulators are also used during anti-terrorism courses to practice the proper technique for decontamination of hazardous materials such as mustard gas or airborne infectious agents like anthrax. Realism in these situations originates from the scenario the learners confront rather than the simulator itself. The simulator does not respond to any action or provide any findings other than being the right size and weight of an adult male.

Anatomic Pathologic Simulators

Anatomic pathologic simulators include models for breast examination, examination of the ear and eye, the female pelvis for vaginal examination, and the male pelvis for rectal examination. The advantage of such simulators is that they enable practical teaching without patient imposition, especially about sensitive maneuvers such as the pelvic examination. Macintosh and Chard (1997) studied the use of pelvic simulators to teach the normal female pelvic examination and the ability to correctly identify pelvic findings, including the presence of adnexal masses and prolapse of the uterus. They found that pelvic simulators were useful in demonstrating the process of pelvic and speculum examination but not suitable for training students in abnormal findings. The authors also noted the pelvic simulators are imperfect representations of the clinical situation. When using simulators of lower fidelity it is important to appreciate their limitations and use them in situations that maximize their strengths.

Procedural Skill Simulators

Other simulators are used to learn, practice and assess procedural and practical skills. Examples of these simulators include:

- Intravenous access via insertion of a cannula or from surgical cut down
- Catheterization of the male and female bladder.
- Airway management including intubation. Some of these devices, including the Cricothyrotomy Simulator (Armstrong Medical Industries, Lincolnshire, IL) provide practice of catheter oxygenation/jet ventilation via the cricothyroid membrane in cases of laryngeal, pharyngeal, lingual tonsilar and epiglottic pathology. This is important because the clinical opportunities for employing this kind of technique are rare.
- Soft tissue injection and aspiration of knee, shoulder, elbow, and wrist joints
- Ureteroscopy for practice of kidney stone removal

Surgical Simulators

Surgical training is one area that would seem to lend itself to simulator training. Proficiency requires knowledge of underlying anatomy including orientation of organs and tissues and dexterity from repetitive practice to sharpen one's skills. Despite this apparent fit, few studies have examined the use of simulators for surgical training. Examples of available simulators include:

- Simple wound closure including suture tension and accuracy of placement.

- Bowel anastomosis (closure) using suture and staples

- Laparotomy practice

- Episiotomy and third degree tear of the perineum with ability to practice suture repair at multiple levels

- An inflamed toe model that allows a range of procedures to be assessed, including ring block with local anesthesia and wedge resection of the nail bed and total ablation of the nail.

- Skin models that allow practice of cutting and suturing as well as the removal of sebaceous cysts, lipomas, perianal hematomas, and skin tags.

Laparoscopic Simulators

Laparoscopic surgery requires multiple skills including familiarity with instruments and proficiency at ambidextrous maneuvers. Laparoscopic surgery is different from traditional open surgery. Derossis and colleagues (1998) point out these differences:

> "Surgeons must learn to operate with long instruments, which amplify hand tremor and are harder to control than conventional instruments. These same instruments are limited in their range of motion by the trocars through which they must be passed. Furthermore, the constraints of length and width of these instruments have limited engineering design. Optical differences between open and laparoscopic surgery add to the difficulty in learning laparoscopy. Surgeons must learn to operate while looking at a monitor in another direction. Conventional laparoscopic imaging systems provide two-dimensional vision. Thus depth perception is lacking, and surgeons must learn other cues to provide a sense of depth. These cues include the sense of touch, and the interaction of light and shading" (p. 482).

Recently, three-dimensional imaging systems have been developed but preliminary studies do not suggest a clear benefit. Limitations of these three-dimensional models include the need to wear glasses or goggles.

Laparoscopic surgery requires hand-eye coordination, proficiency with both hands, and depth perception. These skills were not learned during residency training for generations of surgeons. Several methods have been developed to assist physicians in developing their skills. Examples of these include courses involving practice with animal models and training with other certified laparoscopic surgeons. In the past few years laparoscopic surgical simulators have been developed to allow surgeons to enhance their motor skills in a safe and controlled environment without risk to patients.

Laparoscopic surgical training has moved from training practicing surgeons to training residents. Early studies assessed laparoscopic knot tying and suturing with an open box and direct vision which led to the use of a laparoscopic camera (Melvin, Johnson, & Ellison, 1996). Other research evaluated intracorporeal suture tying using time as an endpoint (Rosser, Rosser, & Savalgi, 1997). Recent studies with newer simulators have included several skills for training and assessment and measure not only speed but precision as well (Derossis, Fried, & Abrahamowicz 1998; Derosis, Bothwell, Sigman, & Fried, 1998).

One such laparoscopic simulator system is the MISTELS program (McGill Inanimate System for Training and Evaluation of Laproscopic Skills) (Derossis, Fried, & Abrahamowicz 1998). The simulator consists of a laparoscopic trainer box measuring 40 x 30 x 19.5 cm (USSC Laptrainer, Unites States Surgical Corporation, Norwalk Connecticut) covered by an opaque membrane to simulate skin. Two 12-mm trocars are placed through the membrane at appropriate working angles on either side of a 10-mm laparoscope. Four alligator clips within the simulator are used to suspend materials for surgical exercises. The laparoscope and camera are mounted on a stand at a fixed focal length which enables each examinee to work independently. The optical system consists of the laparoscope, camera, light source and video monitor that is placed in line with the operator. Several exercises have been developed, each emphasizing a specific skill essential for proper laparoscopic technique. Users are required to:

- Lift pegs from a pegboard with one " hand," transfer the peg to the other hand, and then placed the peg back into the pegboard to assess *hand-eye coordination.*

- Hold a grasper in one hand placing the material under tension while cutting with endoscopic scissors using the other hand to assess *cutting technique.*

- Place two hemostatic clips on a tubular foam structure at premaked positions and cut on a mark half way between the clips to *assess placement of surgical clips.*

- Place and tighten a pretied slipknot on a foam tubular appendage to *assess placement of a ligating loop* (such as one required in an appendectomy).

- Place a 5-cm diameter mesh patch over a previously created 4-cm defect in a foam model and secure the mesh to the foam with staples to *assess mesh placement* (such as one used in hernia repair).

- Place a simple suture 13 cm in length through premarked points in a longitudinally slit Penrose drain. The suture is then tied using a specific knot technique to *assess skills of needle transferring, placement of a suture, and knot tying.*

Studies to assess laparoscopic simulators. Derossis, Bothwell, Sigman, and Fried (1998) evaluated forty-two surgeons in training and in practice to determine if there is a correlation between level of training and proficient practice of laparoscopy. The investigators found significant predictors of overall performance were level of training and frequency of skill repetition. In a follow-up study by the same group, 12 surgical residents were randomized to either five weekly practice sessions or no practice. Each group was pretested with the same tasks described earlier. The simulator trained group showed significantly greater improvement compared to controls on four of the tasks and for overall scores. These tasks include those that are acquired only after persistent repetition. Most important, skills in the intervention group did not plateau even after seven practice sessions and improvement in skills increased after each practice session.

The use of such simulators in surgical training and evaluation will increase and surely lead to improved surgical technique. Surgical technique that develops only after repeated practice and mastering specific skills lends itself to simulator use. Curricula for surgical training programs should join simulator training to didactic lessons before animal lab training sessions or use on live patients. Derossis, Bothwell, Sigman, and Fried (1998) demonstrated the effect of practice on performance varies with the complexity of the task to be performed. Those tasks judged to be most difficult (e.g., intracorporeal suturing) correlated most with practice. Perhaps more than any field in medicine, the perfection of surgical skills has the most direct influence on patient care. It is surprising that the development of more sophisticated simulators has only recently been implemented. Reliance of traditional training on an apprenticeship may no longer be the best method to remain technically proficient in an era when technological advances will change the techniques and instruments of surgery.

Advances in laparoscopic simulators. Recent advances have resulted in even more realistic laparoscopic simulators (Limbs n' Things, Inc., U.K.). A model in the shape of a realistic abdominal wall complete with simulated skin, fat, and peritoneum layers provides an external support system by which modular organs, vessels and other soft tissue structures can be substituted. Most of the modular assemblies have fluid-filled vessels that "bleed" when cut. This realistically simulates a real laparoscopic procedure when extraneous fluid can blur and interfere with the visual field. When an operative procedure is complete, the soft tissue module can be removed, the cavity cleaned if necessary and a new assembly can be put in place for the next trainee. Examples of these new models include:

- Hysteroscopic models for practice of endometrial ablation, oophorectomy, salpingectomy, removal of uteral fibroid, dissection of the peritoneum, and removal of an ectopic pregnancy

- Amniocentesis models that include simulated placentas and an umbilical cord filled with fluid for sampling while guided by ultrasound

- Simulators for the most common laparoscopic procedures such as cholecysectomy, direct and indirect hernia repair, lymphadenectomy, and varicocele

The value of these new generation simulators is that they more realistically mimic operative conditions. Surgical procedures are often complicated by less than ideal conditions of uniform anatomy as well as bleeding vessels. The benefit of these simulators is that "complications" can be initiated to assess trainee responses to adverse events. In this way these simulators may soon serve the same purpose as flight simulators. Such anatomic simulators will be joined with multimedia computer systems so that a standardized control and assessment system can provide uniform situations to multiple learners.

AN ADVANCED SIMULATOR

Evaluation of patients with cardiovascular disease requires a skillfully performed physical examination. This is a noninvasive procedure with the widest application in cardiology. Unnecessary laboratory tests are frequently done when an orderly bedside physical examination would yield an accurate diagnosis. In addition, patient information obtained at the bedside should guide the selection and interpretation of more sophisticated laboratory procedures.

There are two requirements for mastery of the bedside examination used in patient diagnosis and care. First, the skills must be practiced repetitively.

Traditionally, this has required a pool of "teaching" patients with diverse diseases at different stages of severity and treatment. Recent changes in health care delivery at academic hospitals such as shorter hospital stays and outpatient testing has cut the pool of teaching patients (Gordon, Ewy, De Leon et al. 1980; Ewy, Felner, Juul et al. 1987). Second, physician trainees must have an orderly examination technique together with knowledge of hemodynamic correlations with bedside findings. Traditionally this has required instruction by experienced physicians who are motivated to teach. The second requirement is difficult to fulfill because increased demands on faculty time for patient care, research, writing, grant proposal preparation, and administrative duties cut teaching time. Recent educational research also shows that clinical teaching rarely occurs at the bedside. Instead, most clinical teaching is in the form if didactic lectures presented in conference rooms (Collins, Cassie & Daggert, 1978; Weinholtz, 1987).

These problems began to surface in the late 1960s. In response, the "Harvey" group—a national consortium of cardiologists, internists and educators—began work over 30 years ago to "build a patient." The intent was to develop a Cardiology Patient Simulator (CPS) capable of reproducing the bedside findings of almost all cardiac diseases instantly, with high fidelity.

"Harvey" the Cardiology Patient Simulator

When the idea was first conceived in 1967 three mannequins, each representing a single heart disease, were designed and constructed. Each early mannequin comprised a torso mounted on an examination table, draped from the waist down by a sheet. In these original models, small electric motors concealed under the table drove pistons that produced venous and arterial pulsations as well as chest wall movements. Recordings of heart murmurs could be heard in the usual fashion by listening to the chest with a stethoscope.

These original mannequins demonstrated the feasibility of using such devices for instruction. They also suggested other uses, such as testing and certification of students and physicians. The primary drawback of the mannequins was that they represented only selected findings of one disease in each of the bodies.

The lack of versatility prompted the design of a single, multiple disease-state simulator that could be electronically programmed to simulate a variety of cardiac diseases. Over the next several years, a multiple disease-state mannequin was designed to simulate the physical findings of almost any cardiac problem. This model had many new features including bilateral peripheral pulses, more chest wall movements, and a blood pressure system. Additional engineering research resulted in a system that automatically synchronized sounds for each of the four classic acoustic areas and all pulsatile movements. The result of this effort was a simulator that could represent almost unlimited cardiac diseases. It was named " Harvey" in honor of Dr. W. Proctor Harvey of Georgetown University, who always nurtured innovation in education and stimulated young physicians to teach through his example.

The University of Miami subsequently licensed a manufacturer to build and distribute the Cardiology Patient Simulator.

While these technical efforts were being made, 20 slide programs were concurrently developed that displayed background information for specific diseases. They provide all the necessary clinical data to lead the physician or student through the formulation of a reasonable, logical diagnosis. Great effort was made to clearly and succinctly describe the physiology of each finding and the rationale and results of each diagnostic test in the slide programs. A manual was also prepared to summarize the findings in each disease. Over the past 20 years three new generations of "Harvey" have been developed. A digital heart sound auscultation system replaced the original four-track tapes. Seven more diseases have been programmed into "Harvey" and added to the curriculum so that the mannequin now simulates nearly every cardiovascular condition. "Harvey" simulates the following cardiac conditions.

- Introductory Program
- Normal
- Innocent Murmur
- Aortic Valve Sclerosis
- Hypertension
- Angina Pectoris
- Mitral Valve Prolapse
- Mitral Stenosis
- Chronic Mitral Regurgitation
- Aortic Stenosis
- Aortic Regurgitation
- Dilated Cardiomyoaphty

- Hypertrophic Obstructive Cardiomyopathy
- Atrial Septal Defect
- Ventricular Septal Defect
- Patent Ductus Arteriosus
- Tetrology of Fallot
- Primary Pulmonary Hypertension
- Acute Mitral Regurgitation
- Ventricular Aneurysm
- Mitral Stenosis & Regurgitation
- Pulmonary Stenosis

- Coarctation of the Aorta
- Acute Pericarditis
- Inferior Wall Myocardinal Infraction

- Anterior Wall Myocardial Infraction
- Acute Aortic Regurgitation

"Harvey" is able to integrate all of the bedside findings and realistically reproduce both common and rare cardiac diseases. Findings simulated include the blood pressure, bilateral jugular venous pulsations, carotid and peripheral arterial pulsations, precordial pulse movements in five areas, and the auscultatory events of each disease state. The acoustic events are heard in the four classic auscultatory areas, and are synchronized to the respiratory cycle and to the various pulses. Even the most complex pulses and auscultatory events may be simulated for a given disease, and the findings vary with respiration. More than one example of a particular variety of disease may be represented, simulating the marked difference in the clinical presentation of a particular disease that depends upon severity of involvement.

The second requirement for a student or physician to learn bedside diagnosis -effective instruction-must also be fulfilled. To that end, the Harvey Group meets quarterly to review, revise, and update the teaching materials that accompany the CPS. The technique of examination is approached in an orderly fashion and ancillary data are provided on slide programs developed for each disease state in a self-assessment format. These include all the elements that should be included in a real patient workup and sequentially present historical, physical, electrocardiographic, radiologic, non-invasive, hemodynamic, therapeutic, pathologic and epidemiologic information on the patient's disease state. Over the last decade, the group has also developed the UMedic Multimedia Computer System that provides the presentation of an interactive real time patient evaluation and documents learner usage and performance. UMedic will be described in detail later.

"Harvey" can teach in different environments and at multiple levels. The simulator can be used for teaching in any environment in which a patient may be examined. The device works best when permanently housed in a room the size of a patient's small hospital room (e.g., 15 ft x 15 ft) because the space is appropriate for bedside rounds with up to 12 students or physicians. The CPS is mobile and may be moved to a lecture room or, with care, transported out of the building in which it is housed for special conferences or use at outlying hospitals.

"Harvey" is presently being used to educate a variety of trainees. The simulator may be used to teach the beginning student (e.g., sophomore medical student or student nurse) such basic techniques as taking blood pressure and recognizing a heart murmur. For the senior medical student or graduate nurse, "Harvey" associates heart sound variation with respiration, provides a variety of carotid and jugular venous pulsations, and correlates physical findings with historical and laboratory data. For the cardiology fellow, it simulates subtle precordial movements, infrequently heard heart murmurs and electrocardiograms, echocardiograms, radionuclide scans, and provides pathologic specimens to analyze. Harvey also has many applications for the postgraduate training of the primary care physician and internist. The technology of the CPS has advanced to the point where electronic stethophones can be connected to the system to educate several hundred persons in a large auditorium. Television monitors display carotid, jugular, venous, and precordial pulsations that allow heart sounds and murmurs to be synchronized with these pulsations. Approximately 800 physicians were taught with Harvey at the annual convention of the American Academy of Family Physicians in 1979 during four separate 4-hour sessions. (Gordon, Ewy, Felner et al. 1981). In this large group setting, audience participation and feedback was enhanced from use of a response system in the form of a small keypad at each seat.

A realistic and reliable cardiology patient simulator provides many educational advantages. It can produce better-trained physicians in less time and at less cost, and it can provide an objective method for measuring the clinical competency of physician-students in patient-oriented examinations. Unlike a real patient, the simulator is always available and is never tired, worried, or feels abused. Interesting, instructive, and even rare "patients" can be summoned in a matter of seconds. Students as well as physicians learn at their own rate while sharpening skills, developing competence, and acquiring cognitive information in a relaxed environment without patient discomfort. Learners can control the number of variables being taught, thus reducing background "noise" that often overwhelms a student dealing with real patients. In addition, the CPS allows beginning students to make mistakes and errors in judgment before approaching real patients.

Studies Involving "Harvey"

"Harvey" has been subjected to rigorous testing to establish its educational efficacy. The most comprehensive evaluation of any simulation technology was the multicenter study of "Harvey" sponsored by the National Heart, Lung, and Blood Institute (NHLBI) (Ewy, Felner, Juul et al. 1987). This project involved 208 students (116 CPS trained and 92 non-CPS trained) at five medical schools. The study compared the level of bedside technical skills and cognitive knowledge of students taught using the CPS with students taught in a conventional patient-dependent program. Skills were tested using actual patients.

The result of this multicenter evaluation indicated that 4th year medical students who used the CPS during their cardiology elective acquired more cognitive information and were better skilled in bedside cardiac examinations than their counterparts who were trained in the traditional manner. On the multiple-choice posttest the CPS trained students scored significantly better ($p<0.01$) than the non-CPS trained students. The CPS trained group also performed significantly better ($p< 0.001$) than the non-CPS trained group on the CPS skills posttest. There were also significant treatment effects on the patient skills posttest. The CPS trained group again performed better ($p<0.03$) than the non-CPS trained group. The level of student and faculty acceptance of the technology was extremely high. All users expressed intent to continue using the simulator as an adjunct to the teaching of patient-centered cardiology. In addition, patients were equally comfortable with the CPS-trained and non-CPS trained students. Maintenance problems were minimal with very little "down" time, and the type of technical support available at any medical center was found to be more than adequate to maintain the device.

The NHLBI sponsored study demonstrated that the skills learned on "Harvey" are transferable to examination of actual patients. It also shows that student behavior toward patients is not adversely affected by exposure to the CPS, and that the device is technically reliable. In addition, the acquisition of knowledge was enhanced for students in the CPS-trained group. The information available in slides and now on computer, although readily available in textbooks and in the literature, provided a valuable condensation that is immediately and efficiently available for the learner and is presented within the context of a given patient.

Another study conducted at the University of Michigan (Wooliscroft, Calhoun, Tenhaken, & Judge, 1987) concluded that "Harvey" significantly improved cardiovascular clinical examination, assessment, and interpretation skills of over 200 sophomores students. This work extends the earlier NHLBI study that showed "Harvey" had a significant impact in clinical skills in fourth-year medical students who completed training sessions. An important observation made during the Michigan study noted the efficiency of "Harvey" in terms of time saved by the faculty as well as students.

These data support the conclusion that simulation technology is a reasonable addition to the medical curriculum. Combining simulation technology with traditional patient-centered teaching prepares medical students to provide better medical care with increased confidence at the bedside.

"Harvey" as a Testing Instrument

The CPS has much potential as an objective tool for testing bedside cardiovascular examination skills. "Harvey" works just as well as testing trainees with actual patients. However, with the CPS there is complete control over the task selected (e.g., a bedside cardiovascular examination) as well as its complexity. Patient findings can be presented uniformly and the process of skills testing can then be standardized and made objective. The NHLBI experimental design called for testing students on a full range of 200 CPS simulations. All conditions were used with equal frequency. This standardization allowed improved sampling of student performance so that any area (e.g., vital signs, non-auscultatory events, auscultation, etc.) could be assessed. In addition, the testing method, while allowing an objective and reproducible evaluation of bedside skills, was administered by personnel with minimal specialized training. Many of the specialty boards have abandoned oral and practical examinations because of the logistical and educational problems inherent in such patient-dependent testing methods. Other studies have used Harvey and support the use of simulation as a valuable aid to testing the performance of physicians (St Clair, Oddone, Waugh et al. 1992; Jones, Hunt, Carlson, & Seamon, 1997).

St. Clair and colleagues at Duke University used "Harvey" in a study designed to assess internal medicine housestaff diagnostic skills (St. Clair, Oddone, Waugh et al. 1992). The study involved a cross-section of 60 residents (post-graduate years 1 through 3 (PGY1-3) who were evaluated on three valvular simulations. These evaluation sessions were conducted at the beginning and end of an academic year. Housestaff learning during the year consisted of traditional training during bedside rounds and clinical consultations. The overall correct response rate for all housestaff for the 3 simulations was 47%. No difference was noted between the two sessions. For 2 of the valvular simulations, correct assessment of specific bedside clues predicted a correct diagnosis ($p<0.001$).

A similar study at Michigan State University assessed cardiovascular physical examination skills of emergency medicine housestaff and attending physicians (Jones, Hunt, Carlson & Seamon, 1997). Forty-six emergency medicine housestaff (PGY1-3) and attending physicians were tested over a 2 month period on three valvular simulations. After an initial evaluation of clinical skills, participants were given a cardiac examination form to prompt them to interpret 23 separate cardiac findings for each simulation. Participants were tested again on the skills to accurately diagnose the three simulations. The overall correct response rate was 41% with no significant differences among the varying levels of training. Like the Duke study, accurate recognition of key bedside findings was associated with a correct diagnosis in each simulation ($p<0.001$). The findings of these studies demonstrate the deficiencies in physical diagnosis skills among the current generation of physicians and illustrate the potential use of a simulation device as an assessment tool.

Computer Assisted Instruction (CAI)

Computer assisted instruction (CAI) is an ideal method for teaching a core of material repetitively. Many programs are interactive, requiring involvement by the student or house officer in the learning process. Students may also use CAI programs individually, at convenient times without the need for faculty supervision. Furthermore, CAI has the potential to improve productivity by individualizing learning and creating a rich and manipulable environment. A study by Garrett and Ashford (1986) demonstrated that a group of medical residents could run microcomputer-based patient simulations independently, which later produced significant increases in their test scores. Patient simulation techniques, especially when linked to CAI systems, can effectively teach basic bedside and problem solving skills that may be transferable to patient evaluations.

UMedic Multimedia Computer System

The consortium of cardiologists, internists, and educators who first developed Harvey and its accompanying slide programs subsequently developed UMedic, a multimedia computer system (MCS). The UMedic MCS has been developed over the last 14 years with features that include computer and video graphics and real-time digitized video and audio. Ten patient-centered case-based programs comprise a comprehensive generalist curriculum in cardiology. The structure of each program includes:

- *The History*

- *Bedside Findings* including appearance, blood pressure, arterial and venous pulses, precordial movements and auscultation, presented by an instructor on videos of "Harvey," the CPS.

- *Diagnosis*

- *Laboratory Data* including blood chemistries, ECGs, X-rays, scintigraphy, and real-time echo-Dopplers and angiograms

- *Treatment* including videos of interventional therapy/surgery

- *Pathology*

- *Discussions* including case reviews by authoritative cardiologists

Learners can choose to study an entire program that includes all of the above sections or choose to study only the bedside evaluation (e.g., a 1st or 2nd year medical student) in which the Laboratory Data and Treatment sections are omitted. The programs operate in 2 modes: (a) self-learning mode for 1 to 5 learners, and (b) an instructor mode for teaching large numbers in a classroom or auditorium with a video projector or multiple monitors. The instructor mode was created to reduce the time and effort teachers invest in preparing their presentations by providing all of the data necessary to teach. It is flexible, providing a menu of over 20 choices from the patient evaluation, and narrative voiceovers are inactivated to allow instructors to make their own teaching points. Each mode may be used as a "stand alone" training program or be linked to "Harvey."

A physician instructor provides demonstrations of bedside findings, gives narrative explanations, and provides feedback about important points throughout each self-learning program. Multiple choice questions are presented during the program to emphasize key teaching points, encourage problem solving, and enhance interactive learning. The learner can pause or review any of the previously presented material as often as desired before answering a question. After a correct response to a test question, an optional "further discussion" of the correct answer may be chosen. When incorrect, a brief review of the incorrect answer and "further discussion" are mandatory. The discussion that follows auscultation also provides a step-by-step "dissection" of heart sounds and murmurs to simplify complex auscultatory findings.

A pre and post-testing system has been developed to assess basic bedside skills and measure learner performance outcomes. An administrative program tracks learners by name and social security number and records their performance and time spent completing the tests. Twenty-seven categories of learners can be tracked. These include medical students, nurses, house officers, fellows, generalists and cardiologists. Based on the success of these programs, similar modules have been developed in oncology and more computer modules are planned for neurology.

Studies Assessing the Effectiveness of UMedic

The first national multicenter study of UMedic was carried out during the 1991–92 academic year. It involved 182 senior medical students at Arizona, Duke, Emory and Miami. This research revealed that 96% of the students felt the programs improved their bedside skills (Waugh, Mayer, Ewy et al. 1995). This study also demonstrated that the UMedic system is well received, easy to use, and reliable. Another multicenter study demonstrated that this system could be integrated into the entire 4-year medical curriculum (Petrusa, Issenberg, Mayer et al.1999). A total of 1586 students at Duke, Emory, Florida, Miami, Illinois and Iowa medical schools completed 6131 programs and favorably rated the educational value of the system compared to other learning materials The study resulted in a recommended 4-year curriculum plan for the UMedic system. A rigorous eight-step process to develop outcome measures in bedside skills was also undertaken. An analysis of a 77 item test taken by 122 senior medical students at two institutions yielded a reliability coefficient of 0.94 (Issenberg, McGaghie, Brown et al. 1998). From this pool of questions, a pretest and posttest were developed with reliability coefficients of .81 and .84, respectively.

A recently concluded national multicenter cohort study (i.e., nonequivalent control group design) (Issenberg, Petrusa, McGaghie et al. 1999) involving senior medical students at 5 institutions compared the UMedic system with traditional methods for teaching bedside skills in cardiology. Three schools served as the intervention schools; two schools served as comparisons. All of the students were individually pretested at the beginning of the elective. In the intervention group, UMedic modules substituted for both the usual patient bedside instruction and the CPS during the first two weeks of the elective. Students were administered the posttest at the end of the two week period. In the comparison group, students were instructed in bedside skills during teaching rounds and individual patient workups and administered the posttest at the end of the four-week elective. All schools used the same pre- and posttest.

There were no significant differences in the demographic data between the two groups (Age, gender, overall MCAT and USMLE step 1 scores.) There was a significant difference in the pretest scores of the UMedic trained students compared to non-UMedic students (47% vs 41%; $p<0.01$), respectively. When the pretest scores were used to adjust posttest scores, the UMedic group (80%) continued to maintain a significantly higher score than the comparison group (47%) (F=115, df=1, 206, $p<0.001$).

A CPS can maximize the efficiency of the teaching effort. A greater demand for health-care personnel, especially primary care physicians who care for a large proportion of patients with cardiac disease, will highlight the shortage of good clinical teachers. Simulators combined with a sophisticated multimedia computer control system can be a partial solution to this problem. It also appears likely that future requirements to certify and recertify physicians will make testing with a simulator and multimedia computer systems even more attractive. The Physical Examination Self- Evaluation Process committee of the American Board of Internal Medicine shares this view. The committee's task is to "develop a multimedia computer-based, self-assessment program to reaffirm the importance of physical diagnosis as a competence in internal medicine."

The American College of Cardiology Task Force on Teaching also endorses the more widespread use of modern teaching tools such as "Harvey" and interactive computer software (Gregoratos and Miller, 1999).

The expanded use of simulators and sophisticated multimedia computer systems in medical education is inevitable. Simulators that can be used by multiple populations and levels of learner will be the most valuable and cost effective. Simulation technology in medical education is becoming a key to "hands-on" skills training. Combined with multimedia computers, these systems will increasingly be used for certification and recertification of all medical professionals.

References

Barrows, H. S. 1993. An overview of the uses of standardized patients for teaching and evaluating Clinical skills. *Academic Medicine* 68: 443-53.

Byrne, A. J., and Jones, J. G. 1997. Responses to simulated anaesthetic emergencies by anaesthetists with different durations of clinical experience. *British Journal of Anesthesia* 78: 553-6.

Collins, G. F., Cassie, J. M., Daggert, C. J. 1978. The role of the attending physician in clinical training. *Journal of Medical Education* 53: 429-31.

Collins, J. P., Harden, R. M. 1998. AMEE Medical Education Guide No. 13: Real patients, simulated patients and simulators in medical education. *Medical Teacher* 20: 508-21.

DeAnda, A., Gaba, D. M. 1990. Unplanned incidents during comprehensive anesthesia simulation. *Anesthesia and Analgesics* 71: 77-82.

Derossis, A. M., Fried, G. M., Abrahamowicz, M,, Sigman, H. H., Barkun, J. S., and Meakins, J. L. 1998. Development of a model for training and evaluation of laparoscopic skills. *American Journal of Surgery*. 175: 482-7.

Derossis, A. M., Bothwell, J., Sigman, H. H., and Fried, G. M. 1998. The effect of practice on performance in a laparosopic simulator. *Surgical Endoscopy* 12: 1117-20.

Ewy, G. A., Felner, J. M., Juul, D., Mayer, J. W., Sajid, A. W., and Waugh, R. A. 1987. Test of a cardiology patient simulator with students in fourth-year electives. *Journal of Medical Education* 62: 738-43.

Gaba, D. M., and DeAnda, A. 1989. The response of anesthesia trainees to simulated critical events. *Anesthesia and Analgesics* 68: 444-51.

Garrett, T. J., and Ashford, A. R. 1986. Computer-assisted instruction in patient management for internal medicine residents. *Journal of Medical Education* 61: 987-89.

Garrison, P. 1986. Flying without wings. *A Flight Simulation Manual.* Blue Ridge Summit, PA: TAB Books, Inc., 1-31, 102-06.

Goodman, W. 1978. The world of civil simulators. *Flight Internation Magazine.* 18: 435.

Gordon, M. S., Ewy, G. A., DeLeon, A. C., Waugh, R. A., Felner, J. M., Forker, A. D., Gessner, I. H., Mayer, J. M., and Patterson, D. 1980. "Harvey," the cardiology patient simulator: pilot studies on teaching effectiveness. *American Journal of Cardiology* 45: 791-796.

Gordon, M. S., Ewy, G. A., Felner, J. M., Forker, A. D., Gessner, I. H., Juul, D., Mayer, J. W., Sajid, A., and Waugh, R. A. 1981. A cardiology patient simulator for continuing education of family physicians. *Journal of Family Practice* 13: 353.

Gregoratos, G., and Miller, A. B. 1999. Task Force 3: Teaching. *Journal of American College of Cardiology* 33: 1120-1127.

Issenberg, S. B., McGaghie, W. C., Brown, D. D., Mayer, J. W., Gessner, I. H., Hart, I. R., Waugh, R. A., Petrusa, E. R., Safford, R., Ewy, G. A., and Felner, J. M. 1998. Development of multimedia computer-based measures of clinical skills in bedside cardiology. *Proceedings of the 8th International Ottawa Conference on Medical Education and Assessment,* 12-15 July 1998. Philadelphia, Pennsylvania.

Issenberg, S. B., Petrusa, E. R., McGaghie, W. C., Felner J. M., Waugh, R. A., Nash, I. S., Hart, I. R. 1999. Assesement of a computer-based system to teach bedside cardiology. *Academic Medicine,* in press.

Jones, J. S., Hunt, S. J., Carlson, S. A., and Seamon, J. P. 1997. Assessing bedside cardiologic examination skills using ìHarvey,î a cardiology patient simulator. *Academic Emergency Medicine* 4: 980-5.

Keys, B., and Wolfe, J. 1990. The role of management games and simulations in education and research. *Journal of Management* 16: 307-36.

Macintosh, M. C. M., and Chard, T. 1997. Pelvic manikins as learning aids. *Medical Education* 31:194-6.

Mangione, S., Nieman, L. Z., Gracely, E., and Kaye, D. 1993. The teaching and practice of cardiac auscultation during internal medicine and cardiology training: a nationwide survey. *Annals of Internal Medicine* 119: 47-54.

Mangione, S., and Nieman, L. Z. 1997. Cardiac auscultatory skills of internal medicine and family practice trainees: a comparison of diagnostic proficiency. *JAMA* 278:717-22.

Melvin ,W. S., Johnson, J. A., and Ellison, C. 1996 Laparoscopic skills enhancement. *American Journal of Surgery* 172: 377-9.

Office of Naval Research. 1973. *Visual elements in flight simulation.* Washington, D.C.:National Council of the National Academy of Science.

Penta, F. B., and Koffman, S. 1973. The effectiveness of simulation devices in teaching selected skills of physical diagnosis. *Journal of Medical Educaiton* 48: 442.

Petrusa, E. R., Issenberg, S. B., Mayer, J. W., Felner, J. M., Brown, D. D., Waugh, R. A., Kondos, G. T., Gessner, I. H., and McGaghie, W. C. 1999. Multi-center implementation of a four-year multimedia computer curriculum in cardiology. *Academic Medicine* 74: 123-9.

Ressler, E. K., Armstrong, J. E., Forsythe, G. B. 1999. Military mission rehearsal: from sandtable to virtual reality. In *Innovative Simulations for the Evaluation of Professional Competence*, edited by A. Tekian, C. McGuire, and W. C. McGaghie. Chicago: Department of Medical Education, University of Illinois Medical Center.

Roldan, C. A., Shively, B. K., and Crawford, M. H. 1996. Value of the cardiovascular physical examination for detecting valvular heart disease in asymptomatic subjects. *American Journal of Cardiology* 77: 1327-31.

Rolfe, J. M., and Staples, K. J. 1979. *Flight Simulation.* Cambridge: Cambridge University Press.

Rosser, J. C., Rosser, L. E., and Savalgi, R. S. 1997. Skill acqusition and assessment for laproscopic surgery. *Archives of Surgery* 132: 200-04.

Sajid, A., Magero, J., and Feinzimer, M. 1977. Learning effectiveness of the heart sound simulator. *Journal of Medical Education* 52: 25.

Schwid, H. A., and O'Donnell, D. 1992. Anesthesiologistsí management of simulated critical incidents. *Anesthesiology* 76: 495-501.

St. Clair, E. W., Oddone, E. Z., Waugh, R. A., Corey, G. R., Feussner, J. R.1992. Assessing housestaff diagnostic skills using a cardiology patient simulator. *Annals of Internal Medicine* 117: 751-6.

Society of Photo-Optical Engineers. 1975. Simulators and simulation. *Society of Photo-Optical Engineers* 59 (Session 4): 141.

Streufert, S., Pogash, R., and Piasecki, M. 1988. Simulation-based assessment of managerial Competence: reliability and validity. *Personnel Psychology* 41: 537-57.

Wachtel, J. 1985. The future of nuclear power plant simulation in the United States. In: DG Walton (ed.), *Simulation for Nuclear Reactor Technology.* Cambridge: Cambridge University Press.

Waugh, R. A., Mayer, J. W., Ewy, G. A., Felner, J. A., Issenberg, S. B., Gessner, I. H., Juul, D., Mayer, J. W., Sajid, A., and Waugh, R. A. 1995. Multimedia computer-assisted instruction in cardiology. *Archives of Internal Medicine* 155: 197-203.

Weinholtz, D. 1987. *Bedside teaching rounds: A manual for attending physicians.* Iowa City, IA: University of Iowa Medical School.

Woolliscroft, J. O., Calhoun, J. G., Tenhaken, J. D., and Judge, R. D. 1987. Harvey: the impact of a cardiovascular teaching simulator on student skill acquisition. *Medical Teacher* 9: 53-7.

10

The Individual as a Member of a Working Group: Evaluating Team Performance in Aviation and Medicine*

Robert L. Helmreich

Professional failure is all too often due not to lack of individual knowledge or skill, but rather to inappropriate interaction among members of a working group. This chapter cites a number of specific examples from aviation (crew performance) and medicine (surgical teams) that have resulted in major tragedies. It describes illustrative simulation exercises being developed for training and testing of teams of professionals, addresses problems associated with the formal evaluation of group performance, and explores ways to resolve these difficulties. The need to augment simulation with formal training in human factors is stressed. The role of simulators

* The research reported here was supported by a grants from the Federal Aviation Administration, Robert Helmreich, Principal Investigator, and the Swiss National Science Foundation.

*for training in aviation and medicine is discussed, including their expanded use for training in team performance. The need to augment simulation with formal training in human factors is stressed. Problems associated with the formal evaluation of **team** performance are addressed.*

High fidelity simulators have a growing place in training for technology based endeavors. The history of simulator use in aviation illustrates the multiple and complementary functions that simulators fill. Training flights for the qualification of pilots were one of the most dangerous aspects of aviation. Crewmembers were required to perform hazardous maneuvers such as losing an engine on take off, landing with two (of four) engines inoperative in actual flight. Many lives were lost and many aircraft destroyed in the name of training.

With the development of high fidelity simulators in the late 1970s, these activities were accomplished in the simulator. Ultimately, it became possible for all aspects of initial qualification to be completed in the simulator. In theory, a newly qualified pilot could show up at the gate to fly passengers as his first flight in the plane. (In practice, pilots do fly the airplane and must complete a number of supervised flights before being released for independent operation.) The evidence is clear—pilots trained in simulators are better qualified since they have the opportunity to practice conducting dangerous, but essential, maneuvers such as recovery from stalls and windshear as well as coping with a variety of mechanical failures in a simulator that is firmly attached to the ground. At the same time, the number of accidents associated with training for commercial aviation has dropped to near zero. Outside the United States, however, training exercises in the aircraft still result in accidents. For example, in 1996, a DC-8 crashed in South America while making a training landing with two engines inoperative.

The modern simulator provides a faithful representation of the environment of flight. By moving in six axes, it can fool the senses into experiencing acceleration and deceleration as well as climbing and diving. Operational sounds are also faithfully reproduced as are all flight controls and instruments and the sounds of flight. Visual graphics provide a realistic view of the scene outside the cockpit windows—scenery, other aircraft, and even ground personnel to aid in parking at the gate.

At a lower level of fidelity, part-task trainers that simulate a portion of the cockpit environment are also used for training. For example, the programming and operation of the Flight Management Computer in advanced technology aircraft can be conducted in a desktop simulation. Such simulation can also be used to establish initial qualification of trainees.

The second major development in the use of simulators in aviation was the shift of much formal evaluation from the airplane to the simulator. In all major and most regional U.S. airlines, the annual Proficiency Check is conducted in the simulator. This check addresses the individual, technical competence of the pilot and is based on the execution of a required set of technical maneuvers. In addition to the Proficiency Check, pilots also receive an annual Line Check — formal observation of their performance in the aircraft during normal line operations.

Simulators have also found a place in medicine. Instrumented, computer-controlled mannequins can allow anesthesiologists to practice intubation and anesthesia and to deal with a number of crisis situations on a completely compliant patient with no propensity for filing malpractice suits. Anesthesia simulators that approach the fidelity of flight simulators have proliferated in the last decade. Installations are found in the United States at Stanford University, the University of Florida, Harvard University, the University of Pittsburgh, Pennsylvania State University, the University of Rochester, Syracuse University, and the University of Washington (e.g., Gaba & deAnda, 1988). Outside the U.S., anesthesia simulators have been developed and installed at Kyushu University in Japan and at universities in Basel, Switzerland, Toronto, Canada, Copenhagen, Denmark, and Leiden, the Netherlands (e.g., Chopra, Engbers, Geerts et al., 1994; Christensen, Laub, & the Sophus Group, 1995; Good, Lampotang, Gibby, & Gravenstein, 1988). Similarly, laparoscopic simulators can allow surgeons to practice the techniques of this type of surgery using devices that contain, for example, a pig's liver.

Desktop simulation for anesthesiology that allows users to administer different agents in response to computer-presented stimulus situations is also used for training and evaluation. However, the focus of this chapter is on high fidelity simulation.

Extending the Range of Training

In the late 1970s, researchers at NASA completed a study of the causes of commercial airline crashes since the introduction of the highly reliable turbojet transport in 1959 (for a review see Helmreich & Foushee, 1993). The study reached two disturbing conclusions. First, more than 70% of the accidents involved human error rather than failures of the aircraft or environmental causes such as weather. Second, of the human error, the majority of these involved failures in the interpersonal aspects of flight—leadership, communication, decision making, and shared awareness of the situation. A thoroughly studied accident illustrates the intersection of a difficult situation with poor communication and coordination.

In 1982, the crew of an Air Florida Boeing 737 crashed a perfectly airworthy plane on take off at Washington National Airport. The plane took off with ice on the wings and a sensor blocked by ice that caused the instruments to overstate the aircraft's speed. Because of the erroneous speed indication, too little power was applied. As the following dialogue indicates, the first officer sensed a problem with the instrument readings and power setting, but he did not communicate his concerns clearly, as is shown in this flawed exchange between the crewmembers just before they crashed.

First officer:	Ah, that's not right.
Captain:	Yes it is, there's eighty (referring to ground speed).
First officer:	Naw, I don't think it's right. Ah, maybe it is.
Captain:	Hundred and twenty.
First officer:	I don't know.

Shortly after take off, the plane stalled and hit the 14th Street bridge over the Potomac.

NASA researchers presented their earlier findings at an industry conference in 1978 that was attended by representatives of airlines from many countries (Cooper, White, & Lauber, 1979). The immediate outcome of awareness of the research findings was the initiation of new training for flight crews that dealt with the interpersonal aspects of flight. This training was known initially as Cockpit Resource Management or CRM. It has two major phases. The first phase is a seminar that introduces the basic concepts of effective communication, leadership, and teamwork. CRM seminars also use case studies of accidents and incidents to illustrate the life and death importance of the issues addressed in training. The second phase of CRM centers on recurrent practice and training in the application of human factors concepts. This annual training uses the flight simulator as the central element. Human factors training in the simulator is known as Line Oriented Flight Training or LOFT (Butler, 1993). It involves full crews conducting one or two complete flights in the simulator. The flights begin with the necessary paperwork (releases, weather, etc.) and pre-flight briefings. The training is conducted by an instructor with special training in evaluation of group performance. An essential component of LOFT is its non-jeopardy nature. Unlike formal evaluation in the simulator, LOFT is training and pilots are free to experiment with new behaviors without placing their qualification at jeopardy. Sessions are videotaped and, on completion, are thoroughly debriefed by the instructor who uses the video to illustrate effective and ineffective human factors practices.

Rethinking CRM and LOFT

Participants' reactions to CRM and LOFT are highly favorable. The training is generally perceived as relevant and as contributing to safer and more effective flight operations (Helmreich & Foushee, 1993; Helmreich & Wilhelm, 1990). However, it was recognized by the mid-1980s that the focus of training was too narrow. Flight crews operate in a complex environment that includes air traffic control, cabin personnel, company operations, and other aircraft. Cockpit Resource Management was soon renamed Crew Resource Management (retaining the acronym). Training began to address the systemic influences on crew performance and LOFT began to include interactions with (simulated) air traffic control and flight attendants. Many organizations have also initiated joint CRM training that includes pilots and flight attendants.

A characteristic of effective CRM and LOFT programs is their reliance on data to guide curriculum development and to validate training effectiveness. Anonymous surveys are widely used to diagnose the organization and to determine pre-training acceptance of the concepts of teamwork and coordination that form the bases of CRM. Confidential observations of crew performance in line operations provide information on how much of that which is taught finds its way from the schoolhouse to the air (Helmreich & Foushee, 1993). Post-training data from both surveys and observations help determine topics that should be stressed in recurrent training. Further information relevant to training comes from analyses of the human component of accidents and incidents occurring within the organization. This emphasis on using data to guide a continuing program differentiates CRM/LOFT from typical managerial development programs, which also tend not to be recurring in nature.

Expanding the Scope of Human Factors Training in Medicine

The use of simulators for the training of anesthesiologists soon moved beyond purely technical training to include the interpersonal aspects of surgical anesthesia as pioneered by David Gaba and his associates at Stanford (Howard, Gaba, Fish, Yang, & Sarnquist, 1992). This training, often called Anesthesia Crisis Resource Management in recognition of its links to CRM in aviation, is being conducted at most facilities with anesthesia simulators.

The late Hans-Gerhard Schaefer, an anesthesiologist at the University of Basel/Kantonsspital in Switzerland, was an early convert in recognizing the importance of human factors and human factors training in the operating room (OR). Schaefer spent a sabbatical as a visiting scientist with our research group at the University of Texas. During his stay, he became familiar with the use of simulators for human factors training in aviation and with the systematic observational methodology used to assess flightcrew behavior. I subsequently joined him as a visiting professor in the Department of Anesthesia in Basel. He and I observed interactions in the OR and noted instances of error, flawed decision making, and interpersonal conflict. *The most salient finding from our observations was that the most serious human factors issues arise in interactions between the professional disciplines in the OR—surgical and anesthesia teams* (Helmreich & Schaefer, 1994; Schaefer, Helmreich, & Scheidegger, 1995). The implication of this is that simulator training that only involves one component of the OR environment—whether surgeons or anesthesiologists—cannot address the most critical human factors issues.[1] Schaefer's conclusion was that the most effective training should take place in a full OR simulator that can allow all members of medical and support teams to interact while conducting a realistic, simulated operation.

With financing from the Swiss National Science Foundation and the enthusiastic support of the Chairs of Anesthesia and Surgery, a complete OR simulator was developed and installed.[2] The simulator consists of a room equipped as an OR with surgical table, lights, etc. An anesthesia mannequin (naturally named Wilhelm Tell) developed by the Sophus group in Copenhagen is linked to a laparoscopic simulator. A complete anesthesia machine is driven by a Pentium personal computer. The OR is also equipped with multiple video cameras. The computer and video recorders are located in an adjacent room with one way glass walls allowing operators to view the operation. The video record also includes critical patient parameters from the anesthesia monitor.

Simulations are scheduled on the hospital's regular surgical schedule. On the day of a simulation, a complete team consisting of surgeons, anesthesiologists,

---

[1] Actors are commonly employed in pure anesthesia simulation to role-play surgeons. However, the training is only being given to one subgroup of the OR.

[2] Professors Daniel Scheidegger and Felix Harder provided the organizational support essential to this project.

nurses, and orderly arrives at a conference room in surgical garb. A human factors briefing that discusses relevant issues and the goals of the simulation precedes a review of Wilhelm Tell's medical records. Following the briefing, Wilhelm Tell is anesthetized and the laparoscopic surgery starts. During the surgery a number of problems can be introduced that require coordination and decision making—for example, pneumothorax, severe bleeding, etc. Following the simulation, a thorough debriefing is conducted by the human factors team. The debriefing addresses both the positive and negative human factors of the operation. It is made salient by selective review of the video recording of the operation.

Participant evaluations indicate that the training is viewed as important and useful (Sexton, Marsch, Helmreich, Betzendoerfer, Kocher, & Scheidegger, in press). After the tragic death of Hans-Gerhard Schaefer, the program continues to be an important component of training at the Kantonsspital.

Simulation is Not Enough

One of the strong conclusions that can be drawn from aviation research is that human factors training through simulation is not enough to effect significant behavioral change in either flight crews or medical teams (Davies & Helmreich, 1996; Helmreich & Schaefer, 1994). Each group operates in a complex organizational environment that can facilitate or impede effective team performance. To achieve optimum results, the organizational culture and current OR practices must be assessed and addressed. This can be done through several methods, best applied in concert. The organizational culture and staff attitudes about teamwork and communication can be measured through surveys of participants (Helmreich & Davies, 1996). Systematic observations (confidential audits) of team performance in the OR can also provide essential data and provide baseline for the measurement of change over time (Sexton, Marsch, Helmreich, Betzendoerfer, Kocher, & Scheidegger, 1998). A third essential source of data comes from confidential, critical incident reporting systems that address the human factors associated with adverse events (Staender, 1997; Staender, Davies, Helmreich, & Kaufmann, in press). In addition, more formal, didactic training in human performance issues is needed to place simulator training in a meaningful context. The human factors program at the University of Basel, now directed by Dr. Stephan Marsch has been supplemented by data from each of these sources.

The Evaluation Enigma

As I have noted, simulators now provide controlled environments in which individual technical competence can be evaluated. In aviation, the simulator is the primary venue for individual performance assessment leading to qualification and re-certification. Similar opportunities for individual technical assessment are becoming more feasible as the fidelity of simulators increases.

However, since most errors in aviation that result in crashes involve *team interactions*, it follows that the assessment of *team performance* should be an essential element of qualification. Despite its potential value, formal evaluation of *team* behavior raises a number of issues and is a source of resistance and considerable anxiety for those subject to disqualification. Some of the objections posed to team assessment are:

Assessment of group behavior is subjective and subject to bias.

- If one member of a team shows substandard performance while all others are adequate, should the *team* fail?

- What qualifications are required for evaluators to fairly judge interpersonal behaviors?

- If a team commits an error, but traps and manages it well, should this be grounds for disqualification?

- Does placing the team at jeopardy during simulation destroy its training value?

One of the basic premises of LOFT training in aviation has been that it is without jeopardy, allowing participants to experiment with new behaviors. There is a general consensus that the training component of simulation should continue this policy.

Organizations that conduct LOFT have initiated formal training in performance assessment for both trainers and evaluators. Research has shown that team behavior can be classified in terms of specific *behavioral markers* that can be reliably assessed by trained observers and that the subjective nature of team evaluation can be eliminated (Helmreich & Foushee, 1993).

Two issues remain troublesome. The latest generation of CRM training focuses on the management of human error (Helmreich, 1997). The basic premise of the training is that error is inevitable and ubiquitous and that the goal of training is to provide behavioral countermeasures to reduce the frequency of errors, to trap errors before they become consequential, and to mitigate the consequences of those that occur. The dilemma for evaluation is how to weigh the commission of error versus the effective management of those errors that occur. The second problem is how to deal with a crew where the performance of only a single member is unacceptable. In an individualistic society such as ours, the focus has always been on individual responsibility.

The Federal Aviation Administration is moving cautiously toward the implementation of team evaluation in the simulator (called LOE or Line Operational Evaluation to distinguish it from LOFT, which remains without jeopardy). LOE is part of a voluntary set of regulations for training and qualification, called the Advanced Qualification Program. Most major U.S. airlines are moving to operate under these regulations. Initial results suggest that it can provide better training and more meaningful evaluation.

My conclusion is that we must continue to stress the interpersonal component of performance in domains where teams must interact with technology. We must provide crews with training in this as well as the technical aspects of their jobs. To make training effective, individuals and teams must receive accurate feedback on this aspect of their performance. *The logical extension is to make formal evaluation of interpersonal behavior a component of qualification.* Ultimate success, though, requires a solid research base and an equitable evaluation system that protects the individual in the team.

References

Butler, R.E. 1993. LOFT: Full-mission simulation as crew resource management. In *Cockpit Resource Management*. Edited by E.L. Wiener, B.G. Kanki & R.L. Helmreich. San Diego: Academic Press. pp. 199-223.

Chopra, V., Engbers, F.H.M., Geerts, M.J., Filet, W.R., Bovill, J.G., & Spierdijk, J. 1994. The Leiden anaesthesia simulator. *British Journal of Anaesthesia* 73:287-292.

Christensen, U.J., Laub, M. & the Sophus Group 1995. The Sophus anaesthesia simulator. *British Journal of Anesthesia* 5: Supplement 1 A72.

Cooper, G.E., White, M.D. & Lauber, J.K. 1979. *Proceedings of the NASA Workshop on Resource Management Training for Airline Flight Crews* (CP-2120). Moffett Field, CA: NASA-Ames Research Center.

Davies, JM & Helmreich, RL. 1996. Simulation: it's a start. *Canadian Journal of Anaesthesia* 43: 425-9.

Gaba, D.M. & DeAnda, A. 1988. A comprehensive anesthesia simulating environment re-creating the operating room for research and training. *Anesthesiology* 69:387-394.

Good, M.L., Lampotang, S., Gibby, G.L. & Gravenstein, J.S. 1988. Critical events simulation for training in anesthesiology. *Journal of Clinical Monitoring* 4:140.

Helmreich, R.L. 1997. Managing human error in aviation. *Scientific American* May, 62-67.

Helmreich, R.L. & Davies, J.M. 1996. Human factors in the operating room: Interpersonal determinants of safety, efficiency and morale. In A.A. Aitkenhead (Ed.), *Bailliere's Clinical Anaesthesiology: Safety and Risk Management in Anaesthesia. London: Balliere Tindall.* pp. 277-296

Helmreich, R.L. & Foushee, H.C. 1993. Why crew resource management? Empirical and theoretical bases of human factors training in aviation. In *Cockpit Resource Management.* Edited by E.L. Wiener, B.G. Kanki & R.L. Helmreich. pp. 3-45.

Helmreich, R.L. & Schaefer, H.G. 1994. Team performance in the operating room. In: Bogner MS (Ed.) *Human Error in Medicine*, Hillsdale, New Jersey: Erlbaum. pp. 225-253.

Helmreich, R.L. & Wilhelm, J.A. 1991. Outcomes of Crew Resource Management training. *International Journal of Aviation Psychology* 1: 287-300.

Howard, S.K, Gaba, D.M., Fish, K.J., Yang, G., & Sarnquist, F.H. 1992. Anesthesia crisis resource management training: teaching anesthesiologists to handle critical incidents. *Aviation, Space, & Environmental Medicine* 63: 763-770.

Schaefer, H.G., Helmreich, R.L. & Scheidegger, D. 1995. Safety in the operating theatre B Part 1: Interpersonal relationships and team performance. *Current Anaesthesia and Critical Care* 6: 48-53.

Sexton, B., Marsch, S., Helmreich, R.L., Betzendoerfer, D., Kocher, T. & Scheidegger, D. 1998. Participant evaluations of Team Oriented Medical Simulation. In L. Henson, A. Lee, & A. Basford (Eds.) *Simulators in Anesthesiology Education.* New York. Plenum.

Sexton, B., Marsch, S., Helmreich, R.L., Betzendoerfer, D., Kocher, T. & Scheidegger, D. 1998. Jumpseating in the Operating Room. In L. Henson, A. Lee, & A. Basford (Eds.) *Simulators in Anesthesiology Education.* New York. Plenum.

Staender, S. 1997. Critical Incident Reporting System (CIRS), http://www.medana.unibas.ch/ENG/CIRS/Cirs.htm

Staender, S., Davies, J.M., Helmreich, R.L. & Kaufmann, M. (in press). Critical incidents, culture changes and the Internet. *Anesthesiology.*

Papers and links to other related sites can be found on the University of Texas Aerospace Crew Research Homepage: http://www.psy.utexas.edu/psy/helmreich/nasaut.htm

11

Military Mission Rehearsal: From Sandtable to Virtual Reality*

Eugene K. Ressler, Jr., James E. Armstrong, Jr., George B. Forsythe

Today, as never before, the armed forces of the United States rely on simulation and modeling to ensure defense readiness. This chapter explores the many uses of simulation in Army training, assessment, and concept analysis. We begin by presenting a taxonomy for discussing simulations that includes three dimensions— purpose, scope, and type. Next, we offer several examples of on-going work with simulations to illustrate our taxonomy. We highlight examples of virtual, constructive, and live simulations used for individual and collective training, formative assessment,

---

* The views and opinions expressed herein are solely those of the authors and do not represent the official view of the United States Military Academy, the United States Army, or any other agency of the United States Government.

and concept analysis. Finally, we identify from the US Army's experience a number of issues and challenges associated with the use of simulations. We comment specifically on organizational, pedagogical, and technical considerations.

The year is 1972; the place is a classroom in an Army barracks somewhere in West Germany. The leaders of Bravo Company are preparing for divisional maneuvers; their mission is to cross the Rhine River and secure a bridgehead for the passage of a mechanized brigade. Bravo Company's officers and senior sergeants stand huddled around a large children's sand box on saw horses; a model of their sector of the river carved neatly in the sand. The first platoon leader explains his operational plan for the attack. As he talks through each phase of the crossing, his commander asks the tough "what if" questions. "Okay Mike, what if you receive sniper fire from the upper left window of this house right here just as your first landing craft hits the far shore?" the company commander asks, pointing to a likeness of the actual house constructed from blocks. "What are your actions and orders?" The platoon leader and his platoon sergeant then brainstorm alternative actions to this hypothetical situation. During their analysis, they test the applicability of their standing operating procedures against the potential actions of the enemy. A lively discussion of tactical doctrine and company procedures ensues with all the leaders participating. Weeks later, they have the opportunity to do it on the ground, but this time, there are no enemy troops in the house on the other side of the river—the actual residents wisely lock up and take vacation in the Hartz Mountains during the maneuvers.

The year is now 1987; the place is the high desert of the National Training Center (NTC) at Fort Irwin, California, the Army's equivalent of Top Gun school. The Bravo Company Commander from West Germany now commands a mechanized infantry battalion preparing for its third battle in five days with the mighty OPFOR, a Soviet-style mechanized brigade of American soldiers. For the battalion commander and his soldiers, this is as close to real combat as they have ever been. Both opposing forces have MILES equipment, laser devices that register actual hits from direct fire weapons—from rifles to tanks.

Simulated artillery rounds fall with all the sound and fury of the real thing. The tanks and infantry fighting vehicles have laser locator devices so that every movement can be tracked and stored in a centralized computer in the "Star Wars" building. The entire battle is recorded by a computer (some portions are also video taped) for playback during the after action review. The battalion commander and his officers still hold "what-if" drills before coming to fight at the NTC, but they are now conducted with sophisticated computer simulations. Before deploying to the NTC, the commander and his staff rehearse a number of tactical operations using computer simulations and mathematical models to practice command and control procedures and test the effects of alternative battle plans. They also conducted extensive terrain studies of the battle area using virtual reality aerial reconnaissance. Tank and mechanized infantry crews rehearse every possible engagement in combat simulators before deploying to battle the OPFOR. And now, once the battle begins, the enemy stays home to fight and each step of the operation is reviewed and critiqued over and over again.

Today, as never before, the armed forces of the United States rely on simulation and modeling to ensure defense readiness. The experiences of the battalion commander illustrate just how technologically refined military training has become in the past twenty years. Although many factors account for the Desert Storm victory, most military observers agree that our armed forces' high state of training contributed to success on the battlefield. For the Army, our soldiers fought and "bled" in countless peacetime simulated battles to learn the lessons of combat before the war so they would survive the fighting and win on the battlefield. As a complement to simulated combat at all echelons from tank crew to corps, defense planners modeled and tested operations and logistics plans, mobilization scenarios, and deployment schedules long before Saddam Hussein invaded Kuwait.

This chapter explores the various uses of simulation in Army education and training. To set the context, we first present a conceptual framework for discussing simulations. Next, we offer several examples of on-going work with simulations to illustrate components of our framework. Finally, we identify from the Army's experience a number of issues and challenges associated with the use of simulations.

Conceptual Framework

In 1995, the Department of Defense published a master plan for modeling and simulation, which specifies policies, organizational procedures, and management procedures for coordinating, modeling, and simulation activities

A Conceptual Framework for Simulations

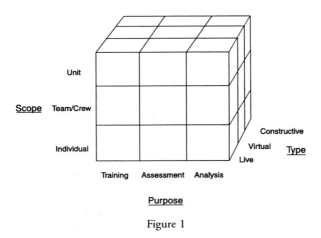

Figure 1

within the Defense Department. In addition, this document offers a set of dimensions for thinking about simulation from which we derive our typology in Figure 1.

Purpose. Although there may be a variety of applications for simulations, the three most common uses of simulations in the Army are identified in Figure 1. Not surprisingly, simulation is an essential feature of Army training, especially for war-fighting tasks, where they support the development of combat skills and expertise for individual soldiers, crews, teams, and units. Simulations also play a role in individual and unit assessment, although assessments are most often formative in nature, supporting the training purpose. We note limited use of simulation for summative assessment in the Army, as is the case for certification and licensing in other professions. Finally, simulations help Army planners analyze operational plans and logistical support by testing mathematical or other logically represented models. Thus, they play a key role in the formulation of doctrine that eventually guides training and education.

Scope. The scope of Army simulations covers tasks and procedures for all echelons, from individual soldier skills, such as tank gunnery, to collective skills, such as battle staff procedures and task force operations. This broad scope permits training, assessment, and analysis at all organizational levels.

Types. The Department of Defense Master Plan (1995, p. A-7) discusses three types of simulations which vary in terms of the degree of human involvement and the degree of equipment realism. *Virtual* simulations involve real people operating simulated systems, such as a tank gunner engaging simulated targets in a computer-based gunnery simulator. *Constructive* simulations involve simulated people operating simulated systems, such as computer war games.

Live simulations involve human actors working with real systems, such as the force-on-force battles at the National Training Center.

In the next section, we describe in some detail several virtual, constructive, and live simulations currently in use to support training, assessment, and concept analysis in the Army.

Military Simulation Examples

Virtual. Current examples of virtual simulations used or planned for use by the Army include the Simulation Networking Trainer (SIMNET), the Close Combat Tactical Trainer (CCTT), the Battle Lab Reconfigurable Simulator (BLRSIM), and the Crewman's Associate. As you might expect, these examples of virtual simulation technology imitate the operation of ground combat vehicles and close support attack helicopters in synthetic battlefield environments. The Army developed SIMNET for training multiple crews to perform as teams. To do this the Army realized it had to connect multiple virtual simulations together so that crews could practice coordinating their fire on enemy targets in a synthetic battlefield. Thus SIMNET stands for *simulation network*.

Simulation Networking Trainer. SIMNET, as shown in Figure 2, looks like a collection of big iron boxes painted Army green. Wires connect the boxes, and each box has a door or hatch. Opening the hatch and climbing inside the boxes reveals the world of today's high technology warfighters—the controls and displays of a modern Abrams tank, an Apache attack helicopter, or a Bradley infantry fighting vehicle—three of the Army's major tactical weapon systems.

SIMNET: A Virtual Picture of Army Combat Platforms

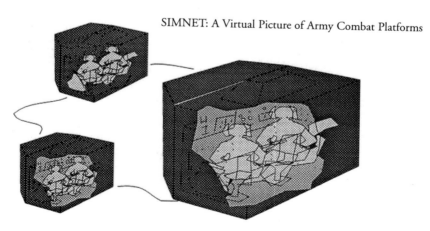

Figure 2

Close Combat Tactical Trainer. As experience with SIMNET grew, the Army realized that virtual simulations were also very useful for training crewmembers on both individual and crew tasks. As a result, the Army's follow-on to SIMNET, CCTT, has much higher fidelity in its representation of the individual crewmember's tasks and the battlefield environment that the crew sees and interacts with. The CCTT, Figure 3, is a high fidelity, multi-echelon full crew trainer. It can be used for precision gunnery training. For example, the tank simulator replicates every task, both individual and crew, that must be performed to detect and engage targets, even including the individual task associated with loading a tank main gun round. The terrain database of the simulation also has much higher fidelity. In SIMNET, driving into a forest puts the tank crew inside a gray canopy, but in CCTT the tank crew is confronted with the problem of maneuvering and firing around individual trees.

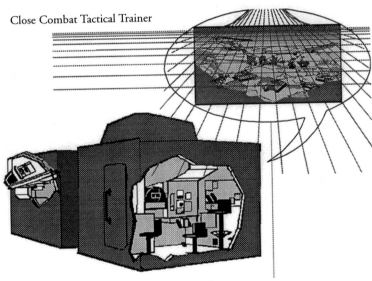

Close Combat Tactical Trainer

Figure 3

Battle Lab Reconfigurable Simulator for Concept Analysis. The combat developments version of CCTT is the Battle Lab Reconfigurable Simulator (BLRSIM). The BLRSIM, Figure 4, is a relatively low-cost and space required virtual, man-in-the-loop simulator which may be rapidly and easily reconfigured to represent current and future combat vehicles and other weapon system platforms to varying levels of fidelity. BLRSIM will provide the US Army's Battle

BLRSIM: A Battle Lab Reconfigurable Simulator

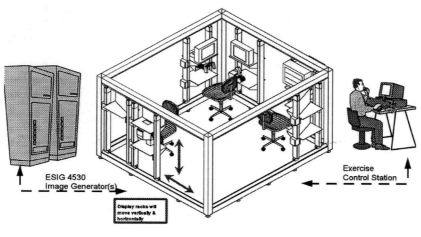

ESIG 4530
Image Generator(s)

Display racks will move vertically & horizontally

Exercise
Control Station

Figure 4

Labs with reconfigurable simulator technology for performing analysis of advanced concepts and requirements. The Battle Labs are research facilities where the Army experiments with new tactical concepts and technology.

The BLRSIM has five configurations: ground combat vehicles such as a tank or infantry fighting vehicle; rotary wing aircraft or attack helicopters; command, control, communication, and intelligence systems; dismounted infantry soldiers; and combat service support systems. This means that Army analysts will use BLRSIM to experiment with changes to Army requirements for doctrine, training, leader development, organization, material, and soldiers. The simulation work envisioned for BLRSIM will be based on the classical scientific method including rigorous experimental design, control, data collection and analysis. The reconfigurable simulator technology, which uses an object-oriented software architecture with common hardware components, will also provide the Army with a capability for research, development, and acquisition testing and evaluation.

Crewman's Reasearch and Development

Crewman's Assoicate Crewstation

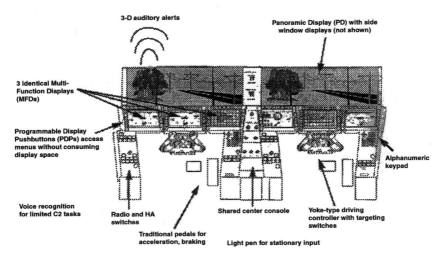

Figure 5

Crewman's Associate for Research and Development. An excellent example of the way virtual simulations are being used to save time and money in research and development projects is the Crewman's Associate. As shown in Figure 5, the Crewman's Associate is a high fidelity research environment that is leading the Army's effort to reduce the size of the tank crew from four to three or two members, yet increase overall weapon system capability.

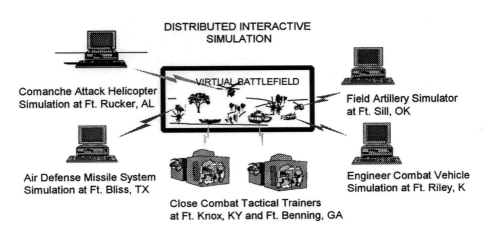

Figure 6

Distributed Interactive Simulation for Telenetworking. The Army's vision is that all the virtual simulators—SIMNET, CCTT, and BLRSIM—will be interoperable so they can be integrated into the same synthetic battlefield exercise even though they are dispersed geographically at different locations across the United States and around the globe. The technology that enables this interoperability is called "distributed interactive simulation" or DIS. Standard interfaces and protocols, common hardware and software architectures, and seamless, error-free communications are essential components of DIS currently in development. The purpose of these DIS initiatives is to enable Army, Navy, and Air Force simulators and simulations to work together so that simulations faithfully reproduce complex interactions among services that mark modern military operations. The success of DIS will permit units that fight together in wartime to conduct peacetime training exercises and mission rehearsals together, even though they may be stationed far from each other.

Constructive. Battle Command Training Program (BCTP) is a combination constructive-live simulation training exercise used for the education and assessment of Corps, Division, and Brigade staffs. Traditionally, this type of training exercise is known in the Army as a command-post exercise or CPX where only the commanders or key leaders with minimum support personnel and equipment deploy to field or simulated field locations. BCTP is partly a live simulation because the training experience involves real people, the battle command staff officers, using much of the real command and control equipment and procedures that they would use in actual combat situations.

Staff officers work with each other and communicate with other command post staffs. They solve complex tactical and logistical problems under the time pressure of simulated battlefield events. BCTP is also a constructive simulation training exercise because a constructive simulation called Corps Battle Simulation (CBS) is used to drive the various battlefield events.

Corps Battle Simulation (CBS). CBS is a low resolution, event driven, interactive combat simulation whose quality benefits from the use of both stochastic and deterministic components. The stochastic parts employ embedded models with pseudo-random variables to produce varied outcomes. The deterministic parts always produce the same outcome for a given simulated situation. CBS is interactive because the outputs of CBS depend on periodic inputs from the decisions and plans of the staff officers. Resolution for Army combat simulations refers to the size of the smallest military unit considered when resolving the outcome of clashes among systems, units, or forces. CBS is considered to be a low-resolution simulation because combat is resolved by

Lanchester-type[1] attrition models at the battalion level, 500 to 1000 people and their equipment.

In contrast to CBS, a simulation that represents combat in detail at the individual soldier or weapon system level would be a very high-resolution model. Interactive refers to the way the simulation operates and is controlled. CBS is interactive because inputs and orders are entered while the simulation is running. This means that CBS is a "man-in-the-loop" simulation, which requires a trained user staff and site support team to operate it (U.S. Army TRADOC Analysis Center, 1990).

Live. The final example is the live simulation training exercises at the National Training Center (NTC) used to educate and assess Army combat battalions and their associated combat support elements. We illustrated simulated combat at the NTC in the chapter's introduction.

Common Features. Preparation, control, and feedback are three important features common to all of the above simulation training examples. Army leaders and soldiers prepare for a simulation exercise in much the same way that they prepare for combat. Mission orders are received, operations plans are drawn up, and equipment undergoes pre-combat checks. Mission rehearsals are often conducted.

Preparation. Simulation plays an important role during preparation for training exercises, war-fighting experiments, research and development/testing, and evaluation analyses. For example, a constructive simulation of land combat called JANUS is used extensively in all three simulation domains. JANUS is an interactive, two-sided (friendly and enemy), stochastic, ground combat simulation featuring both precise statistical and animated output with color graphics. Units preparing for training at the NTC use JANUS to practice deploying and controlling their forces over two-dimensional terrain graphics that represent the terrain they will see later. A JANUS screen of NTC terrain is depicted in Figure 7. Similarly, Division and Corps battle command staffs use JANUS to prepare for BCTP. Company commanders and platoon leaders of tank crews use JANUS to practice maneuvering and positioning units to maximize coordinating fire. Interestingly, though JANUS today has a large role in training, it was originally developed to support force analysis and development requirements.

---

[1] Lanchester applied differential equations to the study of attrition in warfare. Many combat simulations use kill rates derived from some variation of Lanchester's equations.

JANUS Screen Showing National Training Center Terrain

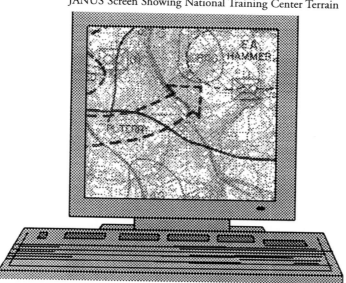

Figure 7

Control. Control of simulation training is exercised by observer-controllers who are specially selected and schooled to monitor and facilitate simulation training. They are important because they make observations and provide insight that instrumentation devices cannot. They also help to ensure that simulation training occurs on schedule and that the participants observe safety rules. The expertise that observer-controllers acquire from watching many different simulation exercises is helpful in providing feedback to the participants during the after-action reviews.

Feedback. Feedback or after-action reviews (AARs) are key to the education and training value of simulation-based training experiences. In these sessions, the participants meet with the observer-controllers and discuss the simulated combat they have just experienced. Often simulation vignettes of the exercise are re-played so the participants can see their "good, bad, and ugly" performance as it is discussed. The focus during these sessions is on learning and not on evaluating performance or placing blame.

Examples in Context. A good way to sum up the Army's view of the importance of simulation can be found in three simple phrases, "Simulate before building, simulate before buying, and simulate before fighting." According to General Max Thurman (1994), "Everything short of combat is simulation." The Army simulates even after fighting in order to validate simulation models and interpolate details of combat reports. For example, after

167

the Gulf War, the Battle of 73 Easting was recreated in a virtual 3-D simulation. This battle was an early success of the ground war. A U.S. Army armored cavalry company ran unexpectedly into an entire Iraqi Republican Guards armored regiment (three times larger) and soundly defeated it. The purpose of the simulation was to capture the battle in a form that could be studied to increase our understanding of what went right and what might have gone wrong. The courageous leader of the U.S. Army's attack force at 73 Easting said that even though it was his first real battle, he and his soldiers were confident in their abilities due to the many simulated battles they had fought.

Issues and Challenges

Despite the Army's overall success and confidence in using simulation for training, it is not surprising that fundamental organizational, pedagogical, and technical issues have arisen as the Army has proceeded to embrace it. The use of simulation in training represents a quiet revolution in thinking and procedures for the Army. From their first days in service, soldiers train in basic skills by practice repeated until the required skill is automatic, executable under great stress and other adverse conditions. The main peacetime mission of military units is to gain and maintain effectiveness by exercising the competencies expected of them. When a specific "real world" mission is at hand, a unit prepares itself by anticipating all imaginable contingencies and rehearsing plans to deal with them. At a more personal level, military culture reveres training in the form of experience. The uniform itself testifies to the combat and peacetime experience of the wearer through decorations and service patches. Certain training is prerequisite for leadership positions, and training is regarded as perhaps the most important single responsibility of leadership. Army jargon is replete with training-related terms and acronyms. At the deepest level, experience in training leads to comfort, security, and ultimately the confidence necessary to stake one's life on personal and unit prowess. Simulation has become, rather suddenly, integral to all of this.

Organizational Issues

The overarching organizational issues confronting the Army and its units regarding simulation have hinged on decisions about *where* and *how* to "buy in" to simulation in training people to fight wars.

Cost vs. Benefit. The great hope for simulation has been that it will "achieve more with less." In the setting of military training, this translates to better-trained units costing fewer dollars. Specifically, simulators save dollars by replacing the operation of very expensive equipment and the firing of live ammunition with the operation of less expensive simulators firing virtual weapons or lasers.

Beyond cost savings, simulators break through old barriers in training. U.S. Army units do not fire live ammunition at other units in training for obvious safety reasons, but they *can* fire laser weapon simulators, achieving at least some measure of the experience of being under fire. Training areas are frequently limited in size and availability, but a simulation can cover any amount of virtual terrain. Live training in darkness or special weather conditions must wait for night or the weather to cooperate, but virtual simulations can create arbitrary conditions instantly.

Conversely, the dollar costs of simulation can be large. Development costs for equipment simulators are often a significant fraction of the cost of developing the equipment itself. Only in operating costs are simulators at a strong advantage over equivalent fleets of real equipment. Hence "low density" items, that is, those present in small numbers in the Army inventory, may not be good candidates for simulation trainers.

Another important cost of simulators involves the precise terrain databases that support the creation of virtual battlefields. To simulate firing from behind a stand of trees, information on the trees must be stored in the simulator. Such databases are large and complex to produce. Older methods involving aerial photography and ground reconnaissance were extremely labor intensive. Economical production has been achieved only through the merging of technologies for detailed multi-spectral remote sensing from space satellites and computer processing of the satellite data.

A more subjective cost of simulation is the opportunity cost of traditional training that will be missed *in lieu* of training with simulation. When the simulation simply adds value, as for MILES laser devices added to a live exercise, this is not a problem. When a command post exercise on real terrain is given up in favor of a simulated operation on virtual terrain, however, opportunity cost is real and bears careful consideration.

Role of simulation for assessment. The Army views simulation as merely a part of the complex process of assessing the training readiness of units and people. There are few instances other than flight training where performance in a simulated environment stands alone as a certificate of proficiency. Rather, the outcome of training exercises and experiences has always been used to provide feedback, usually immediate, on individual and unit success in training. Simulation adds detail and objectivity to this feedback, making it far more valuable. The healthy sense of competition and desire to excel fostered in the

Army culture translates such feedback into a constructive force for development and change. Thus, success or failure of a tank battalion at the National Training Center in a simulated battle against the OPFOR holds no formal weight as a measure of unit effectiveness. Yet everyone in the battalion and its superordinate division likely "knows the score" and looks forward to the opportunity to try again. This positive approach is viewed as highly successful by Army and national leaders.

Pedagogical Issues

The discussion of benefits and roles of simulation leads naturally to detailed consideration of how the benefit occurs, hence to the learning process that simulation reinforces. Training is, after all, teaching and learning.

Trainee-centered framework. The pedagogy of training must center on the experience of the person being trained. During training, a soldier receives *inputs* as perception and interpretations of the training environment. The soldier formulates strategies and plans for action and then acts. The action—firing a weapon, making a radio request for support, commanding a unit to move—comprises the *output*. The output affects the training environment, hence future inputs. Benefit accrues in training if the plans and actions taken, along with the mental and physical performance experienced, result in learning which is useful later, in real mission situations.

Simulation superimposed on the training process affects both trainee inputs and outputs, hence the validity of the training experience. The qualities of a simulation that produce valid training experiences comprise issues in themselves. They fall into three broad categories.

Correctness. The correctness of a simulation is the degree to which it corresponds to the world. All simulations contain an internal representation of the simulated world, a *simulation model*. For a battle tank simulator, for example, the model includes the tank's current engine and overland speed, the positions of controls, the amount of ammunition on board, and a highly detailed description of the terrain where the simulated tank is operating. For a constructive simulation of division operations like JANUS, the model contains unit and weapon systems locations and status information and less detailed terrain information. On the trainee's input side, a correct simulation provides information about the model that is also feasible in the world that the model represents. The tank simulator reflects reasonable speed on its gauges. JANUS shows a map with fighting units drawn where they should be. For outputs, a correct simulator accepts the trainee's actions and makes changes in the model that correspond to what would happen in the corresponding world situation.

Advancing the tank simulator's throttle leads engine speed to increase. Ordering an artillery attack on an enemy unit in JANUS causes unit strength to decrease. A high degree of correctness is a baseline requirement for successful training.

Completeness. The completeness of a simulation is its level of detail. A simulation can be correct yet incomplete. An incomplete simulation does not present inputs to the trainee that are rich enough to provide the desired training experience. For instance, a simulation with a terrain database that omits vegetation is likely to be incomplete, even if all the information that is in the database (on elevation, cultural features, etc.) is correct. Completeness is usually a more difficult issue than correctness because the level of completeness necessary to achieve desired training is a matter of judgment in simulation design.

Fidelity. Experiential fidelity is the quality of a simulation that inspires attention and emotional involvement of the trainee. It often corresponds to realism in the devices that communicate directly with the trainee's senses—the controls of a tank simulator, the graphics of a JANUS scenario, the pace at which inputs are provided to the trainee and outputs are expected. A simulation may have high fidelity even if lacking in correctness and completeness. Video games exist to involve their players, yet they have little training value for real systems. The fidelity required of a simulation is extremely difficult to judge because the effect of emotional involvement on training is not clear.

Technical Issues

Design. The design of simulations for training involves finding technical solutions to the pedagogical and organizational challenges described above in the form of hardware and software systems. Though engineering principles support this process, much of it remains art. The designer's art is to gain enough understanding of the problem at hand to create a system that solves the problem in the sense that the benefits achieved are maximized and, of course, larger than costs.

System design has proven extremely difficult for large, complex problems, including military simulations. The reasons center on limitations of human and organizational communication and comprehension. Successful design depends on the ability of the "customer" to describe and communicate fully the problem to be solved, here the situation to be simulated, the ability of the designer to comprehend it, and her skill at creating alternative solutions. The customer-designer team must evaluate costs and benefits of alternatives correctly to choose the best one. For this, the designer must be able to communicate the capabilities and underlying assumptions of alternative designs back to the customer. Evaluation criteria and methods must be correct and well-understood. Moreover, the customer and designer, which are frequently large organizations, must be uniformly dedicated to a common vision for the result. All this is a tall order when the problem is complex and/or there are many people involved.

"It's what you don't know that you don't know that will kill you." The risks in simulation systems design stem from the possibility of failures in the processes above. Failures of communication, comprehension, or development and evaluation of design alternatives can have three adverse outcomes. First, the design effort can fail to produce a useable system. Second, the effort can produce a useable system with known flaws and limitations, which must be considered in its use. Hence "man-in-the-loop" designs can result when an autonomous simulation was intended. These two difficulties, while undesirable, are insignificant compared to the third. A flawed design process can also yield a system with *unknown* defects, e.g. in correctness, completeness, or fidelity or in true costs that exceed benefits. In our case, the immediate result is a flaw in the process where the simulation is embedded: a poor training experience, a bad acquisition, or an erroneous analysis.

Good system and software engineering practice reduces the probability of design failures of the first two types above. The nature of simulations, that they are models of reality, tends to make description and communication of simulation problems fairly routine. Modern methodologies and tools such as object-oriented design and computer languages further reduce the chances of a known-bad design.

On the other hand, the danger of producing a simulation with hidden flaws is considerable. Perhaps the most important example is a new manifestation of the old saying that "an army trains for the war it last fought," the presumption being that the next conflict will be so different as to find the army unprepared to fight. In simulation design, the danger is that tacit assumptions about the last war will be built into the simulations without due consideration. A straightforward example is that early versions of JANUS assumed two combatants—red and blue forces—based on Cold War assumptions. This proved invalid for Army missions after the disintegration of the USSR. New versions of JANUS are re-engineered to allow for six factions, which may participate as friendly, opposing, or neutral forces. Neutral "forces" can be used to model refugee movements, which were altogether missing from the earlier versions, yet would have been very important in a European conflict.

Integration. The Department of Defense faces enormous challenges in meeting its goals to make simulations interoperable over long distance communication networks. The good news is that the existing computer and computer science literature provides solid theoretical foundations to build upon, and the engineering goals are very clear. The full integration sought is achievable if sufficient resources and leadership are dedicated to see it through.

Implementation. Ironically, the technical issues in implementing simulation systems stem mainly from a human and cultural consideration, namely the technical expertise and orientation it requires of soldiers. Warfare is an ultimate test of human capability, perhaps the most physically and emotionally demanding human endeavor. Classical training for individual soldiers focuses on these demands, emphasizing physical training, marches and movements, and small unit tactical exercises to develop unflinching disciplined response to orders. All this is still important, yet stands in sharp contrast to the intricate expertise required to participate in, say, a BCTP-supported training exercise. Hence the Army has adopted fundamentally new demands for soldiers related to the technical expertise needed to participate in simulations.

Fortunately, related trends have made this cultural shift toward a technically literate Army fairly painless. First is that modern life entails ever-greater familiarity and comfort with technology. Soldiers entering the Army arrive predisposed to accept and use computers and other machines. Second, since society has come to value technical skills, soldiers often volunteer for Army service specifically to gain technical expertise. They are motivated to attain it. Third and perhaps most important is that simulation is merely one example of the military's broad and deep commitment to technology. The U.S. more than any other nation seeks to use technology to minimize risk of life and limb for soldiers while maximizing their ability to win wars. Thus modern American soldiers are immersed in technology because they need it to do their peacetime and wartime jobs. Simulation is merely one more dimension of that technology.

Summary

Simulation has wrought profound change in the way the Army prepares for war. A thorough yet measured integration of simulation in the Army's training programs is still in progress, but has already netted important improvements in overall military readiness. This chapter gives a useful framework for organizing Army simulation applications and shows where some existing examples of simulations fit in this framework. Though there are organizational, pedagogical and technical issues and challenges involved, none have proven insurmountable. The Army is committed to simulation as a technique to achieve more and better training for soldiers, hence a more effective and efficient force. Progress toward wider, deeper use of simulation in training is occurring apace.

References

Department of Defense, Office of the Under Secretary of Defense for Acquisition and Technology. 1995. *Modeling and Simulation (M&S) Master Plan*. Washington, D.C.

Thurman, M. 1994. *Third TMSA Conference on Synthetic Environments*. September 22-23. Washington, D.C.

US Army TRADOC Analysis Center. 1990. *Matrix of Combat Development and Training Models*. Fort Leavenworth, Kansas: Training Simulations Directorate.

Part Three: Challenges and
Opportunities

Part Three: Challenges and Opportunities

Introduction

I n Part One, we examined the essential nature and common characteristics of simulation and the basic considerations for its use in professional competence assessment. Part Two explored prototypic simulations from the professions in assessing cognitive skills; communication, technical, and affective responses; and integration of performance skills and knowledge. Part Three, discusses the new challenges and unprecedented opportunities that technological advances have created for the use of sophisticated simulation methodologies in the instruction and assessment of professionals. We also consider the measurement issues that the application of cutting edge simulation research has highlighted in the use of simulation for testing professional competence.

In Chapter 12, Richard Satava examines the technological revolution within the field of medicine and the role these new technologies play in the continued development of simulations of various surgical, diagnostic and other medical procedures. As the Industrial Era has given way to the Information Age, conventional surgery is being replaced by a host of minimally invasive therapies and non-invasive procedures. So, too, are the traditional pedagogical tools of medical rounds, practicums, and laboratory cadavers being replaced by 3-D visualization imagery, virtual reality technology, and reliance upon electronic or digital representations of real world objects or physical actions. Eventually, Satava argues, certification procedures and assessment of professional competency will ultimately be based upon performance measures using simulation technology rather than more traditional testing formats such as essay and multiple choice questions and oral examinations.

With simulation already being employed in many licensing examinations, and more widespread use likely in the near future, issues about the psychometric properties of simulation exercises need to be examined. John Norcini (Chapter 13) addresses six major measurement concerns involved in the use of simulation for professional testing: fidelity, case generation and test development, reproducibility, scoring and standard setting, test security, and equivalence. For each of these areas, the issues involved in the use of simulation for testing are outlined, and strategies for resolving them are presented and discussed. Norcini believes that with appropriate attention to these issues, simulations can ultimately be made applicable to every instance of professional licensing or performance evaluation in all professions.

Chapter 14 offers a prospective agenda for potential users of simulation to consider. In this chapter, Ara Tekian examines the philosophic and ethical concerns surrounding the use of simulation in the assessment of professional competence. Tekian outlines the various aspects of professional competence best assessed by simulations and provides a glimpse of the expenditure in time and money required to design and implement effective simulations. Potential contaminating factors, as well as the consequences of simulation testing, are discussed. Ethical issues involved in creating realistic simulations, while maintaining adequate public knowledge and disclosure and allowing for proper subject "consent" prior to testing, are identified.

As with any assessment technique, users of simulation must consider problems of implementation, validity of results, benefits for certifying agencies and for candidates, quality of feedback to examinees and examiners, appropriateness for different purposes, as well as possibly unique ethical issues some forms of simulation pose. In the final chapter, McGuire and Tekian argue that although much still needs to be done, it appears from existing studies that simulation approaches yield more useful data than more traditional methods of assessing problem-solving, interpersonal, technical, and communication skills. Current exploratory work suggests that simulation technology opens the possibility of assessing such aspects of competence as team skills, creativity, stress management, and other features of performance not readily assessed by other means.

Part Three demonstrates that simulation-based assessment is a rapidly developing area. On the one hand, it can provide more complete and accurate assessment of many important aspects of competence for which conventional testing methods are now used. On the other hand, simulation offers the only opportunities to investigate individual and team performance in "high risk" situations, (e.g., operating rooms, flight cockpits, space flight) where reality itself is too dangerous, too costly or simply inaccessible. Neither practitioners nor theoreticians can afford to be uninformed about the philosophical, ethical, technical, and psychometric concerns involved in its use.

Ara Tekian

12

The Future Is Now:
Virtual Reality Technologies

Richard M. Satava
Shaun B. Jones

The Information Era is here and with it the computer power necessary to create an entire new dimension of educational and training tools, the most valuable of all being surgical simulators. Based initially upon data from the Visible Human data set, and enhanced with physically based modeling, these early simulators can create cartoon-like images capable of simulating simple surgical tasks. As computer power increases, the level of visual fidelity and complexity will permit even more realistic appearing models, and more complete operations. In addition, tracking of individual motions using sophisticated haptic devices will permit analysis of hand motions and surgical strategy that will execute comparison of a student performance with that of a "teacher." Eventually, analysis of these data will enable certification of professional competence to be based upon actual individual performance. The timetable for such evolution is approximately a decade, with the limiting factor not being the technology, but the funding for research and support from all the stakeholders of the surgical education community.

The field of Medicine continues to evolve so rapidly that before one change has been accepted and perfected, another even more dramatic change promises to replace it. What had been a century of evolution has, in the past decade alone, become a revolution. Laparoscopic surgery, which provided the "wake up call to the information age" as the leading edge technology, has become the accepted standard of medical practice (see Chapter 9). Now even more advanced technologies promise to further improve the practice of medicine.

Many authors have written about revolutionary times; however there are revolutions and then there are Revolutions. The first great Revolution in medicine occurred in surgery in the late 1800s when the Giants in Medicine still walked the earth. Many names can be cited, however there were few visionaries who truly understood the magnitude of change and were able to give birth to the new discipline of Surgery. Among them were Bilroth, Lister, Virchow, and Moore. This disparate group never worked together but it was the integration of their research and clinical skills which gave birth to the disciplines that made modern surgery possible. For it was the convergence of their visions and technologies that enabled Surgery to mature, not a single event. Thus Bilroth brought the new skills and surgical instruments, Lister the asepsis, Virchow the pathology, and Moore the anesthesia. Without the synergy of all areas, modern Surgery would never have happened. Whether ancient myth, mysticism or empirical fact, thousands of years of medicine proved the sanctity of the human body was inviolate to the knife, that a patient could not be voluntarily operated upon and survive. Yet the magical tools of the Industrial Age enabled the impossible, and science gave birth to Surgery. And in a relatively short period the foundations of Surgery were laid for the next generation of pioneers to lead-the clinicians who exploited the technologies and advanced the art of Surgery.

There have been many discoveries since these early beginnings, and many remarkable advances. These have been noteworthy in their own right, but none have changed the entire foundation of medicine as the inception of Surgery. The understanding of shock, cardio-pulmonary bypass and cardiac surgery, and transplantation have all had enormous impact upon the practice of Surgery, but they have fostered the development of a new niche, splintering off a new specialty rather than change the very fabric of medicine. Other new areas have been created, in infectious diseases and chemotherapy for example, yet these are merely evolutions of the ancient art of the pharmacopoeia.

It is interesting yet obvious that the changes that led to the birth of Surgery were contingent upon the discoveries that ushered in the Industrial Age. And just as the Industrial Age is waning, so too is the Golden Age of Surgery. The Industrial Age is being replaced by the Information Age, and conventional Surgery is being replaced by a whole host of minimally invasive therapies and non-invasive procedures. Because we are currently in the middle of transition, it is unclear at this time how the shape of the next generation of Medicine and Surgery will appear, though the trends in the technologies are toward low power, miniaturized, low cost yet highly "intelligent" systems that will eventually transform Surgery from minimally invasive into non-invasive procedures and whose development depends upon the emerging Information Age technologies. This is not to say that surgeons will no longer perform open or minimally invasive surgical procedures in the future, but rather that "conventional" Surgery will recede to a niche, and non-invasive procedures will predominate. Laparoscopic (or minimal access) Surgery is not an endpoint, but rather it is a transitional phase, between the radical approach of "open" Surgery and the emerging forms of non-invasive procedures. But it was the seminal event of laparoscopic surgery that triggered the wake up call to the Information Age, the realization that a revolution is occurring and that physicians must extend their horizons to discover the direction of the future.

But in order to have a revolution, all facets of the discipline must be impacted, rather than a single specialty such as Surgery. And a revolution must also reflect the same changes that are occurring in other scientific areas as well as society as a whole. It must be consistent with the global predictions that are proffered, such as The Third Wave of Alvin Toffler (1991), MegaTrends of John Naisbitt (1997), and most importantly Being Digital of Nicholas Negroponte (1996). While the former two authors gave us a peek into the power and magnitude of the revolution, it was Negroponte's concept of "bits instead of atoms" that brought the concept to fruition. He emphasized that what we do on a daily basis has, in previous times, required using actual physical objects (atoms); whereas the new technologies emphasize using information (bits) to accomplish the same task we had previously completed using the physical object. His classic example is that up to and including the Industrial Age, information in documents and letters were mailed physically from point to point (sending atoms across the country), whereas during the Information Age the same information is sent by e-mail (bits) at a much faster rate and lower cost. In translating this to the medical world, I will refer to "equivalents,"which are electronic or digital representations of real physical world objects or actions.

The magnitude of the importance of the Information Age for medicine was revealed during a National Science Foundation workshop on medical Applications of Virtual Reality in 1994, where the question was asked "How much of what a physician does on a daily basis is really information management?" If you use the most liberal interpretation, the conclusion is about 80 to 90%. For example, during laparoscopic surgery, the surgeon looks not at the actual organs but at the video monitor (electronic image or information equivalent of the organs). When surgery is complete and the patient is visited in the recovery room, the surgeon glances at the physiologic monitor for the blood pressure, pulse and other vital signs (equivalent of sense of touch). The visit is recorded into the electronic or computer medical record (rather that writing on paper). X-rays, CT scan and other visual images are all becoming digital images (instead of film, microscope slides, etc.), and our entire surgical education process is incorporating computer-aided instruction, multimedia, and even virtual reality for simulation and training. Laboratory experiments in telesurgery have converted our hand motions to electronic signals, such that when the surgeon's hand moves, the electronic signal (information) is sent to the tip of the instrument, and the scalpel cuts—it's no longer blood and guts, it's bits and bytes. The importance is that in making this mental leap of the physician interacting with information as a substitute for real world objects, the capability exists to perform things not possible in the physical world. For example, using Doppler ultrasound to display the false color images on a video monitor we have given our surgeons the long dreamed of capability to "see into the body with x-ray vision," which in this case is ultrasound vision of actual blood flow. In order to display the image, Dr. Jonathan Prince (Chinnock, 1995), has created one of the first 3-D true suspended holographic image (hologram) for anatomic visualization. With the imaginative concept of information equivalents, the challenge is to discover in daily practice ways of enhancing capabilities for patient care.

The potential of this innovative approach to medicine can be best illustrated by the results of a "blue sky" brainstorming session in late 1995. This rudimentary idea is referred to as the "Doorway to the Future"and touches upon how information equivalents tie the fabric of medicine together. It was inspired by the many technologies under investigation, and integrates them into a meaningful system of complementary technologies. The following scenario is used to illustrate how the future could be 20, 50, or perhaps 100 years from now.

A patient enters a physician's office, and passes through a doorway, the frame of which contains many scanning devices, from CT scan to MRI to ultrasound to near infra red and others. These scanners not only acquire anatomic data, but also physiologic and biochemical (like the pulse oximeter) data. When the patient sits down next to the physician, a full 3-D holographic image of the patient appears suspended upon the desktop-a visual integration of the information acquired just a minute before by the scanners. When the patient expresses the complaint of pain over the right flank, the physician can rotate the image, remove various layers, and query the representation of the patient's liver or kidney regarding the LDH, SGOT, alkaline phosphatase, serum creatinine or other relevant information. This information and more is stored in each pixel of the patient's representative image (a "medical avatar") such that the image of each structure and organ (such as the liver) stacks up into a "deep pixel" all the relevant information about the structure. Each pixel contains not only anatomic data but biochemical, physiologic, past historical, etc., so that information can be revealed directly from the image rather than searching through volumes of written medical records or a prolonged computer database search. Should a problem or disease be discovered, the image can be immediately used for patient education, instantly explaining to the patient on their own avatar what the problem might be. Should a surgical problem be discovered, this same image can be used by the surgeon for preoperative planning, or imported into a surgical simulator to practice a variety of different approaches to a difficult surgical procedure that will be performed upon the patient the next morning. At the time of operation, the image can be fused with a video image and used for intraoperative navigation or to enhance precision, as in stereotactic surgery. During the post operative visits, a follow-up scan can be compared to the pre-operative scan, and using digital subtraction techniques, the differences can automatically be processed for outcomes analysis. Since the avatar is an information object, it can be available and distributed (through telemedicine) anytime and any place. Thus, this single concept of replacing the written medical record (including x-ray and other images) with the visual record of a medical avatar permits the entire spectrum of health care to be provided with unprecedented continuity.

The time could not be more perfect, for we now have the right type of physician and health care provider to take advantage of this new technology. First it was the "Nintendo surgeon" for laparoscopic surgery; now it is the "Digital Physician." These are our younger generation who have grown up in the video/electronic era-not only are they comfortable with the new technology, now they are demanding it. They play video games, "surf" the Internet and the "information super highway" or become educated with computer aided instruction, multi-media and virtual reality. To them, the future is Now, and it is all digital.

The Paradigm Shift

Just as at the end of the 19th century, now is the time many separate elements (laparoscopic surgery, telepresence, virtual reality, digital imaging and networking) are coming together. Today, the common focal point is the video monitor at a physicians workstation (Satava, 1993). The video monitor is the portal into the entire world of information; this "electronic interface" will bestow power beyond imagination. Although the current portal into this information rich arena is the video monitor, in the future, other display technologies such as head mounted displays (HMD), video-glasses, holograms, palmtop computers, etc. which are currently working in the laboratory or are commercially available may be the interface. This interface is also the point of intellectual enhancement, for it here that all the information can coalesce and be presented to the individual as knowledge, not data. This interface can not only bring in information but can also send out information or commands for action in the real world (teleoperation or remote manipulation enables a person to work at a distance). Intelligent software and sophisticated algorithms are making possible the conversion of data into action. The resulting hierarchy works this way: that massive data is processed into information, which is then collated into knowledge, which interfaces with other knowledge databases to become wisdom, which is then applied to interfaces (instruments, effectors, etc.) to create a specific action-data, information, knowledge, wisdom, action. As an example, a surgeon could be at the monitor during a real operation, doing a surgical procedure in the next city, and collaborating with another surgeon on the same patient. Eventually it might be possible to operate at a place which is too distant or dangerous, such as the space station or third world country. In taking this approach, we are able to "dissolve time and space," the physician can "be" at a distant place at the same time as another person without needing to travel there. But of utmost importance is the fact that the physician can simultaneously bring in many different digital images, such as the patient's CT or MRI scan, and fuse them with real time video images, giving the surgeon "X-ray vision." Before doing a surgical procedure, the surgeon could sit at the workstation and practice on a virtual patient (see below) to simulate the operation, then flip the switch and begin operating on the real patient with precisely the same workstation-this is the power of the electronic interface and the core technology for the medical revolution. The following represents the current status of many of the new information applications in medicine.

Surgical Applications

In the area of remote surgery, Dr. Philip Green, of SRI International has invented the Green Telepresence Surgery System. This system restores to the surgeon those native and intuitive abilities which have been lost with laparoscopic surgery: 3-D vision, dexterous precise surgical instrument manipulation, and the sense of touch from input of force feedback sensory information (Satava, 1992; Green, Hill & Satava, 1991). The system consists of a surgical workstation (Figure 1) which has a 3-D monitor, responsive instrument handles and force feedback for touch (Figure 2), while the remote worksite has a 3-D camera system, dexterous manipulators and sensory input (Figure 3). Although this is actually telepresence rather than VR, the surgeon's abilities are enhanced and surgery can be performed with greater skill and precision. The current generation system is a two-handed very dexterous system with paired cameras for stereovision; the next generation will have a stereoscopic laparoscope to replace the fixed cameras. The system is engineered in such a way the surgeon actually feels as if the surgery were being performed directly in front of him, when in reality the remote site (and patient) could be yards, miles, or even hundreds of miles away. Because the system was designed to mimic open surgery, there will be essentially no special training required, thus permitting surgery with all the feeling, dexterity and 3-D vision of open surgery.

Another telepresence surgery system (Figure 4) created by Hunter et al., (1993), focuses upon expanding the capabilities of human performance. In retinal surgery, the telepresence system scales the motion of the hand up by a hundredfold, so 1 mm of the surgeon's hand motion moves the laser-scalpel 10 microns, and vision magnifies the retinal vessels to the size of a finger. By applying sophisticated signal filtering techniques through the computer interface, the normal intention tremor of the human hand can be removed, thereby permitting accuracy and precision to 10 microns, twenty times more accurate than the unaided hand.

3-D Visualization

The cognitive aspects of surgery are enhanced by 3-D visualization of images. By taking CT or MRI scans and generating full 3-D volume renderings of the patient's specific anatomy, the surgeon is able to conduct a number of essential surgical skills on the "information equivalent" of the patient, before actually operating on the patient. Today, diagnosis is made by looking at flat, 2-D films or performing an endoscopic procedure. Then preoperative planning is done with matching templates or diagraming with pen or pencil. If the operation is extraordinary, the only opportunity to practice the procedure would be on animal models. During a procedure there are few aids to precise navigation or positioning. However, with a 3-D representation of the patient, all these capabilities can be attained.

In the area of diagnostics, the 3-D image can be used for virtual endoscopy (Vining et al. 1994; Vining et al. 1993; Jolesz et al. 1994). This begins by taking CT or MRI 2 dimensional slices, and reconstructing 3-D images which could be rotated, layers peeled away, and individual organs separated and isolated (referred to as "segmentation"). The result is an imaginary reconstruction of a specific portion of a patient's anatomy, in essence a virtual reality brain or colon. Based upon these successes, and taking the next generation of CT scans (spiral or helical CT scan) which can generate much more accurate images, radiologists are segmenting out even more organs, such as the aorta, ear, sinuses, esophagus, and trachea. Using sophisticated flight tracking programs from the military, these virtual segmented organs can actually be "flown" through the way a fighter pilot would follow a computer generated "path" to a target (Lorensen et al. 1995). The result is an image which is exactly the same as doing flexible endoscopy (Figure 5). There is the added advantage that in the virtual anatomy, the point of view is not limited, so that views behind folds or around difficult flexures can be visualized. In addition, if a tumor is encountered, you could "poke your head"through the lesion to see the amount of penetration in the wall, or possibly in the future, look around for nodal metastases. At this time therapeutic procedures cannot be performed, however with newer imaging modalities, an "optical" biopsy could be performed using various forms of multi-spectral analysis of the quality or intensity of the image. Thus "virtual endoscopy" could replace a significant number of "routine screening" flexible endoscopic procedures, leaving the majority of endoscopy to be performed for known diseases or therapeutic procedures. Reconstruction of cardiac structures, whether difficult congenital abnormalities or complicated coronary lesions can now be portrayed in full volume rendering and viewed from any angle or direction.

The current state of the art of virtual endoscopy is very simple, because the segmentation processes have not become sophisticated enough to generate high resolution images equivalent to the resolution of video endoscopy and because simple CT or MRI scans do not have color data, which is important to determine subtle differences in mucosa that indicate disease. Recent digital signal processing algorithms have shown how intensities (for example Hounsfield units) can be used to determine tissue characteristics—in essence a "numerical biopsy" as coined by Dr. Rich Robb of the Mayo Clinic. This, along with the explosion of other new information technologies promise to roll back many of these limitations. The imaging tools of the future will replace many of our invasive or minimally invasive diagnostic procedures of today.

Before performing a procedure, a surgeon can pre-plan an operation with the same image used for diagnosis. Dr. Joseph Rosen (1993), of Dartmouth University Medical Center, has a VR model of a face with deformable skin which allows the practicing of a plastic surgical procedure and demonstration of the final outcome before making the incision on a patient. Dr. Scott Delp (1992), has a virtual model of a lower leg upon which he can practice a tendon transplant operation and then "walk" the leg to predict the short and long term consequences of the surgery (Figure 6). Likewise, Dr. Altobelli (1999), of the Brigham Woman's Hospital has developed a system that creates 3-D images from the CT scan of a child with bony deformities of the face (craniofacial dysostosis); using this 3-D model, the bones can be correctly rearranged to symmetrically match the normal side of the face, permitting repeated practice of this extremely difficult procedure. In neurosurgical applications, Dr. Ferenz Jolenz (1992), of Brigham Woman's Hospital has provided the capability for 3-D MRI scan of an individual patient's brain tumor. At the time of brain surgery, the MRI scan is fused with the video image of the patient's actual skull or brain, thus giving "x-ray vision" of the tumor which is not otherwise visible where it is deeply embedded in the brain tissue (Figure 7). These examples are but the first of many potential applications of VR for medical and surgical therapy.

It is the area of medical education and training where VR may reap the greatest benefits. There are two areas from which VR originated, flight simulation and information visualization (or the need to understand massive volumes of information and databases). Both of these components contribute to medical education. The former can provide training in medical and surgical procedures and the latter will be to help medical students understand through 3-D visualization important physiologic principles or basic anatomy. In addition, VR can be both a didactic and experiential educational tool. A demonstration mode could give a "tour" of the anatomy, and then an exploration mode would allow the student to actually experience the organs and tissues. This method allows not only the reinforcement of information, but promotes initiative in learning through the thrill of discovery. By "seeing" a visual representation of shock or navigating though the arterial tree the student could get a perspective of medicine well beyond anything that could be read from a book or even from dissecting a cadaver. There are currently efforts by Dr. Helene Hoffman (1992) of the University of California, San Diego, to create a 5 dimensional educational tool: the three dimensions of a virtual world (3-D space), the fourth dimension of time (archived information in multimedia format), and a fifth dimension of information (which provides "properties" to the information objects)—in essence, multimedia virtual reality (MMVR). For example, in a MMVR simulator of the gastrointestinal tract, a student could "fly" down into the stomach, see an ulcer and "grab" it as if for a biopsy, this would bring up the histologic micrograph of an ulcer, or play a video tape of a Bilroth 2 operation for ulcer disease, or perhaps demonstrate (predict) the healing in response to medication. In this fashion the multiple layers of understanding could be rolled into one, the properties and textures of the tissues could be felt, and the change of the processes over time can be graphically represented and personally experienced. Virtual environments can satisfy the need for training in surgical procedures. For decades, pilots have been training on flight simulators which have become so sophisticated and realistic that hundreds and thousands of "perfect" take-off and landings can be safely performed before their first real flight. So too will the surgeon of the future be able to perfect surgical skills before operating on the first patient. There are a few VR surgical simulators now appearing in response to the need to train surgeons in laparoscopic surgery by McGovern (1994), and Merril (1999). These consist of a simple plastic torso into which the handles of laparoscopic instruments are mounted (to provide force feedback); the virtual abdomen (liver and gall bladder) are graphically demonstrated upon the video monitor, and the apprentice surgeon can practice the specific laparoscopic surgery procedure. A different approach has been taken by Satava (1993); a virtual abdomen has been created for the immersive, traditional helmet mounted display (HMD) and DataglovTM. Using virtual scalpel and clamps, the abdominal organs can be operated upon. This same abdomen can be "explored" by a student in the manner described above. The realism of the graphics of all simulators are cartoon level; but then flight simulators took 40 years to go from the carnival ride model of Edwin Link to the ultra realistic 747 simulators of today. Hopefully the surgical simulators will progress faster as computing power increases. Today the simulations must trade off (e.g., less realism for more real-time interactivity) because of limited computing power, but the future holds promise of a virtual cadaver nearly indistinguishable from a real person (see medical avatar above).

A final area of information technology is the use of virtual prototyping. Dr.

Kenneth Kaplan of Massachusetts Institute of Technology (MIT) is beginning to apply VR to architectural design in a project for the operating room (OR) of the future (Kaplan et al. 1995). The great change in medicine and surgery alluded to above requires an OR and hospital that is not only worthy of this advanced technology but capable of supporting it. An entirely new environment must be created based upon radically different concepts and the implementation of surgical and minimally invasive (or even non-invasive) therapies. Entirely new space configurations, the use of smart materials and intelligent equipment, and the integration of information infrastructure, knowledge-based decision support, imaging systems and advanced therapeutic modalities will be required to support the new generation of surgeons and interventional therapists. In order to afford the widest possible opportunities to assess the impact of current and future technologies, the OR of the future will be entirely planned using virtual prototyping, giving architects, hospital administrators, surgeons, anesthesiologists, operating room personnel and other key individuals the opportunity to "test" the OR before building it. Not only will the focus be designing an entirely new environment, but it will be patient oriented, insuring that the OR will be integrated into the whole of hospital care and be focused upon human scale and sensitivity.

CONCLUSIONS

Without doubt, not all of these technologies will be able to be developed in precisely the manner indicated above, and many other technologies not mentioned will impact even greater than those currently envisioned. We now have information tools which can fundamentally and totally revolutionize our approach to patient care, tools which exist today and are based upon known and provable science. While it is true that we must stringently evaluate the technologies and concepts with all known scientific rigor, we must not discard these powerful ideas because of our Industrial Age preconceptions.

The intent is to provoke a sense of awe at the incredible opportunities that face us at this moment in history, a moment richer than any other in the past. We must use the scientific information in the advanced technologies to extend our innate abilities beyond the fetters of the past. It truly is time to recreate the future. We are leaving the Golden Era of Surgery where procedures are only performed directly with the hands and entering the next era where a convergence of Information Age technologies such as computers, micro-machines, remote manipulators, energy directed therapies, human interface technologies, 3-D visualization and virtual reality are enhancing both the manual and cognitive abilities of physicians through information equivalents. Advanced technology is enabling many aspects of medicine.

However, the ultimate direction and outcome will not be determined by the state of the technology but the intangibles of personal behaviors, social and cultural preferences, and political will. And as we ride this crest of enthusiasm, it is essential to not forget our fundamental roots, our reason for entering the profession. Physicians and all health care providers are first and foremost humanists, attending to the entire care of the patient, from emotional to technical. It must be remembered that technology is neutral-it is neither good nor evil. It requires human intellect and compassion to breathe the ethical and moral life into technology to enhance the art as well as science of medicine. We must be ever mindful that, no matter how wonderful the technology might appear, it is of absolutely no value unless it provides better care for each and every patient.

Illustrations

Figure 1. Surgeon seated at the surgical workstation of a Green Telepresence Surgery System. (Courtesy of Dr. Jon Bowersox, SRI, International, Menlo Park, CA)

Figure 2. Instrument handle device for the surgical workstation of a Green Telepresence Surgery System. (Courtesy of Dr. Jon Bowersox, SRI, International, Menlo Park, CA)

Figure 3. Remote manipulators of a Green Telepresence Surgery System across from the assisting medic. (Courtesy of Dr. Jon Bowersox, SRI, International, Menlo Park, CA)

Figure 4. Enhanced dexterity system for eye surgery. (Courtesy of Dr. Ian Hunter, Massachusetts Institute of Technology, Cambridge, MA)

Figure 5. Transverse colon view from a virtual endoscopy of the colon, derived from a helical CT scan of a patient. (Courtesy of Prof. W. Lorensen, GE Medical Research Corp., Schenectady, NY)

Figure 6. Virtual reality surgical simulator of tendon transplant that provides opportunity to test the results of surgery before performing the operation. (Courtesy of Dr. Scott Delp, MusculoGraphics, Inc, Evanston, IL)

Figure 7. Fusion of the 3-D reconstruction of a brain tumor (in green) over the patient's skull preoperatively. (Courtesy of Drs. F. Jolesz, and R. Kikinis, Brigham Women's Hospital, Boston, MA)

Figure 1

Figure 2

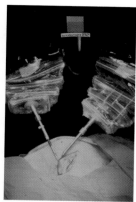

Figure 3

Figure 4

Figure 5

Figure 6

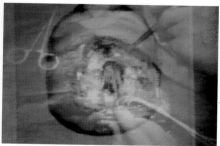

Figure 7

References

Altobelli, D. E., Kikinis, R., Mulliken, J. B., et al. 1999. Computer Assisted Three Dimensional Planning in Craniofacial Surgery. *Plastic & Reconstructive Surgery*, in press.

Chinnock, C. 1995. Holographic 3-D Images float in free space. *Laser Focus World* June:22-24.

Delp, S. L., and Zajac, F. R. 1992. Force and moment generating capacity of lower limb muscles before and after tendon lengthening. *Clinical Orthopedics and Related Research* 284:247-59.

Green, P. S., Hill, J. H., and Satava, R. M. 1991. Telepresence: Dextrous procedures in a virtual operating field.(Abstr). *Surgical Endoscopy* 57:192.

Hoffman, H. 1992. Developing network compatible instructional resources for UCSD's core curriculum. *Proceedings of Medicine Meets Virtual Reality*. San Diego, CA. June 1-2.

Hunter, I. W., Doukoglou, T. D., Lafontaine, S. R. et al. 1993. A Teleoperated Microsurgical Robot and Associated Virtual Environment for Eye Surgery. *Presence* 4:265-80.

Jolesz, F., Shtern, F. 1992. The Operating Room of the Future. *Proceedings of the National Cancer Institute Workshop*, 27: 326-28.

Jolesz, F. A., Lorensen, W. E., Kikinis, R., Seltzer, S. E., Silverman, S. G., Phillips, M., and Geiger, B. 1994. Virtual Endoscopy: Endoscopy-like Viewing and Exploration of Three Dimensional Image Data. *RSNA*, Chicago, Illinois.

Kaplan, K., Hunter, I., Durlach, N. I., Schodek, D. L., and Rattner, D. 1995. A Virtual Environment for a Surgical Room of the Future. In *Interactive Technology and the New Medical Paradigm for Health Care*, edited by R. M. Satava, K. Morgan, et al. Washington DC: IOS Press.

Lorensen, W. E., Jolesz, F. A., and Kikinis, R. 1995. "The Exploration of Crosssectional Data with a Virtual Endoscope." In *Interactive Technology and the New Medical Paradigm for Health Care*, edited by R. M. Satava, K. Morgan, et al. Washington DC: IOS Press.

McGovern, K. 1994. The Virtual Clinic: A Virtual Reality Surgical Simulator. *Proceedings of Medicine Meets Virtual Reality II.* San Diego, CA. Jan 27-30.

Merril, JR., Merril, GL., Raju, R., et al. 1997. Photorealistic Interactive 3-D graphics in Surgical Simulation. In *Interactive Technology and the New Medical Paradigm for Health Care,* edited by R. M. Satava, K. Morgan, et al. Washington DC: IOS Press.

Naisbitt, J. 1997. *MegaTrends.* Asia Philadelphia: Simon & Schuster.

Negroponte, N. 1996. *Being Digital.* New York: Vintage Press.

Rosen, J. 1992. From computer-aided design to computer-aided surgery. *Proceedings of Medicine Meets Virtual Reality.* San Diego, CA. June 1-2.

Satava, R. M. 1992. Robotics, telepresence and virtual reality: a critical analysis of the future of surgery. *Minimally Invasive Therapy* 1:357-63.

Satava, R. M. 1993. Surgery 2001: A Technologic Framework for the Future. *Surgical Endoscopy* 7:111-13.

Satava, R. M. 1993. Virtual Reality Surgical Simulator: The First Steps. *Surgical Endoscocpy* 7:203-05.

Toffler, A. 1991. *The Third Wave.* New York:Bantam.

Vining, D. N., Padhani, A. R., Wood, S. et al. 1993. Virtual bronchoscopy: a new perspective for viewing the treacheobronchial tree. *Radiology* 189:438.

Vining, D. N., Shifrin, R. Y., Grishaw, E. K. et al. 1994. Virtual colonoscopy. *Radiology* 193:446.

13

Measurement Issues in the Use of Simulation for Testing Professionals: Test Development, Test Scoring and Standard Setting

John Norcini

This chapter addresses five major measurement issues involved in the use of simulation: test development, reproducibility, scoring and standard-setting, security, and equivalence. For each of these topics the issues for simulations are outlined and strategies for resolving them are suggested. As regards test development, the opportunities include focusing problems or cases, developing computer-based tools to write and debug problems, trying to disguise cases or problems and trying to model cases or problems. With respect to reproducibility, opportunities exist in focusing cases, and in sequential and adaptive testing. For holistic scoring, application of statistical methods, training, structuring the task and simply increasing the number of examiners may improve the results; aggregate scoring and decision-theoretic methods could help with other types of scoring problems. A few opportunities exist in standard setting, but current methods are sufficient to the task. Security problems can be reduced with large pools of cases and various forms of case and/or problem disguise. Finally, item response theory and rescaling experts' standard-setting judgments are areas that merit further attention for equivalence.

Over the first part of the century, assessment in the professions relied mainly on written essay questions and the oral examination. Multiple choice questions followed, and along with the oral examination they still dominate testing for licensure and certification in the United States. Although some forms of the traditional oral examination are high fidelity simulations, interest increased with the introduction of patient management problems in the 1960s and the wider availability of computers in the 1970s (McGuire and Babbott, 1967; Bunderson, Inouye, and Olsen, 1989). This has been followed by steady growth and innovation to the point where simulation is currently being used in some certifying and licensing examinations and where more widespread use is likely in the near future. The purpose of this chapter is to outline some of the measurement issues involved in the use of simulations including test development, reproducibility, scoring and standard-setting, security, and equivalence. For each, the issues will be described and opportunities will be presented.

There is no agreement on exactly what constitutes a simulation and there is even a good argument to be made that multiple choice questions are consistent with Webster's (1977) definition, "the imitative representation of the functioning of one system or process by means of the functioning of another." To avoid confusion, this chapter will focus on the high fidelity, response-contingent simulations, bearing in mind that even for this smaller class of measurement devices the issues addressed here will not be equally applicable to all professions. The chapter draws heavily on previous publications on related topics (Norcini and Swanson, 1988; Norcini, 1996).

Test Development

Fidelity versus Breadth

Description. Some authors have argued that the best item formats are those that reproduce criterion tasks with the greatest fidelity (Lindquist, 1951; Frederiksen, 1984; Fortune and Cromack, 1995). For testing in the professions, this means that a practice analysis is done and tasks for the simulations are chosen from among the frequent and important activities of job incumbents (Knapp and Knapp, 1995). Once chosen, detailed recreations of the tasks or problems are developed. Because of constraints on the amount of testing time available, an examination is often composed of relatively few problems but each of them is treated in great depth and with great fidelity. This is consistent with the belief that fidelity is of paramount importance. However, the narrow sampling of tasks or problems significantly limits the degree to which scores generalize to the domain of interest.

Traditional fact-based MCQ examinations provide a vivid contrast to most examinations composed of simulations. Developers of these tests also perform a practice analysis and draw their content from the activities of job incumbents (LaDuca, Downing, and Henzel, 1995). However, they believe it is of paramount importance that the content of a licensing or certifying examination thoroughly represent the demands of the occupation. Given constraints in testing time, they use formats that treat each task or problem in a less realistic, more superficial fashion than simulation, but these formats permit a much broader sampling of problems or tasks. The low fidelity of the format limits the degree to which scores generalize to the domain of interest.

Issue. Neither of these extremes produces the best licensing or certifying examination. An exclusive emphasis on fidelity undermines the generalizability of scores just as much as the traditional focus on broad but superficial sampling of content. The two competing demands of fidelity and breadth must be balanced when developing a licensing or certifying examination and neither emphasis alone has any more virtue than its competitor.

Opportunities. Simulations faithfully reproduce the real world and all of its redundancy. Much of what the examinees do when they take a simulation is routine or repetitive. Consequently, getting to the testing point of a case or problem takes considerable time. Where it does not damage the simulation, one strategy is to shorten the cases or problems and focus them around the testing point or critical incident. The work done in this area to date has been encouraging and where the content permits, it is at least useful to include some focused cases or problems (Shatzer, Waldrop, Williams, and Hatch, 1994; Rothman, Cohen, and Bilan, 1996).

Case Generation

Description and Issues. One of the major issues in the use of simulations is case or stimulus generation. Cases are much more difficult to write than MCQs for at least three reasons. First, the selection of topics is hard. Content is derived from a job analysis, but to be useful in an examination a task or case should also 1) have clearly identifiable correct and incorrect responses, 2) be appropriately difficult, 3) separate good examinees from bad, and 4) be sufficiently broad and important to justify the amount of testing time that will be devoted to it.

Second, the actual creation of the case is difficult. There is typically more than one acceptable way to solve a design problem, treat a patient, fly an airplane, perform an operation, or conduct a military mission and all options need to be available to examinees. Likewise, the responses of the simulation (i.e., patient, airplane) to the actions of the examinee need to be specified in advance of testing. Moreover, a range of incorrect options or pathways need to be available. For the more plausible but incorrect courses of action, this is hard but it is even more difficult to imagine, prior to simulation tryout, what actions the less able examinees might take.

Third, it is difficult to refine cases. Once a case has been written, it is very time consuming to obtain knowledgeable reviews because the experts must find their way, or be led, through all of the pathways and they must consider interactions among the potential examinee responses (e.g., responses that conflict or have a synergistic effect). Similarly, it is difficult to predict how examinees will respond to the case and several rounds of tryouts with examinees of various levels of ability necessary before cases are ready for implementation.

Opportunities. Some of the developers of simulations have made efforts to address these issues, but considerable work remains. First, it is essential to develop good tools to create and debug new cases. Ideally, these would 1) be computerized, 2) lead the author through a structured case writing task, 3) include default information, and 4) signal potential internal conflicts and inconsistencies. Even with such tools, extensive case tryout will remain a necessity.

Second, even with good tools it is important to develop means for generating cases more efficiently; case disguise and case modeling might be useful. Disguise entails changes in the non-essential aspects of cases or problems, so that they will not be recognized as similar by examinees. For example, it is easy to envision a medical problem that is unaffected within reasonable limits by the age, gender, race, occupation, and weight of a patient. Cosmetic changes of this type could mask content without substantially changing case difficulty.

In contrast, case modeling entails systematic and substantive changes in case content to generate a family of problems in the same area. For example, in medicine it is possible to take the same patient and alter some of her signs and symptoms (i.e., weight loss, fever, nature of pain) to change which disease she has. Modeling has been successfully used with MCQs in medicine and other scientific disciplines (LaDuca, Templeton, Holzman, and Staples, 1986; Shea, Poniatowski, Day, Langdon, LaDuca, and Norcini, 1992).

Finally, in the general measurement literature more research effort has been devoted to how to score and set standards, than it has to how to write good examinations. The simulation literature is the same and while scoring and standard-setting certainly merit attention, ultimately they are of less importance than the quality of the test material and the ability to generate it efficiently. Therefore, research in the area of test development presents the greatest opportunity and should be the highest priority.

Reproducibility

Description. An important attribute of any test is its reproducibility or consistency in producing the same result if it is repeated (Brennan, 1983). It is important to know that if we gave the same examinees the same test two weeks apart, and they learned nothing in the meantime, they would get the same scores. Reproducibility is especially important in making licensure and certification decisions because it directly influences the number of false negative decisions (examinees whose true ability is sufficient for licensure or certification, but who fail anyway because of errors of measurement) and false positive decisions (examinees whose true ability is not sufficient for licensure or certification, but who pass anyway because of errors of measurement).

Issues. All other things being equal, simulation scores and pass-fail decisions are much less reproducible per unit of testing time than those based on MCQs and similar formats. The poorer reproducibility of scores is a product of what Elstein, Shulman, and Sprafka (1978) call the content specificity of problem-solving skills. Performance on one problem or case does not predict performance on others, so a large number of cases or problems must be sampled to obtain a reproducible score or pass-fail decision. Content specificity is not a disadvantage for MCQs, because a large number of items can be administered in a short period of time. In contrast, simulations, especially the high-fidelity formats, are more time-consuming, so far fewer simulated cases can be administered in a fixed amount of time and scores are less reproducible (Norcini, Meskauskas, Langdon, and Webster, 1986).

This issue of content specificity of problem-solving skills is exacerbated for simulations by two other factors, complexity and controversy. Evaluation of complex skills usually takes more time than evaluation of simple skills, and simulations are more often used to assess the former. For example, in medicine it is less time consuming to obtain a reproducible estimate of a physician's ability to correctly interpret heart sounds than his or her ability to interview a patient and develop an initial plan for treatment. Therefore, a simulation of simple skills will usually require less testing time than a test of a complex skill (Norcini and Swanson, 1989).

Controversy is also a factor that adversely affects the reproducibility of scores and pass-fail decisions. Experts do not always agree on what constitutes acceptable performance on the same case or problem. Sometimes this variability is a product of accepted and substantive differences among experts in how to approach a problem and in other instances it reflects less substantive differences in style or preference. Regardless of its source, controversy leads to variability in identification of the correct responses to simulations and also mirrors variability in candidate performance, therefore lowering reproducibility (Mazzuca and Cohen, 1982; Norcini, 1987).

Opportunities. If the reproducibility of a test is too low, the typical solution is to increase the number of cases or problems that examinees face. Because this is generally not feasible with simulations, at least two other options exist: focus the cases/problems or use a sequential or adaptive administration strategy.

As mentioned earlier, much of what the examinees do when they take a simulation is routine or repetitive. Consequently, getting to the testing point takes time. When it does not damage the simulation, shortening the cases or problems and focusing them around the testing point or critical incident or key features should permit broader sampling and higher reproducibility (Bordage and Page, 1987; Shatzer, Waldrop, Williams, and Hatch, 1994; Rothman, Cohen, and Bilan, 1996).

The second possibility for improving reproducibility in a licensing or certifying setting is to use some form of sequential or adaptive testing. In sequential testing, all examinees are given a short examination. The test is over for those whose pass-fail status is estimated with enough precision, and the remaining examinees take a second test (Cronbach and Gleser, 1965). This conserves resources overall, while improving the reproducibility of scores where it is most needed—around the pass-fail point. Preliminary applications of this methodology to simulations in medicine have been fruitful (e.g., Colliver, Mast, Vu, Barrows, 1991)

Adaptive testing is best suited to computer-based simulations (Wainer, 1990). After each simulation, software estimates the ability of the examinee and then selects a new case or problem that is targeted to his or her level of ability. This circle of ability estimation and case/item administration continues until there is confidence that the examinee's level of ability has been estimated with enough precision to make a pass-fail decision. Preliminary applications of sequential and adaptive tests have been instructive and indicate that these methods could be applied more broadly.

Scoring and Standard-Setting

Scoring and standard-setting for simulations have been the focus of considerable research. Despite this effort, much confusion exists and much work remains. One of the major reasons for the lack of progress is confusion over terms. For studies of some simulations, observers are used to score and set standards simultaneously. For studies of other simulations, mechanical scoring is used and standard-setting is considered separately.

For purposes of this chapter, scoring will be defined as the act of assigning a numerical grade to a performance (Norcini, 1994). It is the answer to the question, "How good was the performance?" Two types of scoring, holistic and mechanical, will be considered separately since they raise somewhat different issues. For this chapter, standard-setting will be defined as the act of determining the lowest score that connotes acceptable performance (Norcini, 1994). It is the answer to the question, "What performance is just good enough to pass?"

Holistic Scoring

Description. In holistic scoring, one or more global assessments are made of an examinee's performance on a simulation (Millman and Greene, 1989; Fitzpatrick and Morrison, 1971). This assessment is typically conducted by an expert who observes (in real time or later) the interaction between the examinee and simulation. In some ways, this is the ideal method of scoring since observation and assessment of an expert can ensure that the richness of the interaction is captured in the grading process.

Issues. There are two issues raised by this type of scoring. First, examiner-experts do not necessarily agree with each other, even when they observe the same event (i.e., they differ in stringency). Some of this variation is good; it reflects legitimate differences in values and appropriate attention to different aspects of the interaction between the examinee and the case or problem. It may also bespeak reasonable differences in standards and emphasis. On the other hand, differences among examiners do matter to examinees, especially if they are caused by any of a number of undesirable things. They may come from experts' broad based knowledge deficits, issues of style, or factors such as the appearance, race, gender, and ethnicity of the examinee.

Second, and related to the differences in stringency, is the interaction of the expert with the examinee, case/problem, or both. Here again, some of the variability can be good, like when the expert has special knowledge in an area or a particular perspective on cases of a certain kind, say Alzheimer's patients in medicine. On the bad side are issues like a lack of knowledge in the problem area, higher standards than are reasonable for a particular examinee, or some form of personal bias.

Opportunities. There are at least three opportunities for addressing one or both of these issues. One way is to employ a statistical model that removes differences among experts (Engelhard, 1996). The models make reasonably strong statistical assumptions about the data and it is important to ensure that the assumptions are met. In addition, they may remove some of the good effects of having different perspectives contribute to the grading, along with the bad effects of stringency differences. Nonetheless, promising work has been done in this area and more is needed.

The second strategy is to train the evaluators intensely in the area to be evaluated or structure the task, perhaps by simply giving them longer lists of behaviors to observe (Noel, Herbers, Caplow, Cooper, Pangaro, and Harvey, 1992; Kroboth, Hanusa, Parker, Coulehan, Kapoor, Brown, 1990). It is important that the experts not be trained to agree simply for the sake of agreeing, nor do we wish to take away from them the ability to observe, synthesize, and interpret a performance from different perspectives. Although it is unlikely to have a major impact, more work on the development of effective and efficient training methods is needed.

Finally, simply increasing the number of experts involved in the evaluation may be best when it is feasible. This reduces the effect of some of the less desirable reasons for expert variability, still gives voice to the different perspectives, and ensures that the ultimate judgment is balanced. The best deployment of experts is to ask each to evaluate the performance of the examinee on a different case or problem (Brennan, 1983).

Mechanical Scoring

Description. Mechanical scoring procedures (sometimes called category or component scoring) typically require experts to identify in advance of test administration, the behaviors that examinees might exhibit and that should be included in their score (Millman and Greene, 1989; Fitzpatrick and Morrison, 1971; Swanson, Norcini, and Grosso, 1987). These behaviors are often sorted into different categories or components, weighted (e.g., to form an answer key), and then combined to form one or more overall scores for an examinee. In the traditional test development approach, scorers who are experts in the content area meet as a group and discuss each task until they reach a consensus about what constitutes acceptable performance. These judgments are then turned into a series of weights (which include zero).

During test administration, examinees' behaviors are captured in a variety of mechanical ways. In some instances, checklists are completed by non-experts and in others devices like the computer record examinees' responses. This allows the test to be administered over time and place without the expense and logistical problems associated with expert observation of the examinees interacting with the simulations. Mechanical scoring methods sacrifice richness in the grading process for improved standardization and feasibility (e.g., experts do not need to observe every interaction).

Issues. There are some difficulties in using mechanical scoring methods. First, as mentioned above, there are usually several acceptable and unacceptable alternatives in solving a design problem or treating a patient. Before a test can be given, all of these pathways through the problem or case have to be anticipated. Identification of the less desirable responses is usually difficult for the experts who create the answer key because of their extensive knowledge.

Having identified the possible pathways, the next difficulty is in assigning them weights or values. The weighting process is typically time-consuming and arbitrary. Moreover, research in medicine has shown that when asked to identify the important behaviors in a test (i.e., those that should receive positive weight), physicians identified twice as many actions as they themselves actually did when facing the same problem in practice (Norman, Neufeld, Woodward, McConvey, and Walsh, 1985).

Finally, in a simulation as in the real world, there are often redundant clues to solving a problem. If these are uncontrolled in scoring, they will produce higher scores for examinees whose test-taking style is to be very active and to take a large number of actions. This artificially inflates estimates of reproducibility (Norcini and Swanson, 1988), reduces the validity of the measure, and hides a potentially serious problem.

Opportunities. To counter some of these difficulties, answer keys for simulations can be constructed using aggregate scoring (Norman, 1985). In this method, a group of experts takes the simulation just as the examinees do. The weight for each action is the proportion of the expert group doing it. For example, if the entire group selects an option, it is given a weight of 1.0, if half of the group selects an option it is given a weight of .5 and if no one selects the option it is given a weight of 0. This method has been applied with some success to a variety of simulations but additional work is needed (Norcini, 1987; Norcini and Shea, 1990; Norcini, Reshetar, and Lipner, 1997).

Another possibility is the use of decision-theoretic approaches to scoring, which have been experimentally applied to medical problems (Friedman and Downs, 1996). Basically, a probabilistic model of a case or patient is constructed. It begins with a description of the patient's presenting problem and then requires specification of the likelihood that the problem is caused by a variety of different diseases. A utility is assigned to each of these diseases, reflecting the value to the patient of deciding it is the actual cause of the problem. Scores could be based on the average expected value of an examinee's actions and/or the expected utility of the final diagnosis. This method of scoring is still in its infancy and considerable work remains both on the method within medicine and on whether it generalizes beyond medicine. Nonetheless, it has some promise for overcoming the problems with traditional methods of mechanical scoring.

Standard-Setting

Description. In licensing or certifying settings the pass-fail point identifies, as a test score, how much a practitioner needs to know to be considered minimally competent. Since a series of articles in the late 1970s, it has generally been conceded that standards are arbitrary (Glass, 1978; Popham, 1978). On one hand, this makes it hard to establish that the passing score for a particular examination is correct and to rule out reasonable alternatives. On the other hand, it means that the particular method chosen to set standards is of less concern since the final result will be arbitrary anyway (Norcini, 1994; Norcini and Shea, 1997).

Issues. No generally acceptable methods have yet been developed for setting standards on simulations. However, a good method should rely primarily on the judgment of the experts, it should incorporate examinee performance data, and it should be easily explained to examinees, standard-setters, and the public. It should demonstrate diligence, but the process should be limited in scope to standard-setting so that it does not undermine decisions made as part of test development and scoring. Finally, the resulting standard should be reproducible over different judges and it should support reliable pass-fail decisions.

Opportunities. Some of the traditional methods for setting standards have been adapted for use with simulations. For example, Ebel's (1972) and Angoff's methods (1971) have been experimentally applied to simulations in medicine (Norcini, Stillman, Regan, Haley, Sutnick, Williams, and Friedman, 1993). These work well but they tend to be time-consuming and somewhat cumbersome. Newer methods for use with simulations and performance assessments have been proposed by Jaeger (1995), Putnam, Pence, and Jaeger (1995), and others. Some of these do not meet the criteria outlined above but they lay the groundwork for future developments.

Despite these opportunities, the use of simulations should not be limited by progress in this area. The traditional methods are cumbersome but they produce credible results. Furthermore, standard-setting is a process for making an arbitrary decision, so substantive advances are not even possible. While improvements in the processes for setting standards will certainly develop over time, the use of simulations need not await these refinements.

Security

Description and Issues. The most important of the measurement characteristics of a test is its validity, that is, whether the inferences based on test scores are correct and meaningful (Wainer and Braun, 1988). A large part of the motivation to use simulations is the belief that their fidelity enhances the validity of scores. There are a variety of factors that affect validity and this chapter does not seek to identify them. Instead, it will focus on one issue, security, that has special relevance to the use of simulations.

Test security is essential since prior knowledge of the simulations and/or the correct course of action makes scores completely meaningless (Swanson, Norman, and Linn, 1995). This threat to validity is of increasing concern as the stakes for licensure and certification increase and the methods for breaching test security become more sophisticated. In some ways, simulations are more immune to security breaks than typical written examinations. No single examinee will become familiar with all of the pathways through a case or the solutions to a problem. In addition, some would argue that even if they have the case material, examinees would not be able to look up or fake the correct responses.

However, memorization and sharing of test material must remain a major security concern. First, written examinations can be administered to all examinees simultaneously. Because simulations tend to be resource intensive, a rolling administration process is not uncommon, allowing examinees time to report on the content of their test. Second, many fewer cases or problems can be administered in an examination composed of simulations. Even if the cases are more elaborate than written examinations, there will be so few of them that examinees will have little trouble remembering their experiences.

Opportunities. The primary way to combat security problems is to have a pool of cases or problems large enough to generate many different forms of the test. In addition, case or problem disguise (that is, changes to the non-essential aspects of cases or problems so that they are not easily recognizable) would be useful. This is especially true if it enabled the administration of cases/problems of equivalent difficulty and content over different forms of the test.

Equivalence

Description. Licensing and certifying examinations must be administered over time and for a variety of reasons different versions of the same test are needed. If the pass-fail decisions on these examinations are not equivalent, it is unfair to examinees who might have passed an easier version of the test. In addition, it is confusing to the public because the meaning of the same license or certificate varies in unknown ways over time.

To ensure the equivalence of pass-fail decisions, the content of the different test forms needs to be similar, their difficulty should be comparable, and some form of statistical adjustment should be used (Shea and Norcini, 1995).

Issues. Simulations pose some special challenges in this regard. First, it is difficult to assure comparable content and difficulty when the number of cases or problems on the test is relatively small. This is especially true when the simulation is targeted at skills within relatively broad disciplines like medicine, law, and architecture. Second, the limited sampling of cases also makes it more difficult to apply some of the statistical techniques used to equate scores. The traditional common item linear and equipercentile methods may be difficult to apply because the number of common cases or problems may be too small.

Opportunities. There are some opportunities in response to these problems. The disguise and modeling strategies for developing cases or problems may make it easier to produce test forms that are comparable in content and difficulty. In addition, there are some developments in terms of statistical methods used to equate scores. Specifically, one method equates standard-setting judgments rather than scores and another applies item response theory models to simulations (Baker, 1992; Norcini, 1990). Both of these are promising but they require additional study.

Summary

In summary, there are five major issues in the use of simulations as tests: test development, reproducibility, scoring and standard-setting, security, and equivalence. Opportunities to make testing more feasible exist in a variety areas. For test development they include focusing problems or cases, computer-based tools to write and debug problems, case/problem disguise, and case/problem modeling.

For test administration opportunities exist in sequential and adaptive testing. For scoring, standard-setting, and equivalence, aggregate scoring, decision-theoretic models, item response theory, and rescaling experts' standard-setting judgments are areas that merit further attention.

References

Angoff, W. H. 1971. Scales, Norms and Equivalent Scores. In *Educational Measurement*, edited by R. L. Thorndike. American Council on Education: Washington D.C.

Baker, F. B. 1992. Equating tests under the graded response model. *Applied Psychological Measurement* 16: 87-96.

Bordage, G. and Page, G. 1987. An alternative approach to PMPs: The "key features" concept. In *Further developments in assessing clinical competence*, edited by I.R. Hart and R.M. Harder. Monreal: Can Heal Publications.

Bunderson, C.V., Inouye, D. K., and Olsen, J.B. 1989. The four generations of computerized measurement. In *Educational measurement*, edited by R.L. Linn. Washington, D.C.: American Council of Education.

Brennan, R. L. 1983. *Elements of generalizability theory.* Iowa City: ACT Publications.

Colliver, J. A., Mast, T. A., Vu, N. V., and Barrows, H.S. 1991. Sequential testing with a performance-based examination using standardized patients. *Academic Medicine* 66: S64-S66.

Cronbach, L.J. and Gleser, G.C. 1965. *Psychological tests and personnel decisions.* Urbana: University of Illinois Press.

Ebel, R.L. 1972. *Essentials of educational measurement.* Englewood Cliffs, NJ: Prentice-Hall.

Elstein, A.S., Shulman, L.S., and Sprafka, S.A. 1978. *Medical Problem Solving: An analysis of clinical reasoning.* Cambridge: Harvard University Press.

Engelhard, G. 1996. Evaluating rater accuracy in performance assessment. *Journal of Educational Measurement* 33: 56-70.

Fitzpatrick, R. and Morrison, E.J. 1971. Performance and product evaluation. In Thorndike, R.L. (Ed.) *Educational measurement.* American Council on Education: Washington, D.C.

Fortune, J. and Cromack, T. 1995. Developing and using clinical examinations. In J.C. Impara (Ed.), *Licensure testing: Purposes, procedures, and practices.* Lincoln, NE: Buros Institute of Mental Measurements.

Frederiksen, N. 1984. The real test bias: Influences of testing on teaching and learning. *American Psychologist* 39: 193-202.

Friedman, C.P. and Downs, S.M. 1996. Alternatives to current methods: Decision-analytic approaches. In *Computer-Based examinations for board certification,* edited by E.L. Mancall, P.G. Bashook, and J.L. Dockery. American Board of Medical Specialties: Evanston, IL.

Glass, G.V. 1978. Standards and criteria. *Journal of Educational Measurement* 15: 237-261.

Jaeger, R.M. 1995. Setting performance standards through two-stage judgmental policy capturing. *Applied Measurement in Education* 8: 15-40.

Knapp, J. and Knapp, L. 1995. Practice analysis: Building the Foundation for Validity. In *Licensure testing: Purposes, procedures, and practices,* edited by J. C. Impara. Lincoln, NE: Buros Institute of Mental Measurements.

Kroboth, F.J., Hanusa, B.H., Parker, S., Coulehan, J.L., Kapoor, W.N., Brown, F.H., et al. 1990. The inter-rater reliability and internal consistency of a clinical evaluation exercise. *Journal of General Internal Medicine* 5: 214-217.

LaDuca, A., Downing, S.M., and Henzel, T.R. 1995. Test Development: Systematic item writing and test construction. In *Licensure testing: Purposes, procedures, and practices,* edited by J. C. Impara. Lincoln, NE: Buros Institute of Mental Measurements.

LaDuca, A., Templeton, B., Holzman, G.B., and Staples, W.I. 1986. Item-modeling procedure for constructing content-equivalent multiple choice questions. *Medical Education* 20: 53-56.

Lindquist, E.F. 1951. Preliminary considerations in objective test construction. In *Educational Measurement*, edited by E. F. Lindquist. Washington D.C.: American Council on Education.

Mazzuca, S.A. and Cohen, S.J. 1982. Scoring patient management problems. *Evaluation and the Health Professions* 5: 210-217.

McGuire, C.H. and Babbott, D. 1967. Simulation technique in the measurement of problem-solving skills. *Journal of Educational Measurement* 4: 1-10.

Millman, J. and Greene, J. 1989. Performance and product evaluation. In *Educational measurement*, edited by R.L. Linn. Washington D.C.: American Council on Education.

Noel, G.L., Herbers, J.E., Caplow, M.P., Cooper, G.S., Pangaro, L.N., and Harvey, J. 1992. How well do internal medicine faculty members evaluate the clinical skills of residents? *Annals of Internal Medicine* 117: 757-765.

Norcini, J.J. 1987. The answer key as a source of error in examinations for professionals. *Journal of Educational Measurement* 24: 321-331.

Norcini, J.J. 1990. Equivalent pass/fail decisions. *Journal of Educational Measurement* 27: 59-66.

Norcini, J.J. 1994. Research on standards for professional licensure and certification examinations. *Evaluation and the Health Professions* 17: 160-177.

Norcini, J.J. 1996. Psychometric Issues in Computer-Based Testing. In *Computer-Based examinations for Board Certification*, edited by E.L. Mancall, P.G. Bashook, and J.L. Dockery. Evanston, IL: American Board of medical Specialties.

Norcini JJ, Meskauskas JA, Langdon LO, Webster GD. 1986. An evaluation of a computer simulation in the assessment of physician competence. *Evaluation and the Health Professions* 9: 286-304.

Norcini, J.J., Reshetar, R.A., and Lipner, R.S. 1997. The answer key as a source of error in performance assessment. *Assessment in Health Sciences Education* 1:103-110.

Norcini, J.J. and Shea, J.A. 1990. The effect of level of expertise on answer key development. *Academic Medicine* 65: S15-S16.

Norcini, J.J. and Shea, J.A. 1997. The credibility and comparability of standards. *Applied Measurement in Education* 10: 39-60.

Norcini, J.J., Stillman, P.L., Regan, M.B., Haley, H., Sutnick, A.I., Williams, R.G., and Friedman, M. 1993. Scoring and standard-setting with a performance test for physicians. *Evaluation and the Health Professions* 16: 322-332.

Norcini, J.J. and Swanson, D.B. 1988. Factors influencing testing time requirements for written simulations. *Teaching and Learning in Medicine* 1: 85-91.

Norman, G.R. 1985. Objective measurement of clinical performance. *Medical Education* 19: 43-47.

Norman, G.R., Neufeld, V.R., Woodward, C.A., McConvey, G.A. and Walsh, A. 1985. *Journal of Medical Education* 60: 925-934.

Popham, W.J. 1978. As always provocative. *Journal of Educational Measurement* 15: 297-300.

Putnam, S.E., Pence, P., and Jaeger, R.M. 1995. A multi-stage dominant profile method for setting standards on complex performance assessments. *Applied Measurement in Education* 8: 57-84.

Rothman, A.I., Cohen, R., Bilan, S. 1996. A comparison of short- and long-case stations in a multiple-station test of clinical skills. *Academic Medicine* 71: s110-s112.

Shatzer, J.H., Waldrop, J.L., Williams, R.G., and Hatch, T.F. 1994. Generalizability of performance on different-station-length standardized patient cases. *Teaching and Learning in Medicine* 6: 54-58.

Shea, J.A. and Norcini, J.J. 1995. Equating. In J.C. Impara (Ed.), *Licensure testing: Purposes, procedures, and practices*. Buros Institute of Mental Measurements: Lincoln, NE.

Shea, J.A., Poniatowski, P.A., Day, S.C., Langdon, L.O., LaDuca, A. and Norcini, J.J. 1992. An adaptation of item modelling for developing test-item banks. *Teaching and Learning in Medicine* 4: 19-24.

Swanson, D.B., Norcini, J.J., and Grosso, L.J. 1987. Assessment of clinical competence: Written and computer-based simulations. *Assessment and evaluation in higher education* 12: 220-246.

Swanson, D.B., Norman, G.R., and Linn, R.L. 1995. Performance-based assessment: Lessons from the Health Professions. *Educational Researcher* 24: 2-11.

Wainer, H. 1990. *Computerized adaptive testing: A primer.* New Jersey: Lawrence Erlbaum.

Wainer, H. and Braun, H.I. 1988. *Test validity.* New Jersey: Lawrence Erlbaum.

Webster's New Collegiate Dictionary. 1977. G&C Merriam: Springfield, MA.

14

Philosophical and Ethical Concerns: Benefits, Limitations and Unexpected Consequences of Simulation in Professional Assessment

Ara Tekian

The use of powerful and costly exercises in the education and assessment of professionals requires that attention be given to questions beyond the usual issues surrounding the validity, reliability and generalizability of inferences based on performance in test situations (see Chapter 13). The questions include: What aspects of professional competence can be better assessed by simulation technique than by other means? What are the extra costs of simulations in terms of money, time, sample size and the like? What contaminating factors do simulations introduce into the test situation, not present in other approaches? What are both the long-and short-term consequences (positive and negative) of participating in simulation exercises as examinees, simulators, and members of the public who may inadvertently be involved? How can ethical requirements of informed consent and "doing no harm" be met without jeopardizing the "reality" of the situations? In addressing such questions, this chapter will provide an agenda for prospective users of simulation.

Seven men sit stiffly in uncomfortable white plastic chairs in a sterile room made of steel and glass. A middle-aged man in a black suit faces them. "We're looking for one of you. Just one. What will follow is a series of simple tests for motor skills, concentration, stamina." A short while later these seven men are placed in a special simulation chamber. Lights flash, creating a disorienting effect. The men, armed with loaded guns, attempt to shoot several grotesque simulated creatures as they come into view. One of the seven hesitates until everyone else has fired several shots at the monsters, then he takes aim and fires once. As the lights return to normal, the simulation coordinator, the same middle-aged man as before, approaches the lone gunman.

"Edwards, what the hell happened?"

Edwards turns, concerned, to face the coordinator. "Hesitated."

"May I ask why you felt little Tiffany deserved to die?" The coordinator presses a remote control and the figure of a little girl carrying physics textbooks slides forward out of the shadows into plain view. She has a single bullet-hole in the middle of her forehead.

"Well," says Edwards straight faced, "she was the only one who actually seemed dangerous at the time, sir."

The coordinator looks thoughtful. "How'd you come to that conclusion?"

"Well, first, I was going to pop this guy hanging from the street light," Edwards points out a long-tailed monster which is clinging to a simulated lamppost. "And then I realized, you know, he's just working out; and how would I feel if somebody came running into the gym and busted me while I was on the treadmill. Then I saw this snarling beast guy," (he points to another beast with its fanged mouth wide-open and clutching what appears to be a handkerchief in its claws) "and I noticed he had a tissue in his hand

and I realized he's not snarling, he's sneezing, you know, no real threat there. Then, I saw little Tiffany. I'm thinking, you know, eight-year-old girl, middle of the ghetto, bunch of monsters, this time of night with quantum physics books? She's about to start something, sir. She's about eight years old. Those books are way too advanced for her. If you ask me, I say she's up to something. And to be honest I'd appreciate it if you eased up off my back about it." There is a moment of silence as the coordinator stares appraisingly at Edwards, who begins to look sheepish. "Or do I owe her an apology?" (Solomon, 1997).

* * *

On a weekday in May, 1997, 200 people stand in line inside an FAO Schwarz store, waiting for the latest shipment of 360 Tamagotchi virtual pets. A late delivery truck has delayed the shipment by three hours, but this seems only to have heightened the excitement of the crowd. Most of the people in line are adults, ranging from their early twenties to mid-fifties. A *Boston Globe* reporter is also present, collecting a variety of different opinions about the latest virtual craze.

"I heard about them from another therapist who said: "I think we have a really good tool here," says a family therapist. "In today's society, everyone wants to be nurtured, but no one knows how. Everyone who's thinking of having a child should have one of these."

Despite the fact that virtual pets have been on the market only a few weeks, some people have already begun collecting Tamogotchis and are waiting in line in an attempt to purchase one of the rare white egg-shaped toys. Still others have less pleasant intentions. An MIT freshmen, when asked why he wants a virtual pet, replies that he and three of his friends are buying them so they can hold a contest to see who can kill theirs first (Cobb, 1997).

* * *

Maryanne Williamson is a forty-two year old lawyer whose mother, Polly, has been in a persistent vegetative state (PVS) since a massive heart attack three months ago. Although Polly is not on a ventilator, she requires tube feeding and does not appear to be improving. In fact, the prognosis for PVS patients who have been in this state for more than three months is very poor in terms of useful recovery.

This being the case, Polly's physicians have just told Maryanne that it is time to think about removing nutritional support. Maryanne believes that this is the best course of action, but not everyone in the family agrees.

215

Although Maryanne is an only child, her husband is against any such action as are her teenage son and some of her cousins. On the nurse's recommendation, she decides to visit the hospital social worker's office. She has just gotten off the phone with her husband and, after a bitter argument with him, feels a tension headache coming on. Generally an outgoing person, she finds herself reluctant to open herself up to a stranger in this matter and by the time she reaches the social worker's door has almost decided to leave the hospital. She hesitates in the doorway.

Just before she turns away, the social worker, a young man with kind eyes, looks up from his desk and says, "Oh, you must be Ms. Williamson. Please, come in and make yourself comfortable."

* * *

Of the preceding dramatized scenarios, only the second is based on an actual event. The first is a scene from the science-fiction adventure film "Men in Black" and the third is an example of a standardized patient case study, the subtext from which the actor creates his/her character. All three, however, are examples of simulations, the first and last of which are used for the purposes of assessing professional competence. The second example, that of the virtual pet, has, as the therapist mentioned, the potential to be used in certain training exercises, but is perhaps more interesting for its emphasis on artificial life. Ethical implications, both explicit and implicit, are involved in all of these sample simulations.

On the explicit level, for example, the obvious questions present themselves: What are the potential ramifications for a law-enforcement trainee who freezes in a hostile situation and shoots an innocent bystander in his confusion? Despite the fact that we are dealing with simulated life, is there not something perverse in people holding contests to see who can kill their virtual animal most quickly? Is it the right thing to do in certain cases to "pull the plug" on someone in a PVS state? These types of questions have been addressed to some degree by other chapters in this book. For example, in Chapter Eight, Christine McGuire discusses the driving simulation in which she almost hit a child and the attendant emotional distress she experienced. Of course, this was only a side-effect of the main purpose of the simulator, which was to test her driving skill under difficult situations. The point of simulation is to train and assess one's capacity to perform the right actions in difficult physical, often ethically complex, situations.

Beneath the surface, however, lies a whole new set of difficulties, namely the ethical implications of simulations. To return to our first three examples, we might ask the following questions: Exactly what aspect of law-enforcement competence was the "Men in Black" simulator assessing? To what extent were its participants informed of the coordinator's expectations? What is the purpose behind creating simulated life, such as the virtual pet? In what ways is simulated life superior to real life? What are the disadvantages of relying on simulated life over real life? In the case of the standardized patient, how close to reality is the designed case study? Finally, what unforseen side-effects or consequences might result from working in any of these simulation settings? In order for simulations to be both effective and ethically acceptable, these types of questions need to be asked and answered by simulation designers.

To answer them, it is instructive to address some larger, overarching issues, which will put the ethical and philosophical issues into a broader context. These issues fall into five general categories which have been addressed in earlier chapters. These categories are: (a) What aspects of professional competence can be better assessed by simulation technique than by other means? (b) What are the extra costs of these benefits in terms of money, time, sample size, and the like? (c) What contaminating factors do simulations introduce into the test situation, not present in other approaches? (d) What are both the long- and short-term consequences (positive and negative) of participating in simulation exercises as examinees, simulators, and members of the public who may inadvertently be involved? (e) How can ethical requirements of informed consent ("doing no harm") be met without jeopardizing the "reality" of the simulation? Finally, in the conclusion, I will suggest some ideas for an agenda that users of simulations should consider.

What aspects of professional competence can be better assessed by simulation technique than by other means?

Simulation technology is best used to complement, not duplicate, other assessment methods. Assessment of an individual's fund of acquired knowledge is done best using a test composed of multiple-choice questions. Procedural skills, such as field stripping a military weapon, are evaluated most efficiently by expert observers, usually following a detailed checklist. However, assessment of *proficiency in human interaction* such as doctor-patient communication, requires using standardized patients (SPs) who not only present simulated medical encounters but also record trainee responses to the simulated problems (Swanson, Norman, and Linn, 1995).

A good general rule to follow in the use of simulations for training or assessment in any profession is as follows: any performance aspect requiring an immediate response in an interactive mode is best assessed by a simulation. For example, considering Edwards from the scenario, we see a performance aspect that requires an immediate response, namely when and when not to shoot and the ability to assess in a split-second whether or not the situation is hostile. The interactive aspect is encountering the aliens and dealing with them (in this case shooting or not shooting them). In similar, more realistic and complete simulations, the FBI Academy's training center (Hogan's Alley) provides numerous simulations for law officers in training. For example, one of the exercises involves a simulated investigation of a bank robbery. The scenario includes interviews, crime scenes, and arrest and search situations. Trainees must be able to document the findings of their case as if it were an actual one and they will later have to "live with their mistakes" when they take the witness stand in a mock court trial (Pledger, 1988).

The assessment of human interaction is a very important aspect of simulations. Orientation sessions that rely on trainees watching a videotape and then writing post-viewing evaluations will never be able to test and teach human values and skills, as well as a simulation can. Videotapes can be employed effectively if they are used to record a simulation process and are then presented to the trainee after s/he has completed the simulation. Videotapes work best when more than one session is recorded and when viewing is supplemented by written summaries which identify strengths and weaknesses (Dinham and Stritter, 1986). This has been shown to be especially true in the use of SPs with medical interns.

Videotaping is, however, only a method of recording the examinee's response to a simulation. The most significant aspect of simulation training and assessment is what is being assessed, namely human action and interaction in professional settings that often require split-second, potentially life-saving decisions. Robert Helmreich, in his chapter on simulation in aviation and medicine (Chapter 10), as well as in his previous work (Helmreich, 1997), discusses the value of simulations in teaching people the importance of teamwork in flying. The Crew Resource Management (CRM) programs of the Federal Aviation Administration (FAA) have been created to train flight crews to communicate in crisis situations. This became imperative after research revealed that *seventy percent* of all airline accidents were caused not by mechanical problems as much as by human error, due primarily to failure on the part of crew members to communicate with one another or to behave as a team. CRM focuses not only on the cockpit crew, but also includes flight attendants, air traffic controllers, and support staff (Helmreich, 1997).

According to Helmreich there are three cultures that affect performance in the cockpit. The first is the *professional* culture of airline pilots which is best expressed in terms of rugged individualism. In addition, "many pilots strongly deny susceptibility to stress—they are unwilling to acknowledge that fatigue and sudden danger can dull their thinking and slow response times" (Helmreich, 1997). The *corporate* culture of an airline can also cause difficulties, especially if unacceptable procedures become established among the airline's crews; e.g., nonstandard checks when taking safety precautions. *Nationality* is the third culture affecting pilots. In a survey performed in an Asian country, *thirty-six* percent of pilots agreed that crew members should have a voice in establishing and reviewing safety precautions. In a Western country *ninety-eight* percent of pilots and crew members echoed this view (Helmreich, 1997). Clearly, some Asian cultures and Western cultures do not have similar views about shared authority in the airline cockpit.

In situations where hundreds of lives may be at stake, the "baggage" created by these cultures is a very serious impediment to safety. Simulations that stress cooperative effort can show the consequences of the lack of teamwork vividly and immediately. The chief value of using a simulation is that it produces directly observable results. Thus, the simulation coordinator can observe and record mistakes and take corrective action immediately.

What are the extra costs of these benefits in terms of money, time, sample size and the like?

Simulation technology has two major costs: (a) development and, (b) maintenance. Costs are not restricted to money. Costs also involve time needed for research, Beta testing, and field trials.

The use of simulated (standardized) patients (SPs) is now widespread in the health professions. Effective use of SPs for education and evaluation requires thoughtful faculty attention to case development, SP training for case presentation and data recording, and staff preparation. These are all development costs. Similar costs are associated with development of sophisticated computer-based simulations for architecture (Chapter 4), medicine (Chapters 3, 6, 9 and 12), aviation (Chapter 10) and the military (Chapter 11). Development costs for these applications can consume dollars in the millions.

In the Maryanne Williamson scenario, hours had to be spent researching PVS patients and the chances of recovery. This probably involved consultation with numerous physicians. Social workers and/or psychologists would also need to be interviewed in order to determine the variety and depth of emotional responses Maryanne could possibly experience. Once the most significant variety of factors is determined, then the SP scenario must be narrowed down to a very specific set of details which, if accurately probed by the social worker in training, can reveal the student's competency in the field. Tamblyn and Barrows (Chapter 6) discuss SP examination development in detail. They stress that once relevant SP case information is collected, the data must be rank-ordered before being used for an actual simulation. After the desired goals are set for the scenario, the SP must be trained. The general assumption is that such training requires a great investment of time. In fact, it generally does not take very long, typically no more than two to three hours (Barrows, 1993). However, the total monetary cost of SP simulations may be quite high.

At the University of Illinois at Chicago Clinical Performance Center, SPs are paid between $10 and $15 per hour, depending on whether they are trained to act as an instructor after the exercise has been completed. In the latter case, the SP must have sufficient training to assess the student's performance accurately and to provide clear and thorough feedback. Some fees may be higher. According to Group Discussion *Highlights* about SPs in *Academic Medicine* (1993), payment to SPs can range as high as $50 per hour, depending on the case circumstance. Sensitive SP encounters (e.g., pelvic, breast, male UGR exams) require higher SP payment rates.

Expensive corrective action may be needed if the scenario as originally designed does not adequately assess what it intends to measure. For example, the Standardized Patient Project (SPP) of the National Board of Medical Examiners (NBME) has been developing SP scenarios for inclusion in the United States Medical Licensure Examination (USMLE) Step II. This has involved substantial startup costs to cover expenses for physician case developers, SP acquisition and training, pilot tests, and administrative overhead. The SP development phase has already consumed four years, with an anticipated startup date for the SP component of USMLE II targeted for 2001. This nationally standardized test was scheduled for revision because the old paper-and-pencil format is useful only for assessing a fraction of the skills needed by a competent clinician. The NBME's idea of using SPs for examination purposes will not only provide evidence that future doctors have the technical skills necessary to perform their jobs, but will also test their (a) ability to handle difficult and sensitive situations, (b) general level of sociability, and (c) recognition of ethical issues. In short, a well-designed simulation can assess several important factors that are needed by doctors—factors which cannot be measured by a paper-and-pencil exam.

Simulations can also be costly to maintain. This may involve expenses for standard operations, trainee and staff time, and costs involved in hardware and software upgrades as in the case of the "Harvey" cardiac simulator (Chapter 9).

A dramatic example involves the difficulties encountered by the space station MIR which are due, in part, to the fact that the station is eleven years old. MIR was not designed to last so long. But part of the maintenance costs are due to human error (Kluger, 1997; Thomson, 1997). When the station lost power in June and again in July 1997, questions arose about commander Tsibliyev's competence including the adequacy of his training (Specter, 1997). According to one news article the commander was complaining of heart problems. What effect might this have on the performance of his duties in space (Lemonick, 1997)? To what extent could one have any heart condition and still perform duties as an astronaut? These are questions which can only be answered with continuing research. In addition, Ground Control personnel could be better trained. In November 1997, Ground Control failed to notice a drop in the power supply during a test of one of the station's solar panels. The oversight led to a power shut down. Fortunately, the astronauts were resourceful and within two days they were able to restart the computer and reset the gyroscopes so that the station was operational once again (Isachenkov, 1997). Such an oversight might have more serious consequences in the future. Was this a breakdown due to flawed individual judgment or was it a problem based on poor teamwork? Simulation training or the application of simulation assessment could be essential in maintaining a competent Ground Control staff who are responsible for astronaut lives. Monetary and time expenditures may be high, but the loss of human life is a much higher cost.

In a world where standardized tests have become so critical, there are numerous ways to "beat the system." One can attend classes, often sponsored by the organization that issues the exam, so that one can learn the "tricks" of the test and pass by a respectable margin. The Educational Testing Service (ETS), in addition to charging students for the exam itself, offers numerous courses, for a fee, to prepare for the Graduate Record Examination (GRE). Clearly this reduces the overall value of the examination.

What contaminating factors do simulations introduce into the test situation, not present in other approaches?

We have looked briefly at the different kinds of interpersonal and interactive factors that simulations can assess. We have seen that designing, maintaining and updating simulations frequently requires a sizeable investment of time and money. Furthermore, no test is ever completely objective. Our world views cannot help but bias all that we do, but such contaminants can have an especially pernicious influence when we are designing simulations. There are also contaminants in the scoring of simulations. For example, there is considerable diversity in what experts see as relevant data for a case. Even when numerous people work together to design the scenario, to set the criteria for judging performance on it, and to create the checklist for rating that performance, a disturbing level of subjectivity still exists depending on the perspective of the rater, e.g., physicians, participant SPs, or observer SPs.

Tamblyn and Barrows assert there are three types of raters who assess student performance in SP assessments. These are (a) physician observers, (b) the SP who is worked-up in the scenario, or (c) a second SP who is observing the interaction. Raters vary in their recordings about the situation. Physicians tend to rate student skill based on technical expertise, whereas the SP will tend to evaluate based on more "socio-emotional aspects," such as interpersonal skills. Thus, the student's score will depend on what each rater perceives to be the most important factor being tested. *This is a type of contamination (response bias) that does not occur in paper-and-pencil examinations.* Recent scholarship in this field reflects an awareness of this subjectivity and discusses means of lessening its impact. Paula Stillman, for example, suggests that checklists of relevant criteria should be highly specific, not general. This will make it easier for the raters to assess student performance (Stillman, 1993). If there is agreement among evaluators, particularly SP and physician raters, then those who assess the student's performance will be working from the same set of rules.

Contamination also results from the artificiality of the simulation. Simulations are approximations of reality. This does not mean that simulations lack fidelity. But there is usually an awareness that simulations are unreal which can influence those who cannot or will not suspend disbelief.

Since some degree of artificiality is unavoidable, the question arises about the consequences of the examinees' awareness that they are responding to an unreal situation. Failure to take simulations seriously can have a variety of implications. In aviation, for example, CRM has been essential in promoting teamwork necessary for airline crews to handle crises efficiently. Yet not all pilots agree. Approximately 5% of pilots reject the centrality of teamwork, presumably viewing a teamwork simulation as inconsequential. Such pilots present a serious safety risk (Helmreich, 1997).

The artificiality of simulations can have detrimental effects even when people take them seriously. In the case of SPs who are used for training and evaluating clinical practitioners, students generally find the experience valuable. However, the trainees know they are being observed and monitored. Although this is necessary for feedback which is administered during the debriefing process, student awareness of the observer can skew the assessment results. Students may work extra hard to do their best and work to fulfill perceptions of observer expectations. This is not a serious source of bias if (a) the student applies learned technical and interpersonal skills correctly, and (b) students take the feedback from the exercise and apply it to their real-life skills. However, if students only perceive the standardized patient encounter as "another hurdle," the lessons learned are seriously compromised. It is very difficult to gauge how much a student will take away from an exercise and apply practically. It is possible to assess what someone has learned from simulation-based education by assessments done later. To illustrate, the use of unannounced standardized patients to assess practicing family physicians shows great promise (Carney and Ward, 1998). Here, artificiality is present, but is not apparent to the person being tested.

Alternatively, taking the simulation too seriously is also a source of bias. Some students have difficulty with SP-based examinations due to evaluation apprehension. Trainees can become immobilized and perform poorly, especially when SP-based examinations are for "high stakes." Practice and experience with these new assessment formats should reduce evaluation apprehension among clinical trainees.

What are both the short- and long-term consequences (positive and negative) of participating in simulation exercises as examinees, simulators, and members of the public who may inadvertently be involved?

We have seen how simulations affect some people and do not affect others. For the purposes of this section, I will deal only with the former group since the consequences are minimal for those who are detached. For others there are: (a) short-term consequences, (b) long-term consequences, and (c) unexpected side-effects.

Short-term consequences. The primary short-term outcome of simulation training is trainee motivation. A good simulated exercise, such as an encounter with an SP or the "Harvey" CPS (Chapter 9) produces a learning opportunity that grows in power as it approximates reality. Students are more likely to be engaged in training and education if they feel their application of knowledge produces immediate, tangible results. This feeling is reinforced by feedback from the simulation itself or an instructor/observer/examiner.

Charles Petranek suggests that the simulation process can be broken down into three parts: participation, debriefing, and writing. After the simulation is finished, oral debriefing should occur, addressing what Petranek calls "the four Es:" events, emotions, empathy, and explanations. The oral debriefing process should be interactive, allowing participants to describe the events that occurred and the emotions surrounding them. If participants have difficulty discussing emotions, the debriefer, acting as facilitator, should gently suggest several possible emotions to stimulate discussion. The debriefer should encourage participants to empathize with each other and to see different viewpoints. This leads into the explanation of the simulation in which the debriefer guides participants through an analysis of the exercise (Petranek, 1992). This interactive format, although initially intended for sociology and anthropology course simulations, can be applied to other simulations as well. The debriefing process is useful in helping clinical trainees learn, in a non-threatening setting, where and why they made mistakes in an SP encounter. Such an approach is far more engaging than a score of correct/incorrect or simple lecture about what the student did and did not do. Not only does simulation involve technical and interpersonal skills, it also fosters interest and engagement. In short, a simulation that is carefully constructed, administered, and explained can stimulate students to improve their skills.

Other scholars have found simulations to be highly motivating for students. Since 1990, in his anthropology course at Northern Arizona University on human interaction, Reed Riner has found simulations motivationally useful. For example, one simulation involved creating a virtual culture for a permanent settlement on the planet Mars. This required each student to develop a persona which would interact with other student personas in a Multiple User Domain (MUD), a text-based virtual reality program that is linked with the Internet. Students collaborate to create virtual constitutions, legal systems, and other sociopolitical features. The emphasis on role playing, and the general spirit of play that was emphasized, encourages students to research different ideas and then apply them to their virtual culture (Riner, 1996). This illustrates the idea expressed by Christine McGuire that at its root, simulation is a form of play.

Anxiety is a potentially negative short term consequence of simulations. Some people do not perform well in a simulated environment, especially in simulations which apply to training or assessment such as an SP encounter. While some individuals are good at "blocking" awareness of an observer, others cannot. Trainees can grow anxious, forget technical information, make mistakes, and occasionally blunder socially. This is the same type of anxiety as exam panic, which most people have experienced. It is "blanking" on the test. One can become so nervous that even simple information becomes impossible to retrieve from memory, creating more anxiety. Few exams carry the stigma that failing an SP encounter does for physicians in training.

Long-term consequences. If the immediate result of simulation is motivation, what are the long-term effects of participating in a simulation? Research shows that motivation and engagement produce better outcomes during professional assessment, whether the assessment is done in a simulated environment or by standard written examinations (Linn and Gronlund, 1995; Glenn, 1996). There is a growing body of evidence, presented throughout this volume, that simulations in many forms are highly effective for teaching and assessing professional skills, attitudes, and responses to stressful situations.

The hidden strength of simulation training may reside in its qualitative potential, rather than its quantitative outcomes. Repeated exposure to different SP scenarios gives the clinical practitioner an experiential database to work from. The more scenarios the trainee is exposed to, the larger the database. Having such a base of experience has potentially positive and negative consequences. On the positive side, having a large number of cases from which to draw analogies allows the clinician to make connections quickly in patient diagnosis. On the negative side, a large memory file may encourage practitioners to make uncritical connections when working up patients.

Automaticity is a desired outcome of deliberate practice using simulation technology (Ericsson, Krampe, & Tesch-Romer, 1993). A well-educated clinician, trained by repeated exposure to SPs and other simulations, may be able to quickly diagnose a patient's problem by mentally manipulating memory files, engaging in pattern matching. When pattern matching works, the problem can be correctly assessed and treated promptly.

In fields beyond medicine having such a database of crisis scenarios can prevent disaster. Take, for example, an airline pilot who is flying a simulated DC-10. Disintegration of an engine has severed the hydraulic lines which transmit fluid to the rudder and other equipment which maneuver the aircraft, thus leaving the pilot unable to control the plane's direction (Helmreich, 1997). In such a situation, the trained and experienced pilot would deal with the crisis automatically. If the database of simulated situations is large and practiced thoroughly, attempts to deal with real emergencies have a higher probability of success. This appears to have happened in the scenario just described. In 1995 a real DC-10 landed just short of the runway in Sioux City, IA. Of 296 people, 185 survived. The National Transportation Safety Board investigated the crash and singled out the pilot and crew for their crisis performance and lauded their CRM training (Helmreich, 1997). In Chapter 11, Ressler, Armstrong, and Forsythe highlight the confidence level of the leader of the U.S. Army attack force at 73 Easting during the Gulf War. Although it was his first real battle, the leader and his soldiers felt confident due to the number of simulated battles they had already fought. These examples illustrate the feeling of competence that professionals can develop from deliberate practice and assessment in high-fidelity simulators.

The negative aspect of *automaticity* occurs when an individual makes an inaccurate connection with their prior training and so reacts inappropriately. In the simulation of the uncontrollable airplane described above, thirty-four minutes elapsed from the time the hydraulic lines were severed to the time of the crash (Helmreich, 1997). In many real airplane disasters there is much less time. There may be only a few seconds to assess a situation accurately and react appropriately. An inaccurate assessment of the situation could spell disaster for crew and passengers—and this is not all that unlikely since no matter how close a simulation is to reality, it is never an exact duplicate; every situation has specific unique factors.

Unexpected Side-effects. All human endeavors have unexpected side effects – both benign and adverse. In the case of simulation the effects on four constituencies need to be considered: (a) the author/creator of the simulation; (b) the respondent (learner, examinee); (c) the simulator, when one is used and (d) the public when they may be impacted.

Authors/creators may become so invested in their work that they resist updating the scenario and/or the scoring to reflect scientific developments. Alternatively, they may become so inspired that they research the area to the point where their highly specialized expertise gets in the way of their developing problems at a suitable level, and setting standards appropriate for the generalist.

Respondents may be so overwhelmed by powerful simulations, especially those that imitate potentially dangerous situations and/or those on which they have performed badly, that they become obsessed with the situation to the point of developing disabling nightmares and fantasies; alternatively, they may find some scenarios so instructive that they tend to apply their learning, even in situations in which it is not appropriate.

Simulators may find that they have learned so much about the problem they were simulating that they tend to "instruct" experts whom they are consulting (for example an SP may prompt a physician who has neglected an important element in the history). Also those who play the same role repeatedly may be at risk of taking on, in real life, aspects of the persona they are depicting. For example, adolescent SPs may be particularly vulnerable, but even adults who play the role of a depressed patient, or an unreasonably aggressive one, may carry some behaviors they have simulated into real life. Users of simulation for both teaching and testing purposes will need to be sensitive to potentially adverse effects of these kinds.

Finally, as we have seen, in the case of military, police, emergency preparedness and other large scale simulation exercises, it is almost impossible to avoid impacting the public. Those conducting such exercises are ethically responsible to take every feasible means to avoid potential difficulties and/or to warn the public in advance, when avoidance cannot be assured.

How can ethical requirements of informed consent, "doing no harm," be met without jeopardizing the "reality" of the situation?

Is it possible to create a simulation that is so real to participants that they actually suffer trauma? According to McGuire (Chapter 8), an unnamed corporation is currently being sued by some of its employees who were convinced of the reality of a robbery simulation and claim to be suffering from post-traumatic stress syndrome. This story raises issues of ethics in simulation design and implementation. If simulations are to be effective for training and assessment, they must reflect reality as accurately as possible. Yet if a simulation is so close to reality that participants suffer numerous side-effects identical to the real situation, is it doing more harm than good? The dilemma, in short, is mirrored reality and trauma versus apparent artificiality and ineffectiveness.

Although the distress created by an unexpected turn of events in a controlled, simulated environment may be less than that which occurs in reality, the coordinator should be cautious about using deception, even in the former case. While deception may be a necessary feature of the simulation in some situations, in others it can violate trust and create a barrier between teacher and learner or examiner and examinee. Charles Petranek discovered this the hard way when, during a simulation designed to instruct students in a social psychology course, the students discovered a built in deception to the game. It took Petranek the better part of the rest of the semester to win back some of the students' trust. This has led him to make the seventh rule of simulation work: "Do not deceive the participants" (Petranek, 1994). This is, I believe, a valid warning to instructors who would use simulation technology. This is not to say that simulations should avoid probing sensitive areas such as emotional responses to certain procedures (HIV testing, for example) or the ability to choose between two undesirable split-second decisions (the impossible dilemma), either of which may result in a loss of life. Depending on how a person defines deception, simulation scenarios may seem rife with it. There is a way, however, to carefully control the level of deception used in a simulation.

Consider, for example, Patricia Carney's attempt to evaluate HIV preventive practices among family nurse practitioners and family physicians by introducing unannounced SPs into their clinical practices. None of the professionals being assessed was any longer in a learning environment; all were in practice. How then could one actively assess their competence in a given area without some form of deception? One solution: informed consent. All participating practitioners had agreed earlier to the conditions of the simulation. This meant that within three to four months of their consent to participate they would be visited by someone portraying a potentially at-risk individual who wanted to be tested for, and learn more about, HIV (Carney and Ward, 1998). A similar study was conducted by Carney several years earlier to assess primary care physicians' ability to perform physical examinations and to provide cancer prevention services for unannounced SPs portraying an asymptomatic fifty-five year old woman (Carney et al. 1993). Both studies revealed much variation in preventive practices among the study clinicians. Both studies also demonstrated deficiencies in physician practices; of the eleven physicians who agreed to take part, none attempted to assess the patient's sexual history or mentioned the word "condom" in their discussion of safer-sex practices (Carney and Ward, 1998).

These studies are success stories. However, their findings have only limited utility. Informed consent means willing participants. In the HIV preventive practice scenario, eighty physicians were deemed eligible from a stratified random sampling in Washington state, but only fourteen agreed to participate. This number was later reduced to eleven, giving the research coordinators only 12.5% of the total eligible physician population to study (Carney and Ward, 1998). Informed consent rarely yields a representative sample. Furthermore, persons giving informed consent are likely to be more interested and better informed in the area being investigated than the average individual, thus skewing the results even further (Carney et al. 1993).

While relicensure or recertification has already been mandated in most medical specialities and in some other health professions, it would be naïve to think that many other professions are ready to adopt such controls. In the meantime it will be necessary to educate both other professionals, as well as the public, regarding the importance of assessing continuing competence. As has already been demonstrated in aviation, simulations will prove especially useful in relicensure and recertification. Meanwhile, continuing expansion in the use of simulation during training will familiarize future practitioners to their value and will, over time, diminish objections to their post-training utilization. In either situation (during or post-training) "deception" will need to be carefully monitored and appropriate "informed consent" obtained.

Conclusion: Notes for Users of Simulations

We have seen what aspects of professional competence are best assessed by simulations. We have noted expenditures in time and money required to design and implement effective simulations. Potential contaminating factors and long- and short-term consequences have been mentioned, along with some of the problems surrounding the issue of implied consent. Where then, do we go from here? Have the above questions really been answered, or have the explanations simply raised more questions?

Development of simulations for use in professional education and assessment is frequently a major undertaking. This is especially the case for simulations that rely on advanced computer technologies and virtual reality environments. Such developmental work can be done only in highly specialized centers that have the personnel and technical resources to (a) invent and manufacture innovative simulations, (b) test simulation *efficacy* under controlled laboratory conditions [Alpha testing], and (c) test simulation *effectiveness* in field trials [Beta testing].

Professional educators in any field—military, medicine, law, architecture, aviation—need to be critical consumers of simulation technology that is used for developing and assessing competence. Educators should insist on rigorous evaluations of these technologies before they are adopted for widespread use, especially for "high stakes" professional personnel evaluations.

Innovative simulations have the potential to make significant contributions to professional education and assessment. The educational community needs to enjoy this potential but also to recognize the limits of simulations.

References

Barrows, Howard S. 1993. An Overview of the Uses of Standardized Patients for Teaching and Evaluating Clinical Skills. *Academic Medicine* 68 (6):443-51.

Carney, Patricia A., et al. 1993. The Periodic Health Examination Provided to Asymptomatic Older Women: An Assessment Using Standardized Patients. *Annals of Internal Medicine* 119 (2):129-135.

Carney, Patricia A. and Ward, Deborah H. 1998. Using Unannounced Standardized Patients to Assess the HIV Preventive Practices of Family Nurse Practitioners and Family Physicians. *The Nurse Practitioner* 23 (2):56-76.

Cobb, Nathan. 1997. Pets' Spur a Virtual Feeding Frenzy. *The Boston Globe* May 23.

Dinham, Sarah M. and Stritter Frank T. 1986. Research on Professional Education. In Merlin C. Wittrock, ed. *Handbook of Research on Teaching* 952-70. New York, New York: Simon and Schuster Macmillan.

Ericsson, K. Anders, Krampe, Ralf T., and Tesch-Romer, Clemens. The Role of Deliberate Practice in the Acquisition of Expert Performance. *Psychological Review* 1993; 100: 363-406.

Glenn, Jerry. 1996. A Consumer-oriented Model for Evaluating Computer-assisted Instructional Materials for Medical Education. *Academic Medicine* 71 (5):251-55.

Helmreich, Robert L. 1997. Managing Human Error in Aviation. *Scientific American* May, 62-67.

Highlights of Group Discussion of Technical Issues of the Logistics of Using SPs. 1993. *Academic Medicine* 68 (6):469-70.

Isachenkov, Vladimir. Human Error, Again: Mir's Latest Woes Short-Lived. *Associated Press* November 17.

Kluger, Jeffrey. 1997. Patching up the Ship. *Time* September 1, 62-63.

Lemonick, Michael. 1997. Adrift in Space. *Time* July 28, 46-48.

Linn, Robert L. and Gronlund, Norman E. 1995 *Measurement and Assessment in Teaching* (7th ed.). Englewood Cliffs, N.J.: Prentice-Hall.

Linsk, Nathan L. and Tunney, Kathleen. 1997. Learning to Care: Use of Practice Simulation to Train Health Social Workers. *Journal of Social Work Education* 33 (3):1-17.

Petranek, Charles. 1989. Knowing Oneself: A Symbolic Interaction View of Simulation. In *Communication and Simulation,* edited by D. Crookall and D. Saunders, pp.109-16. Clevedon, England: Multilingual Matters.

Petranek, Charles. 1994. A Maturation in Experiential Learning: Principles of Simulation and Gaming. *Simulation and Gaming* 25 (4):513-522.

Petranek, Charles, Corey, Susan, and Black, Rebecca. 1992. Three Levels of Learning in Simulations: Participating, Debriefing, and Journal Writing. *Simulation and Gaming* 23 (2): 174-85.

Pledger, James R. 1988. Hogan's Alley: The FBI Academy's New Training Complex. *FBI Law Enforcement Bulletin,* 5-9. Quantico, Virginia: FBI Academy.

Riner, Reed D. 1996. Virtual Ethics - Virtual Reality. *Futures Research Quarterly* 12:1, 57-72.

Solomon, Ed. 1997. Men in Black. Columbia Pictures in association with Amblin Entertainment Corp.

Specter, Michael. 1997. Troubled Mir's Crew Leaves, Landing Safely in Kazakstan. *The New York Times* August 15.

Stillman, Paula. 1993. Technical Issues: Logistics. *Academic Medicine* 68 (6):464-68.

Swanson, David B., Norman, Geoffrey R., and Linn, Robert L. 1995. Performance-based Assessment: Lessons from the Health Professions. *Educational Researcher* 24 (5):5-11, 35.

Thomson, Dick. 1997. A New Fix-It Crew Checks In Aboard Mir. *Time* August 18, 59.

15

Conclusions and Recommendations: A Suggested Strategy

Christine H. McGuire
Ara Tekian

As with any assessment technique, users of simulation must consider problems of implementation, validity of results, benefits for certifying agencies and for candidates, quality of feedback to examinees and examiners, appropriateness for different purposes and, possibly, unique ethical issues some forms of simulation pose. Further, it is essential, especially in "high stakes" testing, that each set of exercises be carefully studied and appropriately modified to establish the reliability and validity of inferences drawn from performance on that specific test. While some broad generalizations may be made about the overall nature of the competency measured in different types of simulations, it is nonetheless necessary to analyze the meaning of performance of particular groups on specific tests. Though much still needs to be done, it appears from existing studies that simulation approaches yield more useful data to all concerned than do more traditional methods of assessing problem-solving, interpersonal, technical and communication skills. Further, current exploratory work in a number of professions strongly suggests that simulation technology opens up the possibility of assessing such aspects of competence as team skills, creativity, stress management, response to ethical dilemmas and the like, not readily assessed by any other means. Despite high costs, work in these important areas should continue in order to resolve many issues regarding scoring, setting of standards, interpreting results and establishing the psychometric properties of various types of simulations. Finally, as this volume clearly demonstrates, experience in one profession has significant applications in many other, sometimes quite different, professions. The implications of this finding, both for improved quality and increased cost-effectiveness, cannot be overestimated.

T he value of simulation for purposes of *instruction* has been long recognized and widely exploited. Such is not the case regarding the application of simulation technology in *assessment*, where its introduction has, until recently, been slow, hesitant and limited, especially in high stakes tests administered for the purposes of licensure and/or certification.

Reasons for Delayed Adaption of Simulation

The reasons for this apparent delay in the use of what would seem to be such a valuable tool are numerous. First, and probably among the most important, is the fact that a set of exercises used for purposes of assessment must meet certain psychometric standards with respect to validity, reliability, generalizability etc., not required of instructional exercises. Second, "bug-free" simulations are significantly more difficult to create than conventional test exercises. Third, typical simulations require more response time from examinees, per exercise, than do traditional questions, and hence, give rise to both logistical and sampling concerns. Fourth, and related to these issues, is the fact that, just as in real life where generalization from a few observations is risky, so also limitations on the inferences that can be responsibly drawn from an examinee's responses to one or a few simulation exercises, must be carefully considered.

Advantages of Simulation in Licensure and Certification

The reasons to extend the use of simulation technology in high stakes testing are, however, even more compelling. First, such exercises are simply more interesting, more enjoyable and more informative than conventional examinations. Second, they focus the examinee's attention on what is genuinely important. Third, if the exercises are well constructed, respondents learn from their mistakes. And, fourth, they have the appeal of what we once called "face validity;" i.e., on the "face of it" they require the candidate to demonstrate that he can perform tasks that are relevant to the demands of professional life.

Characteristics of "Well-Constructed" Simulations

However, these benefits apply in full force only to "well-constructed" simulations, i.e. ones that meet the following criteria:

- The behavior being sampled constitutes a critical performance requirement of the profession (e.g., an architect must be able both to interpret and to create blue prints).

- The simulation exercise replicates the *salient features* of real life (e.g., inferences about a physician's history-taking skills requires that the candidate be observed actually taking a history from a real and/or a simulated patient who responds to the examinee's inquiries in a realistic way).

- The exercise provides opportunities for the respondent to make the kinds of mistakes that such professionals often make in real life (e.g.,the pilot stalls the simulated plane when the "tower" instructs him/her to abort a landing and/or perform a "go around").

- On the other hand the exercise does *not* furnish unintended cues to an optimal response, unlikely to exist in real life.

- The simulation reflects a typical situation in the profession, neither so routine as to be obvious, nor so rare and/or exotic as to be relatively unimportant in the real world.

- The total set of simulations to which a candidate is asked to respond, is representative of the range of situations the examinee is likely to encounter in professional practice.

- The available bank of simulation exercises is sufficiently large and varied so that examiners can be reasonably sure that candidates are responding to a situation which is new to them, not merely reacting on the basis of what they have heard about, or personally experienced in, previous administrations of the test.

Compromises and Trade-Offs

A certifying process that furnishes evidence, derived either from real life or "well-constructed" simulations, about each important aspect of competence would, in most circumstances, be unacceptably expensive and impossibly time-consuming for both examinees and examiners. And so each certifying body will need to develop explicit criteria for trade-offs between cost (both time and money) on the one hand vs. utility and validity on the other.

In making decisions about these trade-offs, licensure agencies will need to be very clear about (a) what aspects of competence it is essential to assess, (b) whether they wish that assessment to yield information about the candidates' typical levels of performance or their maximum capabilities, and (c) the way in which assessment results are to be reported.

For example, in response to the first issue, an individual's fund of knowledge can, in most instances, be more quickly, economically and reliably measured by straight forward traditional-type tests that require the examinee merely to recall or recognize isolated bits of information. At the other extreme, such tests are, for all practical purposes, useless (possibly even misleading) as sources of relevant evidence about an individual's ability to function as a member of a team; *valid* evidence about most aspects of team performance can be derived only from observations (including reports by other team members) of an individual's behavior in germane group situations, both real and carefully simulated.

Answers to the second issue—assessment of *typical performance* vs. *maximum capability* – will affect the size and nature of the behavioral sample required for responsible judgments about an individual's competence in the specific area of concern. Furthermore, clarity about this issue (typical vs. maximum performance) becomes especially critical in attempts to evaluate affective responses to situations for which the "politically correct" behavior is fairly obvious. In such cases it may be necessary to employ "stealth" stimuli to obtain valid evidence of typical performance—a procedure that, in turn, raises unique ethical issues (see Chapter 8 and below).

Decisions about the third issue—the reporting and use of evaluation data— will dictate how examinee responses to test exercises of each type are to be summarized (i.e., "scored"), interpreted, combined, and judged (i.e., by what "standard"); decisions about these issues will, in turn, influence and be influenced by cost, feasibility and other logistical constraints.

Ethical Considerations

All evaluation of individuals—whether for admission to advanced education, promotion, graduation, licensure, employment, etc.—is expected to meet certain professional standards with respect to quality, appropriateness, confidentiality of results and the like. Nonetheless, private corporations and some government agencies have, for decades, employed special, unidentified persons to pose as customers or clients to gauge the quality and courtesy of employee service. Nowadays, we are accustomed to the telephone warning that "this call may be monitored for purposes of quality control." We have also known for years of the "stealth shoppers" hired by management to create problem situations in order to determine how well a new employee handles difficult situations.

More recently we have heard of cases in which, in order to determine what, if anything, participants had learned from a typical continuing education course, mock "patients" were subsequently introduced unannounced into the regular practices of the physician/therapist/pharmacist/nurse attendees to see if they were applying what they had learned in responding to typical patient inquiries. In most such programs the organizer informs learners about the plan for program evaluation and obtains at least their tacit consent.

But the ethics of the situation changes dramatically when the object of the evaluation is the *individual*, not the *program*. And yet, that is precisely what is proposed in Chapter 8 as an especially useful method for obtaining accurate information about typical behavior, and perhaps the only method of assessing an individual's basic values and his/her ability to manage unexpected stress.

Various suggestions have been made for handling the ethical dilemmas created by using stealth stimuli in individual assessment. Among the most interesting is the possibility of implementing a type of advance "informed consent," analogous to that physicians and hospitals regularly get from patients, prior to performing any procedure. If that model were to be followed, individuals applying for any privilege (e.g., admission to a school, employment, licensure, etc.) would be "invited" to sign a release authorizing the use of certain unannounced and unidentified procedures for their assessment under specified conditions. At present there is no clear consensus about the best way to resolve many such ethical dilemmas inherent in certain applications of simulation technology.

A Proposed Strategy

The vivid illustrations of simulation technology offered in Part Two of this volume and their obvious utility and applicability throughout the professions, constitute a strong motivation for credentialing agencies to incorporate them as soon as possible into their official procedures. To maximize the likelihood of success in that endeavor, it is recommended that, whenever such a move is contemplated, the following steps be taken:

First, the credentialing body develop a clear and detailed set of specifications of the critical performance requirements for practicing the profession.

Second, optimal sources of evidence (e.g., interview, observation of performance, recommendation from supervisors or mentors, records, tests, etc.) about the extent to which individuals have achieved each type of competency should be identified.

Third, for those competencies for which tests appear to be the method of choice, the kinds of tasks that the candidate should be asked to perform will need to be enumerated.

Fourth, at this point it will be possible to give rational consideration to issues related to test format – oral vs. written vs. practical exercises, individual vs. group exercises, simulations vs. traditional type exercises, etc.

Fifth, for those tasks for which simulation appears to be useful, evaluation planners would be well advised to undertake a reasonably detailed cost-benefit analysis. What will performances on simulation exercises tell you about the candidates' levels of competency and their patterns of deficiencies that more traditional exercises will not reveal? What are the relative time requirements, for both examiner and examinee, of the alternate formats? Which format will convey the most accurate information to the applicant about what is really important to know and to be able to do in this field?

Sixth, some simulation exercises should be created, reviewed by colleagues, and compulsively "de-bugged" for those areas where it is anticipated that the cost-benefit ratio will be highest.

Seventh, following adequate orientation about the new-type exercises, a few may be incorporated in an up-coming assessment cycle, preferably on an experimental basis.

Eighth, results from the experimental administration of the simulation exercises should be rigorously studied to determine (a) the reactions of various constituencies to the new type of exercises; (b) the extent to which the anticipated pay-offs have, indeed, occurred; (c) the unanticipated difficulties encountered and the actions needed for their remediation.

Ninth, assuming this initial experience yields positive results, the use of simulation may be gradually expanded by developing exercises which simulate diverse situations that are more representative of overall professional experience in the designated area (e.g., for pilots, simulated take-offs in varied wind, weather, terrain, traffic and emergency conditions).

Tenth, repeated iterations of steps one through nine are required to maintain quality control and, over time, improve the entire evaluation process.

A Research Agenda

The strategy outlined above identifies a number of issues that will require ongoing research. These, together with the many specific questions raised in previous chapters, suggest a set of priority areas for study. Among the most urgent are the following:

- Difficulties in scoring and limitations of various approaches to scoring have emerged in most forms of simulations; these need to be systematically studied and the relative merits of alternative approaches documented.

- Related problems have been encountered in setting standards of satisfactory performance; research to resolve these problems is urgently needed in any situation where simulations are used as part of a certifying process.

- More explicit attention needs to be given to choice of the appropriate types of simulation. For example, it has often been noted that, in comparison with computer-based simulations of clinical problems, standardized patient simulations are ineffective in assessing patient care over time and inefficient in assessing diagnosis and treatment. Clearly, research on the comparative utilities of alternative simulation techniques in this and other arenas is needed.

- Similarly, much more study is needed to determine what features of reality it is important to simulate with high fidelity (even what constitutes "high fidelity"), in assessing different aspects of competence.

- Among the frustrations frequently suffered by persons attempting to introduce simulations into high stakes testing programs is the fact that these innovative tests do not conform to the assumptions of classical test theory (e.g., item independence, etc.). Hence conventional methods for determining their true psychometric properties (e.g., reliability, validity, etc.) are inappropriate. This gives rise to serious problems in interpreting and utilizing performance data from such tests. These problems need to be addressed in a comprehensive research agenda.

- As a component of that agenda, appropriate methods are urgently needed for determining the number and variety of exercises required to yield reproducible test results.

- Simulation has proved costly in time and money; if the use of this valuable technology is to be fully exploited, then more economical and effective tools for creating and de-bugging new exercises must be developed.

- New applications of simulation technology will present new issues requiring on-going investigation. For example, can simulation be profitably employed in re-licensure and re-certification? If so, how should the process differ from initial certification? What general types of modifications, if any, will need to be made in the nature, quantity, diversity and scoring of simulation exercises, to accommodate differences in practice patterns that occur among professionals over time? How will differences in practice and experience affect interpretation of performance?

- Simulation also offers interesting possibilities for evaluating numerous important aspects of competence that are difficult to assess with conventional tools currently available. The application of simulation to such areas as the evaluation of creativity, reaction to stress, response to ethical dilemmas and the like should be investigated.

- Finally, it should be noted that in the further development of simulation technology, it will be especially important to give systematic attention to the creation of new simulation techniques, their extension to new areas of assessment, and their applicability for a variety of purposes and in diverse fields.

Conclusion

The use of simulation for evaluation is still in its pioneer days. As such, it presents an ambitious and exciting vision of the future and offers many stimulating, challenging and rewarding opportunities to evaluators. And, as in any field, progress at this stage will be determined in large part by the level and nature of communication among evaluators experimenting with the new technology. This volume is offered as one example of such communication. We hope it will stimulate much, much more.

Author Biosketches

Author Biosketches

Lieutenant Colonel James E. Armstrong, Jr., Ph.D., is an Associate Professor in the Department of Systems Engineering at the United States Military Academy at West Point, where he has also served as Director of the Operations Research Center. He received his Ph.D. in industrial and systems engineering from the Georgia Institute of Technology. Lt. Col. Armstrong is a career officer in the U.S. Army, and his research interests include combat modeling, simulation, distributed decision making, decision support systems and command-and-control.

Howard S. Barrows, M.D., is currently Professor and Chairman, Department of Medical Education at Southern Illinois University School of Medicine. He received his B.A. in Zoology from the University of California at Berkeley and his M.D. from the University of Southern California. Dr. Barrows has carried out research into the problem-solving skills of physicians, pioneered the development of the simulated/standardized patients and a variety of printed simulations of patient problems, and the development of problem-based learning as a structured teaching/learning method.

David E. Blackmore, Ph.D. is the Director of the Evaluation Bureau of the Medical Council of Canada, which provides testing services for the council's paper and pencil, clinical skills assessment, and computer-based examinations. His areas of interest include examinations that are used for licensure or certification.

Brian E. Clauser, Ed.D., is Senior Psychometrician at the National Board of Medical Examiners. He received his doctoral degree from the University of Massachusetts at Amherst, specializing in measurement and evaluation methods. He has published numerous articles on psychometric issues in performance assessment. His current responsibilities at the National Board of Medical Examiners include research related to implementation of computer-based case simulations as part of medical licensure assessment.

Stephen G. Clyman, M.D., is Director of the Computer-Based Case Simulation Project at the National Board of Medical Examiners, where he has worked since 1986. A graduate of Jefferson Medical College, he completed an internship in internal medicine and went on to earn a Master's degree in medical information science at the University of California at San Francisco. His research interests include the application of computers to testing physician readiness to practice medicine.

Dale Dauphinee, B.Sc., M.D. is a medical graduate of Dalhousie University who has been active in medical education and assessment for over twenty-five years. He has been the Executive Director of the Medical Council of Canada since 1994 and previously was the Chair of Medicine at McGill University and Director of the McGill Center for Medical Education. His current medical education research interests are educational outcomes and the methods of clinical assessment.

Colonel George B. Forsythe, Ph.D., is Vice Dean for Education and Professor at the United States Military Academy. He has also served as the Director of the Center for Leadership and Organizations Research and as the Associate Dean for Academic Affairs at the United States Military Academy. Col. Forsythe earned a Bachelor of Science degree from the United States Military Academy, as well as a M.A.C.T. degree in social psychology and a Ph.D. in education from the University of North Carolina at Chapel Hill. His current research interests include leadership education, training, development, and assessment.

Robert L. Helmreich, Ph.D., is Professor of Psychology at the University of Texas at Austin, where he has taught since 1966. He also serves as Visiting Professor at the University of Basel/Kantonsspital in Switzerland. He received his Bachelor's, Master's and Ph.D. degrees in personality and social psychology from Yale University. He is currently principal investigator of two major research projects: Individual and Team Performance in Aviation and Surgery; and The Influence of Organizational and National Culture on Behavior.

S. Barry Issenberg, M.D., is Assistant Professor of Clinical Medicine and Director of Educational Research and Technology at the Center for Research in Medical Education (CRME) at the University of Miami School of Medicine. A graduate of the University of Miami School of Medicine, he completed a residency in Internal Medicine the Universities of Alabama and Miami. He currently directs all projects at the CRME related to the development of teaching and assessment systems using simulation technology. His research interests include the creation of outcome measures to assess the teaching effectiveness of simulation technology, including "Harvey," the cardiology patient simulator and the UMedic multimedia computer system.

Shaun B. Jones. M.D., is the Program Manager for Unconventional Pathogen Countermeasures in the Biological Warfare Defense Program at the Defense Advanced Research Projects Agency (DARPA). He is aggressively pursuing the application of today's most advanced technologies to counter biological warfare. After receiving his M.D. from the Uniformed Services University of the Health Sciences, he completed a residency otorhinolaryngology—head and neck surgery at the National Naval Medical Center.

Jeffrey F. Kenney, M.Arch., is former Director of Professional Development for the National Council of Architectural Registration Boards, where he was responsible for the planning and operation of the Architect Registration Examination, used in the U.S. and Canada as part of the qualifications for initial licensure. At present, he is at the Professional Development Partners, Inc. (PDP) in Washington, D.C. He is licensed as an architect in Colorado, New Mexico, and Virginia. He received a Bachelor of Architecture degree from the University of Tennessee and a Master of Architecture and Urban Design degree from Washington University.

William C. McGaghie, Ph.D., is Professor of Medical Education and Professor of Preventive Medicine at Northwestern University Medical School in Chicago. His research and scholarly interests include evaluation of medical student academic and clinical achievement, competence evaluation in the professions, and medical student knowledge structures in the basic and clinical sciences. He has authored or edited six books including (with J.J. Frey) *Handbook for the Academic Physician* (Springer-Verlag New York, 1986) and more than one hundred scholarly journal articles and textbook chapters. Professor McGaghie has also served as a national officer in several professional organizations and as a consultant to the National Institutes of Health, private foundations, universities, and medical schools.

Christine H. McGuire, M.A., is Professor Emerita of Medical Education at the University of Illinois at Chicago College of Medicine; she is also Professor of Medical Education at George Washington University School of Medicine. She pioneered introduction of new and improved techniques of evaluating professional competence, including the development and validation of simulated problems in patient management. She is the co-author and/or editor of a number of standard reference books and monographs, including the *Handbook of Health Professions Education* and *The International Handbook of Medical Education*. Professor McGuire is a continuing consultant to the World Health Organization and to numerous medical schools, professional associations, and licensure authorities around the world.

Donald Melnick, M.D., is Senior Vice President at the National Board of Medical Examiners (NBME) and Vice President, Division of Evaluation Programs. He received his M.D. from Loma Linda University. He has published numerous articles on the assessment of physicians' clinical competence during his tenure at the NBME. Dr. Melnick led developmental efforts for the NBME's two research and development activities in clinical skills assessment: the computer-based case simulation, and standardized patient projects. He was primarily responsible for the implementation of the United States Medical Licensing Examination and is leading efforts to enhance that examination through computer-based testing and improved clinical skills assessment.

John J. Norcini, Ph.D., is Executive Vice President for Evaluation and Research and Senior Associate to the President at the American Board of Internal Medicine. He has worked on the measurement characteristics of a number of different simulations in medicine, including written patient management problems, video-based assessment of the interpretation of echocardiograms and arteriograms, standardized oral exams including CASE and CBX, and standardized patients. His recent work focuses on the effects of various factors on standard setting, more efficient designs for collecting expert judgments, and methods for generating equivalent pass/fail decisions.

Lieutenant Colonel Eugene K. Ressler, Ph.D., is Academy Professor and Associate Dean for Information and Educational Technology at the United States Military Academy(USMA), West Point. He received a Bachelor's degree from West Point, a Master's degree in computer science from the University of California, Berkeley, and a Ph.D. in computer science from Cornell University. He has provided the USMA with Internet presence policy and implementation, Internet access for cadets, USMA-standard math tool (MathCAD), and strategy and implementation of technology for course support. His research interests include the use of technology in undergraduate education and for intelligence agents in military simulation applications.

Richard Reznick, M.D., M.Ed., is a colorectal surgeon and Director of Surgical Education at The Toronto Hospital, as well as the Director of the Centre for Research in Education and Associate Professor of Surgery at the University of Toronto Faculty of Medicine. He divides his time between surgery and medical education research. His major efforts in medical education have been in the field of assessment. He has also been involved in the incorporation of a clinical skills examination into medical licensure in Canada and has run a research program on teaching and testing technical skills.

Arthur I. Rothman, Ed.D., is Professor of Medicine at the University of Toronto. He also holds a cross appointment in the Ontario Institute for Studies in Education. He was the first full time permanent appointment in Medical Education in a Canadian Faculty of Medicine. For over thirty years he has had a distinguished career as a leader and consultant in medical education throughout the world. His research interests include curriculum development and methods of clinical assessment.

Colonel Richard M. Satava, M.D., is Professor of Surgery at Yale University School of Medicine and Program Manager of the Advanced Biomedical Technology Program of the U.S. Army Advanced Research Projects Agency. He serves on the White House Office of Science and Technology Policy (OSTP) committee on Health, Food and Safety and on the Emerging Technologies, Resident Education, and Informatics committees of the American College of Surgeons. He has been continuously active in surgical education and surgical research, with over 125 publications and book chapters in diverse areas of advanced surgical technology, including surgery in the space environment, video and 3-D imaging, telepresence surgery, and virtual reality surgical simulation.

Sydney M. Smee, M.Ed., is Manager of the Medical Council of Canada's clinical skills examination and has been working with standardized patients in medical education for 25 years. Her research interests include multi-site OSCEs, professional development for SP educators, and OSCE checklist design and scoring.

Jane Peterson Smith, J.D., is Director of Testing for the National Conference of Bar Examiners. She has principal responsibility for developing the Conference's four national examinations. She also serves as Associate Dean at the University of California, Hastings College of the Law, teaches English at the University of San Francisco, and practices law in Oakland. She was responsible for the development and grading of the California Bar Exam while she was Director for Examinations for the California Bar Examiners.

Robyn Tamblyn, Ph.D., is an epidemiologist who holds an appointment as a Medical Scientist in the Clinical Epidemiology division of the royal Victoria Hospital and a position as Associate Professor in the Department of Medicine and the Department of Epidemiology and Biostatistics at McGill University. She obtained her Ph.D. in epidemiology and biostatistics at McGill in 1989. She has been funded as a Quebec research scholar by the FRSQ, and more recently as a National Research Scholar by NHRDP. She currently leads the *Quebec Research Group in Medicare Use in the Elderly* (USAGE), and a provincial team that is carrying our research program on the relationships between medical education, medical practice and patient outcome.

Ara Tekian, Ph.D., MHPE, is Head of International Programs and Associate Professor of Medical Education at the University of Illinois at Chicago College of Medicine. He received his Ph.D. in Neuroscience from the American University of Beirut, and earned a Master's degree in Health Professions Education (MHPE) from the University of Illinois at Chicago. Dr. Tekian has served for the past two decades as a consultant to the World Health Organization Eastern Mediterranean Regional Office for projects in the division of the Development of Human Resources for Health. He has established a number of medical education departments or units in medical schools throughout the world and consulted in more than 30 countries. Most of his recent publications and research are focused on international health professions education, student assessment and innovative testing methodologies, instructional technology, and selection and retention of underrepresented minorities in medical schools.

Subject Index

Subject Index

A

Adaptive testing, 200-201
Administration, 40, 66-68, 238
    of Computer-based Case Simulation (CCS), 40
    of Multistate Performance Test (MPT), 66-68
AIDS/HIV Prevention, 10, 228
American Bar Association, 62
American Board of Internal Medicine, 17, 89
Anatomical simulation, 128-129
Anesthesia simulation, 149, 151-153
    Interpersonal aspects of, 151-152
    William Tell, 152-153
Architecture Registration Examination (A.R.E.), 43-58
    and Computer assisted design (CAD), 45
    Graphic divisions, 48, 51
    Vignettes, 47-56
Army, 157-173
Assessment, 8, 79-81, 86, 90, 154, 169, 217-218, 234
    Center, 8
    in Military mission rehearsal, 169
    of group behavior in Aviation, 154
    with Standardized patient (SP), 79-81, 86, 90
Automaticity, 225-226
Aviation (*see also Flight simulation*), 147-155
    Advanced Qualification Program, 155
    Line check, 149
    Proficiency check, 149

B

Bar examinations, 59-70
Battle Command Training Program (BCTP), 164-166
Battle Lab Reconfigurable Simulator (BLRSIM), 160-162
Bulldozer strategy, 88

C

California Committee of Bar Examiners, 61
Certification, *see Licensure*
Close Combat Tactical Trainer (CCTT), 160-161
Cockpit Resource Management (CRM), 150-151
Computer assisted design (CAD), 45
Computer-based case simulation (CCS), 29-40
    Allied Health Professions, 40
    and Standardized patients, 33
    Comparisons with other measures, 33-34, 38-39
    Items, 36-37
    Limitations, 32
    UMedic multimedia system, 140-143
Corps Battle Simulation (CBS), 165
Crew Resource Management (CRM), 151, 218-219, 222, 225
Crewman's Associate, 161, 163

D

Department of Defense Master Plan, 159-160
Distributed Interactive Simulation for Telenetworking, 164

E

Educational Testing Service (ETS), 45-48, 53, 56, 58, 220-221
Emergency Medical Skills Training, 128
Equivalence, 206-207
Essay questions, 60-61, 69
Evaluation, 31, 79, 154-155, 240
    in Computer-based case simulation (CCS), 31
    in Flight simulation, 149, 154-155
    with Standardized patient (SP), 79
    Technology, 15-17

F

Federal Aviation Administration (FAA), 155, 218
Feedback, 6, 66-67, 167
  with Military mission rehearsal, 167
  with the Multistate Performance Test (MPT), 66-67
Fidelity, 170, 197-198
  in Military mission rehearsal, 170
Flight Management Computer, 149
Flight simulation, 147-155
  Cockpit Resource Management (CRM), 150-151
  Crew Resource Management (CRM), 151, 154-155, 218-219, 222, 225
  Team interaction, 150-151, 154-155

G

Generalizability, 109, 234
  and Objective Structured Clinical Examination, 109
Graduate Record Examination (GRE), 221
Green Telepresence Surgery System, 185, 190-191

H

Hamburger University, 119
"Harvey" cardiology patient simulator, 134-140
Hogan's Alley, 218

I

Interpersonal skills, 89-93, 217-219
Intervention, 78, 81
Item response theory model (IRT), *see Rasch Model*

J

JANUS, 166, 170-171

L

Laparoscopic surgery, 130-133, 149, 180-182, 184-185, 188
Legal education, 59-70
Licensure, 78, 80, 235, 237-239
  in Architecture, 43-58
  with Standardized patient (SP), 78, 80, 105-112

Line Operational Evaluation (LOE), 155
Line Oriented Flight training (LOFT), 150-151
Low-tech simulation, 117-119
  Impossible dilemma, 117-118
  Role-playing, 117-119
  Stealth stimuli, 117, 119

M

Medical Council of Canada, 105,106
  in Objective Structured Clinical Examination 105-106, 108-112
MILES equipment, 158, 168
Military mission rehearsal, 157-173
  Battle Command Training Program (BCTP), 164-166
  Battle Lab Reconfigurable Simulator (BLRSIM), 160-162
  Close Combat Tactical Trainer (CCTT), 160-161
  Corps Battle Simulation (CBS), 165
  Crewman's Associate, 161, 163
  Distributed Interactive Simulation for Telenetworking, 164
  JANUS, 166, 170-171
  MILES equipment, 158, 168
  National Training Center (NTC), 158
  Simulation Networking Trainer (SIMNET), 160-161
Military simulation, See *Military Mission Rehearsal*
MIR Space station, 221
Multimedia Virtual Reality (MMVR), 188
Multiple choice questions (MCQs), 33-34, 38-40, 60-61, 196-200
  Advantages, 33
  and Computer-based case simulation (CCS), 33-34, 38-40
  Disadvantages, 33-34
Multiple User Domain (MUD), 224
Multistate Bar Examination (MBE), 59-61, 64
Multistate Essay Examination, 60
Multistate Performance Test (MPT), 61-69
  Item development, 66
Multistate Professional Responsibility Examination, 60

N

NASA, 149-150
National Board of Medical Examiners
    (NBME), 29, 38, 40, 45, 220-221
National Conference of Bar Examiners
    (NCBE), 59-60, 62-63
    and ACT, 63-64
National Council of Architectural
    Registration B45-48, 51-53, 55-58
    and Educational Testing Service (ETS),
    45-48, 53, 56, 58
    and National Board of Medical
    Examiners (NMBE), 45
National Council on Measurement in
    Education, 64
National Science Foundation, 182
National Training Center (NTC), 158, 166,
    169
Nuclear power plant, 13-15

O

Objective Structured Clinical Examination
    (OSCE), 79, 105-112
    Data analysis, 107
    Feasibility, 110
    Format, 106
    Results, 108
    Standard setting, 108
    Structure, 107
OPFOR, 158-159, 169

P

Patient compliance, 90
Patient education, 90
Patient history, 32-33, 80-81, 85-88
    in Computer-based case simulation
    (CCS), 32-33
    with Standardized patient (SP), 80-81,
    85-88
Physical examination, 32-33, 80-81, 85-87
    in Computer-based case simulation
    (CCS), 32-33
    with Standardized patient (SP), 80-81,
    85-87
Portfolio assessment, 113, 115
Post-traumatic stress disorder (PTSD), 119-
    120, 227
Primum CCS, 30-38
Provincial licensing authorities, 106

R

Rasch model, 37
Raters, 84, 87-88, 93-94, 222
    with Standardized patient (SP), 84, 87-
    88, 93-94
Reliability, 39, 107-109, 234
    in Computer-based case simulation
    (CCS), 39
    in Objective Structured Clinical
    Examination, 109-111
Reproducibility, 199-201
Research, 45, 57, 61-62, 78-79, 239-240
    in Architecture Registration Examination
    (ARE), 45, 57
    in Multistate Performance Test (MPT),
    61-62
    of National Conference of Bar
    Examiners, 62-65
    Standardized patient (SP), 78-79

S

Scoring, 34, 36-38, 51-57, 66, 201-205,
    222, 239
    Holistic scoring, 201-203
    in Architecture Registration Examination
    (ARE), 51-57
    in Computer-based case simulation
    (CCS), 34, 36-38
    in Multistate Performance Test (MPT),
    66
    Interpretation, 236
    Mechanical scoring, 203-204
Security, 205-206
Shared decision-making, 90
Simulation Networking Trainer (SIMNET),
    160-161
Standardized patient (SP), 8, 33, 77-94,
    215-217, 219-226
    Advantages, 33, 78
    and OSCE, 79
    Cases, 81, 85-86, 90-92
    Checklist, 82-83, 87, 92-93
    Data collection, 80-88
    in health professional training programs,
    78
    Interpersonal skills, 89-93
    Limitations, 93
Standard setting, 108, 204-205
Swiss National Science Foundation, 152

T

Task Force on Law Schools and the
Profession, 62-63, 65
Teamwork, 149-155
Test development, 197-199
Three dimensional visualization (*in Surgery*),
130-133, 186-189
Treatment, 32-33, 81, 86
with Computer-based case simulation
(CCS), 32-33
with Standardized patient (SP), 81, 86
Typology, 11-13, 159-160

U

United States Coast Guard, 116
United States Medical Licensing
Examinations (USMLE), 40, 220
and Computer-based case simulation
(CCS), 40

V

Validity, 37-39, 46, 110-112, 205-206, 234
in Architecture Registration Examination
(ARE), 46
in Computer-based case simulation
(CCS), 37-39
in Objective Structured Clinical
Examination, 110-112
Virtual endoscopy, 186-187, 190-191
Virtual pets, 215-217
Virtual prototyping, 188-189